Law and Justice

Law and Justice: *Essays in Honor of Robert S. Rankin / edited by Carl Beck*

Duke University Press *Durham, North Carolina 1970*

© 1970, Duke University Press
LCC card no. 74-86476 ISBN 0-8223-0213-6
Printed in the United States of America
by the Seeman Printery, Inc.

Contents

Preface

The preface for this volume of essays in honor of Professor Robert S. Rankin had to be written in the days immediately following the third major political murder that occurred in the United States in the last five years—the slaying of Senator Robert F. Kennedy. This murder caused an immediate outcry and set forth actions that can only be viewed as a counterpose to Senator Kennedy's dedication to law and justice, a dedication shared by both President Kennedy and Dr. King.

How easily during this period American political leaders and commentators accepted and glorified the term "order." To those of us who studied political science at Duke University, "order" had come to be associated with police states and totalitarian monoliths. The civil society, we had learned, is marked not by a passion for order but by a passion for justice.

A passion for justice has been the hallmark of the man whom we salute in this volume. We, who are his students, know that in his teaching, his research, and his civic actions, Robert Rankin has been constantly motivated by a commitment to justly improving man's relationship with man. To some this meant that Professor Rankin was a conservative; to others, that he was a radical. It was events and the perceptions of others that bring these attributions to his academic and civic career. These attributions are to him irrelevant.

The theme of this volume emerged naturally. Each contributor was asked to develop an essay appropriate to the occasion. All of us recognized that law and justice were the academic threads to which we must constantly refer.

There are many who could express their appreciation to Robert Rankin more eloquently than we his students. But it is fitting that we who are his students come together in the best way that we know: in a volume of essays in his honor. This we have done with respect and pleasure.

It is a pleasure also to acknowledge the assistance of those who helped in the preparation of this volume. The original suggestion stems from Taylor Cole and John Hallowell; I am grateful to the staff of Duke University Press for assistance and diligence in the preparation of this volume; and secretarial assistance was given by three persons on whom I have come to depend continually during the past two years: Mrs. Suzanne Sega, Miss Patricia McGeary, and Miss Linda Fey.

I can think of no more fitting gesture than to dedicate this book to the children of all of us with the hope that they will live in a society marked by civility in human relationships, and law and justice in the government's relationship to its citizens.

Carl Beck
June 16, 1968

Robert S. Rankin—A Biographical Sketch

After forty-two years of dedicated service to Duke University, Professor Robert S. Rankin now approaches retirement. Bob, as he is affectionately known to his friends and colleagues, can look back upon his personal and professional achievements with justified pride. If institutions are but the lengthened shadows of men then Duke University owes a great deal of gratitude to Bob Rankin whose forty-two years of teaching, scholarship, and community activity have contributed to making Duke the great university which it is today.

Robert Stanley Rankin was born on November 17, 1899, in Tusculum, Tennessee, the son of Thomas Samuel Rankin and Mary Isabel Coile Rankin. His father was a Professor of Latin at Tusculum College for forty-five years. Bob graduated from Tusculum College with an A.B. *summa cum laude* in 1920. He went to Princeton University to pursue graduate studies in politics following his graduation. It was there that he encountered a great teacher and scholar, Professor Edward S. Corwin, who was to have significant influence upon his professional career. He was awarded an M.A. degree in 1922 and the Ph.D. degree in 1924. From 1924 to 1927 he taught political science at Tusculum College. In 1927 he was called to Duke University as an Assistant Professor. Although he taught occasionally at other universities, including Columbia and Stanford, he remained at Duke throughout his professional career. In September 1933, he married Dorothy Newsom. They have two children, Dorothy Battle and Robert Stanley, Jr. Both children are lawyers.

Shortly after coming to Duke, Bob Rankin was appointed Assistant Dean of the Graduate School. He held this position until 1936. Early in his career, Bob, together with other friends in the profession, founded the Southern Political Science Association, one of the most active of the regional associations. Its quarterly publication, *The Journal of Politics*, has made a significant contribution to the development of the discipline of political science. Bob served as the Book Review Editor of this journal from 1942 to 1945. He was elected President of the Southern Political Science Association in 1931. At its

annual meeting in Atlanta that year he delivered an address on "Interstate Agreements as a Means of Dealing with Economic Problems."
At the same meeting, Professor Edward S. Corwin, then President of
the American Political Science Association, also gave an address.

Bob Rankin's teaching and research interests have focused upon
problems of constitutional law and of state and local governments.
His interest in the problems of state and local government is reflected
not only in his bibliography but in his activities as a consultant and
politician. In 1949 he was asked to serve as project director of the
Connecticut Commission on State Government. He also helped to
develop a new program of government for the District of Columbia.
As recently as 1967, he was appointed to a state commission to study
local government in North Carolina.

But it was perhaps as an elected member of the Durham City
Council that Bob became most intimately involved in problems of
local government. He was elected to the Council as a member at large
in 1955 and served in this capacity until 1960. During that period
he was elected permanent chairman of the Durham City-County Charter Commission. The Commission proposed a plan for city-county
consolidation that unfortunately was defeated at the polls. Speaking
at the time of his retirement from the Council, the then Mayor E. J.
Evans said: "His wise judgment, thorough knowledge of governmental
affairs and keen understanding of the problems of the people have
been a source of inspiration to all of us."

Bob's retirement from the City Council coincided with his appointment by President Eisenhower as a member of the United States Civil
Rights Commission. Shortly after the establishment of the Commission in 1957, Bob had been asked to serve as a consultant to that Commission. In this capacity he helped to prepare and edit the Commission's 1959 report entitled "With Liberty and Justice for All." Gordon
Tiffany, the staff director of the Commission, has said: "Bob Rankin's
influence permeated the 1959 Report which this Commission sent to
the Congress. It was, therefore, peculiarly appropriate that the President should choose him to replace Governor Battle on the Commission
when the Governor resigned early in 1960. During the course of Commission meetings and in the work of the Commission staff, we, again
and again, find ourselves turning to Bob Rankin for advice, for the
exercise of his keen judgment, and for the use of his felicitous pen."

Increasingly in recent years Bob Rankin's teaching and research interests have focused upon civil liberties. In 1963 he was invited to give the annual Edmund James Lecture at the University of Illinois, and he chose as his theme "The Impact of Civil Rights upon Twentieth Century Federalism." In response to those who were critical of federal activity in the supervision of state elections, Dr. Rankin replied that "States rights advocates would win more victories with better causes." In 1964 Bob was one of nine distinguished scholars selected for the Phi Beta Kappa Visiting Scholar program. In this capacity he lectured on civil rights at a number of colleges and universities throughout the nation. In 1967 he was invited to give the commencement address at Duke University, and he chose as his topic "The Roots of the Tree of Liberty."

In addition to his activity as a member of the Durham City Council and more recently as a member of the United States Civil Rights Commission, Bob has taught a full schedule as a professor of political science. At one time Bob taught courses in state government, American political institutions, and American constitutional law. Much of his significant research was done at a time when a twelve-hour teaching load was considered normal. In recent years Bob has concentrated his teaching in the area of American constitutional law and civil liberties. Student demand for his courses has necessitated his offering two sections of the same course. A recent student evaluation of his courses describes him as "a delightful personality and an outstanding professor." His keen sense of humor is appreciatively noted, and he is described as "heavily interested in the human side of the law."

Robert Wilson and Bob Rankin are the two architects of the Department of Political Science at Duke. Political science was first taught at Duke by Alpheus T. Mason, recently retired from Princeton University. At that time political science courses were offered in the Department of Economics. Mason was joined by Robert Wilson in 1925 and by Bob Rankin in 1927. Robert Wilson and Bob Rankin had been roommates at Princeton. A separate Department of Political Science was established in 1934 with Robert Wilson as chairman. Robert Wilson served as chairman of the department from 1934 to 1948, and Bob Rankin served as chairman from 1949 to 1964. Under their leadership the department grew both in numbers (to its present size of twenty-one) and in professional stature.

During this period of thirty years, the department had awarded by January of 1963, 126 M.A. and 69 Ph.D. degrees. (To date the number of Ph.D. degrees awarded has climbed to 107). Bob Rankin has supervised the dissertations of approximately twenty-six students. Many of the graduates of the department have made distinguished records. Among them are at least three college presidents, several past or present chairmen of political science departments (Illinois, Kentucky, Wellesley, Fordham, Lafayette, Maryland, East Carolina, West Virginia), recognized scholars, and public officials.

Bob Rankin's activities, both personal and professional, reflect a life of dedication to education and public service. In addition to the activities mentioned above, he is a ruling elder of the First Presbyterian Church, a past president of the Durham Rotary Club, a trustee of Tusculum College (which honored him with an LL.D. degree in 1958), and the faculty representative on the Duke Athletic Council. The last mentioned post was more than honorific, for Bob has long been interested in athletics at Duke and has made constructive suggestions for their nurture.

As a teacher, administrator, and public servant, Bob Rankin has made significant contributions to Duke, to Durham, to North Carolina, and to the nation.

R. Taylor Cole and John H. Hallowell

Law and Justice

Floyd M. Riddick / State and Local Government: Scholar and Participant

The public career of Professor Robert S. Rankin is a testament to that portion of the Declaration of Independence "that all men . . . are endowed by their Creator with certain unalienable Rights; that among these are Life, Liberty, and the pursuit of Happiness. That to secure these rights, Governments are instituted among Men, deriving their just powers from the consent of the governed."

To accomplish this end more nearly, Dr. Rankin taught that the governed must place emphasis on and turn their attention unstintingly to government at the local level because it is there that the individuals have the best opportunity to make their influences felt, and because it is there that the average citizen can best understand and cope with the problems of self government. He has directed most of his attention over the past forty years to this phase of our governmental system, although he has also concerned himself with government on the national level. He has written much on state, municipal, county, and local government and has directed numerous dissertations in these fields for doctoral candidates.

As early as 1934, articles by Professor Rankin on methods of improving local government appeared in nationally recognized periodicals such as the *National Municipal Review*. These articles heralded what was then a fairly new approach to local government—the county-manager plan. Using Durham County as his model, Dr. Rankin demonstrated convincingly how the businesslike methods available by the adoption of the county-manager plan of government could lift a county from the financial disaster column and place it in a position of fiscal responsibility. As he pointed out, under this county-manager plan, Durham County, which had been operating at a deficit in 1930, with an outstanding debt of $2.3 million, in four years achieved financial surpluses, and reduced its outstanding debt by almost half a million dollars.[1]

1. See Rankin *et al.*, "The County Manager Plan Proves Itself." *National Municipal Review*, XXIII (Oct. 1934), 511-513.

With the events of the 1930's bringing the very tenets of self government into question, Professor Rankin wrestled not only with the problems of the administration of local government but also with the theory underlying the importance of strong local government. In an address before the Durham Real Estate Board in 1940, Professor Rankin posited the statement that "democracy depends upon the maintenance of good local government."[2] With this hypothesis, he examined in turn the three possibilities facing our country and the rest of the world.

First, to paraphrase his conclusions, democratic government could be abandoned as a noble but failing experiment, much as prohibition had been abandoned almost a decade before with the repeal of the Eighteenth Amendment. Secondly, there could be a transfer of all powers to the central government in an attempt to save democratic government from itself as well as from outside enemies.

Dr. Rankin proceeds to analyze the flaws in this remedy, pointing out that local government provides the education for government needed in a democracy much as the root system of trees provides sustenance for its highest branches. Further, certain functions of government at the local level simply cannot be shifted to the central government. If such an attempt were made, these functions would simply die off, leaving the citizens that much the poorer. Dr. Rankin further points out that community spirit and local pride are very often intimately associated with the governments of these communities. To destroy local government would be tantamount to destroying this spirit and pride.

Unable to find a satisfactory solution in the first two, Dr. Rankin turns to a third possibility as an answer for the survival of local and democratic governments that would entail improvements in local government itself. Of primary importance in this prescription is the ingredient of increased care in the selection of local officials. Since local government is the proving ground for officers and employees from which state and national officials are chosen, each local official should be selected carefully and with the idea that this man or woman may some day be called upon to perform governmental functions of the highest order. Rankin also suggests that "if the local citizenry wished to improve the quality of local government they should cease the perpetual

2. Durham *Morning Herald* (Feb. 16, 1940), p. 3.

battle of trying to acquire 'special favors' in their own behalf": to support this charge he cites the Recorder's Court as a popular site for such favor seeking. Another contention is that the governed do not voice constructive criticism, an element that Dr. Rankin believes would give a needed stimulant to prod the local government into appropriate action and the acceptance of its responsibility. These hypotheses, of course, anticipate an informed citizenry; the governed would be expected to keep abreast of local governmental activity in order to be in a position to criticize intelligently any action or inaction by its local government. If these ends were to be accomplished, Professor Rankin feels that the democratic governments would have a chance in their fight with the forces of "totalitarianism."[3]

In July, 1940, Professor Rankin wrote an article which seemed to be a refinement and crystallization of his thoughts on the future of our form of government and which reasserted his belief that the "bulwark of democracy is local government."[4] Thus he joined hands with a long line of distinguished commentators on government, whom he had often quoted and used as authorities in his lectures. In this article he quotes, for example, Blackstone, as writing "that the liberties of England may be ascribed above all things to her free local institutions. Since the days of their Saxon ancestors, her sons have learned at their own gates the duties and responsibilities of citizens."[5] He quotes William Bennett Munro at greater length to the same effect:

Democracy is said to have an educative value. Its eulogists are fond of asserting that it enlightens the people. But the educative value of a democracy depends very largely upon the nature and spirit of its local institutions. The county, the town, and the parish are potential schools of citizenship, as both England and America have long since discovered. It is in the ward caucus and in the town meeting that people most easily learn the first lessons in the art of governing themselves. Until you learn to govern, or be governed by, your own neighbors it is futile to expect that you can successfully govern people afar off. The complications and difficulties of government increase as the square of the distance. It is for this reason that the tree of liberty is more firmly rooted in English-speaking than in Latin Countries. Local institutions in England and in the United States are more truly democratic than in the countries of continental

3. *Ibid.* (Feb. 17, 1940), p. 3.
4. Robert S. Rankin, "The Roots of the Tree of Liberty," *South Atlantic Quarterly*, XXXIX (July, 1940), 276.
5. *Ibid.*

Europe, they stand more firmly upon their own feet, have a greater degree of independence, and contribute more substantially to the political education of the people.[6]

In spite of the truth in this theoretical position, however, Dr. Rankin noted an increasing trend in the United States toward centralization of powers in the respective state governments or in the hands of the federal government at Washington. Some of this shift in power, he feels, is a result of the improvement in "transportation and communications facilities." This improvement has fostered the transfer of some "functions that formerly could have been better performed by the State" or national governments but which have been left with the county because of lack of these facilities.[7]

Another impelling force for the centralization of power can be found in the "inefficiency of our local units of government."[8] Dr. Rankin cites such areas as road building, public welfare, and education as aspects of government in which local units are "sadly lacking." Finally, he notes the baneful effects of political machines on the confidence of people in their local government.

Reacting to the circumstances and picture depicted above, Professor Rankin examines the alternatives: The first question: Can an answer be found by shifting to a fascist or socialist state? For those who feel that it cannot happen in the United States, Professor Rankin calls to their attention the following quotation from the then Secretary of the Interior Harold Ickes:

One by one, in other lands, the lamps of reason are going out. Whether they will be relighted in our time, or in our children's time, no one may dare say. Will they grow dim in our own country too? Five years ago, when the darkness first began to settle over Europe, no intelligent man or woman in this country would have taken the question seriously. Tonight no intelligent man or woman can think of much else.

Countries that today enjoy the blessings of liberty under democratic forms of government tomorrow may find themselves deprived of those liberties by a totalitarian dictatorship. Concentration camps and liquidations have become common expressions on the tongues of supposedly humanitarian and liberty-loving peoples. Men and women whose unfortunate lot is to live under a modern despotism are not permitted to seek happiness as individuals. They are pawns of a totalitarian state, cannon fodder, political robots, sterilized intelligences who may not live their own lives

6. *Ibid.*   7. *Ibid.*, p. 277.
8. *Ibid.*

in their own way; who may not express their thoughts freely; who may not worship God according to their own consciences; who may not vote unless they are prepared to say "yes."

And let us make no mistake. Totalitarianism is on the march. We are not safe. Totalitarianism is insidiously boring today from within the temple of our liberties as well as assaulting it from without.[9]

Putting this approach aside as an inappropriate answer, Dr. Rankin rejects, for the already mentioned reasons, the centralization of powers, making a plea for the strengthening and cleansing of local governments as the last best hope of preserving our system of government. Filled with eternal optimism, he concludes that already the reaction against centralization of power is turning the tide in favor of local government.[10]

In the 1950's, Professor Rankin further sharpened his focus on state government, this time with an article in the "Tar Heel Social Studies Bulletin,"[11] followed by the publication of a definitive study on *The Government and Administration of North Carolina.*[12]

In the article, he pointed out that certain reforms or improvements were desirable in order to improve North Carolina's political life. As summarized by the Durham *Morning Herald,* they included:

1. "The State's administrative machinery greatly needs overhauling. North Carolina's government is the largest business in the State, employing 60,000 persons and spending annually more than four hundred million dollars. . . .

"Complex as it has become, our State's government has never had a planned administration organization. Bureaus and boards, departments and commissions have been added in haphazard fashion."

Dr. Rankin points out that a commission is now studying the State's governmental administration and is making recommendations.

2. "Real need exists for constitutional revision . . . much of the present State Constitution is obsolete in spite of numerous worthy provisions."

3. "Reapportionment of the General Assembly, particularly the Senate, should be made immediately. Although the State Constitution provides for reapportionment each decade, none has been made since the census of 1940. As a result the General Assembly has lost much of its representative character."

For example, Cleveland County with a population of 64,000 has one representative, as does Tyrrel County with 5,000 residents. In the State

9. *Ibid.,* pp. 278-279.   10. *Ibid.,* p. 280.
11. See Durham *Morning Herald* (Jan. 16, 1955), Sec. 1, p. 6.
12. New York, 1955. American Commonwealths Series, ed. W. Brooke Graves.

Senate, one senator represents 48,253 constituents while a fellow senator's home district has 196,160 persons.

4. "Education and highways should remain under control of the State. These services have become matters of statewide, as well as local concern."

5. "It is high time that sound financial planning be made for the future. A sudden drop in revenue would leave the state in an impossible financial situation. . . ."[13]

In the book on North Carolina government, Dr. Rankin discusses not only the problems of state government but returns to the field of local government, pinpointing some of the new developments in local government and the problems associated therewith. The growth of the suburbs is one such area to which he gives much attention. He notes that the people on the fringes of the metropolitan areas "remain dependent upon the municipality and thereby in effect increase its population and the demands upon its government, without, at the same time, contributing toward taxes." To illustrate the point, Dr. Rankin reminds the reader of municipal fire protection which sub-urbanites expect to receive from the city fire departments without contributing toward upkeep through taxes.[14] Annexation, of course, would be a partial answer to such problems, but as Dr. Rankin points out, there are always many barriers to annexation which prevent it from being a cure-all.[15] Finally, he once again returns to what is a recurrent theme in his writings on local government—the benefits of the council-manager form of government.[16]

Toward the end of the 1940's, Professor Rankin began to utilize his scholarship in political science in the field of government—Rankin, the professor of political science began to merge with Rankin, the political practitioner. In 1949 he was appointed one of three project directors for the Connecticut Commission on State Government organi-zation. The commission was assigned the task of studying state high-way, health, and military agencies. Professor Rankin was assigned the study of military agencies.[17]

The year 1955 was a landmark in Professor Rankin's involvement in local government. Not only had he been a contributor to publica-tions but in March of that year he announced his candidacy for coun-

13. Durham *Morning Herald* (Jan. 16, 1955), Sec. 1, p. 6.
14. Rankin, *Government and Administration of North Carolina*, p. 339.
15. *Ibid.*, pp. 340-341.
16. *Ibid.*, p. 352.
17. See Durham *Morning Herald* (Aug. 21, 1949), Sec. 1, p. 4.

cilman-at-large on the Durham city council. He won this first quest for public office with a total of 3,140 votes—the largest number of votes cast for any candidate for that post.[18] Thus, he began a five-year tenure of office on a city council[19] which was destined to make many crucial decisions affecting the future of Durham and the surrounding area.

The Durham *Morning Herald* characterized the powers of this council as follows:

In legal respects, the City Council is the City of Durham.

All of the powers conferred upon and delegated by the Legislature to the city are invested in the Council—with only a few minor exceptions.

Under the City Charter, the policy-making body has the power "to make such ordinances, rules and regulations as it may deem necessary for the proper government of the city and to promote and safeguard the health, morals, safety and general welfare and convenience of the public."

It also is given the power to provide means of enforcing such ordinances —by the use of fine, imprisonment, or otherwise.

On a more common level, the City Council serves as a sounding board for the public's desires and proposals. Constituents of the six members from wards do not hesitate to bring their requests or complaints to their representative.

And the six members elected at-large receive the same type of communication from the entire city.[20]

In July, 1955, the council proposed an $8 million bond issue for water, sewer, and street improvements.[21] The following year a five-man commission was set up with Dr. Rankin as a member to study the feasibility of building a National Guard Armory. The commission filed a favorable report, with Professor Rankin voting in the affirmative.[22] A somewhat more controversial issue arose in 1957—the fluoridation of Durham's drinking water. Joining with the majority of the council, by a vote of 7 to 5, he went along with the council to put fluoride in the water.[23] But this did not prove to be the last word on this subject. A post card poll on fluoridation was held, which resulted in a two-to-one vote against the council's action. As a result, the city council backtracked in early 1958 and dropped the whole idea. Al-

18. Durham City Council, *Minutes*, May 16, 1955.

19. In April, 1959, Professor Rankin filed for a second term and was re-elected. See Durham *Morning Herald* (April 15, 1959), Sec. A., p. 1, for announcement of candidacy for re-election.

20. *Ibid.* (April 16, 1960), Sec. C, p. 1.

21. *Ibid.* (July 6, 1955), Sec. 2, p. 1.

22. Durham City Council, *Minutes*, Aug. 20, 1956, p. 498.

23. Durham *Morning Herald* (May 7, 1957), Sec. A, p. 1.

though Rankin agreed that "fluoridation [is] . . . a dead issue,"[24] he "was 'disappointed' in the council's handling of the issue." "Rankin said the council should not let the poll determine the outcome."[25]

In June, 1958, the council voted unanimously, but against the advice of the city manager, to create an urban renewal commission.[26] In July of the same year, Dr. Rankin was named by Mayor E. J. Evans to head a city council committee to "study the city's retirement and pension programs."[27] In the same month his deepening responsibility in city affairs was made evident by his appointment by Mayor Evans "to the city council's legislative committee. . . . The group [was] . . . charged with the responsibility of preparing for Durham county's legislative delegation any new laws or changes in existing statutes that would be beneficial to the city."[28]

A detailed plan for urban renewal to eliminate the city's slums was approved by the council in November, 1958.[29] Early in 1959, the council approved a bond issue for airport improvements, and voted to set up a planning group for the highly successful Research Triangle Park.[30]

In July, 1959, the committee on the retirement system for city employees, appointed by the mayor in 1958, and chaired by Dr. Rankin, made a report which was discussed by its chairman on WTVD, the local television station. The Durham paper reported that the chairman of the committee had said:

"Provisions for retirement in so far as city employees are concerned are not quite fair to the employees now. . . . We do have a retirement plan, but the stipends aren't sufficient.

"People have been forced to work until they are really quite old, to obtain the necessities for living," he continued.

Dr. Rankin's committee is working toward a two-fold goal: to find a suitable means of increasing the amount of retirement pay without undue cost to the city, and to set a definite age for retirement purposes.[31]

That same month another commission was set up by the council to study the possible merger of Durham county government with that

24. *Ibid.* (Jan. 3, 1958), Sec. A, p. 1.
25. *Ibid.*
26. *Ibid.* (June 10, 1958), Sec. B, p. 1.
27. *Ibid.* (July 11, 1958), Sec. B, p. 1.
28. *Ibid.* (July 12, 1958), Sec. B, p. 1.
29. *Ibid.* (Nov. 18, 1958), Sec. B, p. 1.
30. *Ibid.* (April 3, 1959), Sec. B, pp. 7-8.
31. *Ibid.* (July 20, 1959), Sec. A, p. 1.

of the city of Durham.[32] This commission was also chaired by Professor Rankin.[33] But before this last study was completed, he accepted
a call to service in the national government: he was appointed to the
U.S. Commission on Civil Rights. This position cut short his role in
local government. In a ruling handed down by the Attorney General
of North Carolina, it was concluded that by accepting the post on the
U.S. Civil Rights Commission he had vacated his seat on the City
Council.[34]

When Mayor Evans was informed of the decision of the Attorney
General, he stated that it:

"is a great disappointment to Dr. Rankin as well as to myself and other
members of the council.

"Dr. Rankin was very devoted to his service on the council and proud
of the role he was playing for the future development of our country.

"His wise judgment, thorough knowledge of governmental affairs and
keen understanding of the problems of the people have been a source of
inspiration to all of us."[35]

This verdict did not conclude his interest in local government,
however. As recently as June, 1967, in his commencement address at
Duke University, he devoted most of his speech to the subject of government. As might have been expected, he used this important occasion for his summation of observations and conclusions of a lifetime in
political science with particular attention to the area of local government. The following excerpts from the address speak for themselves:

The pervading fear of "big government" in Washington . . . has reached
epidemic proportions. It is not my intention to assuage this fear by assur-
ring you that there is no reason for concern over the continued proliferation of power in Washington. To do so would be to ignore the whole
history of the development of our system of government, which has been
marked by suspicion of, and resistance to, centralized authority.
    . . . Our forefathers, although well aware of the potential dangers of
centralized government, nevertheless recognized the need for flexibility in
our system of government in order to cope with inevitable changes in our
society. It is my contention, then, that while we should be always vigilant
against encroachment on our liberties by the central government, such
vigilance does not mean blind and unreasoning opposition to any new
program or exercise of power by the federal government.

32. *Ibid.*, Sec. B, p. 1.
33. *Ibid.* (Aug. 16, 1960), Sec. A, p. 1.
34. Durham City Council, *Resolution Book II*, p. 212.
35. Durham *Morning Herald* (Aug. 16, 1960), Sec. A, p. 1.

Instead, what is called for is first a thoughtful appreciation that there are areas in which only a strong central authority can act effectively. Secondly, in areas where we feel the federal government's role should remain limited, we must not merely parrot the phrase "states' rights" but rather present effective and meaningful alternatives at the state and local level.

Many of the country's problems are truly national in area and dimension, and the limited resources of the separate states simply cannot deal with them effectively.

. . . As the government at Washington increases in size and power, the states and local units have lost influence in certain notable areas. You will notice that I said the states have *lost influence*, not *withered away*. . . . From 1950 to 1963, the federal government gained 431,111 new employees while the states were gaining 2,903,000. State budgets have grown just as rapidly. . . . However, in the fields of education, health, welfare, and others, there has been a shift in power away from the states.

. . . Another reason for increased power of the central government is that the states and the local units of government have too often failed to meet the social, economic, and political issues of this generation.

. . . Yet I believe that to despair of state and local governments because of their past inadequacies is as shortsighted as believing that "states' rights" is a panacea for all the strains and stresses of modern life.

There are many signs of revitalization of state and local governments. . . . I believe there must be an increasing awareness on the part of federal officials in Washington that there are limits to the effectiveness of the federal government in dealing with local disturbances and problems, and that increasing efforts should be made to work with, not against, local officials. Finally, federal officials, such as Secretary Gardner, have stressed the need for creative federalism, in which the federal government would rely on local governments and local citizens to administer federal programs.

But if there is to be a revitalization of local governments, the states and their subdivisions must meet this challenge with new and creative programs and with competent and intelligent local officials.

. . . The major problem confronting the states today is that of law enforcement. . . . To combat it requires dispatch, and also impartial and positive action. Making the job of law enforcement even more difficult, some people believe that it is permissible to disobey a law simply because they do not like it. If this were true, I wonder how much money the government would garner from the personal income tax. The right of revolution, as developed by our forefathers, was never intended to justify citizens' disobeying laws they do not like. . . .

There are other functions of government such as education and health care that lend themselves to local control. . . .

Equally as important as the proper performance of the responsibilities placed on our states and their subdivisions is the modernization of these units of local governments to enable them to achieve the basic standards of social, economic, and political justice. For instance, in North Carolina, there are one hundred counties. Why? Chiefly for the rule of thumb that was responsible for their creation. This rule required that counties be small enough in size to enable a citizen to milk his cow, travel to the county seat to transact his business, and return to his home by milking time in the evening. If the same rule were followed today, at least eighty of the hundred counties could be eliminated. Local pride, debts, and differing tax rates stand in the way.

Let us get closer home. Citizens of the City of Durham, located in the County of Durham, have a dual government where only one is necessary. There exist within the County of Durham, which includes the City of Durham, two school systems, two police systems, two governing bodies, two governmental managers, two tax offices, and two tax bills for the residents of the City of Durham to pay. Granting that the unification of these two units of government might not afford the tax relief that some of us would desire, the resulting one unit of government should be more efficient and effective. Yet a few years ago a plan for this unification was turned down by the citizens, and the vote was not even close. Some piecemeal unification has occurred since then, but it is high time that the matter be reconsidered.

. . . Finally, by improving the quality of local and state government in the United States, we preserve our democratic system of government. . . .

To participate effectively in local government and community activities requires a change in attitude by many college graduates. Up to now many of you have been critical of office-holders in government, of the policies of those in power, and of the instruments of government. There is no doubt that these persons and agencies have been open to criticism, and I hope they have profited by your critical remarks. Good and thoughtful criticism is always valuable. . . .

. . . Your participation in community government demands very little, but the rewards are great. By fulfilling these responsibilities of citizenship, you will not only aid in the preservation of our federal state, but you will be maintaining the democratic character of our American government.

S. Sidney Ulmer / Searches, Seizures, and Military Justice*

I

When the Uniform Code of Military Justice (UCMJ) was enacted in 1950,[1] Congress was responding to insistent demands for revising the system of military law then prevailing in this country. Such an occurrence was neither new nor unwarranted. Substantial changes in the Articles of War were legislated in 1806, 1874, 1916, 1920, and 1948.[2] The last two revisions in this series came about largely as a consequence of complaints from "citizen-soldiers," many of whom experienced military "due process" during the two world wars. These complaints ran the gamut from inhuman treatment in military prisons to unfair trial and pretrial procedures.

During World War I, American military police in Paris were charged with using strong-arm methods in making wholesale arrests of American soldiers. Once arrested, the prisoners were frequently subjected to maltreatment, which allegedly included such tortures as being struck by guards or forced to swallow lighted cigarettes, and "encouraged" to confess by physical and psychological coercion. At trial, the military defendant ran some of the same risks as the indigent defendant in a civil court, i.e., the possibility of having inexperienced counsel assigned for his defense. Shortly after World War I, it was suggested in Congress that an enlisted man who "ignorant of his rights, unappreciative of the consequences, is placed on trial before a court-martial for his life, and has assigned to him for his defence a newly joined second lieutenant who stands before the court more like a culprit than the accused himself, frightened, inexperienced, knowing nothing of life, knowing nothing of law, and less than nothing about courts-martial procedure, . . ."[3] cannot possibly receive a fair trial.

* The research on which this paper is based was supported by the Institute of American Freedoms.

1. U.S., *Statutes at Large*, LXIV, 129 (1950).
2. *Ibid.*, II, 359 (1806); XVIII, 274 (1847); XXXIX, 587 (1916); XLI, 787 (1920); LXII, 627 (1948).
3. U.S. *Congressional Record*, Feb. 27, 1919, 65th Cong., 3d Session, p. 4505.

While this characterization of assigned counsel might not have been an accurate one, there seems little doubt that inexperienced counsel were frequently assigned in court-martial cases. More important, however, is what the legislators believed.

During United States involvement in France, Congress was deluged with reports of military commanders who followed no set rules of procedure, convicted innocent men, and dispensed unjust sentences. As a contemporary writer put it: "The picture is that of a military tyrant sitting haughtily in his office with a trembling soldier before him; a complaint against the soldier for an infraction of Army rules; a hurried, summary questioning of the accusor and one or two subordinates, no thorough investigation; no opportunity to the accused to secure counsel, speak for himself or obtain witnesses; no standard of proof which must be met; no impartial judge or jury but rather a tyrant"[4] who stands ready to convict and punish severely for trivial violations. This picture, undoubtedly overstated, was accepted by a number of congressmen. In responding to the complaints received, Congress quickly reached the conclusion that new legislation was needed. This in spite of the fact that, given the validity of many of the charges, the malfeasance was attributable to the individuals involved rather than to the Articles of War and the procedures established under them.

Legislation enacted in 1920 failed to prevent numerous complaints in World War II. During that war, the death penalty was pronounced for such acts as refusing to obey the order of a superior officer. Officers, themselves, were not above maltreatment. In one case, a second lieutenant was discharged after a court-martial conviction on charges served on him an hour and twenty minutes before trial. In 1945 Senator Wayne Morse held military courts guilty of "the grossest types of miscarriage of justice."[5]

The number of men involved in World War II greatly exceeded the number participating in World War I. This resulted in a much greater absolute number of courts-martial. The rate of such trials in World War II, however, was three per thousand as against nine per thousand in World War I. Moreover, in World War II approximately

4. G. C. Bogert, "Courts-Martial; Criticisms and Proposed Reforms," *Cornell Law Quarterly* (1919), pp. 35, 19. The writer did not subscribe to this view, considering it overdrawn.
5. New York *Times* (Nov. 7, 1945), p. 8.

40,000 lawyers, or one-fourth of the American bar, was in the service. Many of these lawyers served in the Judge Advocate General's Corps and, undoubtedly, had some impact on procedures in the military legal system. Yet, many of the 80,000 men convicted by courts-martial in World War II objected to the treatment accorded them. In one survey of five hundred servicemen, 18 per cent complained of inadequate counsel, faulty procedures, or the structure of the court. During the war itself, concern over court-martial procedures and practices was subordinated to winning the war. General Eisenhower remarked in 1947 that when forces were mobilized in some distant part of the world to fight under "fearful conditions," there was need for "autocratic government" in those forces "as severe as we have ever had on this earth."[6] This view is not inconsistent with the restoration of the death penalty in 1942 for desertion, advising or abetting desertion, and misbehavior of a sentry on duty. Courts-martial imposing this sentence were required to indicate whether death was to be by hanging or shooting, with the former being considered the more ignominious.

While recognizing the need for strong measures to deal with certain kinds of misbehavior, the government was not insensitive to the abuses and irregularities which the stresses of war can cause. From 1941 to 1945, 102 men paid the death penalty. For these men, irregular procedures discovered after the fact were irrelevant. But as early as 1943 President Roosevelt was called upon to review many court-martial decisions. Shortly thereafter, Secretary of War Robert P. Patterson announced that the Army would reconsider 27,500 court-martial cases. Special clemency boards were established to review all sentences of general court-martial prisoners then in confinement and those overseas upon return to the United States. If this task were carried out carefully, Patterson said, "with due regard for the individual differences in offenders and offenses, with the desire to deal as justly as possible with the offender, but at the same time not forgetting the vast majority who maintained an honorable record, the Army will retain, and deserve to retain, public confidence in its system of military justice."[7] The confidence to which Patterson referred was not to be realized.

In May, 1947, the Undersecretary of War, Kenneth C. Royall,

6. *Ibid.* (Jan. 21, 1947), p. 18.
7. *Ibid.* (Nov. 17, 1944), p. 19.

identified the alleged deficiencies in the court-martial system during
World War II as (1) discrimination between officers and men, reflected
particularly in the prohibition that enlisted men may not serve on
courts-martial, (2) excessive initial sentences, (3) command control, and
(4) insufficient use of legally trained officers. By implication, two of
these problems were due to improper use of discretion. Sentences were
not required to be excessive and legally trained officers could have been
used to better advantage. Command control and the discrimination
between officers and enlisted men, on the other hand, were both built
into the system by the Articles of War. A former officer on General
Eisenhower's wartime staff has been quoted as saying that "I do know
from experience in two wars that without violating a comma of Article
37 [pertaining to trial irregularities] I, as a commanding officer, could
get any verdict I wanted from any court chosen from my command."[8]
This ability was the result of the fact that courts-martial were appointed and convened by the commanding officer of the person to be
tried—the same officer who controlled promotion and other forms of
advancement for many of those who might be appointed to such courts.
Discrimination between officers and enlisted men has always been a
fundamental part of the military system of justice. This is seen in
the 1806 provision that officers under arrest were to be confined to
quarters while enlisted men were to be stockaded, as well as in the
prohibition in the 1920 legislation that officers were not to be tried
by summary courts-martial. Consequently, when Congress began to consider new legislation in the late forties, proposals to meet both these
problems and to alleviate others were presented.

The 1948 revisions made by Congress involved no changes in Article 37, and command control was retained in Articles 8 through 11
governing the appointment of courts-martial, Judge Advocates, and
defense counsel. The new legislation, however, specifically granted enlisted men the right to serve on a court-martial and an enlisted defendant the right to have up to one-third of the court that tried him
composed of non-officers. Other discriminations were retained. Thus,
officers were not to be tried by Summary Courts and enlisted men were
not to be appointed to such courts. As a consequence, many of the
arguments about excessive command control, rank discrimination, and

8. U.S., Congress, House, Committee on the Armed Forces, *Report of Sub. No. 1.*
81st. Cong., 1st Session, 1949, p. 717.

other shortcomings were not quieted by the 1948 changes. The following year, Secretary of Defense James V. Forrestal appointed a committee to study the desirability not only of incorporating new and better provisions promoting military justice in a new code but also to consider the possibility of a single code to cover all the services. The committee produced the UCMJ passed by Congress in 1950.

II

The significance of "civilian-soldier" status in promoting reform lay in the heightened sensitivity of the draftee to disparities in civil and military justice—disparities which, for the professional military man, either went unnoticed or occupied a low priority in his population of "problems." The notions of due process or fair play instilled in American citizens from earliest school days and reinforced through later direct or vicarious contacts with government are likely to be so ingrained by adulthood as to become pronounced expectations. As President Johnson has learned in recent years, frustrated expectations may produce greater pressures on and problems for government than the specific contents of the problems themselves. In any event, it has been suggested elsewhere that "in a political system in which individual preferences are given equal weight, the value of priorities adopted in the system will inevitably encroach upon the variant values of any sub-system involving substantial numbers of citizens who participate in both systems."[9] This is to be expected if what is valuable in one setting is worth preserving in another. Admittedly, the context of due process, procedural rights, and personal liberty may mediate their value. But the degree of mediation will depend on the extent to which differences in context are considered relevant and significant variables in evaluating personal rights.

For the professional military man, encroachments on individual rights may be viewed as necessary if the goals of military organization and activity are to be attained. It may be argued that there can be no victory without command; no command without discipline; and no discipline without legal procedures suited to the regulation of military life, even if such procedures are insensitive to the refinements which

9. S. Sidney Ulmer, *Military Justice and the Right to Counsel* (Lexington: University of Kentucky Press, 1969).

federal and state bills of rights exhibit. For the amateur and temporary citizen-soldier, who constituted the bulk of our forces in World Wars I and II, such allowances for the exigencies of the military system may seem excessive. If this perspective is correct, one would expect Congress, in legislating a new military code, to direct its efforts toward bringing the values of the civil and military systems into a relationship of greater coincidence.

The disparity between military and civil procedures for regulating personal behavior should not come as a shock to anyone familiar with the historical development of military law in the United States. The Republic was born out of fear of and reliance on military power. We responded to that fear by subordinating military power to civil authority. On the second dimension, however, we allowed, nay perpetuated, the development of a military legal system conceptually apart and with little interference from the civil courts. Article I of the Constitution empowers Congress to "make rules for the government and regulation of the land and naval forces." This provides authority for the Articles of War and the *Manual of Courts-Martial*,[10] which together constituted the "Constitution" of the Armed Forces until 1950. But action taken under the Articles was never subject to review in the civil courts in a manner similar to that prescribed for action taken under other congressional statutes. From the beginning, the Articles established a legal system of military courts and appellate bodies in which decisions were viewed as "final" and not subject to review by civil courts. While federal civil courts have habeas corpus jurisdiction over applications from persons confined by military courts, the scope of matters open for review has always been more narrow than in civil cases.

In *Burns* v. *Wilson*,[11] the Supreme Court pointed out that:

Military law, like state law, is a jurisprudence which exists separate and apart from the law which governs in our federal judicial establishment. This court has played no role in its development; we have exerted no supervisory power over the courts which enforce it; the rights of men in the armed forces must perforce be conditioned to meet certain overriding demands of discipline and duty, and the civil courts are not the agencies which must determine the precise balance to be struck in this adjustment. The framers expressly entrusted that task to Congress.

10. The Manual of Courts-Martial (MCM), traditionally, has been a gloss on the Articles of War. It is promulgated by executive order in accordance with prevailing military law as enacted by Congress.

11. 346 U.S. 137, 140 (1953).

As a consequence of this trust, the enactments of Congress are of especial importance for the rights of the serviceman.

Historically, Congress has shown less concern for the criminal defendant before military courts than that accorded the civilian defendant by the Supreme Court. Yet Congress has not been entirely oblivious to the need for protecting the serviceman within the confines of the military legal system. The 1806 Articles of War, which established General and Regimental Courts for trying criminal cases, prohibited trials between the hours of 3 P.M. and 8 A.M.; limited the length of time that prisoners could be held before being brought to trial; granted protection against double jeopardy; provided a modified statute of limitations for one accused of violating military law; gave the accused the right to challenge members of the court; and instructed the Judge Advocate or his deputy to protect the defendant against self-incrimination and leading questions to witnesses.

Changes of 1874 placed further limitations on punishment and forbade branding and tatooing of those convicted. The 1916 revision established General, Special, and Summary Courts with their scope of jurisdiction and severity of punishment clearly delineated. The right of the military defendant to be represented by counsel of his own choosing was specified. Counsel rights were extended further in 1920, at which time appointed counsel in all General and Special Courts became a statutory right. A prohibition against cruel and unusual punishment was adopted. Of considerable importance was the establishment of a Board of Review in the office of the Judge Advocate General. This board, composed of three officers, was given authority to vacate or set aside either finding or sentence in whole or in part. Restrictions on pre-trial confinement and the right to a pre-trial investigation were added. And a prohibition against bringing an accused military person to trial before a General Court within five days subsequent to the preferring of charges was adopted.

Enlisted men were authorized to sit on General and Special Courts in 1948. Law Members were also required for all General Courts. These specialists were members of the Judge Advocate General's department or officers who were members of the federal bar or the bar of the highest court for a state. In addition, each Law Member was to be certified by the Judge Advocate General as qualified to sit on a General Court. This guaranteed that during General Court proceedings, at least one official present would be familiar with judicial processes in civilian courts and be in a position to prevent or at least ameliorate procedural abuse. Going further toward eliminating the distinctions traditionally made between officers and enlisted men, the 1948 legislation subjected officers for the first time to special courts-martial in non-capital cases. To the earlier Board of Review, a Judicial Council was added to serve as an appellate body. To reduce command influence, a separate Judge Advocate General's department with a separate promotion list was established. Being one of the more controversial provisions of the legislation, this section was vigorously resisted by the Army. But in fact, it affected only the control of central Army administration over members of the Judge Advocate General's department. It was of little consequence for the relationship between the convening authority and those appointed by him to participate in courts-martial as members, and as defense or trial counsel.

The qualifications of defense and Trial Judge Advocates were also given increased attention. While non-lawyers could be appointed as Trial Judge Advocates or defense counsel in General and Special Courts, it was stipulated that in cases in which the Trial Judge Advocate was a lawyer or a member of the Judge Advocate General's department, the appointed defense counsel was to possess the same qualifications. In a new article, the military defendant to be tried by a General Court was to be represented at all pre-trial investigations by counsel of his own selection, civil if he chose, or military if reasonably available, or by appointed counsel.

Certainly, enactments of military law between 1800 and 1950 substantially improved the status of the criminal defendant tried by courts-martial. But, in general, the rights of the serviceman lagged behind those of his civilian counterpart. On those occasions on which revisions in the serviceman's "Bill of Rights" were made, Congress usually added one or more privileges traditionally accorded the civilian in federal, and to some extent in state, courts. Yet, despite some growth and some "progress" through the years, the inadequacies revealed in World Wars I and II and the emotion-charged reactions to them were sufficient to move Congress to new legislation in 1950.

The UCMJ went somewhat beyond all earlier legislation in providing protection for the serviceman charged with a crime. In addition to retaining the major provisions of the 1948 Code and earlier protections of individual rights, the Code requires lawyer-counsel to be furnished for all general courts-martial. If the accused has counsel of his own selection, the appointed defense counsel may be excused, but this requires the consent of the defendant. This salutary provision does not turn on the indigence of the defendant—a frequent question in civilian courts. The indigent defendant, in fact, is a concept unknown to military law in the United States. All defendants in General and Special Courts are furnished counsel without request and without question as to their ability to provide individual civilian counsel. Even if such counsel are provided, appointed counsel may still serve as an associate to the civilian attorney. While counsel must be appointed in General and Special Courts, the lawyer-counsel requirement does not extend to the special court-martial. It is an understatement to say that this omission remains a major bone of contention among those who seek further modifications in the Code itself.

The most innovative provisions of the 1950 Code refer to appellate procedures. For the first time, the military legal system was provided with a high court of three civilian judges appointed by the President for fifteen-year terms. This court reviews all cases in which a death sentence has been approved by a Board of Review or in which a general flag officer has been sentenced. In addition, it takes all cases forwarded by the Judge Advocate General after appropriate action by a Board of Review and, may accept, at its discretion, other cases on petition of the accused.

III

What has happened to the civil rights of the serviceman since the last major congressional enactment of military law? In the remainder of this essay, we shall examine the work of the United States Court of Military Appeals (USCMA) in interpreting the Uniform Code of Military Justice. Our purpose is to acquire some "feel" for the sensitivity of this court to individual rights as reflected in contractive or expansive rulings in relevant cases. Since the USCMA sits as the Supreme Court of the military and the UCMJ is the Constitution of the serviceman, we may introduce a comparative dimension by relating the work of the USCMA to that of the United States Supreme Court. This will permit us to ask, in the period from 1950 to 1967, how

the rights of the serviceman compare with those of the civilian defendant and whether differences have been narrowed or broadened. Since
limitations of space require that we narrow our focus to a single substantive area, we shall examine decisions dealing primarily with questions of search and seizure—questions that have been in significant
contention in both civil and military life during the period under
study. While this will not permit any additional statements about the
civil rights of the contemporary serviceman in general, it is a first
step in that direction and, perhaps, will encourage greater attention
to other aspects of the problem than political scientists have been prone
to give.

The UCMJ provides no prohibition against search and seizure,
reasonable or otherwise. Nevertheless, there is no question that the
Fourth Amendment is applicable in the military legal system. The
relevant portion of that amendment states that "The right of the
people to be secure in their persons, houses, papers, and effects against
unreasonable searches and seizures, shall not be violated, and no warrants shall issue, but upon probable cause, supported by oath or affirmation, and particularly describing the place to be searched, and the
persons or things to be seized." The congressional expansion of this
protection in the civilian system has also been extended to the military system. That expansion occurs in the 1934 Communications Act
which says simply that "no person not being authorized by the sender
shall intercept any communication and divulge or publish the existence, content, subject, proport, effect or meaning of such intercepted
communication to any person. . . ."[12]

The *Manual of Courts-Martial* specifies certain privileged communications, defined as those incidental to a confidential relation which
it is public policy to protect. Military courts are expected to exclude
evidence of such communications unless the protection is explicitly
waived. Among the communications covered are those made by in-
formants to criminal investigators, the deliberations of courts and grand
and petit juries, diplomatic correspondance, certain communications
between husband and wife, client and attorney, penitent and clergy-
men, and confidential or secret information produced by Inspectors
General of the various armed forces. But more important, the *Manual*

12. U.S., *Statutes at Large*, LXVIII, 1103, Sec. 605 (1934). Cf. *U.S. v. Gebhart*, 10 U.S.
C.M.A. 606 (1959).

explicitly forbids the use of evidence obtained by an unlawful search and seizure where federal agents are involved or where evidence is secured in violation of the 1934 Communications Act. This represents an adoption, in 1951, of the so-called exclusionary rule which the Supreme Court affirmed in *Weeks* v. *United States*.[13]

The Exclusionary Rule

In the Weeks case, the Supreme Court ordered the suppression, in federal courts, of evidence illegally seized by federal agents. Since the Fourth Amendment was applicable only against the federal government, the rule was not imposed on the states. Thirty-five years later the Court decided that although the Fourth Amendment applied to the states through the Fourteenth Amendment, the exclusionary rule was not required. Of course, some states adopted such a rule much earlier. Iowa had it in 1903, and by 1949 sixteen other states had similar rules in force.[14]

Shortly after its establishment, the USCMA decided *Dupree* v. *United States*,[15] a case interpreting paragraph 152 of the *Manual of Courts-Martial*. That paragraph, among other things, lists lawful searches as: (1) one conducted under a lawful search warrant, (2) a search incident to lawful apprehension, (3) a search to prevent the removal or disposal of what is believed to be criminal property, (4) a search made with consent of one who owns the property searched, and (5) a search of property owned or controlled by the United States or its agents. The paragraph also authorizes commanding officers to delegate their authority to search and explicitly states that the list of approved searches is merely illustrative. Nevertheless, the clear implication is that searches under conditions not listed carry a heavier burden of proof for validation than those mentioned.

Dupree was convicted of possessing an opium derivative and sentenced to a dishonorable discharge, total forfeitures, and four years' hard labor. On appeal, he charged that a package of narcotics had been removed from his person illegally and should have been excluded as evidence at court-martial. In ruling on this contention the USCMA observed that neither the Fourth Amendment nor the exclusionary

---

13. 232 U.S. 383 (1914).
14. Jacob W. Landynski, *Search and Seizure and the Supreme Court* (Baltimore, 1966), p. 145.
15. 1 U.S.C.M.A. 665 (1952).

rule were made mandatory in the military system by Constitution or statute. Nevertheless, it adopted the federal rule as stated in the *Manual*. The *Manual* is promulgated by the President but does not supersede and must be consistent with the Code. If the Code does not require the exclusionary rule, the *Manual* could not do so. The Military Court's acquiescence in Paragraph 152 of the *Manual*, then, was of some importance. For it represented a more liberal stance than that of most states—a position taken nine years before the state courts were forced to follow federal practice by the Supreme Court's decision in *Mapp* v. *Ohio*.[16]

Under the holding of the Supreme Court in *Wolf* v. *Colorado*,[17] evidence illegally seized by state officers was constitutionally permitted in state prosecutions. Under the "silver platter" doctrine, such evidence was also admissible in federal trials.[18] But in 1960 a federal court conviction in Oregon on wire-tapping charges brought an appeal to the Supreme Court in *Elkins* v. *United States*.[19] The Oregon police uncovered the evidence used in the federal trial while searching the house of another person on a separate offense. Oregon courts found Elkin's conviction invalid, holding the officers' search warrant faulty. This, however, created no problem for the federal prosecutor who proceeded to get a conviction in the federal district court.

In the Supreme Court, the exclusionary rule, said Justice Stewart, was necessary to compel respect for the Fourth Amendment by removing the incentives to disregard it. Noting that statistical data to evaluate its effectiveness was lacking, he then proceeded to speculate, not on the effects of the rule, but on the fact that no apparent ill effects from its use were evident. Pragmatic evidence for this proposition was found in the experiences of the Federal Bureau of Investigation and the administration of criminal justice in the federal courts. Moreover, the steadily increasing adoption of the rule by the states suggested to Stewart that they evaluated the experience with the rule in the same way. Thus he had no difficulty in reaching a conclusion that evidence unconstitutionally obtained by state officers was inadmissible in federal trials, given a timely objection by the defendant.

The Court reached a further stage of development in *Mapp* v. *Ohio*. Here the search and seizure involved forceable entry, "roughing up"

16. 367 U.S. 643 (1961).   17. 338 U.S. 25 (1949).
18. *Lustig* v. *United States*, 338 U.S. 74 (1949).
19. 364 U.S. 206 (1960).

of the defendant, and a search of bedrooms, closets, a living room, kitchen, dinette, and basement. In the basement a trunk containing obscene materials was found, for possession of which Miss Mapp was ultimately convicted. Ohio courts concluded that the search was reasonable, even though it appeared that no search warrant was secured. The Ohio Supreme Court went on to say that, in any event, evidence obtained by an unreasonable search and seizure was admissible in a state court for a state crime and that a failure to exclude such evidence did not violate the Fourteenth Amendment. This put the issue squarely to the Supreme Court, which then adopted a new rule. Justice Clark's opinion for the court asserted that the Fourth Amendment guaranteed a right to privacy that is enforceable against the states. Such a right was said to prohibit "rude invasions by state officers" and to require means of enforcement sufficient to prevent it not from becoming but from remaining "an empty promise." Thus, via an "implied powers" kind of reasoning, the Court enunciated the rule that all evidence obtained by searches and seizures in violation of the Constitution is inadmissible in state courts.

On the military side, neither *Mapp* nor *Elkins* caused any appreciable changes in prevailing practices. *Mapp* concerned state officers and state courts, factors not present in the military system. *Elkins* would by analogy bar, in courts-martial, the use of evidence illegally seized by state officers. But military authorities have never relied to any significant extent on such evidential sources. At the same time the exclusionary rule appears to have been written into the Constitution by the rulings in *Mapp* and *Elkins*. Thus the military court's earlier position that the exclusionary rule was required by neither Constitution, Code, nor statute may have been undermined.

Search by Private Party

Since the prohibition against the states is through the Fourteenth Amendment, state action is necessary to make a search and seizure by state personnel inadmissible under the holdings in *Elkins* and *Mapp*. What is sometimes overlooked is the admissibility of evidence, however obtained, in state and federal courts and in courts-martial provided there is no involvement of state or federal officials. In 1921 the Supreme Court found no violation of the Fourth Amendment when the wrong done was the act of an individual in taking the property of another.[20] A federal district court in Washington, D.C., held as recently as 1964 that the exclusionary rule does not apply to evidence seized wholly by private persons.[21] This ruling was announced about the time that "Slammer" Dorsey found himself in difficulty with his roommate—Carter.[22] "Slammer" was the heavyweight boxing champion of the Third Army. After missing $145 from his trousers' pocket, Dorsey proceeded to extract a confession from Carter by physical force, recovering his money in the process. At the court-martial, Dorsey's report of his "discovery" was not challenged. On appeal, the defense counsel argued that the Law Officer should have struck Dorsey's testimony, urging that the evidence had been illegally seized, and that it represented a coerced confession.

In *Dupree* the USCMA refused to entertain a claim of unreasonable search and seizure raised for the first time at the appellate stage. But here, the issue of timeliness was bypassed and a ruling on the substance of the claim itself was made. The case presented the question of the interplay between the Fourth and Fifth Amendment—a question with which the Supreme Court has dealt in some recent cases. In *Mapp*, for example, the Court suggested that an illegal search and seizure was "tantamount to coerced testimony." In *Schmerber* v. *California*,[23] it was clearly stated that the privilege against self-incrimination applied only to evidence of a testimonial or communicative nature and was operative only when the individual was compelled to be a witness against himself. Taking of blood by the state for chemical analysis was held not to represent such compulsion. The interplay between the Fourth and Fifth Amendments flows from the conceptualization of any evidence used against a defendant as compelled testimony when consent to its use is not freely given.

In *Carter* the USCMA went to some length to spell out its position on this issue. Pointing to the Supreme Court's holding in *Curcio* v. *United States*,[24] which distinguished the Fourth and Fifth Amendments, the military court held the amendments to be separate and distinct with separate and distinct requirements. Thus, while an incrimi-

20. *Burdeau* v. *McDowell*, 256 U.S. 465 (1921).
21. *United States* v. *Frank*, 225 F. Supp. 573 (1964).
22. *United States* v. *Carter*, 15 U.S.C.M.A. 495 (1965).
23. 384 U.S. 757 (1966).
24. 354 U.S. 118 (1957).

nating statement obtained by coercion is inadmissible against a military defendant in a court-martial, irrespective of how the evidence was obtained, the exclusionary rule does not make inadmissible evidence of a criminal act illegally seized by a private party. Consequently, Dorsey's testimony, while illegally seized, was not excludable under the Constitution, the Code, or the *Manual.* This ruling left open the possibility that a violation of the Fifth Amendment had occurred. Such a question hinges on whether non-verbal evidence is to be viewed as of a testimonial or communicative nature. Judge Ferguson in the Military Court and Justices Black, Douglas, and Fortas in the Supreme Court are on record as subscribing to the view that compelled non-verbal evidence in certain circumstances violates the self-incrimination prohibition. But in neither court has that view found majority support.

The significance of admitting evidence in criminal trials that has been illegally seized by a private party lies in the ease with which such a procedural gap can be exploited. It is undoubtedly more difficult to establish that public authorities instigated private searches than that such authorities have engaged in illegal search. Moreover, it seems to leave open the possibility that private citizens can initiate all manner of illegal exploratory searches, freely providing public authority with whatever criminal evidence may be found. While this possibility may be thought so remote that a rule to deter it is unnecessary, it is not difficult to conceive of situations in which such behavior might be motivated. A private party who hires an investigating firm to prepare evidence for divorce proceedings may make use of criminal evidence discovered for criminal prosecution, blackmail purposes, spite, or for other reasons. Or a corporation under attack by critics of automobile safety may find it useful to see if its private investigators can turn up evidence of criminal acts committed by its critics. While it is necessary and in the public interest to oppose crime and ferret out those who perpetrate it, it seems illogical to impose restrictions on the officers charged with that responsibility while permitting other less responsible parties to operate free of similar restrictions.

In general, we may say that the Fourth Amendment and the exclusionary rule developed to implement it are equally applicable in state, federal, and military courts and that the prohibitions which they represent are limited to public authority in all three instances. Like the

Supreme Court, the USCMA has distinguished the Fourth and Fifth
Amendments by limiting the Fifth to compelled verbal or communicative testimony and conceptualizing its coverage to all parties, public
or private.

Authorization for a Search

In recent years the Supreme Court has frequently encountered what
might be called "sophisticated searching"—or searching which involves
complex electronic devices or intricately planned forays using inform-
ers or spies. Federal officers have monitored telephone and other conversations through a spike mike attached to a heating duct of a house[25]
(evidence inadmissible). They have used a wire recorder hidden on
the body of an Internal Revenue officer to record evidence of a bribery
attempt[26] (evidence admissible). State officers have "bugged" a room
at a jail set aside for conversations between prisoners and visitors[27]
(evidence admissible) and installed recording devices on private premises to secure evidence of bribery attempts[28] (evidence inadmissible).
In two recent cases that gained some notoriety, the federal government
used an informer to secure incriminating statements from James
Hoffa,[29] the labor leader, and a tape recorder hidden on an informer
to secure evidence of bribery in a related case.[30] In the same year the
federal government used an undercover man to purchase narcotics from
a "pusher."[31] In all three cases the informer was a welcome guest but
under false pretenses. Nevertheless, in all, the evidence seized was
admitted. In each, factors relevant for decision were not limited to
the method of search. But the cases illustrate a manner of searching
which has not characterized military cases.

In military proceedings involving search and seizure, the nature of
the questions controverted have to some extent been the consequence
of military organization and the disparities between the customs of
military society and the larger society of which it is a part. Unlike
state and federal police officers, the property searched by military officials is usually owned or controlled by the United States. While a

25. *Silverman v. United States*, 365 U.S. 505 (1961).
26. *Lopez v. United States*, 373 U.S. 427 (1963).
27. *Lanza v. New York*, 370 U.S. 139 (1962).
28. *Berger v. New York*, 87 S. Ct. 1873 (1967).
29. *Hoffa v. United States*, 385 U.S. 293 (1966).
30. *Osborn v. United States*, 385 U.S. 323 (1966).
31. *Lewis v. United States*, 385 U.S. 206 (1966).

civilian may have government property in or on his private premises, this may not be known until a search has commenced. In such circumstances, civilian courts have upheld the right of government officers to seize such property. In the military system, it is well established that property owned or controlled by the government is subject to search by the commanding officer having jurisdiction of the place concerned. Thus a post commander may search a post, a squadron commander a squadron, and a group commander a group. In this connection, the commanding officer stands in relation to military personnel under his command as the magistrate to civilians in his jurisdiction.

The person who issues the search warrant (authority to search) in the civilian system must be a judicial officer who is interposed between the citizen and the policeman as an impartial judge of the facts in a given situation. Before granting authority to search, he must be presented not only with the allegation of a crime but also with the facts establishing a probable cause to believe that a crime has been committed. This requirement grew out of our experiences with the infamous general warrants which omitted the name of the person to be arrested and the writs of assistance which granted authority to search any suspected place and to seize any person or property. The reaction to these procedures was to ban them in state and federal constitutions. Thus, while evidence necessary to establish guilt is not required, good faith on the part of the officer is insufficient. Succinctly put—"probable cause exists if the facts in circumstances known to the officer warrant a prudent man in believing that the offense has been committed."[32] The Supreme Court has held recently that the smell of opium from behind a closed door,[33] the mere loading of cartons into an automobile,[34] the observation that an automobile "sat low" in the rear,[35] and the assertions of an informer without adequate factual support, did not establish probable cause.[36]

Commanding officers in military installations and naval commanders on ships have always possessed the authority to order shakedown inspections or searches in the interest of safety and security.[37] The shakedown inspection is usually designed to test an individual's readi-

32. *Henry v. United States*, 361 U.S. 98, 103 (1959).
33. *Johnson v. United States*, 333 U.S. 10 (1948).
34. *Henry v. United States.*
35. *One 1958 Plymouth Sedan v. Pennsylvania*, 380 U.S. 691 (1951).
36. *Aguilar v. Texas*, 378 U.S. 108 (1964).
37. *United States v. Lange*, 15 U.S.C.M.A. 486 (1965).

ness to carry out his military duties and the condition of his equip-
ment. This power of the CO and his subordinates to order what is in
a sense a search of an individual's quarters and his belongings without
the restrictions of the Fourth Amendment sharply distinguish the position of the commanding officer from that of the civilian magistrate.
While the magistrate is required to see that certain conditions are met
before issuing a warrant, the CO can call an inspection at his unen-
cumbered discretion given proper motivation. Proving improper
motivation is not a simple matter. In the early period, the USCMA
was fairly lenient in deciding such questions.

An illustrative case is that of *United States* v. *Swanson*.[38] Swanson
was accused of stealing $73 from a fellow soldier. On the morning
after the alleged theft, an empty billfold was found in the area and
returned to the first field sergeant. He ordered a formation and announced that if the person who took the money would simply throw
it to the ground as the group dispersed, the matter would be dropped.
When the money did not appear, the sergeant ordered an inspection
during which the missing funds were found in Swanson's helmet liner.
The Court held the sergeant possessed the authority to order a search
in these circumstances—not because the inspection was properly motivated—but because there was probable cause to believe a crime had
been committed. It should be noted, however, that the individual to
be searched in such a situation is not identified in advance and that
a search that occurs via an inspection is a search of all persons and
property on the premises. The premises, in turn, may be anything
from a barracks to an entire post. Consequently, establishing a probable cause to believe that a given individual has committed a crime
and authorizing a search of that person and his property is preferable
to accomplishing the same ends through an inspection procedure.

In more recent years, the USCMA has been a little more restrictive
in this area. In *United States* v. *Battista*[39] a naval court-martial found a
dental officer on shipboard guilty of inducing seamen under the influence of drugs to disrobe, practice fellatio, and pose in the nude for
photographs. The conviction was based on photographs developed
from films seized in the dental officer's stateroom. The court held the
evidence inadmissible, saying that the captain lacked probable cause

38. 3 U.S.C.M.A. 671 (1954).   39. 14 U.S.C.M.A. 70 (1963).

to believe the stateroom contained instrumentalities or fruits of the crime or other proper objects of search.

This ruling was followed two years later by an opinion in *United States* v. *Hartsook*[40] which circumscribed still further the discretion of commanding officers to authorize searches. Hartsook was a participant in a bingo game in 1963 who won a thousand dollars in a game of "coverall." Upon investigation, it was determined that the winning card had been subjected to modification. When United States agents requested permission from the commanding officer to conduct a search, they were told to go ahead but to check in with the batallion commander. The batallion commander not only approved the search but later accompanied the agents in implementing it. At trial, the defense counsel objected to the seizure in Hartsook's quarters of certain materials used to doctor the bingo card and the use of such items as evidence at the court-martial. He urged that neither officer was sufficiently informed by the agents of the things to be seized or of the grounds for believing these things located in the place to be searched. In upholding this objection on appeal, the USCMA seemed to equate the civilian magistrate with the commanding officer. Thus it was said that commanding officers must have probable cause to believe the things to be seized are on or within the premises to be searched, that the things to be seized must be described with the same particularity as that required for the magistrate, and that, in general, the CO must be informed to the same extent as the magistrate before granting authority to search. This suggests a closer scrutiny of the way in which commanding officers exercise their discretion in ordering searches than in the past.

The restrictive ruling in Hartsook came at a time when the Supreme Court was beginning to relax its restriction on "things to be seized." In April, 1967, the Court dropped its prohibition against the seizure of "mere evidence."[41] In earlier cases the Court had allowed the seizure of instrumentalities, fruits of the crime, or contraband.[42] After the robbery of a taxi cab office in Baltimore, a jacket and trousers similar to those described on the fleeing gunman were found in a basement washing machine. Although in *Schmerber* the Supreme

40. 15 U.S.C.M.A. 291 (1965); see *United States* v. *Brown*, 10 U.S.C.M.A. 482 (1959).
41. *Warden* v. *Hayden*, 87 S. Ct. 1642 (1967).
42. *Boyd* v. *United States*, 116 U.S. 616 (1886); *Gouled* v. *United States*, 255 U.S. 309 (1921).

Court had permitted the seizure of "mere evidence" in allowing blood to be taken, it did not consider in that case the distinction between instrumentalities, fruits, or contraband and "mere evidence."

In *Hayden* the mere evidence rule was said to have derived historically from a superior governmental claim in the property seized. If a search and seizure were legal only when the government had a superior property claim, then items not so characterized, though useful as evidence, were not subject to seizure. Justice Brennan pointed out that "the principal object of the Fourth Amendment is the protection of privacy rather than property . . ."[43] and that the Court had "increasingly discarded fictional and procedural barriers rested on property concepts."[44] Consequently, he concluded, the government may seize evidence simply for the purpose of proving crime.

It may be noted that both the mere evidence rule and the authority of a commanding officer to search are based upon the same ground: i.e., the superior governmental claim to property. If, as Justice Brennan suggests, "fictional and procedural barriers rested on property concepts" are to be discarded, the customary authority of a commanding officer to search may undergo some circumscription at the hands of the USCMA. At least that may be expected if the Military Court follows the lead of its civilian counterpart. The opinion in *Hartsook* could certainly be read as a move in that direction. But were this to occur, we would have an anomalous situation in which by diminishing the importance of property concepts, we enhance the protection of the serviceman against arbitrary search while impinging still further on the protection afforded the civilian.

Like civilian law enforcement officials, the commanding officer has traditionally possessed the power to inventory the effects of one who is in custody. In civilian practice this is normally restricted to clothing, money, and other items taken from the person who is incarcerated. The military situation requires more since the military prisoner leaves space and possessions in a barracks to which other tenants have access. Some step must be taken to protect these possessions until disposition of the prisoner. There may be materials or items among a criminal defendant's possessions which constitute a danger to other occupants of his barracks. Or the space which the possessions occupy may be needed for other purposes. The question is whether these considera-

43. *Warden* v. *Hayden*, p. 1648.   44. *Ibid.*

tions, irrelevant in the civilian setting, should serve to reduce the right of the military person against unreasonable search and seizure.

In *United States* v. *Kazmierscak*[45] the USCMA provided an answer to this question. Kazmierscak was convicted of stealing mail. While in confinement, his belongings were inventoried in accordance with long-standing military practice. Letters addressed to other parties were found in his quarters during the inventory. The opinion for the Court noted that "in recent decades, the scope of constitutionally protected rights and privileges of the individual has been substantially redefined . . ."[46] and that "a thick code of tradition . . . is not assurance of constitutional acceptability."[47] However, it also suggested that "in the interplay between the exercise of governmental power and the exercise of a constitutional right by the individual, reason must be the arbiter"[48] and that "Time and circumstance may require a balance to be struck at one point in the civilian community, but at another in the military."[49] Thus to the Frankfurtian doctrine of "balance" between governmental power and individual rights, the opinion added an additional dimension—the distinction between the military and civilian societies. While it is not clear from this opinion whether the Court believed that the military person's rights should always have less weight in the scale than those of the civilian when balanced against the rights of government, its ruling that the inventory was routinely legal and that evidence found during such a procedure may be seized and used in court-martial proceedings takes us beyond the approved encroachments on civilian rights.

Judge Ferguson stressed in dissent that the arguments for the inventory were sound and that such procedures should not be barred. But he vigorously opposed using evidence secured by such means to obtain a criminal conviction. In Ferguson's view, this would constitute a search without probable cause since all the commanding officer is required to do, judging from the majority opinion in *Kazmierscak*, is to confine and rummage at will using what he finds as evidence. The majority, however, required good faith on the part of the commanding officer. Thus, if it can be shown that he confined and rummaged without good faith, evidence from a particular inventory may not be

45. 16 U.S.C.M.A. 594 (1967).
47. *Ibid.*
49. *Ibid.*

46. *Ibid.*, 599.
48. *Ibid.*, 599-600.

admissible. The majority seemed to follow the lead of the Supreme Court in *Frank* v. *Maryland*[50] where community interest was found to justify an encroachment on the periphery of Fourteenth Amendment rights and in *Abel* v. *U.S.*[51] where evidence found in a hotel room formerly occupied by one in confinement was admitted in a criminal trial. The *Abel* decision, by analogy, is supportive of the *Kazmierscak* holding. But in *Abel*, the hotel room was searched by FBI agents immediately after Abel had paid his bill and vacated the room. At that point possession returned to the hotel management, which then gave permission for the search. *Kazmierscak*, on the other hand, did not vacate his quarters of his own free will. Certainly it is arguable whether such a distinction should be ignored. As it stands the civilian right has not been similarly reduced.

To say that the gap between the authority of the civilian magistrate and that of commanding officers to authorize searches has been reduced is to say no more than that. The CO remains differentiated by his power to call inspections and to inventory the possessions of a confined serviceman, even though those possessions may be some distance removed from the point of a valid search. Civilian magistrates have no such authority and the Supreme Court has imposed restrictions on the area that may be searched as an incident to a valid arrest. The commanding officer is also differentiated by his power to delegate to his subordinates the right to authorize a search. No civilian magistrate may delegate such power to one who is not given a legal authority to exercise it. That authority in turn flows not from the Fourth Amendment, which is silent on the subject, but from statutes. Congress has delegated the power to make rules on the subject to the Supreme Court. That Court has formulated a rule requiring that search warrants be issued only by state and federal judges, and United States Commissioners "within the district wherein the property sought is located."[52] The CO, on the other hand, may enable a number of different people in his command to "issue warrants." This delegation does not devolve automatically on a subordinate during a temporary absence of the commander. The general expectation has been that the delegation of authority to search must be specific or at least of a nature to imply that delegation was intended.

50. 359 U.S. 60 (1959).   51. 362 U.S. 217 (1960).
52. Rule 41, Federal Rules of Criminal Procedure.

Since a CO may delegate the authority to order a search, the burden of showing lack of delegation falls on the complaining party. While this may seem to give the commanding officer considerable leeway in delegating his power and encourage widespread delegation, other restrictions prevent the CO from "ducking" his responsibility to make what may be "hard" decisions. In the first place, a delegation which represents an abandonment of discretion is not permissible. A commander cannot delegate the power to authorize searches to each and every member of his command. And he can no more give such authority to persons employed primarily in police work or criminal investigation than can the civilian magistrate to a civilian police officer. But a Board of Review has held that a valid delegation may be communicated in any reasonable manner and that a written authorization is not required.[53] This holding is of some importance since the board declined the opportunity to require documentation which in time might have grown to "search warrant-like" proportions.

The principle underlying the assignment of the power to issue warrants to a judicial officer is that such decisions should be made by an impartial arbiter who can determine objectively whether on the facts presented to him there is probable cause to warrant a search. In the military system, a similar view prevails: i.e., that while the CO may delegate the power to authorize searches, such delegation must be to parties who, like the CO, can effectively assume the role of an objective judge. Specifically, it has been said that delegations should be limited to those whose rank, duties, responsibilities, and discretion assure dispassionate and impartial consideration in exercising the delegated power. Currently, this distinction satisfies only two of the three judges sitting on the USCMA. Judge Ferguson has vigorously argued the position that the authority to order a search is a judicial function and, in the military, only the commanding officer can legitimately exercise such a "magisterial" role.[54] Thus he is opposed to any and all delegation. While this argument has some appeal, it seems insufficiently sensitive to the demands on the time of a CO of a large service installation. On such posts some delegation is likely to be a necessity.

53. *United States* v. *Barker*, 35 C.M.R. 779 (1964).
54. *United States* v. *Drew*, 15 U.S.C.M.A. 449 (1965) (dissenting opinion).

Consent to Search

Private searches and seizures which escape the restrictions of the Fourth Amendment and the exclusionary rule do not exhaust the situations in which the persons searched may receive less than ideal protection. Although officers have no search or arrest warrant and no probable cause to believe a crime has been committed, a search and seizure may still be made, given the consent of the appropriate party. Since the protection against unreasonable search is personal, one cannot object to the searches of another's property if the latter consents to the search. It has been held that where a suspect's mother consents to a search of his room in his absence, evidence seized is admissible.[55] And the Supreme Court has denied certiorari in a situation in which the owner of a house gave consent to search the room of a guest.[56] The Court of Appeals below held that the guest had no right to object to evidence seized and used against him under these circumstances. However, it seems unlikely that situations of this type would be approved by the present Supreme Court.

In recent years the Court has held that the search of a hotel room with the manager's consent after the departure of a guest is permissible.[57] However, the Court has also indicated that when a pass key furnished by the manager of an apartment building is used to enter an occupied apartment, the entry is the legal equivalent of a "break in" and must be justified on grounds other than consent.[58] A year later the Court detailed the rights of one who occupies a hotel room.[59] The search involved was conducted without a warrant of any kind but with the permission of the hotel clerk who freely opened the room for the searches. Recognizing that when a person rents a hotel room, he impliedly consents to entry by such persons as maids, janitors, or repairmen, the Court concluded that the clerk was not in this privileged group and had no authority to authorize the search of an occupied room. Evidence from the search was held to be inadmissible. In a related holding the Court has condemned the search of a tenant's house authorized by the owner[60] and the search of hotel rooms with the

55. *Gray* v. *Commonwealth,* 249 S.W. 769 (1923).
56. *McGuire* v. *State,* 92 A.2d 582; cert. den. 344 U.S. 928 (1953).
57. *Abel* v. *United States,* 362 U.S. 217 (1960).
58. *Ker* v. *California,* 374 U.S. 23 (1963).
59. *Stoner* v. *California,* 376 U.S. 483 (1964).
60. *Chapman* v. *United States,* 365 U.S. 610 (1961).

consent of the proprieter.[61] And in *On lee* v. *United States*[62] the consent of On lee to the entry of a government agent carrying a concealed transmitter was a factor in the Court's decision that no Fourth Amendment rights were violated.

A more contentious question concerning consent to search is: When has consent been given by one who is legally authorized to give it? Any constitutional right may be waived, and consent to a search, even though unreasonable, may constitute a valid waiver of the Fourth Amendment right. The problem lies in determining when a reported consent by the party to whom the right is personal is freely given and when it is coerced. Where questions of this nature are controverted, courts are forced to draw inferences from surrounding facts. Thus a valid consent will often turn on the circumstances. Generally, the presumption lies against consent and the burden is on the prosecuting authority to establish it. Where a suspect is frightened, has attempted to escape, is threatened, has low intelligence, or has been arrested first, valid consent is hard to establish. This is not to say that arrest or any of these factors rules out the possibility of consent. The Supreme Court has denied certiorari in a case in which arrest occurred first.[63] But local authorities are ill-advised to depend on their ability to establish consent in many if not most search and seizure situations. The "practice pointers" for governmental authorities suggested by a writer in the *American Law Reports* is informative on this point. Speaking like a modern judicial behavioralist, the author offers the following advice: "The morals for the government lawyer seem clear: urge the law enforcement officers in his jurisdiction to secure a warrant before making a search, rather than take a chance on talking the suspect into consenting to a search; instruct them in the basic requirements of a valid warrant, and the proper method of executing it, and do everything possible to establish cordial relations between individual officers and the magistrates authorized to issue search warrants in the jurisdiction."[64]

On the military side, the question has usually been of this latter type—i.e., did the party consent to the search of his own free will? As in other courts, the USCMA has adopted the rule that failure to raise

61. *Stoner* v. *California*.   62. 343 U.S. 747 (1952).
63. *Schaffer* v. *State*, 184 A.2d 689, cert. den. 374 U.S. 834 (1962).
64. 9 A.L.R.3d 867.

the issue of consent at trial is to waive the right. The position taken, essentially, is that the mere appearance of a government agent illegally taints any consent later alleged to have been given. Permitting government agents to enter and search a house occupied by a suspect is not necessarily a valid consent to search. In *United States* v. *Heck*[65] a warrant officer admitted military police to his quarters after midnight. The search of the quarters revealed the presence of a woman in violation of Army regulations. At the court-martial, the woman testified that she was, indeed, in the quarters at the time. A Board of Review, however, held her testimony inadmissible on the ground that no valid consent to search had been given. In *United States* v. *Justice*[66] the USCMA noted that submission to color of law or acquiescence in an officer's announced intention to search is not sufficient proof of consent.

In some civilian jurisdictions, the difficulties of ruling on consent have seemed to push courts in the direction of deciding on the basis of "legally irrelevant" considerations—such as the subject matter involved. In California, for example, it has seemed easier to establish consent to search in narcotics cases than in those involving a less obnoxious subject matter.[67] Obviously, it is difficult to find a formula for deciding such questions. The USCMA has complained about the problems of determining consent and has, in its choice of language, seemed to discourage reliance by searchers on the consent doctrine. In *Justice* the Court remarked, "It would certainly lessen the frequency of dispute and ease the burden of decision if law enforcement agents made crystal clear to persons whose premises are to be searched that they have no official authorization, and that they cannot search in the absence thereof, unless they have free and knowing consent to enter into and search the premises."[68] At the same time, the Court complained that "Specificity of such advice and consent is, however, seldom found."[69]

If we compare the military posture on consent with that taken by civilian courts, the military appellate bodies appear to impose more severe standards on those who would prove consent. But in general, neither civilian nor military jurisdictions encourage the use of consent

65. 6 C.M.R. 223 (1950); see *United States* v. *Cook*, 1 C.M.R. 850 (1951).
66. 13 U.S.C.M.A. 31 (1962).
67. *People* v. *White*, 218 Cal. App.2d 267 (1963); cert. den. 376 U.S. 926; *People* v. *Randall*, 226 Cal. App.2d 205 (1964).
68. P. 34; see *United States* v. *Whitacre*, 12 U.S.C.M.A. 345, 347 (1961).
69. *Ibid.*

as a means of legitimizing searches and seizures otherwise illegal. This, of course, is quite consistent with the Supreme Court's recent stance in *Escobedo* v. *Illinois,*[70] *Miranda* v. *Arizona,*[71] and other cases in which additional protections for the individual against the coercive pressures of law enforcement officers have been established.

Search Incident to Arrest

The Fourth Amendment protects against arbitrary arrests as well as against arbitrary searches and seizures.[72] This is reflected in the coupling of the words "persons and things" to be seized and is consistent with the history of events which produced the amendment. Under subsequent court holdings, those who have the authority to make arrests are rewarded for making a legitimate apprehension through the "search incident to arrest" doctrine. A valid arrest makes what would otherwise be an illegal search perfectly constitutional. American courts, in the development of this principle, have been influenced by the same considerations that led to its incorporation in English Common Law. A search incident to an arrest may be justified to insure against the escape of the party arrested, to protect the life of the arresting officers, or to prevent the destruction of evidence of the crime.

Today, the search of the person arrested occasions no great difficulty in the courts. But the search of his property or the environment in which the arrest takes place is another story. As early as 1925 the Supreme Court indicated that it was permissible to search the place where the arrest is made.[73] But the search was confined to the area under the immediate control of the prisoner. This rule was expanded and contracted in subsequent years. Sometimes the area of permissible search consisted of the premises used for the unlawful venture[74] or, perhaps, the premises under the prisoner's control.[75] In *Trupiano* v. *United States*[76] the Court refused to sanction the seizure of articles in plain view of the arresting officers, holding that a search warrant could have been obtained and that the reasonableness of a search

70. 378 U.S. 478 (1964).   71. 384 U.S. 436 (1966).
72. *Giordenello* v. *United States,* 357 U.S. 480 (1958).
73. *Carroll* v. *United States,* 267 U.S. 132 (1925).
74. *Marron* v. *United States,* 275 U.S. 192 (1927).
75. *Harris* v. *United States,* 331 U.S. 145 (1947).
76. 334 U.S. 699 (1948).

should be tested by the availability of a search warrant where it is feasible to obtain one. This, in turn, was overruled two years later in a decision permitting the search of the room in which the arrest had occurred including the safe, desk, and cabinets located in it.[77] In later cases the Court has held good the search of a whole house and the hotel room and adjoining bath occupied by the person arrested.[78]

One who seeks from these cases some formula by which it may be explicitly stated what is permissible and what is forbidden under the "search incident to arrest" doctrine has no easy task. Inconsistent rulings have been as frequent as personnel changes. Where men have different views and the law is unclear, a change in personnel may be the equivalent of a change in law. About the most one can say is that for the Supreme Court it is a question of: "What is reasonable under the circumstances" rather than "Is the search incidental to a valid arrest." There is little question that the replacement of Justices Murphy and Rutledge by Clark and Minton was responsible for some of the inconsistent rulings of the Supreme Court in this area. But the vacillating behavior of Justices Douglas and Black was also of some significance.[79]

The USCMA has ostensibly accepted the principle that some kind of search is justified as an incident to a valid arrest. In an early case the Court said: "We are attempting to carry out the congressional intent to grant to military personnel, whenever reasonably possible, the same rights and privileges accorded civilians. Accordingly, we have elected to determine if this search, tested by civilian practice, would be condemned as being unreasonable. If not, it would not, a fortiori, be unreasonable under military law."[80] This case involved a soldier stationed in Korea whose job was to inventory the personal effects of deceased soldiers. After one such inventory list was thought to have omitted certain pay certificates in the possession of two soldiers at their deaths, the commanding officer ordered the suspect to report to his office. There he was interviewed and requested to produce his wallet, which he did. Pay certificates found in the wallet were introduced at court-martial and a conviction resulted.

To the claim that the search was illegal, the USCMA demurred.

77. *Rabinowitz* v. *United States,* 339 U.S. 56 (1950).
78. *Kremen* v. *United States,* 353 U.S. 346 (1957); *Abel* v. *United States.*
79. See the positions of Black and Douglas in *Trupiano, Harris,* and *Rabinowitz.*
80. *United States* v. *Florence,* 1 U.S.C.M.A. 620 (1952).

The Court, acknowledging that the commanding officer has the authority to order a search or inspection of personnel or property under his command, held the search incident to a valid arrest. In order to reach this position, it was necessary to determine the point at which arrest occurs. Here it was said that arrest may be the final step in a series of disassociated acts from receipt of information to confinement, or the "end of a sequence of events so closely interrelated that it is impossible to fix the point of actual deprivation of liberty."[81] In this situation the latter was the case and the initiating step in the arrest was the order directing the accused to report. Consequently, the accused party was arrested and then searched, and the search was valid. A civilian situation analogous to this might be one in which a police department asks a party in for questioning. It is unlikely that a search of a responding party prior to his formal arrest would be upheld in the courts, even though the search occurred in the confines of a police station.

In regard to the place that may be searched, given a valid arrest, appellate military bodies have, on occasion, taken a quite restrictive view. While an arrest on a porch may justify the search of a house, it has been held that an arrest in a latrine fifty yards from the arrested person's barracks does not justify a search of his footlocker located in the barracks;[82] that an arrest in a hallway outside the locked door of the prisoner's room will not validate a subsequent search of the room;[83] and that the search of an automobile on private property is not a search incident to an arrest which occurred on an Army base.[84] This third example provided the interesting spectacle of Army agents who arrested the suspect on the post, took him physically to his automobile off the post, arrested him again upon reaching the vehicle, subsequently carrying out their search. The USCMA refused to countenance this "arrest of convenience" at the site of the search. Since the prisoner had not been released from custody after the first arrest, the second "alleged" arrest was a nullity. Thus, while in general the USCMA has followed the lead of the Supreme Court, it has been slightly more

81. *Ibid.*, 623. In criminal law an arrest signifies the detention of a person for the purpose of assuring that he will be forthcoming to answer for an alleged crime (*Patterson* v. *United States*, 192 F.2d 631, cert. den. 343 U.S. 951 [1952]) and cannot be used as a pretext for a search (*United States* v. *Lefkowitz*, 285 U.S. 452 [1932]).

82. *Gosnell* v. *United States*, 3 C.M.R. 646 (1952).

83. *United States* v. *Wallace*, 27 C.M.R. 605 (1958).

84. *United States* v. *Decker*, 16 U.S.C.M.A. 397 (1966).

restrictive in regard to the area of the search and more consistent in enunciating compatible principles from case to case.

IV

In summation, let it be said that this survey is by no means an exhaustive treatment of the military legal system nor of the principles governing searches and seizures within that system. But our exploration, as far as it has gone, suggests certain tentative conclusions that might be summarized.

We have suggested that the civil rights of the serviceman are no less important than those of his civilian brother.

The fact that these rights are protected in different legal documents and in separate legal systems is a consequence of a historical development reflecting a commitment to the view that military sub-society provides a context for behavior that differs essentially and fundamentally from that of civilian society. The purpose of the military society is security of the larger system, and all other principles must be subjugated to that primary one. The controverted questions have been on the order of: "What is necessary to accomplish that aim?" The answer given is that some encroachments on individual rights are justified, even if the result is to narrow the serviceman's rights as compared with those of the civilian. However, it is quite evident that the "necessary encroachments" have been steadily whittled down, particularly in the period from 1916 to 1950, in congressional statutes enacted for governing the military system. The USCMA, on the other hand, has not been a significant contributor to this development. Our hypothesis that closure between civilian and servicemen's rights is a function of the large-scale use of draftees or citizen soldiers in the modern age has found support in our data.

Subsequent to the establishment of the UCMJ and the USCMA, we have examined the protections of the serviceman against unreasonable searches and seizures. At the same time, recent Supreme Court decisions pertaining to similar rights on the civil side have been noted. Essentially, we found that the exclusionary rule and its limitations apply equally in both military and civilian systems. While the military system came to this rule later than the federal courts, they adopted it much earlier than most state jurisdictions.

In regard to private party searches, no significant distinctions between the Supreme Court and Military Court decisions were found. We suggested, however, that possible shortcomings exist in both systems.

The role of the judicial officer in issuing search warrants was set off markedly from that of the issuing officer in the armed services. We recognized the apparent trend in the USCMA toward conceptualizing restrictions on the commanding officer as analogous to those of the magistrate on the civilian side. Yet, the rights of the CO in regard to governmental property, his power to order inspections and inventories, and his legal right to delegate to others his power to approve searches clearly establishes that he has no closely analogous counterpart in the civilian system. In general, we can say that the commanding officer is less restricted than the magistrate, or that the rights of the serviceman at the authorization of search stage are of less scope than those of a civilian at the same procedural stage.

Consent to search has been a factor of some import in both systems. Military appellate bodies appear a little more difficult to persuade that valid consent has been given. Both the USCMA and the Supreme Court have decided questions of consent "on the circumstances" of each case.

In making rules for searches incidental to arrest, the Supreme Court was found to have vacillated from case to case, depending largely upon the personnel on the Court. No clear-cut formula has emerged for meaningful guidance. The USCMA and various Boards of Review have adopted positions similar to those of the Supreme Court, and like that Court have decided such issues "on the circumstances" rather than by some hard-and-fast rule. The USCMA has defined arrest as "an order to report to a Commanding Officer"—a holding which the Supreme Court has yet to match. Such a holding, of course, is entirely consistent with the efforts of the Supreme Court to push the point at which meaningful constitutional protection is afforded the individual in the direction of the first contact between the individual and law enforcement officials.

In general, we have found the serviceman to have substantial protection against unreasonable searches and seizures—more protection, perhaps, than we anticipated. Nevertheless, the discrepant role of the commanding officer and his powers in searching and seizing from those under his command reveals substantially less protection in this area than is afforded in the civilian system. It is beyond the purpose of this essay to argue the necessity of such discrepancies. But that they should be argued anew may appear certain to those subject to military law.

Claud H. Richards, Jr. / Religion and the Draft: Jehovah's Witnesses Revisited

Eight groups of conscientious objectors are identified by Sibley and Jacob in their study of the World War II period.[1] Perhaps none has proved more troublesome to draft boards and courts than Jehovah's Witnesses. Between October 16, 1940, and June 30, 1946, 6,086 conscientious or professed religious objectors were convicted of violating the Selective Service Act of 1940. Approximately 75.5 per cent, or 4,411, were Jehovah's Witnesses.[2] Moreover, the large number of cases involving the sect heard by federal courts in the postwar period indicates the continuing significance of the problem which they pose for Selective Service officials.

Founded by Charles Taze (Pastor) Russell during the last quarter of the nineteenth century, Witnesses have now spread their gospel and their literature to the far reaches of the earth. According to William J. Whalen, the cult reported only 106,000 members in 1942.[3] Under the leadership of Nathan II. Knorr, however, phenomenal growth occurred. In 1962, Witnesses claimed more than 884,000 adherents, representing a gain of 700 per cent.[4] No other denomination or sect in the United States could claim a growth of more than one-seventh that rate during the same period.

Jehovah's Witnesses deny that they are a religion, sect, or cult.[5] Witnesses are simply those persons, selected by God, who are completely devoted to Him and His kingdom and are diligent and faithful

1. Mulford T. Sibley and Philip E. Jacob, *Conscription of Conscience: The American State and the Conscientious Objector, 1940-1947* (Ithaca, N.Y., 1952), p. 18.
2. Selective Service Monograph No. 14, *Enforcement of the Selective Service Law* (Washington, 1950), chap. vii and Table 18, p. 95.
3. *Armageddon Around the Corner: A Report on Jehovah's Witnesses* (New York, 1962), pp. 15-16.
4. *Ibid.*, p. 16.
5. Good treatments of the religious and social doctrines of Jehovah's Witnesses may be found in Royston Pike Whalen, *Jehovah's Witnesses* (London, 1954), and Anthony A. Hockema, *The Four Major Cults* (Grand Rapids, Mich., 1963). Also see the author's "Jehovah's Witnesses: A Study in Religious Freedom" (unpublished Doctoral thesis, Duke University, 1945), chap. ii. Extended bibliographies of the publications of books, periodicals, and pamphlets published by the Watchtower Bible and Tract Society may be found in all these works.

in carrying out His commands. The chief witness is Christ Jesus, God's first spiritual creation, who agreed to assume human form to ransom mankind from the penalty of death. Abel, however, was the first, and Noah, Abraham, Joseph, all the faithful prophets from Moses to John the Baptist, and the apostles can be counted among their number.

Jehovah's Witnesses were not, then, according to their own doctrine, organized or established by man. They are a part of a theocratic organization ruled by Jehovah God through Christ, His chief executive, who with the "little flock" (144,000 in all) selected since Pentecost will eventually serve as the invisible ruler of a theocratic government to be established at the close of the battle of Armageddon. Some of the flock may still be living today, but no Witness can be sure that he is one of them. Associated with these are a much larger group known as "Jonadabs," "the other sheep," "the multitude," or "people of good will," whose obligations and duties are similar to those of their companions but who have no hope of becoming a part of the spiritual body of Christ. The world-wide activities of the Witnesses is directed by the Watch Tower Bible and Tract Society, a Pennsylvania corporation, with headquarters in Brooklyn.

The present world as viewed by the Witnesses is corrupt and Devil-ridden. Satan, who is the fallen angel Lucifer, his chief deputy, Gog, and other angels who joined Lucifer in rebellion against God are the invisible rulers. The visible agents comprise the unholy trinity—organized religion, government, and big business. The worst of the three is perhaps religion, the first means used by Lucifer to cause Eve and then Adam to sin and forsake God. Every great ruling power from Egypt to the present has been Satan's instrument. All have opposed the government of Christ, and, as Witnesses perceive the future, the final development before the battle of Armageddon will be the joining of democracies with totalitarian regimes in one great federation to plague and torture true followers of Jehovah.

The battle of Armageddon with Jehovah and Christ on one side and the Devil and his forces on the other will be a mighty and bloody affair. Millions will be killed, and seven years will be needed to bury the dead, clear the ruins, and construct the new paradise.

A part of the "new world" to be fully established after the battle of Armageddon has already come into existence. This is the "new

heaven," consisting of Christ Jesus, king of the theocracy, and the
little flock. The visible part of the theocracy, "the new earth," will
not be established until the defeat of Satan. It will consist of the
"Jonadabs," or "the other sheep," who have remained faithful, and
the resurrected prophets of old, who will be their visible rulers. It is
the divine mandate of Jehovah that the Jonadabs marry and fill the
earth with their progeny. This they are commanded to do during a
thousand-year period of probation, at the end of which Satan will reappear to make the final test of their righteousness. Those who succumb to the Devil's trickery will be destroyed with him and his angels.
Those who remain steadfast will inherit eternal life, everlasting peace,
security, strength, and happiness. All racial prejudices, distinctions,
and inequalities will be erased. Everyone will be fully employed.
There will be no oppression of the poor by the rich. Divisive national
boundaries, trade barriers, and tariffs, and colonial exploitation will
no longer exist. Political corruption will be impossible. But the greatest pleasure of the individual will be to know his God.

Wherever the devoted Witness is found, he remains aloof in his
relation to political and social institutions. His citizenship is in the
"theocracy," and as God's ambassador and ordained minister he considers himself no more than an alien in the land in which he resides.
As any other alien he pays his taxes, sends his children to the public
schools, resorts to the courts to defend himself, and abides by all laws
that do not contravene Jehovah's holy mandates. Yet he refuses to
salute the flag, vote or hold public office, to perform jury service, and
to serve in the armed forces. Toward the church, Catholic and Protes-
tant, he displays complete antipathy. The Catholic hierarchy is the
object of his bitterest attacks, and he will have nothing to do with
some of the most revered Christian beliefs and practices—the doctrine
of hell, the concept of the Holy Trinity, and the observance of Christ-
mas and other religious holidays. To the weak, the oppressed, and the
underprivileged he extends his sympathy but feels no obligation to
support those organizations fighting the battle of social and economic
justice. The skills of the medical profession he will use when necessary but is unalterably opposed to blood transfusions on the ground
that the Bible condemns the use of blood as food.

In short, Witnesses are neutrals in a foreign land. Their sole duty
is to proclaim to all mankind the grand eschatological plan of God's

will and to prepare all who will listen for eternal life in an imminent theocratic paradise. This obligation they assume with a devotion and a zeal seldom exhibited among adherents to the more orthodox religions. The street corner and the doorstep are their pulpit, and the community is their congregation. A dedicated Witness spends hours distributing books, tracts, and magazines. He spends additional hours ringing doorbells, making back calls on the interested, and organizing home Bible studies. Since he is unpaid, he must in addition engage in secular employment to maintain himself and his family. These are the people and these are some of the fundamental beliefs that have presented the courts with so many perplexing issues, not only in regard to conscientious objection to war, but in relation to the whole question of religious freedom.

Judicial Review of Classifications

An initial handicap to Witnesses in getting their claims to conscientious objection and ministerial status sustained in Selective Service cases was the reluctance of the courts to review the decisions of local draft boards and appeal boards. During World War I the only way in which a registrant could challenge his classification was through habeas corpus proceedings after induction.[6] During World War II, however, Jehovah's Witnesses consistently contended that classifications could be challenged in criminal proceedings brought against them for refusal to submit to induction. Prior to the decision of the Supreme Court in *Falbo* v. *United States*[7] some courts continued to adhere to World War I practice. This was particularly true in the Fifth Circuit.[8] On the other hand, the Fourth Circuit Court of Appeals held on several occasions that if the order of a draft board was found to lack foundation in law, was unsupported by substantial evidence, or was so arbitrary or unreasonable as to amount to a denial of due process, the courts should "treat it as a nullity in the same way as if the question arose in a habeas corpus proceeding."[9] This view would seem to sub-

6. All registrants under the 1917 act were inducted into the Army regardless of their compliance with induction orders.

7. 320 U.S. 549 (1944).

8. See *Fletcher* v. *United States*, 129 F. (2d) 333 (1942), and *Haberman* v. *United States*, 131 F. (2d) 1018 (1942). To the same effect was *United States* v. *Grieme*, 128 F. (2d) 811 (1942) in the Third Circuit, and *Bronemann* v. *United States*, 138 F.(2d) 333 (1943) in the Eighth Circuit.

9. See *Baxley* v. *United States*, 134 F. (2d) 998 (1934). Also see *Goff* v. *United States*,

stantiate the Witnesses' position. On at least two occasions courts held that judicial review of board action could be had only when all administrative remedies had been exhausted.[10]

In *Falbo*[11] the Supreme Court did little to clarify the issue. Nick Falbo had wilfully failed to obey an order to report for assignment to work of national importance on the ground that his classifications had been arbitrarily made and that he was not obligated to obey an order based upon erroneous action taken by his board. Justice Murphy argued that there was neither express nor implied limitation in the Selective Service Act on the granting of a full judicial review of induction orders in criminal proceedings. Courts, he added, had not hesitated to make such review available in habeas corpus actions following induction, in spite of the absence of express statutory authorization. Where, therefore, induction would never occur, as in Falbo's case, and where habeas corpus procedures were unavailable, it would seem that judicial review in a criminal case was essential, if a petitioner was to receive any protection against arbitrary and invalid administrative action. He failed to see that mobilization of the armed forces would be either impeded or augmented by the availability of judicial review of local board orders in criminal actions. In the rare case in which a person could prove that the action of a board had been arbitrary and illegal, he argued, an induction order should never have been issued, and the armed forces were deprived of no one who should have been inducted. If a defendant was unable to prove such a defense, on the other hand, or if he was forbidden to assert this defense, "the prison rather than the Army or Navy would be the recipient of his presence." But Murphy was in dissent. The majority, through Justice Black, held that the mobilization system which Congress established by the Selective Service Act was designed as one continuous process for the selection of men for national service in the quickest possible manner. Completion of the functions of the local boards and appellate agencies, important as these functions might be, were not, therefore, the end

---

135 F. (2d) 610 (1943), and *Honaker* v. *United States*, 135 F. (2d) 613 (1943). A later case decided after *Falbo* in the same circuit is *Zilkanich* v. *United States*, 139 F. (2d) 1016 (1944).

10. *Johnson* v. *United States*, 126 F. (2d) 242 (1942), and *United States* v. *Kowal*, 45 F. Supp. 301 (1942).

11. *Falbo* v. *United States*, 320 U.S. 549 (1944). For a favorable evaluation of the decision, see Nathan T. Elliff, "Jehovah's Witnesses and the Selective Service Act," *Virginia Law Review*, XXXI (Sept., 1945), 811-834.

of the Selective Service process. A selectee could still be rejected at the induction center, and a conscientious objector might be rejected at the civilian public service camp. The connected series of steps by which one enters the national service was not concluded until the registrant was finally accepted by the Army, Navy, or civilian public service camp. A board order to report was "no more than a necessary intermediate step in a united and continuous process designed to raise an army speedily and efficiently." Even if there were a constitutional requirement that judicial review must be available to test the validity of a local board decision, Black concluded, Congress was under no obligation to provide this remedy prior to induction. That Congress had not done so in the Selective Service Act was adequate justification for refusing to review Falbo's classification.

In general, the courts of appeal adhered, after *Falbo,* to Black's interpretation of judicial review,[12] and there were some decisions in which judges specifically stated that post-induction habeas corpus proceedings were the only means by which classifications could be challenged.[13] The effect of such rulings, as applied to Jehovah's Witnesses, was that no review was possible, since they refused to be inducted.

The Supreme Court did not speak again until 1946, after hostilities had come to an end. In *Estep* v. *United States*[14] Justice Douglas, speaking for the majority, indicated that the Selective Service Act specifically stated that the actions of local boards should be final except as appeals are allowed by rules and regulations prescribed by the Pres-

12. See: *Nicholson* v. *United States (Lowery* v. *Same),* 141 F. (2d) 981 (1944); *United States* v. *Gosciniak,* 142 F. (2d) 240 (1944); *United States* v. *Van Den Berg,* 139 F. (2d) 654 (1944); *United States* v. *Fratrick,* 140 F. (2d) 5 (1944); *United States* v. *Baxter,* 141 F. (2d) 359 (1944); *United States* v. *Longo,* 140 F. (2d) 848 (1944); *Black* v. *United States,* 142 F. (2d) 679 (1944); *United States* v. *Browder,* 140 F. (2d) 315 (1944); *Clayton* v. *United States (Stull* v. *Same),* 141 F. (2d) 494 (1944); *Clayton* v. *United States,* 142 F. (2d) 552 (1944); *United States* v. *Ensley,* 142 F. (2d) 1014 (1944); *United States* v. *Grieme,* 141 F. (2d) 495 (1944); *Gutman* v. *United States,* 142 F. (2d) 555 (1944); *Hampton* v. *United States,* 143 F. (2d) 598 (1944); *United States* v. *Krisfalusi,* 140 F. (2d) 458 (1944); *Lundgren* v. *United States,* 141 F. (2d) 497 (1944); *United States* v. *Meng,* 140 F. (2d) 315 (1944); *Nesselrotte* v. *United States,* 142 F. (2d) 679 (1944); *Giese* v. *United States,* 143 F. (2d) 633 (1944); *United States* v. *Nelson (Same* v. *Gibbs, Same* v. *Schwartz),* 143 F. (2d) 584 (1944); *Koch* v. *United States,* 150 F. (2d) 762 (1945); *Wallace* v. *United States,* 152 F. (2d) 751 (1946); *United States* v. *Madole,* 145 F. (2d) 466 (1944); *Edwards* v. *United States,* 145 F. (2d) 678 (1944); *Penley* v. *United States,* 145 F. (2d) 748 (1944); *Cahoon* v. *United States,* 152 F. (2d) 752 (1946); *United States* v. *Estep,* 150 F. (2d) 768 (1945); *Van Bibber* v. *United States,* 151 F. (2d) 444 (1945).

13. *Giese* v. *United States,* 143 F. (2d) 633 (1944); *United States* v. *Estep,* 150 F. (2d) 768 (1945); *Gibson* v. *United States,* 149 F. (2d) 751 (1945); *Enge* v. *Clark,* 144 F. (2d) 638 (1944); *Albert ex rel. Rocin* v. *Goguen,* 141 F. (2d) 302 (1944); and *Biron et al* v. *Collins,* 145 F. (2d) 758 (1944).

14. 327 U.S. 114 (1946).

ident. He also pointed out that sec. 11 of the Act provided for the trial in the district courts of one charged with wilfully failing to assume any obligation imposed upon him by the Act. No mention was made of defenses, if any, which might be available to a registrant so charged. But, the Justice argued, the decisions of local boards were final only when those decisions were made within the jurisdiction of the board, and it could not be readily inferred that Congress meant to depart so radically from the traditional concepts of a fair trial as to provide that a citizen of the United States should go to jail for not obeying an unlawful order of an administrative agency. The provision making the decision of the boards final meant only that Congress chose not to give administrative action under the Selective Service Act the customary scope of judicial review which obtains under other statutes.

It means that the courts are not to weigh the evidence to determine whether the classification of the local boards was justified. The decisions of the local boards made in conformity with the regulations are final even though they may be erroneous. The question of jurisdiction of the local board is reached only if there is no basis in fact for the classification which it gave the registrant.[15]

The scope of appellate jurisdiction allowed here, then, was not as broad as that allowed in other cases involving review of administrative decisions. In National Labor Relations cases, for example, "substantial evidence" had to be found to establish the board's rulings. In Selective Service cases, however, only some evidence, a "basis in fact," must be found. While there is little proof that the "basis in fact" rule has been used arbitrarily by the courts, it does permit much wider latitude on the part of the judge in upholding board classifications than would be true under the "substantial evidence" rule used in reviewing other administrative decisions. There is much to be said for adopting the latter in deciding questions affecting such vital rights as those related to conscience.

The majority in *Estep* did not foreclose habeas corpus proceedings after conviction as a form of relief, but contended that the very existence of the habeas corpus remedy gave added support to the necessity of the remedy of criminal defense. For to grant the use of the former without the latter would mean that the courts would be sending men

15. *Ibid.*, 122-123.

to jail today "when it was apparent that they would have to be released tomorrow." The courts would be required to "march up the hill when it is apparent from the beginning that they will have to march down again."[16]

In *Dickinson* v. *United States*[17] the Court expanded to some degree its ruling in the *Estep* case. Once a registrant has made a prima facie case, the Court held, a draft board must "search the record for some *affirmative evidence* [italics added] to support the local board's overt or implicit finding that the registrant has not painted a complete or accurate picture of his activities."[18] Furthermore, to dismiss a registrant's claim, supported by uncontroverted evidence, solely on the ground of suspicion and speculation is both contrary to the spirit of the Selective Service Act and foreign to our concepts of justice. It may be questioned whether this rule can be equally applied in cases involving ministerial status where fairly objective standards may be established, and for conscientious objector cases, where any evidence which casts doubt on the registrant's sincerity and good faith might serve to defeat him.[19] Draft boards are not bound by traditional rules of evidence. They may often make their case by reference to hearsay, opinion, affidavits, and other questionable evidence.[20]

A change in the requirement regarding physical examinations for inductees occasioned another ruling by the Supreme Court. In *Dodez* v. *United States*[21] the Court held the change from a post-induction physical to a pre-induction physical meant that all administrative remedies had been exhausted before a registrant actually reported for duty, and no proscription on the right to challenge a board's classification could be imposed on the ground that the assignee had failed to report to camp. The effect of the change left only the tasks of making a formal entry that the registrant had completed the order to report and noting the fact, time, and place of acceptance upon the assignee's papers to be performed at the camp.

In a companion case[22] the government attempted to argue that when a person reported for duty at a public service camp and later deserted, he had gone too far in the administrative process to offer an

16. *Ibid.*, 124-125.   17. 346 U.S. 389 (1953).
18. *Ibid.*, 396.
19. See Carl L. Shipley, "Selective Service: Finality of Draft Board Decisions," *American Bar Association Journal*, XLI (Aug., 1955), 709-712.
20. *Ibid.*, p. 711.   21. 329 U.S. 338 (1946).
22. *Gibson* v. *United States*, 329 U.S. 338 (1946).

arbitrary classification by a local board as a criminal defense. It was the government's position that as in the case of a registrant inducted into a military camp, an assignee to a public service camp became subject to military law once he had reported for duty and consequently had no legal standing in a civilian court except perhaps in seeking a writ of habeas corpus. But the majority of the Court were of the opinion that the two situations were not analogous. The transfer of jurisdiction in the case of the conscientious objector was from one civilian agency to another, both of which are branches of the Selective Service System. There was no actual change of jurisdiction insofar as the courts were concerned. The person remained a civilian. His duties were not military in nature, and he was not subject to military discipline or authority. Consequently, he could not be tried by court-martial or military tribunal for violation of duties or orders imposed on him by camp officials. The analogy relied upon by the government being fallacious, the Court held that a criminal defense should be allowed.

Participation in War in Any Form

While attacks on the constitutionality of the draft have been made in the past and are currently being made in relation to the war in Vietnam, courts have uniformly held that exemption from military service rests not on constitutional right but on legislative will.[23] Nevertheless, Congress in its mercy has consistently considered it wiser to respect a man's religious scruples than to compel him to serve. In 1917 exemption was provided for those who could support their claim as conscientious objectors by membership in a religious group including in its creed provisions for objection to war.[24] Only those who were willing to serve in a noncombatant capacity in the armed forces were protected. No provision was made for the objector to both combatant and noncombatant service. The Selective Service Act of 1940 was more liberal.[25] The reference to religious creed was dropped, and no person conscientiously opposed to participation in war in any form by

23. *Draft Cases, Arver* v. *United States*, 245 U.S. 366 (1918); *Hamilton* v. *Regents*, 293 U.S. 245 (1934); *In re Summers*, 325 U.S. 561 (1945), 572; and *United States* v. *Macintosh*, 283 U.S. 605 (1931), 623-624. Also see cases cited in n. 28, below.
24. Selective Service Law of 1917, sec. 4, U.S., *Statutes at Large*, XL, 78.
25. Sec. 5 (g), U.S., *Statutes at Large*, LIV, 889 (1940).

reason of religious training and belief was to be required to be subject
to combatant training or service in the armed forces. In addition, any
person claiming conscientious objection could, if his claim was sustained by a local draft board, be assigned to noncombatant service or,
if opposed to such service, to work of national importance under civilian direction. Essentially the same provision was incorporated in the
Selective Service Act of 1948,[26] with the exception that the conscientious objector was required to base his objection on a belief in a
supreme being. Exemption was not to be granted the philosophical,
sociological, ethical, moral, or political objector. Neither was any provision made for the absolutist who felt he violated his conscience by
submitting to registration. The clause requiring work of national importance was eliminated, but in 1951 Congress amended the law by
providing that the objector to noncombatant service be ordered by
his draft board, subject to regulations prescribed by the President, "to
perform . . . such civilian work contributing to the maintenance of
the national health, safety, or interest as the local board may deem
appropriate."[27]

As might be expected, the constitutionality of the clause in the
1948 amendment requiring a belief in a supreme being was challenged
in the courts.[28] In each case, however, exemption from military service
was ruled to be an act of legislative grace to be granted on any conditions Congress desired to impose. In *United States* v. *Seeger*[29] the
Supreme Court side-stepped the constitutional issue and gave a broad
interpretation to congressional intent. The test of belief in a relation
to a supreme being, the Court said:

is whether a given belief that is sincere and meaningful occupies a place
in the life of its possessor parallel to that filled by the orthodox belief in
God of one who clearly qualifies for the exemption. Where such beliefs
have parallel positions in the lives of their respective holders we cannot
say that one is "in relation to a Supreme Being" and the other is not.[30]

26. Sec. 6 (j), U.S., *Statutes at Large*, LXII, 612 (1948).
27. U.S., *Statutes at Large*, LXV, 75 (1951).
28. See *United States* v. *Bendik*, 220 F. (2d) 249 (1955); *Clark* v. *United States*, 236
F. (2d) 13 (1956), *George* v. *United States*, 196 F. (2d) 445 (1952); *Etcheverry* v. *United
States*, 320 F. (2d) 873 (1963).
29. 380 U.S. 163 (1965).
30. *Ibid.*, 166. Here the Court was following the broad interpretation which Judge
Augustus Hand gave to the phrase "religious training and belief" in the 1940 law in
United States v. *Kauten*, 133 F. (2d) 703 (1943), rather than the narrow, more orthodox
interpretation of the Ninth Circuit found in *Berman* v. *United States*, 156 F. (2d) 377
(1946). Also see *United States* v. *Jakobson*, 325 F. (2d) 409 (1963), and *United States*
v. *Seeger*, 216 F. (2d) 846 (1964).

Justice Clark could find nothing in the history of the 1951 statute that would prevent this interpretation. In enacting the Military Selective Service Act of 1967, nevertheless, Congress took steps intended to reverse the *Seeger* rule. The phrase "belief in a relation to a Supreme Being" was struck, and the provision of the 1940 law providing for objection based only on religious training and belief was restored. It seems doubtful that the attempt of Congress to limit the Court will have any lasting effect, for if one reads the *Seeger* opinion closely enough, he will find that the Court was just as concerned with the interpretation of the term "religion" as it was with the phrase "belief in relation to a Supreme Being." Tillich, Robinson, and other theologians who certainly cannot be said to be orthodox or traditional in their concepts of religion, were cited with approval. A more severe challenge to Congress is the recent ruling of District Judge Wyzanski of Massachusetts that the 1967 law discriminates unconstitutionally against the non-religious objector to the limited war in Vietnam.[31]

Jehovah's Witnesses are unlike any other group in their objection to war. Their objection stems directly from their unswerving allegiance to Jehovah's theocracy and their neutral attitude toward all things worldly. They differ from the historic peace churches in that they are not opposed to *all* wars. How could they be, when the heart of their message rests dead center on a phophecy of the greatest war of all time—Armageddon? Most Witnesses also admit that they do not accept wholeheartedly the biblical admonition, "Thou shalt not kill." They will, if necessary, use force to defend themselves or brothers in the faith. Basically, then, objection to war by the Witness is objection to earthly wars of the blood and flesh variety waged by Satanic, worldly powers. As an alien and ambassador of God in an unfriendly world, he can take no part in such carnal conflict.

Prejudice undoubtedly has led some local boards to deny conscientious objector status to Jehovah's Witnesses. More often, however, an inability or unwillingness to understand the theological tenets of Witnesses on the part of boards, as well as the Justice Department and courts, has been responsible for the lack of sympathy their claims have received. Writing in the *University of Pittsburgh Law Review* in 1958, T. Oscar Smith, Chief of the Conscientious Objector Section of the Justice Department, and Derrick A. Bell contended that there was no

31. See New York *Times* (April 2, 1969).

indication in the group's literature that the wars in which they would take part would be limited to spiritual wars, but only that they would be spiritually inspired.[32] They also noted that the willingness of Witnesses to use force to defend their brothers and kingdom interests indicated that under certain circumstances they would be willing to fight. Thus, there was, at least in their opinion, a clear inference that theocratic war, as the term is used by the Witnesses, could refer to flesh and blood conflicts and that if a certain war should meet the group's definition of "theocratic," the religious objection would not be applied. The dissents of Reed and Minton in *Sicurella* v. *United States*[33] seem to corroborate this view. To similar effect was *White* v. *United States*,[34] decided before *Sicurella*, and *United States* v. *Jones*,[35] decided after *Sicurella*. In *White* Circuit Judge Pope commented on the fact that White's objection was broader than that to war. It was an objection to any governmental service whatever. Furthermore, White's employment in an aircraft factory holding war contracts with the government seemed to indicate some inconsistency in his claim to objection to all military service.

These opinions, however, are not in accord with the majority view expressed by Justice Clark in the *Sicurella* case. The test in cases involving conscientious objectors, he said, is not whether the registrant is opposed to all war but whether he is opposed, on religious grounds, to *participation* in war. And by war he made it clear that he thought Congress meant "real shooting wars . . . actual military conflicts between nations of the earth in our time—wars with bombs and bullets, tanks, planes and rockets."[36] He could not believe that Congress had in mind theocratic wars or Armageddon between powers of good and evil, where Jehovah's Witnesses fight without carnal weapons. In 1954 the Court of Appeals for the Eighth Circuit had already formulated this rule and had further held that

The words, "in any form," obviously relate, not to "war" but to "participation in" war. War, generally speaking, has only one form, a clash of opposing forces. But a person's participation therein may be in a variety of forms. . . . We think Congress intended this section to exempt those persons from serving in the armed forces whose religious beliefs were op-

32. T. Oscar Smith and Derrick A. Bell, "The Conscientious Objector Program—A Search for Sincerity," *University of Pittsburgh Law Review*, XIX (Summer, 1958), 695-726, at 712-713.

33. 348 U.S. 385 (1955).   34. 215 F. (2d) 782 (1954).
35. 142 F. Supp. 806 (1956).   36. 348 U.S. 385 (1955), 391.

posed to any form of participation in a flesh and blood war between nations.[37]

Circuit Judge Barnes, in *Kretchett* v. *United States*,[38] attempted to limit the *Sicurella* holding. The decision would not apply, he contended, where an individual Witness expressed a willingness to defend himself, his home, or his Christian brothers by killing, if necessary, and to participate in a war involving the use of carnal weapons, if he felt Jehovah or someone he believed to be speaking for Jehovah ordered him to do so. Any permissible belief in warfare on the part of a conscientious objector, in other words, should be limited to spiritual warfare unrelated to killing by man or to the use of carnal weapons. Judge Barnes did not persuade the majority of his court, and other courts have refused to follow him.[39]

Once the scope of exemption for the conscientious objector has been defined, Selective Service authorities and courts have the added task of determining the sincerity of the registrant. This lies at the heart of all conscientious objector controversy.[40] But how does a draft board or judge determine the sincerity of a registrant? Sincerity after all is a subjective quality not easily discerned by one who is asked to judge its existence in the mind of another. Perhaps there is no clear and reliable standard which can be applied, but certain factors have been considered by the courts in attempting to judge the sincerity of Jehovah's Witnesses.

In the first place, courts in the Ninth[41] and Fourth Circuits[42] have held that work in a defense plant may be considered as an indication that the registrant lacks sincerity in his objection to war. The same has been held true for a registrant who has served in the Naval Reserve or has attempted to enlist for military service within a reasonable time before he asked for conscientious objector status.[43] The Court of Appeals for the Ninth Circuit has also held that willingness to accept civilian work in a military reservation is inconsistent with a

37. *Taffs* v. *United States*, 208 F. (2d) 329 (1954), 331.
38. 284 F. (2d) 561 (1960), 566-567.
39. See *United States* v. *Hagaman*, 213 F. (2d) 86 (1954); *United States* v. *Bortlik*, 122 F. Supp. 225 (1954); *United States* v. *Hartman*, 209 F. (2d) 366 (1954); *Shepherd* v. *United States*, 217 F. (2d) 942 (1954); *Ashauer* v. *United States*, 217 F. (2d) 788 (1954).
40. See *Witmer* v. *United States*, 348 U.S. 375 (1955).
41. *Keefer* v. *United States*, 313 F. (2d) 773 (1963).
42. *Blalock* v. *United States*, 247 F. (2d) 615 (1957).
43. *Selby* v. *United States*, 250 F. (2d) 666 (1957); *United States* v. *Salamy*, 253 F. Supp. 616 (1966).

claim of opposition to both combatant and noncombatant service, although such an attitude is not inconsistent with objection to combatant service alone.[44] While admittedly association with immoral persons is no conclusive test of insincerity, the Court of Appeals for the Tenth Circuit has concluded that it is a factor which Selective Service authorities may consider when taken in context with other actions and attitudes.[45] A lack of understanding of the Scriptures or a lack of strong personal commitment, even when Scriptures are extensively quoted, may also reflect a superficial attachment to objection to war.[46] On the other hand, the Tenth Circuit has held that a conscientious objector need not show humility,[47] and the Ninth Circuit has decided that neither aid in filling out a questionnaire nor a charge brought by a fellow religionist that one is a playboy may defeat a claim for objection.[48] The court properly pointed out that to a devout Jehovah's Witness going to a theater, smoking a cigarette, or participating in sports on Sunday might make one a "playboy." Apparently all the fellow Witness meant was that the person he criticized was an unsuitable candidate for the ministry and not that he was a riotous liver.

Section 1625.2 of the Selective Service Regulations provides that a local board may reopen anew the classification of a registrant after an order to report for induction has been mailed to the registrant, but only if the board "first specifically finds there has been a change in the registrant's status resulting from circumstances over which the registrant has no control." Cogent argument may be presented to support the right of the Johnny-come-lately to have his case reviewed.[49] Undoubtedly many late claims, especially after an induction notice has been mailed, may be spurious. After all, the normal registrant has had more than twenty years to reconcile his conscience with his obligation to serve in the armed forces. Nevertheless, many factors may play a part in making a decision. The social disapproval often shown the objector, the fear that any display of doubt at any early stage may cause a board to question the sincerity of the registrant, the imme-

44. *Goetz* v. *United States,* 216 F. (2d) 270 (1954).
45. *Bouziden* v. *United States,* 251 F. (2d) 728 (1958).
46. *United States* v. *Corliss, United States* v. *Heise, United States* v. *Herold,* 280 F. (2d) 808 (1960).
47. *Annett* v. *United States,* 205 F. (2d) 689 (1953).
48. *Parr* v. *United States,* 272 F. (2d) 416 (1959).
49. See "Pre-Induction Availability of the Right to Claim C.O. Exemption," *Yale Law Journal,* LXXII (June, 1963), 1459-1468, at 1463-1464.

diate impact of impending induction on deeply held beliefs—any one
of these—may cause the candidate for Selective Service to postpone to
the latest possible moment the making of a decision as to this course
of action. There are perhaps conversions, even today, on the road
to Damascus. Yet, with some exceptions,[50] courts have usually sustained
denials for rehearings under section 1625.2 on the ground that no
change in status had occurred to warrant reconsideration of classification.[51] Said Circuit Judge Barnes for the Ninth Circuit: "There must
be some end to the time when registrants can raise a claim of conscientious objection to induction, and raise and re-raise an alleged right
to review. Any other conclusion would result in chaos."[52] The District
Court for New Jersey, however, felt that the government's argument—
that a registrant by exposing himself voluntarily to the teachings of
Jehovah's Witnesses and then accepting them and thus bringing about
a change from circumstances over which he had control—bordered on
the naïve.[53] Dissenting in a case in which a rehearing was denied
because a prospective draftee had joined Jehovah's Witnesses three
months before his order for induction, Judge Spencer Bell of the
Fourth Circuit observed: "The statute gives this man exemption, the
Army does not want him, the jail will not change his religious beliefs,
nor will the will of the people to fight for their country be sapped
by a generous adherence to the philosophy behind this law."[54]

Perhaps in conscientious objector cases no better rule for determining sincerity can be devised than that formulated by Judge Soleloff
of the Fourth Circuit:

Human experience has devised no precise guage for appraising a subjective belief lodged in the mind and heart of the person himself and
never truly known by others. Sincerity can be judged only from the individual's demeanor, the consistency of his statements, appraisals by persons
to whom he is known, and other immeasurable factors which may be
deemed significant by some men but not by others.[55]

Justice Clark has stated in *Witmer* v. *United States*: "in all cases where
there was conflicting evidence or where two inferences could be drawn

50. See, for example, *United States* v. *Underwood*, 151 F. Supp. 874 (1955).
51. See *United States* v. *Schoebel*, 201 F. (2d) 31 (1953); *Boyd* v. *United States*, 269
F. (2d) 607 (1959); *United States* v. *Bonga*, 201 F. Supp. 908 (1962); *United States* v
Beaver, 309 F. Supp. 273 (1962).
52. *Boyd* v. *United States*, 269 F. (2d) 607 (1959), 612.
53. *United States* v. *Brown*, 129 F. Supp. 237 (1955).
54. *United States* v. *Beaver*, 309 F. (2d) 273 (1962), 279.
55. *Blalock* v. *United States*, 247 F. (2d) 615 (1957), 618.

from the same testimony, we cannot hold that petitioner was wrongfully denied the conscientious objector classification."[56]

Jehovah's Witness as Minister

That Jehovah's Witnesses couple their concept of the ministry with their objection to military service is clearly seen in several cases in which they have questioned the right of the government to require them to perform work of national importance in lieu of service in the armed forces.[57] As J. B. Tietz, a lawyer who has defended numbers of Jehovah's Witnesses, points out, the Witness is a conscientious objector because he is a minister.[58] As such, although he claims no ordination from man, he has formed a covenant with God to spread in the streets and at the doorstep the news of the imminent advent of Jehovah's theocratic order. If he is compelled to break this covenant by any earthly power, he is doomed to "everlasting death." Since he has no purgatory and no hell, everlasting death is the greatest catastrophe that may befall him. Therefore, most Witnesses protest any alternate service which other conscientious objectors may accept.

In spite of this strong belief, Selective Service authorities and courts have consistently refused to recognize its validity. According to Judge Pope of the Ninth Circuit:

[the Witness's] real objection to noncombatant service would appear to be its interfering with his carrying out the "message" and doing what he chose to call "ministerial work." We think in drawing the line where it did, it cannot be said that the appeal board acted without basis in fact. The board could well understand from appellant's representations that his objections would include such tasks for a government of "this world" as fighting forest fires or building roads. An objection, on religious grounds, to any assignment which would take the registrant away from his missionary activities is not an objection which the [Selective Service] Act recognizes.[59]

Courts have, then, consistently held that a Jehovah's Witness's claim to exemption must be based either on objection to participation to

56. 348 U.S. 375 (1955), 383.
57. See, for example, *Tomlinson* v. *United States*, 216 F. (2d) 12 (1954), and *Leiffler* v. *United States*, 260 F. (2d) 648 (1958).
58. J. B. Tietz, "Jehovah's Witnesses: Conscientious Objectors," *Southern California Law Review*, XXVIII (Feb., 1955), 123-137, at 130.
59. *Tomlinson* v. *United States*, 216 F. (2d) 12 (1954), 18.

war in any form or on ministerial status. Both claims may be presented simultaneously, but each must be considered separately, not as interrelated with each other.

The reason for exempting ministers from the draft is somewhat obscure. Julien Cornell, writing in the *Yale Law Journal* in 1947,[60] speculated that Congress has felt spiritual guidance of ministers in wartime is essential to the national well-being. Or, he said, it may be that Congress was convinced of the basic pacifist character of the Christian religion and did not wish to place those who had dedicated themselves to following the teachings of Christ in a position where they would have to abandon their principles by engaging in warfare. Still another reason might be that many ministers are avowed pacifists and would refuse to be drafted. The imprisonment of such leaders might encourage pacifism, a result to be avoided in wartime.

Whatever the reason might be, Congress has provided in all recent draft legislation exemption for the clergy. The 1940 law provided that regular or duly ordained ministers of religion and students preparing for the ministry in theological or divinity schools recognized as such for more than one year prior to the date of the act's enactment were exempt from training and service.[61] Selective Service regulations defined a "regular minister" of religion as one who customarily "preaches and teaches the principles of religion of a recognized church, religious sect, or religious organization of which he is a member, without having been formally ordained as a minister of religion; and who is recognized by such church sect, or organization as a minister." A duly ordained minister was defined as a man who "has been ordained in accordance with the ceremonial, ritual or discipline of a recognized church, religious sect, or religious organization, to teach and preach its doctrines and to minister its rights and ceremonies in public worship; and who customarily performs those duties."[62] Subsequent legislation has retained essentially the same guidelines for the classification of those claiming ministerial exemption, although in the 1948 law Congress was careful to exclude from the definition of minister those who performed their ministerial duties only irregularly or incidentally

60. Julien Cornell, "Exemption from the Draft: A Study in Civil Liberties," *Yale Law Journal*, LVI (Jan., 1947), 258-275, at 263.
61. Sec. 5 (d), U.S., *Statutes at Large*, LIV, 888.
62. Selective Service Regulations, secs. 622.44 (b), (c).

as an avocation rather than as a vocation.[63] It was made unmistakably clear by the Senate Armed Services Committee that they were fearful that the views expressed in minority opinions in *Cox* v. *United States* might lead to a wholesale exemption of Jehovah's Witnesses and that this was not the intent of Congress.[64] In *Cox*, Douglas, with Black's approval, had argued that unorthodox as well as orthodox sects and religious groups should be treated equally under the regulations of the Selective Service System and that a person might properly be considered a minister even though he found it necessary to engage in secular occupations to meet his financial needs. Part-time ministers, such as Jehovah's Witnesses, "by practical as well as historical standards . . . are the apostles who perform the minister's function" for their respective religious groups.[65] Both in 1951 and in 1967 Congress left the statutory ministerial definition unchanged.

During World War II the British and the Canadians avoided the difficult problem of classifying Jehovah's Witnesses by simply refusing to recognize them as a religious group or sect.[66] There is some evidence that at least some members of local draft boards here in the United States have had similar persuasions.[67] But the Census Bureau, General Hershey, and the courts have all held to the opposite view. In fact, to accept the position of our British and Canadian cousins would hardly seem to be consistent with the American tradition of toleration and the spirit of the First Amendment.

Equally untenable is the contention that lack of education in high school, college, or seminary precludes a Witness from being a minister.[68] Witnesses are adamant in their view that education does not make a preacher. And they can substantiate their claim by reference to the practices of Quakers, Methodists, and Presbyterians, not to mention Baptists, who have not been unknown to accept as ministers those who have done little more than receive the call of the Lord.

63. Sec. 6 (g), U.S., *Statutes at Large*, LXII, 611.
64. Senate Report No. 1268, 80th Cong., 2d Sess., 1948, p. 13.
65. 332 U.S. 442 (1947), 457.
66. Defense of Canada Regulations (Consolidation), 1941, sec. 39C (1), and Report from British Ministry of Labour and National Service, quoted in brief filed for the United States in *Falbo* v. *United States*. Cited in Elliff, pp. 820-821, nn. 35 and 37.
67. See *United States* v. *Henderson*, 223 F. (2d) 421 (1955); *United States* v. *Cheeks*, 159 F. Supp. 328 (1958).
68. *United States* v. *Kezmes*, 125 F. Supp. 300 (1954); *Niznik* v. *United States*, 184 F. (2d) 972 (1950); *United States* v. *Hurt*, 244 F. (2d) 310 (1958); *United States* v. *Stepler*, 258 F. (2d) 416 (1958).

What, then, are the criteria by which the right of Jehovah's Witnesses to be called minister is to be judged? Circuit Judge Wisdom of the Fifth Circuit has suggested three: (1) in line with congressional policy, the ministry must be followed as a vocation rather than an avocation, (2) a substantial part of the Witness's time must be devoted regularly, not sporadically, to religious affairs, and (3) the position of the Witness must be that of a minister to a congregation or of a recognized leader to a group of lesser members of his faith.[69]

In *Witmer* v. *United States*,[70] decided in 1955, the Supreme Court held that unlike conscientious objection, ministerial exemption must be determined on the basis of objective fact rather than the subjective state of a registrant's mind. But it was Judge Wisdom's opinion that the manner in which a registrant views his ministerial activities, "especially as discoverable from outside facts," is at least of probative importance.[71] In *Fitts* v. *United States*,[72] for example, while Fitts claimed ministerial classification, he had on several occasions admitted openly that he considered farming his principal occupation. Furthermore, he acknowledged the fact that he took part in his religious activities only when he had spare time, when the weather was good, and there was no farm work to be done. In *Wiggins* v. *United States*,[73] in contrast, the defendant was a full-time crane operator but put his ministerial duties before his secular labors. On several occasions he changed jobs in order to prevent his secular work from interfering with his religious work.

A question might be raised at this point concerning the weight to be given moral irresponsibility in judging ministerial claims. On at least one occasion a Jehovah's Witness had twice been convicted of stealing and at the time he filed his questionnaire was suffering from venereal disease.[74] Ministerial status was denied, but there is no conclusive proof in the case that the denial was based on the apparent indiscretion of the claimant. Other factors, including secular work, were involved. In addition, the young man in question was convicted on the theft charges at the early age of seventeen, a full year before his ordination, and he assured his draft board that he had contracted venereal disease from an unfaithful wife from whom he was seeking divorce on grounds of adultery. In any case, it would not seem prudent

69. *Fitts* v. *United States*, 334 F. (2d) 416 (1964), 421.
70. 348 U.S. 375 (1955).   71. 334 F. (2d) 416 (1964), 421.
72. 334 F. (2d) 416 (1964).   73. 261 F. (2d) 113 (1958).
74. *Neal* v. *United States*, 203 F. (2d) 111 (1953).

for courts to take upon themselves the responsibility of determining ministerial status on moral grounds. Regardless of personal indiscretion the minister is nonetheless a minister unless he has ceased to be recognized as such by his church, sect, or group.

One other question related to the sincerity of the registrant is posed in *Schumann* v. *United States*.[75] Schumann did not begin his religious studies with the Witnesses until he had registered for the draft and had not sought exemption until after the Korean War broke out. Yet he had given up all secular work and studies and was recognized by his co-religionists as a minister. Therefore, the court held that there was enough evidence to support his claim and that the length of time one has been connected with a faith has no bearing upon whether one is entitled to exemption.

The second of Judge Wisdom's criteria for judging ministerial status has been one of the most persistent themes pursued by the courts in litigation involving Jehovah's Witnesses. It might be called simply the "time-devoted" doctrine. Witnesses, as already noted, receive no pay for their ministry and must, as a result, engage in some secular work to provide the necessities of life for themselves and their families. And according to Witnesses, the fact that a minister may engage in secular work does not defrock him.[76] The apostle Paul was a tentmaker, and many pioneer preachers in the early history of the United States supported themselves largely by work done outside their clerical callings. Even today there are recognized denominations and sects, such as Friends, Mormons, and Brethren, who give no pecuniary reward to their ministers. These, like Witnesses, are compelled to seek employment in non-religious pursuits. Moreover, among such churches as the Baptists and Methodists, which customarily remunerate their preachers, some are so badly paid that they must do other work to secure a livable income. Finally, no minister, regardless of the amount paid him by his congregation, Witnesses aver, devotes all his time to clerical duties. He preaches on Sunday and makes a few calls during the week, but for the most part, the rest of his time is his own to use as he pleases.

Nowhere in the history of congressional legislation since 1940 is

75. 208 F. (2d) 801 (1953).
76. A good statement of the position of the Witnesses may be found in the *Joint Brief for Petitioners, Louis Dabney Smith, Petitioner,* v. *United States of America, Respondent; William Murray Estep, Petitioner,* v. *United States of America, Respondent, Supreme Court of the United States,* October Term, 1945, pp. 153, 172-173.

there any indication that a minister may not engage in secular work. But law does require that a registrant pursue the ministry as a vocation on a regular and customary basis, if he is to be granted exemption. There is the clear implication that Jehovah's Witnesses, orthodox or not, are to be measured roughly on the same scale as the orthodox minister.

How much time, then, must the Witnesses devote to religion to qualify as minister? This is not an easy question to answer. In the *Dickinson* case the Supreme Court stated that "Preaching and teaching the principles of one's sect, if performed part-time or half-time, occasionally or irregularly, are insufficient to bring the registrant under s. 6(g) [of the Universal Military Service and Training Act]."[77] At best this formula is vague, but some courts have interpreted it to mean that a registrant must devote more time to the ministry than he does to secular work.[78] Other courts apparently have been persuaded that where a Witness holds a secular job at which he works full-time, he cannot possibly make the ministry his principal vocation.[79] In other instances judges have established 160 hours as a normal work month and have refused ministerial classification if a Witness did not devote at least that much time to religious activities.[80] Without setting any precise standard, ministerial claims have been favored if secular work was only incidental to ministerial duties. Just what makes work incidental is not exactly clear, but in *Dickinson* the Supreme Court held that a work week of five hours was not too much.[81] And in *United States* v. *Ransom* the Court of Appeals for the Seventh Circuit permitted a Witness devoting one hundred hours a month to his ministry to work one day a week on a family farm for room and board.[82] Where the amount of time devoted to a secular pursuit far outweighs that spent in preaching and teaching, the courts have on most occa-

77. 346 U.S. 389 (1953), 395.
78. See *United States* v. *Kahl*, 141 F. Supp. 161 (1956); *Jeffries* v. *United States*, 169 F. (2d) 186 (1948). The same is implied in *Smith* v. *United States*, 238 F. (2d) 79 (1956).
79. *United States* v. *Pomorski*, 125 F. Supp. 68 (1954); *United States* v. *Schumann*, 119 F. Supp. 640 (1954). In *United States* v. *Carlson*, 248 F. Supp. 1003 (1965), however, it was held that a local board was in error when it denied ministerial classification to a Witness who engaged in secular work and was not paid for religious work.
80. *United States* v. *Kenstler*, 250 F. Supp. 833 (1966), *United States* v. *Stewart*, 213 F. Supp. 497 (1963).
81. *Dickinson* v. *United States*, 346 U.S. 389 (1953).
82. 223 F. (2d) 15 (1955). Also see *United States* v. *Burnett*, 115 F. Supp. 141 (1953), and *Brown* v. *United States*, 216 F. (2d) 258 (1954).

sions been unsympathetic to the registrant.[83] Some courts have included in religious activities time spent in study and preparation,[84]
while others have been willing to include only time actually spent in
the field.[85] The latter approach seems patently unfair, since any minister in one of the orthodox denominations must necessarily devote a
considerable part of his time to study and the preparation of sermons.
Regularity to some judges has meant that religious work must be done
consistently. Yet, one court has held that, even though a farmer engaged in religious activities at odd times when there was no farming
to be done, he could be granted exemption, provided he averaged one
hundred hours a month in the ministry over a period of a year.[86]
Finally, the record of hours devoted to the ministry must be clearly
substantiated. Any ambiguity or contradictions in the evidence will
defeat a registrant's claim.[87]

The third of Judge Wisdom's criteria for judging ministerial status
is perhaps the most important and at the same time the most perplexing. Witnesses refuse to accept the "shepherd-flock" relationship which
exists between minister and parishoner in recognized denominations.
It has already been observed that every Witness considers himself a
shepherd. His pulpit is not found in a church building but in the
street and at the doorstep. His congregation is not a gathering of
dedicated souls in church pews but the crowd on the street or the
man in his home. Everyone is a missionary evangelist. Yet, as a
perusal of legislative policy has already shown, Congress has placed the
mantle of orthodoxy on him and has insisted that Selective Service
boards must distinguish between shepherds and sheep. Courts have
been forced to follow.

Equally as difficult as the problem of applying the "time-devoted"
principle has been the judicial task of interpreting the "leadership"
concept. There are numerous positions in the organizational structure

---

83. *Badger* v. *United States*, 322 F. (2d) 902 (1963); *United States* v. *Blankenship*,
127 F. Supp. 760 (1954); *United States* v. *Beatty*, 350 F. (2d) 287 (1965); *United States*
v. *Bartelt*, 200 F. (2d) 385 (1952); *United States* v. *Bartell*, 144 F. Supp. 793 (1956);
United States v. *Kushmer*, 365 F. (2d) 153 (1966); *United States* v. *Hoepker*, 126 F. Supp.
118 (1954); *Leitner* v. *United States*, 222 F. (2d) 363 (1955); *United States* v. *Clark*, 307
F. (2d) 1 (1962).

84. See, for example, *Wiggins* v. *United States*, 261 F. (2d) 113 (1958).

85. *Tettenburn* v. *United States*, 186 F. Supp. 203 (1960). Also see *Bradshaw* v.
United States, 242 F. (2d) 180 (1957).

86. *Pate* v. *United States*, 243 F. (2d) 99 (1957).

87. *United States* v. *Norris*, 341 F. (2d) 527 (1965); *United States* v. *Hogans*, 253 F.
Supp. 409 (1966); *United States* v. *Kutz*, 199 F. Supp. 205 (1961).

of the Witnesses that might be considered positions of leadership.[88]
There are first of all Pioneers, who are required to devote a minimum
annual average of 1,200 hours to field ministry. There are full-time
Headquarters Servants, or the Bethel Family, who work at Watchtower
Headquarters in Brooklyn. District Servants have supervisory power
over eleven or twelve circuits in each of eighteen districts in the United
States. Each circuit is supervised in turn by a Circuit Supervisor, who
has power to inspect and direct the work of some eighteen to twenty-
five congregations in the circuit. Each congregation is headed by a
Congregational Servant who has full charge of the ministerial work
of the entire congregation of missionaries and ministers. Other servants in each congregation include an Assistant Congregational Servant, a Bible Study Servant, a Theocratic Ministry School Servant,
a Watchtower Study Servant, a Magazine-Territory Servant, a Literature Servant, and an Accounts Servant. At the bottom of the
hierarchy is the Book Study Conductor, who presides over small meetings of a part of the congregation each week. These meetings are held
in private homes and usually have from eight to twenty-five people in
attendance.

In a letter written to General Hershey in 1959, Hayden C.
Covington, general counsel for Jehovah's Witnesses, claimed outright exemption for Pioneers, Headquarters Servants, District and
Circuit Servants, and Congregational Servants.[89] For all the others
exemption was advised if they devoted a substantial amount of their
time to the performance of their duties "as well as to door-to-door
missionary work . . . and do not perform such duties irregularly . . . ,
depending upon the circumstances of each particular case, as to whether
their lives are devoted to the ministry as leaders, and they pursue it
as their vocation, as properly defined in the Act."

There would appear to be sound argument for Covington's position
that Pioneers and top-ranking servants down to the level of Congregational Servant, at least, should be recognized as ministers. Some courts
have been willing enough to accept both Pioneers and Congregational
Servants within the ministerial category, but others have not. The

88. An extended discussion of the various positions of leadership in the organization
of Jehovah's Witnesses may be found in *Tettenburn* v. *United States*, 186 F. Supp. 203
(1960).
89. A reproduction of the letter may be found in *United States* v. *Stidham*, 248 F.
Supp. 822 (1965), 839, n. 9.

dissenting courts have generally reasoned that the intent of Congress can be determined only by draft authorities and the courts. No religious body, in other words, has the authority to define the status of its members under a congressional law. Thus, in the absence of other evidence indicating ministerial activity, Pioneers have been denied exemption.[90] In *United States* v. *Hurt*, however, the Court of Appeals for the Third Circuit observed that Selective Service authorities have recognized that Pioneers ordinarily devote all or substantially all their time to the dissemination of their tenets and beliefs.[91] Where any secular activity is followed merely for subsistence purposes, therefore, the Pioneer should be granted exemption. Hurt was also a presiding minister in his congregation. But, if one is required to be both a Pioneer and a Congregational Servant to qualify as a minister, the Jehovah's Witness is placed not only in an unjust but often an impossible situation. The Pioneer tries to devote as much of his time as possible to field work, and the work of a Congregational Servant, or any servant for that matter, does not contribute in any way to the minimum time required of the Pioneer. There simply may not be enough hours in the day to permit many to be both, particularly if the Witness has to engage in secular work to meet his physical needs.[92] Occasionally boards have refused to grant exemption to vacation Pioneers, who are appointed for a period of from two weeks to three months, but are expected to preach and teach under the same standard imposed on full-time Pioneers. The appointment is usually considered a necessary step to the higher rank. On two occasions in the past few years, courts have reversed such decisions by the boards and have upheld the ministerial claims of these persons.[93]

The most favorable stand in favor of lesser officials among Jehovah's Witnesses has been taken in the Fifth Circuit. In *Wiggins* v. *United States*,[94] Judge Wisdom, relying heavily on *Olvera* v. *United States*[95] and *Pate* v. *United States*,[96] contended: (1) that the Universal Military Service and Training Act by granting exemption to ministers constituted a statute of liberty, (2) that once a registrant makes a showing

90. *United States* v. *Steinhart*, 129 F. Supp. 594 (1955); *United States* v. *Zasadni*, 206 F. Supp. 318 (1962).

91. 244 F. (2d) 46 (1957).   92. See *Tietz*, p. 132.

93. *United States* v. *Majher*, 250 F. Supp. 106 (1966), and *United States* v. *Hested*, 248 F. Supp. 650 (1965).

94. 261 F. (2d) 113 (1958).   95. 223 F. (2d) 880 (1955).

96. 243 F. (2d) 99 (1957).

that the ministry is his vocation, he is entitled, not as a matter of grace, but as a matter of right, to the statutory exemption, (3) that the exemption should be broadly interpreted, and (4) that no pattern of orthodoxy as to pay, lack of secular employment, or traditional position of leadership should be imposed in defining the term "minister." Wiggins had full-time secular employment and spent only about forty hours a month in the ministry, about one-fourth the time devoted to secular work. He was a Book Study Conductor. Yet, he was granted exemption. Judge Wisdom ruled that some allowance in the law must be made for ministers who are gainfully employed, simply because they are not paid for their religious ministry. And if they must work, they should not be penalized for working steadily. A young man such as Wiggins could hardly work less than forty hours a week and hold on to his job. Furthermore, the position of Book Study Conductor is comparable to that of assistant pastor, and Wiggins had performed his religious duties regularly without allowing his secular duties to interfere with his religious work.

This was heady drink for other federal judges, and severe criticism of the *Wiggins* ruling was not long in coming. District Judge Watkins of Maryland just two years later in *United States* v. *Tattenburn*[97] completely repudiated *Wiggins*. He did not agree that a Book Study Conductor was analogous to an assistant minister. Much of Wiggins's time and Tettenburn's time was spent not in missionary teaching or preaching but in study. And while travel time, study time, and attendance at meetings are all in furtherance of the ministry, Judge Watkins was convinced, after a careful review of Witnesses' literature, that in the case of Pioneers as with all Jehovah's Witnesses, such time is not reported in the 1,200 hour annual minimum quota of preaching in the missionary field. The Court of Appeals for the Fourth Circuit held that another Book Study Conductor's role in his congregation was little more than that of all members of his sect—that of spreading among the public the beliefs of Jehovah's Witnesses and of educating those already believers of the faith.[98] In addition, there was no proof that it was a part of his regular task to administer the ordinances or rites of public worship. In contrast, in the *Dickinson* case, decided by the Supreme Court, the defendant was a Company Servant engaged not

97. 186 F. Supp. 203 (1960).
98. *United States* v. *Stewart*, 322 F. (2d) 592 (1963).

only in the normal missionary tasks common to many members of the sect, but he was also responsible for conducting the public meetings of the congregation.

If the present policy of attempting to fit Jehovah's Witnesses into the mold of the orthodox ministry is continued, there is much validity in the Watkins position in the absence of some material manifestation of substantial field work for the lesser servants below the level of Congregational Servant. In their position and role these people strongly resemble deacons, Sunday school superintendents and teachers, and chairmen of committees in other denominational groups. To be consistent, Selective Service boards might find themselves faced with the necessity of exempting the latter if they exempt the former.

Even the Fifth Circuit seemed to beat a slow retreat in *Fitts* v. *United States*,[99] although an effort was made to distinguish *Fitts* from *Wiggins*. In *Wood* v. *United States*[100] the retreat was even more noticeable, even though only an assistant congregational Book Study Conductor was involved.

Conclusions

The history of litigation concerning the obligation of Jehovah's Witnesses to serve in the armed forces points to one conclusion. The basic difficulty in adjudicating their cases stems from a lack of understanding on the part of Congress first of all, but on the part of Selective Service authorities and courts as well, of the theology and practices of this unorthodox group of religious zealots. To the uninitiated their doctrines are all but incomprehensible. They are a cult unto themselves, and to fit them into any pattern of orthodoxy is little less than impossible. There are, at least, four possible alternatives in attempting to deal with them more successfully in the future.

The first of these is to follow the practice of the British and Canadians during World War II and refuse to recognize them as a sect.[101] But as shown earlier, to do so would be contrary to American traditions and concepts of liberty embodied in the First Amendment. Moreover, to follow this course would be unthinkable in view of the fact that for so long they have been regarded as a sect.

99. 334 F. (2d) 416 (1964).　　　　　　　100. 373 F. (2d) 894 (1967).
101. See n. 66, above.

A second possibility is to abandon the Selective Service system in favor of voluntary enlistment. Both Senator Hatfield of Oregon and Senator Brooke of Massachusetts supported this position during the Senate debates on the Selective Service Act of 1967.[102] Obviously, if all inductees in the armed forces were volunteers, there would be no problem with Jehovah's Witnesses. They would never volunteer.

This is not the place to argue in detail the merits of a volunteer army. It may suffice to say that Senator Hatfield contends that such an army, while necessitating higher pay incentives and other advantages to attract young men into the armed services, would nevertheless make the military less costly to the taxpayer. Greater efficiency through the elimination of the high rate of turnover now current among draftees would be encouraged. Furthermore, a voluntary service would be fairer and more democratic, since none would serve against his will. And finally, patriotism is still cherished enough by our young people that securing the required number of inductees would be no problem, provided, of course, we are not engaged in a wholesale holocaust.

Senator Edward Kennedy, on the other hand, has pointed out that according to a recent poll taken by the United States Youth Council, 61 per cent of its members who responded favored a volunteer army, but 58 per cent—almost as many as favored voluntary enlistment—indicated they would not volunteer.[103] In addition, he was fearful that a volunteer army would be largely a Negro army. The rate of re-enlistment for Negroes, he asserted, is 46.6 per cent. For whites it is 21.6 per cent. He feared a situation in which one part of our population, gifted either financially or intellectually, would be free to continue to develop its talents, while another part, less gifted, would fill the ranks of our armed forces. Either this would be true, or the lower ranks would be filled with Negroes, while the staff would be manned by white officers. Senator Kennedy was also convinced that the voluntary system would be a costly one. Even Professor Walter Y. Oi of the University of Washington, a proponent of the system, was quoted as estimating that its operation would cost, in a non-Vietnam situation, between $4 and $7 billion a year. The Defense Department estimated that the cost, in a Vietnam situation, would lie somewhere between

102. *Congressional Record,* CXIII (May 11, 1967), S6734-S6747. Also see James C. Miller, III, ed., *Why the Draft?* (Baltimore, 1968).
103. This and other remarks by Senator Kennedy may be found in the *Congressional Record,* CXIII (May 11, 1967), S6747-S6749.

$10 and $17 billion a year. Finally, Senator Kennedy felt that a volunteer army would make the President so sensitive to popular opinion that he would be seriously handicapped in fulfilling his responsibilities with regard to foreign policy.

At any rate, the time may not be ripe for the type of change Senator Hatfield wants. The Defense and State Departments have been opposed to it. Congress has been unreceptive, and it is doubtful that a majority of the public would press for it.

A third approach is to make certain modifications in the present system. In fairness to the registrant, it would seem desirable to replace, with a substantial evidence test, the requirement that a board produce some affirmative evidence to support a basis in fact for denying objector or ministerial classification. Judicial review in draft cases would then be brought in line with policy followed in reviewing many other types of administrative decisions. The practice by the courts of requiring ministers to spend as much or more time in religious work as they do in secular work or to devote an amount of time equal to a normal work month to the ministry should be abandoned. So long as a Witness spends a reasonable number of hours in missionary endeavor and gives evidence of being sincere in his religious work, he should be granted exemption. The *Wiggins* test of approximately forty hours field work a month and a clear indication of willingness to place religious work before secular work seems realistic.

Improvement in probationary policy could be achieved.[104] A judge may be unable to change a classification but he has considerable latitude in sentencing. About one-third of all defendants sentenced by federal judges are granted probation, but there is apparent reluctance to give the religious objector this consideration on the ground that he is not repentant and would "do the same thing tomorrow." This reasoning is highly questionable.

Jehovah's Witnesses rarely are candidates for probation, since they are committed to serve Jehovah at all times at any place. Ordinarily a judge grants probation only where a job situation has been worked out that clearly shows that the national interest will be more adequately served by having a man employed in it than by jailing him. If religious commitment is sympathetically understood, probation could be given Jehovah's Witnesses on the sole condition that the defendant engage

104. *Tietz*, pp. 135-137.

in his religious work. On occasion this practice has been followed with desirable results.

A final proposal for change in current policy is the most revolutionary of all the possible alternatives. Yet in many ways it deserves the greatest consideration. Both Congress and the courts should discontinue the attempt to distinguish the ministerial status of Witnesses from their status as conscientious objectors. The Witness is a conscientious objector because he is a minister, and one role cannot be separated from the other. Judgment as to his right to exemption, therefore, should be based solely on his objector claim. The test of sincerity would necessarily have to be imposed as in all other objector cases, and objective facts concerning devotion to religious activity would surely be a part of the test. The necessity of separating shepherd from flock, full-time minister from part-time minister, lesser official from higher official would, however, be obviated.

Jehovah's Witnesses may be a poorly understood minority with little respect among most Americans. On the other hand, the vast majority of them are sincere Christians, however strange their tenets and practices may seem to others. A recognition of their unorthodox position and a program of draft exemption suited to that position are essential, if they are to be given those rights which our Constitution and liberal heritage guarantee to other minorities among us.

Francis Canavan, S. J. / Constitutional Casuistry: Cases of Conscience

"Conscience" is again becoming a force in American political life. Crowds march on military induction centers, shouting: "Hell no, we won't go!" Young men burn their draft cards and, on occasion, themselves. Students block access to the tables set up by military recruiters on campuses. When their fellow students vote in a referendum to allow the recruiters to function on campus, the dissenters announce that they will not accept the result of the referendum because it is a political solution to a moral question. Grayer heads express fears that the democratic process may break down under the pressures put on it by those whose consciences will allow no accommodation and no compromise.

By the time these words appear in print, the crisis may have passed and be on its way to being forgotten. The end of the war in Vietnam, were it to come, would end the bitterness and the violence that arise when a political issue turns into a moral one. But the broader issue would still remain with us, as it always will. When the conscience of the individual comes into conflict with social policies that are backed up by the power and the majesty of the law, which shall prevail?

Individual vs. Social Conscience

We cannot assume that the individual is always right, any more than we can assume that society is always right. It is easy and tempting to present the issue as conscience vs. power, conscience being the peculiar property of individuals, and power that of society. But societies are people, too, and they also have consciences. In any given conflict, it may be the conscience of society that is right and the private conscience that is wrong.

A society's laws and policies reflect its conception of its own interests, or the interests of sufficiently powerful and determined groups within the society. Most of what we ordinarily think of as politics is concerned with just such interests and the pressures that are exerted to translate them into public policies. Nonetheless, law and policy also embody the moral convictions held by society as a whole or at least by its dominant part. In this sense, they are expressions of society's conscience rather than of its interest. Society's conscience, of course, like the individual's, may be and often is distorted by its passions and its prejudices. But one should recognize that the clash between society and the individual is sometimes a conflict of consciences. It is not possible always to present it as a struggle of conscience against power.

All societies maintain the superiority of some moral norms to the dictates of dissenting consciences. Our society is no exception. Human sacrifice, ritual prostitution, and polygamy are examples of conduct that we socially disapprove and legally punish. They are examples so extreme that it may seem unfair to use them.[1] But they have been practiced by some of the religions of mankind. Presumably their devotees had the kind of conscience that approved these practices. Yet there is no chance that American law at present would tolerate such doings on the plea of freedom of conscience. Both law and public opinion would condemn them, and it seems idle to pretend that the condemnation would be based on considerations of social utility alone. The practices in question would be punished as violations of a publicly accepted and enforced code of morality.

We have, it is true, a pluralistic society in which some moral norms that were once commonly accepted and legally enforced are now dissolving. It is also true that the freedom of the individual conscience from social coercion is held by our constitutional law as a public value of a high order. The only point made here is that it is not a value of so high an order that every other consideration yields to it. The fact is that our society sometimes resorts to coercion even against the claims of private conscience.

Coercion in matters of conscience admits of several shades of meaning, and it is necessary to distinguish them. The law may prohibit a person from acting according to his conscience. This in turn may mean preventing him from doing what in conscience he thinks he has a right to do, or it may mean preventing him from doing what he thinks he has a duty to do. It makes a difference which kind of law is

1. But the U.S. Supreme Court has used similar examples. See *Reynolds* v. *United States*, 98 U.S. 145, 166 (1878).

in question. We are not greatly impressed by those who argue that they may break a speed limit, or exclude Negroes from their restaurants, or pay substandard wages because their moral judgment tells them that they have a right to act in these ways, despite what the law says. But some of us, at least, would feel a greater reluctance to prevent a man from doing what he felt in conscience he was obliged to do; for example, to engage in some religious practice that was injurious to public health. Though we might enforce the law and stop the man from doing his duty as he saw it, we would recognize that his conscience was more deeply offended than that of a person who was merely stopped from doing what he thought he had a right to do.

We should feel an even greater reluctance to force a person to act against his conscience. Yet, again, a distinction must be made. It is one thing to force someone to do what he believes he has a right not to do. An example would be compulsory paying of taxes beyond what one considers a just limit—the "wrong" of which Mrs. Vivian Kellems complained so bitterly some years ago. It is another thing to force a person to perform what he believes is an immoral action: the classic example is compulsory military service. The man who does under compulsion what he thinks he has a right not to do regards himself as a victim of injustice. But the man who does under compulsion what he believes is morally wrong and prohibited is convinced that he is doing evil and is likely to regard himself as a sinner—even though he does the evil only because of his fear of the consequences of refusing. In this case, coercion directly violates conscience.

Conscience and the Court

The above distinctions are intended to bring out the fact that the respect owed to conscience by social authority poses problems of varying degrees of acuteness. The courts in the United States have long been accustomed to making another set of distinctions in interpreting the freedoms guaranteed by the First Amendment to the Constitution. To state the matter in summary fashion, and without all the qualifications that professional students of constitutional law will doubtless look for, the courts have distinguished (1) freedom of thought or belief, which is absolute in its immunity from governmental interference; (2) freedom of action, which is not absolute, being subject to the requirements of public order; and (3) freedom of speech, which is as absolute as freedom of thought unless the speech is "utterly without redeeming social importance" (*Roth* v. *United States*, 354 U.S. 476, 484 [1957]) or bears so close a relation to illegal action that the state must be permitted to prevent or punish it.

One of the Court's many statements of the basic distinction between freedom of thought and freedom of action is found in *Cantwell* v. *Connecticut*, 310 U.S. 296, 303 (1940), where it said: "The [First] Amendment embraces two concepts—freedom to believe and freedom to act. The first is absolute but, in the nature of things, the second cannot be. Conduct remains subject to regulation for the protection of society." But, stressing the need to limit regulation in the interests of freedom, the Court continued: "The freedom to act must have appropriate definition to preserve the enforcement of that protection. In every case the power to regulate must be so exercised as not, in attaining a permissible end, unduly to infringe the protected freedom."

In *Cantwell*, and indeed in the greater part of the "freedom of conscience" cases it has decided, the Court was dealing with the religious conscience. The conscience whose claims it had to adjudicate was not a purely individual moral judgment, but a judgment formed by the teaching of a church or sect. The issue therefore could have been presented as organized religion vs. the state, or the spiritual vs. the temporal, rather than as the individual vs. the social conscience. But it is in the latter terms that the Court has dealt with the issue. Religion enters a case insofar as it may furnish the content of an individual's conscience; but the right whose limits are to be determined by the courts is the right of an individual.

Under modern conditions of religious pluralism and civil liberty of religion, no church is socially accepted or legally recognized as being fully as public an institution as the state and as more competent than the state to explicate and define the claims of conscience. The Supreme Court's emphasis therefore falls more and more heavily upon the individual conscience simply as individual.

In the years following *Cantwell*, the Court enunciated the doctrine that freedom of religion, together with the other First Amendment freedoms, enjoyed a "preferred position." But the Court has in recent decades abandoned any preference for Christianity or even for theism. There was a time when the Court declared: "This is a Christian nation" (*Holy Trinity Church* v. *United States*, 143 U.S. 457, 471 [1892]; repeated in *United States* v. *Macintosh*, 183 U.S. 605, 625 [1931]). But since the Court began to apply the religion clauses of the First Amendment to the states through the Fourteenth Amendment, it has moved steadily toward a position of neutrality or non-preference between belief in God and non-theistic "religions."

The culmination of this process was the statement in *Torcaso* v. *Watkins*, 367 U.S. 488, 495 (1961): "We repeat and again reaffirm that neither a State nor the Federal Government can constitutionally force a person 'to profess a belief or disbelief in any religion.' Neither can constitutionally pass laws or impose requirements which aid all religions as against non-believers, and neither can aid those religions based on a belief in the existence of God as against those religions founded on different beliefs." A footnote explained: "Among religions in this country which do not teach what would generally be considered a belief in the existence of God are Buddhism, Taoism, Ethical Culture, Secular Humanism and others."

It may be, as Leo Pfeffer has said, that "calling . . . secular humanism a religion does not make it a religion. It is not a religion."[2] But so far as the Supreme Court is concerned, it ranks as a religion. To the extent that the "preferred position" is still the Court's doctrine, what is preferred is the individual's ultimate belief, whatever it may be; all ultimate beliefs, including secular ones, are "religions" in a broad sense of the term and are legally and constitutionally on the same plane.

Religious orthodoxy thus ends up on a somewhat lower level than political orthodoxy. In *West Virginia Board of Education* v. *Barnette*, 319 U.S. 624 (1943), the Court struck down an order of the board making it a legal duty for all public school children to salute the American flag while reciting the pledge of allegiance. According to the Court, the salute and the accompanying pledge were an expression of political faith, a "credo of nationalism." And this, said the Court, no government could constitutionally force anyone to utter. But the Court did not say that the flag salute ceremony could not be conducted by public schools, only that no one could be obliged to take part in it.

A different fate awaited the school prayers that often went along with the flag salute in a single ceremony. In *Engel* v. *Vitale*, 370 U.S.

2. *Catholic World*, CXCVII (1963), 314.

421 (1962), the Court found that a prayer approved by the New York State Board of Regents for use in public schools was an unconstitutional establishment of religion. The prayer was not saved by a provision that those who did not wish to join in it would be excused. "The Establishment Clause," the Court said (*ibid.*, 430), "unlike the Free Exercise Clause, does not depend upon any showing of direct governmental compulsion and is violated by the enactment of laws which establish an official religion whether those laws operate directly to coerce nonobserving individuals or not."

It would seem, therefore, that government may provide for the expression of a common political faith, so long as it does not coerce anyone to join in professing the faith. But government may not profess a religious belief, however broad and general its terms, whether it coerces anyone to join in the profession or not. In public schools (if nowhere else), government must be absolutely neutral in matters of religious belief. It is open to some question whether, given the present structure of American education, this neutrality is truly realistic. The present writer has argued elsewhere that it is not.[3] But however that may be, the Court's intention is clearly to remove government altogether from the realm of religious belief in order to make all consciences equal before the law, independently of their religious content.

It is impossible, however, to remove government entirely from the realm of the moral conscience. There was a time when the Supreme Court was able to assume a commonly accepted moral code supported by the Judeo-Christian tradition and taught by the main body of the country's religious institutions. It is now more difficult for the Court to do this. Yet the Court cannot avoid deciding cases arising out of conflicts between private and public moral standards.

In the brief scope of this paper it will be impossible to review or summarize the large number of cases in which claims of freedom of conscience have been adjudicated. All that can be done here is to present a very small selection of cases for the sake of illustrating the type of problem with which the courts are confronted, and to indicate that, for better or worse, freedom of conscience is not the last word in American law.

3. "Implications of the School Prayer and Bible Reading Decisions: The Welfare State," *Journal of Public Law*, XIII (1964), 439-446.

The Limits of Action

Thus, the Court has upheld the right of government to prevent people from acting in accordance with their consciences when it felt that a sufficiently significant social value was at stake. In the last century, it firmly denied the constitutional right of Mormons to practice polygamy, despite their claim that the teachings of their religion made the practice a duty when circumstances permitted it. In the leading case on the subject, *Reynolds* v. *United States*, the Court said:

As a law of the organization of society under the exclusive dominion of the United States [the Territory of Utah], it is provided that plural marriages shall not be allowed. Can a man excuse his practices to the contrary because of his religious belief? To permit this would be to make the professed doctrines of religious belief superior to the law of the land, and in effect to permit every citizen to become a law unto himself. Government could exist only in name under such circumstance.

It is noteworthy that the reason given why religious doctrine may not be taken as superior to the law of the land is that to affirm the primacy of religion would in effect "permit every citizen to become a law unto himself." In other words, the individualism implicit in a regime of religious liberty makes government, or some agency thereof, of necessity the ultimate judge of conflict of conscience.

As we saw above in *Cantwell*, the bias of the Constitution is toward guaranteeing the freedom of every citizen to act in accordance with his conscience, and toward limiting social regulation of his conduct to what is genuinely necessary for the protection of society. So, in the *Reynolds* case, the Court felt constrained to uphold the legal prohibition of polygamy by asserting that marriage was the foundation of society and that monogamy was, to some extent, necessary for the maintenance of a free system of government. The protection of monogamy was therefore a legitimate social concern which overrode the claims of the private conscience. And it was an agency of government that made the ultimate judgment in the case.

Courts have also supported the social, as against the individual, conscience in matters other than the institution of marriage. In *Harden* v. *State*, 188 Tenn. 17, 216 S.W.2d 708 (1948), a state court upheld a Tennessee law that forbade the handling of poisonous snakes in such a manner "as to endanger the life or health of any person." The mem-

bers of "The Holiness Church" were accustomed to handling rattle-
snakes during their religious services in the belief that, according to
Mark 16:18, they could thereby manifest their faith without suffering
harm. The court remarked that the law did not attempt to prevent
them from *believing* that handling poisonous snakes was a necessary
part of religious worship. But the law did prevent them from *acting*
on this belief—and, said the court, the law did not thereby deprive
them of the free exercise of religion.

In like manner, along with a large number of decisions maintaining the freedom of individuals to act according to their religious beliefs despite state laws and municipal ordinances to the contrary, the
U.S. Supreme Court has in some cases supported the law rather than
the individual. To mention but two examples, in *Prince* v. *Massachusetts*, 321 U.S. 158 (1944), it denied that the free exercise of religion
gave a nine-year-old child the right to sell religious publications of
Jehovah's Witnesses in violation of the Massachusetts child-labor law.
In *Braunfeld* v. *Brown*, 366 U.S. 599 (1961), the Court admitted that
a Pennsylvania Sunday-closing law imposed a financial burden on
Orthodox Jews who felt obliged in conscience to close their shops on
Saturday as well, but it refused to declare that the law either established
religion or deprived the shopowners of the free exercise of their religion.

The Supreme Court has also affirmed the power of the state to
force persons to submit to physical treatment against their moral convictions. In two early cases the issue of freedom of religion was not
raised, doubtless because the Court had not yet declared that the
religion clauses of the First Amendment bind state governments
through the Due Process Clause of the Fourteenth Amendment. In
Jacobson v. *Massachusetts*, 197 U.S. 11, 26 (1905), the defendant argued
(in the Court's paraphrase of his words), that

his liberty is invaded when the State subjects him to fine or imprisonment
for neglecting or refusing to submit to vaccination; that a compulsory
vaccination law is unreasonable, arbitrary, and oppressive, and, therefore,
hostile to the inherent right of every freeman to care for his own body
and health in such way as to him seems best; and the execution of such a
law against one who objects to vaccination, no matter for what reason,
is nothing short of an assault upon his person.

The Court overrode Mr. Jacobson's moral judgment about his inherent right as a freeman with the observation that a compulsory vaccination law was a reasonable exercise of the state's policy power to protect public health.[4] The Court later used substantially the same argument in *Buck* v. *Bell*, 274 U.S. 200 (1927).

This was the case in which Justice Oliver Wendell Holmes, for the majority of the Court, upheld the application of a Virginia compulsory sterilization law to Carrie Buck, an allegedly feeble-minded girl, with the remark: "Three generations of imbeciles are enough" (*ibid.*, 207). Since Carrie Buck was a Catholic, she (or, more accurately, her lawyer) might have argued that submission to sterilization was against her conscience; but this point was not raised by her lawyer or decided by the Court. The substantive issue was whether it was within the constitutional power of the state to deprive a person of his physical power of reproduction. Justice Holmes said that it was, and argued: "We have seen more than once that the public welfare may call upon the best citizens for their lives. It would be strange if it could not call upon those who already sap the strength of the State for these lesser sacrifices, often not felt to be such by those concerned, in order to prevent our being swamped with incompetence."

Professor Walter F. Berns of Cornell University has severely criticized Justice Holmes for his opinion in this case.[5] It is, he says, "surely one of the most 'totalitarian' statements in the history of the Court." "The point should have been made," he feels, "that due process of law *does* require more than certain procedures, and that there are some things which decent government simply should not do. One of these is to perform compulsory surgical operations in order to satisfy the racial theories of a few benighted persons."

If we may believe what geneticists are now telling us that they expect to be able to do in the foreseeable future, the integrity of the reproductive process against state interference will again be a constitutional issue. It seems probable, at any rate, that science's growing capacity for refined technological control of the reproductive process in all its stages will lead to demands for eugenic legislation, and that some of these demands will be successful. If so, under the current interpretation of the Due Process Clause, the legislation will be con-

4. The Court later stated that religious grounds would not avail for exemption from compulsory vaccination (*Prince* v. *Massachusetts*, 158, 166).
5. "*Buck* v. *Bell*: Due Process of Law?" *Western Political Quarterly*, VI (1953), 762-775.

tested in the courts as violative of religious liberty and the rights of conscience. It is doubtful that the Supreme Court will declare such legislation unconstitutional precisely because it violates the rights of conscience. But one may hope that the question of substantive due process will receive a more thorough consideration than it did in *Buck* v. *Bell.*[6]

Blood Transfusion Cases

Some inkling of what the Court might do is furnished in the cases occasioned by the doctrine of Jehovah's Witnesses that to receive a blood transfusion is to "eat blood" and therefore is prohibited by the Bible. The Supreme Court of Illinois decided in 1952 that the religious objections of parents belonging to Jehovah's Witnesses could not bar a court order for a blood transfusion to be administered to their children, when doctors testified that it was necessary to prevent the child's death or permanent mental injury (*People ex rel. Wallace* v. *Labrenz*, 411 Ill. 618, 104 N.E.2d 769; cert. den., 344 U.S. 824). This principle seems solidly established whenever the prospective recipient of the transfusion is a minor.

Cases directly affecting adults are much more recent. The first of them seems to have been one concerning Mrs. Jessie E. Jones. In September, 1963, at the age of twenty-five, she was brought by her husband into Georgetown University Hospital, a Roman Catholic institution in Washington, D.C., for emergency treatment. She was suffering from a hemorrhaging ulcer but, when the doctors declared that only blood transfusions could save her life, both she and her husband refused to consent, on the ground that it would be against their religious beliefs. In a rapid series of legal moves, the university's attorney brought Judge J. Skelly Wright of the U.S. Court of Appeals into the hospital. After talking to the patient and her husband and apparently ascertaining that, if the court took responsibility for authorizing the transfusions, they would not feel that they had acted against their religious beliefs, Judge Wright gave the order for the transfusions on the spot.

His action was criticized some weeks later in a sermon delivered

6. At this writing, the U.S. Supreme Court has substantially the same issue as *Buck* v. *Bell* before it in the case of *Cavitt* v. *Nebraska.*

by the Rev. Kenneth K. Marshall of Davies Memorial Unitarian Church in Washington. If the court order were allowed to stand as a precedent, Mr. Marshall said, it "would lead to erosion of the liberties of other religious groups." He contended that similar court orders could override Christian Science practices and could even force a Catholic woman to have an abortion in order to save her life. The present writer knows from conversation with the authorities at Georgetown University that the same thought had occurred to them and had disturbed them greatly. But, since the situation was an emergency and a decision on the blood transfusion had to be made at once, they decided, as Judge Wright also did, to act in favor of life and to argue the moral and legal points later.

In an opinion written some months later, Judge Wright justified his order with the argument that the patient was near death and in no better mental condition to make a rational decision about a blood transfusion than a child would have been; hence, a court could assume authority to make the decision for her. Besides, she was the mother of a seven-month-old child, whom the state as parens patriae had a right to prevent her from abandoning by death. Judge Wright mentioned other considerations as well, but the above two are the ones that distinguish his decision from opposite ones taken by other courts in other cases.

The full bench of the Court of Appeals later denied Mrs. Jones's appeal for a rehearing, saying that the case was now moot and there was nothing to rehear. But several judges made it plain that they disagreed with Judge Wright's action (*Application of President & Directors of Georgetown College, Inc.*, 118 App. D.C. 80, 90; 331 F.2d 1000, 1010; cert. den., 377 U.S. 978).

In a case arising the following year, 1964, Mrs. William Anderson was brought into a hospital in Neptune, N.J., suffering from complications developed in her seven-and-one-half-month pregnancy. Physicians warned her that she might die at any moment and take her unborn child with her if she did not receive a blood transfusion. She refused on the usual grounds given by Jehovah's Witnesses. Hospital attorneys then obtained an order from the New Jersey Supreme Court (*Raleigh Fitkin–Paul Morgan Memorial Hospital* v. *Anderson*, 42 N.J. 421, 201 A.2d 537), under which a "special guardian" was appointed for the child, with authority to "consent to such blood transfusions

as may be necessary to preserve the lives of the mother and the child."
The court's order was based specifically on the unborn child's right
to the protection of the law, although it was the mother who would
receive the transfusion. Mrs. Anderson appealed the state court's ruling
to the U.S. Supreme Court, arguing that to undergo blood transfusions
was contrary to her "freedom of conscience and freedom of worship
protected by the Constitution." But the Court promptly rejected her
petition for a stay and denied certiorari (377 U.S. 985).

In 1965 in *United States* v. *George* (239 F. Supp. 752), a U.S. district court judge in Connecticut ordered a blood transfusion for an
adult patient, the father of four children. The judge first assured the
patient that the court would not force a transfusion on him. But he
issued the order after the patient stated that he would not resist the
doctors once the order was signed. In explaining its reasons for issuing
the order, the court said that the fact that the patient was coherent
and rational did not distinguish the present case from the Georgetown
College case, whose rationale the court explicitly adopted. It added
that since the patient had voluntarily submitted himself to medical
treatment, he could not use his religious beliefs to dictate to the doctors a course of treatment amounting to malpractice.

But in the same year, in *Re Brooks' Estate* (32 Ill. 2d 361, 205
N.E.2d 435), another court overruled a trial court's order for a blood
transfusion to an adult member of Jehovah's Witnesses, who refused
to receive it despite her clear knowledge that death would probably
result. Since the patient had no minor children, the court said, there
was no such danger to public health, welfare, or morals as would
justify interference with the patient's free exercise of her religion. A
similar decision had been rendered by a New York court in 1962 in
a case involving a completely competent adult patient with no minor
children (*Erickson* v. *Dilgard*, 44 Misc. 2d 27, 252 N.Y.S.2d 705).

As for the attitude of the U.S. Supreme Court, all that is clear is
that it is not seizing opportunities to review blood-transfusion cases.
If the Court should take a case for review, the most liberal precedents
before it would be those in which a court refused to order a blood
transfusion to a patient who was adult, completely *compos mentis*,
and had no minor children dependent on him. The courts are apparently unwilling to admit that the individual's right to follow his

conscience is supreme where the rights of others or the public health, welfare, and morals are concerned.

This conclusion must be qualified by noting that all of the cases mentioned above involved persons who had voluntarily entered hospitals as patients and had submitted themselves to medical care. Nevertheless, these cases offer little ground for supposing that the U.S. Supreme Court would invalidate eugenic or other socially inspired legislation for the sole or principal reason that it was contrary to the consciences of the persons subjected to it.

Conscientious Objection to Military Service

The final problem which we shall consider is that of the conscientious objector to military service. The problem has not ordinarily arisen in constitutional terms because the United States has not been eager to force persons to fight when they had conscientious objections to taking part in war. Since colonial times, exemption from military service has been conceded to those whose religious beliefs opposed such service. The U.S. Supreme Court had no occasion to consider the constitutionality of the exemption until the Selective Service Act of 1917 was contested on several grounds, one of them being that it violated the First Amendment by excusing from service ministers of religion, theological students, and members of religious denominations whose teachings excluded the moral right to engage in war. The Court rejected this contention with the remark that "its unsoundness is too apparent to require" discussion (*Selective Draft Law Cases*, 245 U.S. 366, 390 [1918]).

The exemption, however, is a statutory, not a constitutional right. Even in its moments of greatest concern for the protection of the individual conscience, the Court has not admitted that it would be beyond the power of government to force a man against his conscience into active military service in time of war, if the government deemed it necessary.

In a series of decisions in the late twenties and early thirties, the Court upheld the denial of naturalization to applicants for citizenship who were unwilling to state without qualification that they would bear arms in defense of the United States. The Court made itself look rather silly since the persons involved were a fifty-year-old woman

(*United States* v. *Schwimmer*, 279 U.S. 644 [1929]), a professor of religion at Yale University (*United States* v. *Macintosh*, 283 U.S. 605 [1931]), and a Canadian nurse (*United States* v. *Bland*, 283 U.S. 636 [1931]). Eventually, in *Girouard* v. *United States*, 328 U.S. 61 (1946), the Court adopted an interpretation of the naturalization law that allowed pacifists to become citizens. Congress has concurred by making it plain in subsequent legislation that such was its intention.

But in *United States* v. *Macintosh* the constitutional issue was raised with a degree of clarity that makes the case still worth studying, even though the Court has since reversed its decision there. Mr. Macintosh had professed his willingness to take the oath of naturalization and swear to support and defend the Constitution and laws of the United States against all enemies, foreign and domestic. But he would not do it if the oath were understood to commit him to fight in a future war that he would judge to be morally unjustified. It was, he said, a "fixed principle of our Constitution, zealously guarded by our laws, that a citizen cannot be forced and need not bear arms in a war if he has conscientious religious scruples against doing so."

The Court's majority opinion declared flatly: "There is no such principle of the Constitution, fixed or otherwise." Exemption on grounds of conscientious objection was a privilege derived solely from acts of Congress, not from the Constitution. "No other conclusion is compatible," the Court said, "with the well-nigh limitless extent of the war powers . . . which include, by necessary implication, the power, in the last extremity, to compel the armed service of any citizen in the land, without regard to his objections or his views in respect of the justice or morality of the particular war or of war in general" (*ibid.*, 623-624).

The Court also had an answer to Mr. Macintosh's contention that as a Christian he was obliged to obey God rather than men. Said the Court (*ibid.*, 625):

When he speaks of putting his allegiance to the will of God above his allegiance to the government, it is evident, in the light of his entire statement, that he means to make *his own interpretation* of the will of God the decisive test which shall conclude the government and stay its hand. We are a Christian people, according to one another the equal right of religious freedom, and acknowledging with reverence the duty of obedience to the will of God. But, also, we are a nation with the duty to survive; a nation whose Constitution contemplates war as well as peace; whose government must go forward upon the assumption, and safely can proceed upon no other, that unqualified allegiance to the nation and submission and obedience to the laws of the land, as well those made for war as those made for peace, are not inconsistent with the will of God.

One could hardly find a more forceful or succinct statement of the position that ultimately the law, and not the individual conscience, must be supreme, even in the instance where the law commands the individual positively to perform an action that he conscientiously considers to be morally wrong.

The other view, which was eventually to prevail, appeared in Chief Justice Charles Evans Hughes's dissenting opinion in the *Macintosh* case, in which he was joined by Justices Holmes, Brandeis, and Stone. The Chief Justice carefully narrowed the question before the Court to whether the broad and general language of the naturalization oath should be interpreted as being an unconditional promise to bear arms. Such a construction, in Chief Justice Hughes's opinion, was unwarranted because "directly opposed to the spirit of our institutions and to the historic practice of the Congress" in granting exemption from military service to conscientious objectors (*ibid.*, 627). Hughes went on, however, to rebut the Court's thesis that duty to the state is "paramount" and must be "recognized" even when "it conflicts with convictions of duty to God." He said (*ibid.*, 633):

Undoubtedly that duty to the state exists within the domain of power, for government may enforce obedience to laws regardless of scruples. When one's belief collides with the power of the State, the latter is supreme within its sphere and submission or punishment follows. But, in the forum of conscience, duty to a moral power higher than the State has always been maintained. The reservation of that supreme obligation, as a matter of principle, would unquestionably be made by many of our conscientious and law-abiding citizens.

He then defined "the essence of religion" as "belief in a relation to God involving duties superior to those arising from any human relation"—a phrase that Congress inserted, with some modification, into the Universal Military Training and Service Act in 1948 in order to explain the grounds of exemption from service. Hughes went on to say that one could not properly understand religious liberty "without assuming the existence of a belief in supreme allegiance to the will of God." Even when divorced from particular conceptions of deity, "freedom of conscience itself implies respect for an innate conviction of paramount duty." There was, therefore, a "proper field" in which conscience was supreme. What it was presented "in part a question of constitutional law and also, in part, one of legislative policy in avoiding unnecessary clashes with the dictates of conscience." But it was certainly possible to maintain the supremacy of law in its own field "without demanding that either citizens or applicants for citizenship shall assume by oath an obligation to regard allegiance to God as subordinate to allegiance to civil power" (*ibid.*, 634).

This statement, like the similar one by Justice William O. Douglas in *Girouard* v. *United States* (61, 68), deserves to be applauded. It is more Christian, more civilized, and politically more wise than the opinion of the Court in the *Macintosh* case.[7] But does it resolve, or does it prudently seek to avoid, the problem arising from an irreconcilable clash between the social and the private conscience?

Hughes distinguished the "domain of power" in which duty to the state is paramount from the "forum of conscience" in which duty to "a moral power higher than the state" prevails. This distinction is serviceable if we are dealing with subjects that under our Constitution are recognized as being beyond the competence of the state, e.g., religious beliefs. But the law is concerned with action rather than belief, and many actions fall within both the domain of power and the forum of conscience. In some instances the domain of power may itself be a forum of conscience: government, after all, has a moral as well as a legal duty to protect and promote the general welfare. Government, therefore, has a moral right to require certain public services of citizens. It is repugnant to think that a government might be morally justified in forcing a man to perform, directly and immediately, what he regarded as an immoral act, and one hesitates to admit that such might ever be the case. But a government might, in good conscience, judge some actions so vitally necessary to society that it would require

7. The Court has never again argued the issue of conscientious objection as profoundly as it did in the *Macintosh* case. Its only major pronouncement on the subject in recent years was in *United States* v. *Seeger*, 380 U.S. 163 (1965). Here the Court said the religious belief on the ground of which exemption from military service was granted by act of Congress had to be extended to include any "belief that is sincere and meaningful [and] occupies a place in the life of its possessor parallel to that filled by the orthodox belief in God of one who clearly qualifies for the exemption" (*ibid.*, 166). The Court thus clarified what is the conscience that the law intends to respect and again made it plain that it is conscience, not its specific religious content, that is protected.

individuals who found them morally impermissible to co-operate with them at least indirectly.

Justice Benjamin N. Cardozo touched on such a situation in his concurring opinion in *Hamilton* v. *Regents*, 293 U.S. 245, 266-268 (1934). He noted that, while Quakers and other conscientious objectors had historically been exempted from military service, they had often been required to supply substitutes for themselves or to contribute money to the prosecution of the war. Apparently the lawmakers who granted exemption did not think that they were violating the constitutional rights or the moral claims of objectors by coupling the exemption with these collateral conditions. Then Justice Cardozo remarked:

Manifestly a different doctrine would carry us to lengths that have never yet been dreamed of. The conscientious objector, if his liberties were to be thus extended, might refuse to contribute taxes in furtherance of a war, whether for attack or for defense, or in furtherance of any other end condemned by his conscience as irreligious or immoral. The right of private judgment has never yet been so exalted above the powers and the compulsion of the agencies of government.

And, indeed, it does seem most unlikely that even the most liberal government will exempt conscientious objectors from paying taxes or in other ways indirectly aiding public policies that they judge to be immoral.

Conclusion

The truth is that no government can recognize the freedom of the individual conscience as absolute. Those of us who honor the Machabees and the Christian martyrs believe that Caesar's rights are not absolute, either. But sacred as freedom of conscience undeniably is, it must ultimately be limited by the claims of that other conscience that molds laws and policies of society. It is not enough, therefore, for society to show the utmost possible respect for the individual conscience. Society must itself have a good conscience, for it is this conscience that furnishes the content of law and policy. The Nazis were evil, not merely because they failed to respect the conscience of dissenters, but because they enacted laws and followed policies that were inhuman. They would have been just as evil even if they had genuinely represented the conscience of the greater part of the German people.

The late Justice Felix Frankfurter said in *Bartkus* v. *Illinois*, 359 U.S. 121, 128 (1959): "The Anglo-American system of law is based not upon a transcendental revelation but upon the conscience of society ascertained as best it may be by a tribunal disciplined for the task and environed by the best safeguards for disinterestedness and detachment." Let us resist the temptation to remark that the Supreme Court thus assumes the role of a secular Holy See. What needs to be emphasized is that it is the conscience of society that in the long run determines which values will be embodied in law.

It is society, too, that judges which values are of such paramount social importance that the claims of the individual conscience will not be allowed to prevail against them. A liberal society will try to reduce the number of such extreme cases of conflict of consciences. But there will always be some of them; perhaps, in an increasingly technologized and interdependent world, more rather than fewer of them. That is why it is not enough for society to be liberal in its treatment of dissenters: it must also strive to be moral and to form for itself a social conscience that judges soundly and well the human values that it will maintain by force of law.

As Professor Berns said, there are some things which decent government simply should not do. There are other things that decent government should prohibit. But what those things are is a question—in American constitutional terminology—of substantive due process of law. It cannot be reduced merely to the question of the rights of the individual conscience. If society is going sometimes to impose its conscientious judgment on dissenters, it is important that society's conscience should be right.

Clarence N. Stone / Patterns of Voting on *Mallory*, *Durham*, and other Criminal Procedure Issues in Congress

Though much attention has been given to criminal procedure as a legal issue, few scholars have examined criminal procedure as a political issue. Yet the 1964 presidential campaign served notice that crime, including the procedures involved in the apprehension and treatment of criminal suspects, is a matter of national concern and controversy. Moreover, interest has not subsided since the 1964 election. Equally important, the crime issue did not spring full-grown from the brow of Barry Goldwater during the presidential campaign. Court rulings, especially the *Mallory* decision,[1] had been under attack in Congress for some time. In the Senate itself, a full six years before the Goldwater presidential candidacy, the charge had been made that "enough has been done for those who murder, rape and rob . . . ," that "the rights of criminals have been magnified out of all proper proportion, while the right of society to protection has been ignored."[2] Both inside and outside Congress concerns had been expressed over matters ranging from parole and probation practices to a broadened definition of insanity. Vice presidential candidate William Miller's denunciation of "bleeding-hearts who often center more sentiment and concern on the criminal than the victim," of "this soft-on-crime, society-is-to-blame breed,"[3] then, only brought into sharp focus a long-standing set of specific concerns. In short, criminal procedure bears signs of a major political issue—one that may have been highlighted by the events and personalities of the 1964 election campaign, but one that neither began nor ended there.

There are far too many facets of this complex and still evolving issue for exhaustive treatment here. However, one preliminary step that can be taken at this time is an analysis of congressional voting on

1. *Mallory* v. *United States*, 354 U.S. 449 (1957).
2. Remarks made by Senator Ervin, Democrat of North Carolina, *Congressional Record*, CIV (Aug. 19, 1958), 18481, 18483.
3. New York *Times* (Oct. 10, 1964), p. 14.

criminal procedure questions. Hopefully such a study will provide some understanding of the forces underlying and contributing to national controversy. A few caveats are in order first. Congress has taken up only a very limited number of specific questions. Most of its attention in this area has been directed toward the Mallory decision, though some other matters have been considered. It should also be pointed out that congressional action on criminal procedure matters derives mainly, but not exclusively, from the special responsibilities Congress has for the District of Columbia. At the same time hearings and floor debate indicate that Congress has not regarded the criminal procedure questions before it as issues of local concern only. Quite the contrary, testimony and debate dwell on the national implications of several aspects of the apprehension and punishment of criminals.[4] It is perhaps in order, then, to look at the substance of the issues and the debate in Congress before the roll call votes are analyzed.

Background to the Roll Call Votes: Issues

In June, 1957, the United States Supreme Court overturned the conviction of Andrew Mallory, accused of a rape to which he confessed while being held illegally by the District of Columbia police. Mallory was an illiterate Negro, described in Justice Frankfurter's decision as "a nineteen-year-old lad of limited intelligence." Though the case was remanded, a second trial never occurred because, according to Court critics, the rape victim was unable to undergo the further ordeal of being the major witness in a retrial. The elements of a highly emotional controversy were present and bore fruit.

The facts of the case were as follows. Rule 5(a) of the Federal Rules of Criminal Procedure provide for arraignment "without unnecessary delay." As interpreted by the Court, these rules provide that arrest may not be made on mere suspicion but on probable cause only. Arraignment is to take place "as quickly as possible so that [the arrested person] may be advised of his rights and so that the issue of probable cause may be promptly determined."[5] Mallory had been apprehended

4. Similarly statements and testimony in committee hearings have not been restricted to District officials and organizations. Witnesses have included Chief Parker of Los Angeles and Chicago Police Superintendent Wilson, both nationally known figures. Organizations testifying and submitting statements have ranged from the American Civil Liberties Union to the National Sons of the American Revolution.

5. *Mallory* v. *United States*, p. 454.

between 2 and 2:30 P.M. He denied committing the rape when questioned, was then asked to submit to a lie detector test, and given food and drink. The polygraph operator could not be located at first so the questioning did not begin until 8 P.M. After one and one-half hours of interrogation, Mallory stated to the polygraph operator alone that he was responsible for the crime. Then, after the confession was repeated to other police officers, an unsuccessful attempt was made to find an arraigning officer. Mallory was then examined by the deputy coroner, who found no signs of physical or psychological coercion. Next Mallory was confronted by the rape victim and members of the Sex Squad. The confession was repeated, and between 11:30 and 12:30 that night he dictated the confession. He had not been told of his right to a preliminary examination, of his right to remain silent, of his right to counsel, and he had not been warned that any statement made by him might be used against him. Mallory was arraigned the next morning. The trial was delayed for a year because of doubts about his capacity to understand the proceedings against him. He was convicted and received the death sentence.

The Supreme Court decision was unanimous, the opinion brief and to the point. The Court reaffirmed the rule that adequate enforcement of "the congressional requirement of prompt arraignment" could be accomplished only by making inadmissible "incriminating statements elicited from defendants during a period of unlawful detention."[6] Then the Court held that in view of the surrounding circumstances Mallory's arraignment could not be considered to have taken place without unnecessary delay.[7] Thus, through a more stringent application of an older rule the decision seemed to threaten the interrogation process whereby the police extracted confessions.

A month after the decision *U.S. News and World Report* ran an article entitled "Why Policeman's Job Is Getting Tougher."[8] The

6. *Ibid.*, p. 453. The general rule was laid down in *McNabb* v. *United States*, 318 U.S. 332 (1943), a decision which was also criticized in Congress both when first rendered and during the Mallory debate.

7. *Ibid.*, p. 455.

8. July 26, 1957, pp. 38-40. A check of magazines indicated that over a ten-year period leading up to the 1964 election *U.S. News and World Report* was the one most intensely concerned with the crime issue. Whether *U.S. News* shaped opinion or was simply registering already articulated concern is difficult to determine. It is worth noting that coverage of the crime issue in *U.S. News* during the late fifties and early sixties was strikingly similar in tone and substance to the Goldwater treatment of the issue in the presidential campaign subsequently.

article reported, "Police across the country are threatened now with new restrictions on the questioning of persons under arrest."[9] And the *Mallory* decision was described as part of "a long-time trend in the courts—to add more and more restrictions to the activities of police."[10] Thus the article predicted "a broad new test in this country" between police rights and criminal rights.[11] A few months later, *U.S. News and World Report* ran a cover article, "Easing Up on Murderers —Why?" Again reference was made to the circumstance under which the police "now are sharply limited in their right to get voluntary confessions."[12] Anxiety over a general "tilting of the balance in favor of the criminal" was evident.[13] Meanwhile, in Congress, hearings were held before the *Mallory* decision was a month old.[14] Thus began a ten-year effort to modify the *Mallory* rule.[15]

The bill that was considered and passed by the House in 1958 provided that delay alone would not be grounds for rendering a statement inadmissible as evidence. Suspects were to be informed that they were not required to make a statement and that any statement might be used against them, but other notifications such as the right to counsel were not called for and were rejected when offered as amendments on the floor. This same version of *Mallory* rule modification passed the House in 1959. Both of these efforts, coming through the Judiciary Committee, would have amended the Federal Rules of Criminal Procedure. In 1961 a similar bill came through the District of Columbia Committee, but its application was restricted to the District of Columbia. This same effort was made in 1963 and 1965 as part of an omnibus crime bill for the District of Columbia.[16] In 1967 the D.C. crime bill first omitted direct modification of the *Mallory* rule when an amendment to include this provision was defeated, but the 1967

9. *Ibid.*, p. 38.
10. *Ibid.*, p. 40.   11. *Ibid.*, p. 38.
12. Nov. 29, 1957, p. 33.   13. *Ibid.*, p. 35.
14. A special House Judiciary subcommittee, chaired by Representative Willis of Louisiana, held hearings in July, August, and October, 1957. Senate hearings were not held until 1958, when two separate Judiciary subcommittees conducted hearings.
15. The legislative histories of the various bills, only one of which became law, are very complex, involving everything from Senate filibuster to a presidential veto. Brief accounts may be found in *Congressional Quarterly*. Nothing on later bills equals Walter Murphy's very fine study of the 1958 legislation. See *Congress and the Court* (Chicago, 1962), pp. 177-183, 193-223.
16. The 1963 and 1965 House omnibus crime bills for the District included, in addition to Mallory modification and other provisions discussed below, a provision for the detention of material witnesses, increased penalties for various crimes, and an anti-obscenity title.

bill did include a provision also found in the 1963 and 1965 bills, authorizing investigative arrests. When the 1967 bill came out of conference, it left intact District arrest law but in line with the Senate bill did alter slightly the application of the *Mallory* rule within the District.

Attempts to modify the *Mallory* rule have generated considerably less floor activity in the Senate than in the House. In 1958 the Senate accepted the House bill but with the one crucial change of inserting the word "reasonable" before delay. Thus, the Senate bill was at most a minor modification of the Mallory decision, and perhaps nothing more than a clarification of it.

The issue did not reappear on the Senate floor until 1965, when the Senate version of *Mallory* modification was again much milder than the House version.[17] Statements would be admissible if four conditions were met: (1) the suspect was apprised of all his rights, (2) the suspect was given an opportunity to obtain counsel, (3) interrogation did not exceed an aggregate time of three hours, and (4) the interrogation was recorded. Investigative arrests were excluded from the committee bill as being patently unconstitutional.

The 1967 Senate bill, the version written into law, provided for a three-hour period "immediately following" arrest in which statements would not be inadmissible "solely because of delay." Arrested persons were to be "advised of and accorded" applicable rights, but these were not specified in the bill. As was the case with all of the bills in the sixties, coverage was restricted to the District of Columbia.

Though it did not become an issue in Congress until after the *Mallory* controversy had developed, a 1954 Circuit Court decision on criminal insanity, *Durham* v. *U.S.*,[18] also generated criticism and legislation. Monte Durham, a man with a long history of imprisonment and hospitalization for mental disorders, had been convicted of housebreaking. His only defense was that he was "of unsound mind." His conviction was set aside on two grounds. The trial court was held to have erred first in not applying the rule that, once evidence of mental disorder is introduced, the prosecution must prove sanity beyond a reasonable doubt in order to establish criminal intent. Secondly, the

17. For a brief comparison of the House and Senate bills, see the *Congressional Quarterly Almanac*, XXI (1965), 662.
18. 214 F. (2d) 862.

court rejected the traditional test of criminal insanity as not taking "sufficient acount of psychic realities and scientific knowledge."[19] The ability-to-know-right-from-wrong test supplemented by the irresistible urge test was replaced by a ruling that "an accused is not criminally responsible if his unlawful act was the product of mental disease or mental defect."[20] *U.S. News and World Report* on this occasion also reacted quickly. An article of early 1955 sounded alarm over the possibility that "thousands of defendants will be able to avoid prison if courts across the nation follow the precedent set in Washington."[21] And there was further concern that "not all those acquitted as insane will be committed to mental hospitals."[22] Thus the question was posed: "Are more criminally insane persons going to be turned loose to prey on the public, if the new rules are generally applied?"[23] In 1961 the House District of Columbia Committee held hearings which resulted in a recommendation that both parts of the decision be modified. House critics of the Court decision first made an isolated attempt to alter the *Durham* rule, which resulted in a voice vote,[24] but in 1963, alteration of *Durham* became part of the various House omnibus crime bills for the District of Columbia. A different reaction took place in the Senate District Committee. In 1965 the committee found the *Durham* rule workable and called only for prior notification by the defense when a plea of insanity was to be entered. House attempts to redefine criminal insanity more in line with the traditional rule and to eliminate prosecution responsibility to prove sanity failed to find a place in the 1967 enactment. Only the Senate's prior-notification provision became law.

Two other District of Columbia matters have engendered controversy. In 1962 Senator Morse attempted to have the Congress go beyond simply restricting somewhat the use of the death penalty and have it eliminated completely in the District of Columbia. That same year a struggle developed in the House of Representatives over the juvenile court system. The District of Columbia committee reported out a bill, defeated on the floor, which would have lowered the maxi-

19. *Ibid.*, 874.   20. *Ibid.*, 874-875.
21. Feb. 11, 1955, p. 62.   22. *Ibid.*
23. *Ibid.*, p. 63. Nearly three years later, a chart was published showing the hospital action taken for persons acquitted under the Durham rule—*U.S. News and World Report* (Nov. 29, 1957), p. 35.
24. U.S. *Congressional Record*, 87th Cong., 1st Sess., 1961, CVII, 11169-11179.

mum age for juveniles from eighteen to sixteen and eliminated the juvenile court as a separate division of the municipal court system.

Thus, a range of issues has come before the Congress in the last decade, occasioning a small but significant number of roll call votes. While most of the controversy has been over the *Mallory* case and police handling of suspects, the definition of criminal insanity, the treatment of juveniles, and the place of punishment in combating criminal behavior have also been issues.

Background to Roll Call Votes: Debate

Much of the congressional debate has centered on the civil liberties issue of where to draw the line between individual liberty and the security needs of the general public. When the *Mallory* issue first arose, Senator Cooper, in opposing any legislative action, said: "there is a question of which is prior and which is supreme—the preservation of individual human rights by due process or some unlimited law-enforcement right. I believe under the Bill of Rights, individual rights and due process must be observed."[25] To Senator Ervin, on the other hand, "the main object of criminal laws is the protection of society."[26]

At a less general level the *Mallory* debate concerned the place of confessions in law enforcement. Critics saw the decision as overruling the long-established principle that the only test of the admissibility of a confession was its voluntariness. If a statement was not induced and was therefore "trustworthy as evidence,"[27] restrictions on its use were described as a misplaced punishment of the general public. Senator Ervin charged that the *Mallory* decision and the earlier *McNabb* decision were "based on the theory that the supposed sins of the police officers ought to be visited on society, instead of on the police officers themselves."[28]

Supporters of the *Mallory* decision were somewhat suspicious of police interrogation and confessions in general. Congressman Lindsay described the anti-*Mallory* bill as an attack on the rules that "reflect and embody the fundamental guarantees of the right to counsel, the privilege against self-incrimination, the right to habeas corpus, and

25. *Ibid.*, 85th Cong., 2d Sess., 1958, CIV, 18438.
26. *Ibid.*, p. 18482.   27. *Ibid.*, p. 12694.
28. *Ibid.*, p. 18484.

the right to be detained only on probable cause."[29] He felt that the bill would "gut the presumption of innocence."[30] Because coercion was regarded as something virtually impossible to prove and because prosecution of police officers was deemed "undesirable and impractical," the *Mallory* rule was seen as "the one practical method of assuring police compliance with the arraignment law,[31] as "a realistic and effective sanction against the violation of procedural due process."[32]

As might be anticipated, sharply contrasting views of law enforcement officials and of their handling of suspects were also in evidence. Senator Ervin spoke of "an abiding confidence in the officers of the law who are protecting society against criminals."[33] The opposing side expressed concern over "the tense atmosphere of the police station," the "scowling faces" and "anger" of the police, "truncheons and clubs" being "brandished,"[34] lie detector tests being imposed on suspects,[35] dragnet operations,[36] third-degree methods,[37] and "emotionally unbalanced people" and those "on the psychological borderline" having their minds twisted by "the power of suggestion, stirred up by fear."[38]

It is not surprising, then, that different understandings were evinced of the *Mallory* case and the factual background against which the case was decided. Critics thought the case hinged on the time technicality that several hours elapsed between detention and arraignment. Thus Congressman Cramer declared: "This case deals with a confession that has been given freely and voluntarily without any threat of violence or coercion, other than the fact that the man was held for 7½ hours."[39] By contrast, Senator O'Mahoney said that the confession was, in effect, extorted because a lie detector test was imposed.[40] And Congressman Multer denied that the case turned only on delay in the arraignment of Mallory: "because he was not brought before a committing magistrate without unnecessary delay and apprised of his rights and because this was an illiterate person with low mentality, almost so low a mental-

29. *Ibid.*, 87th Cong., 1st Sess., 1961, CVII, 10070.
30. *Ibid.* Libertarians displayed a recurring concern on other issues as well as Mallory that legislation was weighted too heavily in favor of the prosecution.
31. *Ibid.*, 85th Cong., 2d Sess., 1958, CIV, 18495.
32. *Ibid.*, p. 12697.   33. *Ibid.*, p. 18481.
34. *Ibid.*, pp. 12697-12698.   35. *Ibid.*, p. 18439.
36. *Ibid.*, p. 18490.   37. *Ibid.*, p. 18516.
38. *Ibid.*, p. 18515.   39. *Ibid.*, p. 12700.
40. *Ibid.*, p. 18439.

ity as to be considered mentally incompetent, his confession could not be received in evidence."[41]

Difference factors are salient to different congressmen because there is intertwined with the civil liberties issue a class issue, a question of how law enforcement affects different segments of the population. Senator Hennings explained:

The police do not take the president of the First National Bank to the captain and say, "Now, come clean, buddy, or we'll take you down and cool you off a little longer until you remember some of the details." They do not say that to him. They say to him, "Mr. Jones, apparently you made a very serious mistake. Perhaps you need a lawyer. Here is the telephone. You should get a bondsman, because you are being charged with manslaughter."[42]

It was also argued that the hardened criminal knows his rights and how to assert them, that those who needed protections such as the *Mallory* and *Durham* rules are the poor and discriminated against, those with little education, few friends, and no financial resources. Without stringent libertarian protections, Court defenders felt, "arbitrary and capricious methods" would be used "against the ignorant."[43]

Those who live in slum neighborhoods were believed to be picked up often "merely because they happened to live there."[44] The example was cited of the District of Columbia police undertaking a dragnet operation. After an attack on a woman and on the basis of a statement that the assailant was a "short, stocky Negro" the police arrested "approximately 90 short, stocky Negroes" but "did not find probable cause against a single one who was caught in the dragnet."[45] The police were further regarded as susceptible to the temptation to use " 'third degree' methods to extract confessions from poor, uneducated or youthful suspects."[46]

Even in the matter of punishment it was believed that the poor pay more. On the capital punishment question a study was cited to the effect that the exaction of the death penalty depended more on skin color and financial position than on the gravity of the crime and

41. *Ibid.*, 87th Cong., 1st Sess., 1961, CVII, 10074.
42. *Ibid.*, 85th Cong., 2d Sess., 1958, CIV, 18477.
43. *Ibid.*, p. 18516.   44. *Ibid.*, p. 18476.
45. *Ibid.*, p. 18514.
46. The minority report on the 1963 House omnibus crime bill for the District of Columbia.

the number of victims.[47] Senator Morse quoted one writer in this manner: "It may be exceedingly difficult for a rich man to enter the Kingdom of Heaven but case after case bears witness that it is virtually impossible for him to enter the execution chamber."[48]

Intermingled with both the civil liberties issue and the class issue was a conflict over basic values, a cultural clash between views rooted in the traditional and individualistic morality developed in an earlier period and views associated with the modern and more social-minded morality of the mid-twentieth century.[49] While disagreement was not absolute, much of the debate gravitated around the punitive approach vs. the rehabilitative approach. Other related themes such as personal responsibility vs. social causation and the relative importance of discipline vs. care and understanding as deterrents to criminal behavior were also present.

The bill abolishing the juvenile court as a separate jurisdiction was defended by floor manager James C. Davis of Georgia this way:

The greatest protection the public can have from a robber, murderer, or rapist is punishment to deter him from doing it again, and confinement to remove him from the scene, so he cannot repeat the offense. Yet, these juvenile court people will frankly tell you that this concern is with rehabilitation of the criminal.[50]

In the debate on the 1963 omnibus crime bill for the District of Columbia, Congressman Whitener asserted: "These sociological views which keep cropping up and all of this crying and wailing about the criminals did not bother the subcommittee too much."[51] He argued, "the greatest antidote to crime is punishment."[52] Congressman Kyl charged, "the average 15-, 16-, and 17-year old youngster in the District of Columbia who violated the law in the District of Columbia very definitely lacks a respect for the law because he does not think he is going to have to suffer any consequences for his actions."[53] In general, the view from the non-libertarian side was that crime control

47. U.S. *Congressional Record*, 87th Cong., 2d Sess., 1962, CVIII, 4136.
48. *Ibid.*, p. 4137.
49. Though the various writers have not dealt with crime and law enforcement, general treatments of value cleavage and cultural or symbolic politics may be found in Joseph R. Gusfield, *Symbolic Crusade* (Urbana, Ill., 1963); Daniel Bell, ed., *The Radical Right* (Garden City, N. Y., 1963), and the *Journal of Social Issues* symposium on "American Political Extremism in the 1960's," XIX (April, 1963).
50. U.S. *Congressional Record*, 87th Cong., 2d Sess., 1962, CVIII, 2905.
51. *Ibid.*, 88th Cong., 1st Sess., 1963, CI, 14728.
52. *Ibid.*, p. 14727.
53. *Ibid.*, 87th Cong., 2d Sess., 1962, CVIII, 2938.

requires a hard-line approach. The sentiment was widely held that the time had arrived to be "a little tough on criminals."[54] Representative Smith of Virginia expressed his contempt for the "do-gooders" who are "screaming not to do anything to these poor innocent children."[55] Representative Keating charged that the *Mallory* decision "went too far in coddling criminals."[56] Others struck out against "'love-and-kisses' type of treatment of criminals,"[57] "this bleeding heart business,"[58] "the sob sisters and leftwing organizations,"[59] and "namby-pamby treatment of young hoodlums."[60] Congressman Becker declared that he was "tired of pampering the wicked."[61]

While Court critics believed that effective crime deterrence requires removal of restrictions on the police, punishment of criminal conduct, and a "return to ideas of personal responsibility,"[62] Court supporters maintained that control of crime is best achieved through alleviating the problems of poverty and discrimination. Thus the omnibus crime bill was attacked on the grounds that it proposed "harsh and repressive measures to punish the criminal symptoms of the social and economic misery within the District of Columbia."[63] In contrast to the non-libertarians' suspicion of sociologists, social workers, and psychiatrists, the libertarians displayed great confidence in those with social science training. The effort to modify the *Durham* rule was criticized on the grounds that the hearings had been cursory and did "not include the testimony of medical or psychiatric experts, of specialists in mental health, penology or criminology."[64] Senator Morse cited social science research to counter the belief that capital punishment is an effective crime deterrent, and quoted a criminologist who described the death penalty as "the antithesis of the rehabilitative nonpunitive, nonvindictive orientation of 20th century penology."[65]

One additional dimension of the congressional debate that should be mentioned concerns relations between the legislative and judicial

54. *Ibid.*, 88th Cong., 1st Sess., 1963, CIX, 14747.
55. *Ibid.*, 87th Cong., 2d Sess., 1962, CVIII, 2932.
56. *Ibid.*, 85th Cong., 2d Sess., 1958, CIV, 12695.
57. *Ibid.*, 87th Cong., 2d Sess., 1962, CVIII, 2910.
58. *Ibid.*, 87th Cong., 1st Sess., 1961, CVII, 10070.
59. *Ibid.*, 87th Cong., 2d Sess., 1962, CVIII, 2939.
60. *Ibid.*, p. 2910.
61. *Ibid.*, 88th Cong., 1st Sess., 1963, CIX, 14747.
62. *Ibid.*, 87th Cong., 1st Sess., 1961, CVII, 11176.
63. Minority report of the House District of Columbia Committee, on the 1965 bill.
64. U.S. *Congressional Record*, 88th Cong., 1st Sess., 1963, CIX, 14755.
65. *Ibid.*, 87th Cong., 2d Sess., 1962, CVIII, 4136.

branches of government. Walter Murphy, in his study of anti-Court legislation in the fifties, viewed the anti-*Mallory* bill as part of a general effort to repudiate the moral authority of the Warren Court.[66] Indeed, some of the congressional defenders of the *Mallory* decision, especially in the Senate, saw this legislation the same way.[67] At the very least, institutional rivalry was involved. Critics of the decision made references to "encroachments upon the lawmaking authority,"[68] and "an unrestrained program of usurping legislative authority and making law where they have no jurisdiction to do so."[69] Libertarians defended judicial involvement as well as the substance of court decisions.

Finally, it should be stated that race was a factor, though not overtly so in the debate. Undoubtedly Southern attitudes toward the Supreme Court have been influenced by racial considerations. And, perhaps even more to the heart of the matter, race is an integral part of the class issue. Quite clearly libertarians and other minority group spokesmen believe that the treatment of criminal suspects varies not only according to economic status but according to race as well.[70] Furthermore, the racial composition of the District of Columbia's population has hardly been an incidental factor in the particular concern that Southern congressmen have displayed over crime in the nation's capital. Thus, with race understood to be subsumed under other topics, there are four major dimensions of the debate in Congress: the civil liberties controversy, the class issue, the cultural clash, and institutional conflict.

Criminal Procedure Voting Patterns

For the ten-year period from 1958 through 1967, a time running from the beginning of the *Mallory* controversy to the enactment of legislation, fifteen roll calls were selected for analysis—eight in the House, seven in the Senate. These roll calls were the only ones that involved a clearly predominant criminal procedure question and that also elicited opposition to the majority amounting to at least 20 per

66. *Congress and the Court*, p. 183.   67. *Ibid.*, pp. 201-202.
68. U.S. *Congressional Record*, 85th Cong., 2d Sess., 1958, CIV, 12695.
69. *Ibid.*, p. 12706.
70. See, for example, the findings in the report by the United States Commission on Civil Rights, *Justice* (1961), p. 109.

cent of the votes cast. State and district data were collected so that each vote could be related to constituency characteristics as well as to the party affiliation of and the region represented by the senators and representatives. For reasons of time and space, only the constituency traits of urban-rural character and the proportion of the population that was non-white were included in the analysis discussed below.

Voting on criminal procedure questions divides along the familiar party and sectional lines associated with the conservative coalition. However, as Table 1 indicates, congressional voting on criminal procedure differs somewhat from voting on economic issues. Since Republicans are less consistently and overwhelmingly non-libertarian than Southern Democrats, Republicans occupy the intermediate position.[71] While intermediate, Republicans in both houses of Congress lean to the non-libertarian side, and, except for one Senate roll call, they have voted in larger numbers with Southern Democrats than with Northern Democrats.

Once Southern Democrats are treated separately, describing an issue in partisan terms is open to question. Because Democrats outside the South tend to come from a type of constituency different from Republicans,[72] it is possible that what appears to be partisan conflict is in large measure simply a reflection of constituency differences.[73] The comparisons in Tables 2 and 3 indicate, however, that party differences are real and substantial.[74] The Senate figures need to be

71. The voting pattern resembles that reported in Charles F. Andrain, "A Scale Analysis of Senators' Attitudes Toward Civil Rights," *Western Political Quarterly*, XVII (Sept., 1964), 488-503.

72. A recent presentation of this finding is Lewis A. Froman, Jr., "Inter-Party Constituency Differences and Congressional Voting Behavior," *American Political Science Review*, LVII (March, 1963), 57-61.

73. Continuing research has not supported such an interpretation of legislative politics. See my comment on the above cited article by Froman, "Inter-Party Constituency Differences and Congressional Voting Behavior: A Partial Dissent," *American Political Science Review*, LVII (Sept., 1963), 665-666. For a recent review of pertinent state legislative literature, see Thomas A. Flinn, "Party Responsibility in the States: Some Causal Factors," *American Political Science Review*, LVIII (March, 1964), 60-71. Finally, for an example of how systematic analysis of early roll data has led to a new emphasis on the role of party in Congress, see Joel H. Silbey, *The Shrine of Party: Congressional Voting Behavior, 1841-1852.* (Pittsburgh, 1967).

74. See also, my "Congressional Party Differences in Civil-Liberties and Criminal-Procedure Issues," *Southwestern Social Science Quarterly*, XLVII (Sept., 1966), 161-171. A third constituency characteristic, median education, was also included in the research. Preliminary analysis indicates clearly that this factor accounts for neither the party differences discussed here nor the regional differences discussed below. It might also be noted that legal training for senators and representatives has also been considered as a possible contributor to libertarian voting. Only among House Republicans is there a substantial positive association.

read with extra caution because, due to the small numbers, the two constituency factors were controlled consecutively rather than simultaneously.[75] Party differences are more pronounced on some roll calls than others. Still the over-all tendency is for urban and rural Democrats to resemble one another as do urban and rural Republicans more closely than their party opposites from a like constituency. Similarly, under cross-party comparisons by proportion of non-white population, Democrats remain more libertarian than Republicans. The House comparisons in Table 3 produce wide and stable party differences.

An examination of voting tendencies within the parties reveals that the North-South split is not the only sectional cleavage to appear. Libertarian sympathies are more in evidence among Republicans from the Northeast and Border states than among Republicans from other areas. Table 4 shows that sectional differences among Republicans are a little more pronounced in the Senate than the House but quite evident in both houses.

Deviation from the libertarian leanings of Northern (that is, non-Southern) Democrats is strong among those elected from Border and Rocky Mountain states.[76] Sectional differences are steadier in the House than in the Senate, apparently because House issues have been less varied. In both houses there seems to be a strongly libertarian/moderately libertarian split that coincides with regional groupings. Thus, wide regional differences appeared on the efforts in the Senate to go beyond a partial libertarian victory to defeat even a weakened version of *Mallory* modification and to abolish completely capital punishment for the District of Columbia. On the other hand, regional differences have little opportunity to show up on issues which call only for a limited libertarian stance, as on the Juvenile Court bill in the House and the 1958 efforts to weaken *Mallory* modification in the Senate.

75. Party differences do hold up under further cross-tabulation. On the twenty-eight comparisons that can be made, the median difference between the proportion of Democratic senators voting libertarian and the proportion of Republican senators voting libertarian is thirty percentage points. However, the numbers in several cells are quite small—in the two to four range. Such numbers are far too small to warrant much confidence.

76. Deviance is generally a little stronger among Border Democrats but quite pronounced nonetheless among Rocky Mountain Democrats. I am indebted to Professor Eleanor Bushnell and her research on the reapportionment issue for calling my attention to the Rocky Mountain states as a distinct subregion. See, "Political Arithmetic: Apportionment in the Western States," a paper delivered at the 1966 annual meeting of the American Political Science Association.

Like party differences, regional differences are suspect as being due mainly to underlying differences in constituency characteristics. But again like party, region remains as an important factor even after district character is held constant. Comparisons were done only for the House because the Senate numbers become quite small. For this reason Table 5 contains comparisons for the one Republican low cohesion roll call and for a composite analysis of voting on the *Mallory* and D.C. Crime bills. Table 6 contains comparisons on the two roll calls for which Democratic cohesion was lowest. Republicans' differences are smallest among congressmen from predominantly rural districts with a low percentage of non-white population. In the other categories the percentage point spread is quite substantial. A cross-regional resemblance is also evident among rural Democrats from districts with a proportionately low non-white population. And on the 1965 vote the regional differences between Democrats from urban districts with an intermediate number of non-white residents was not large. Still, while regional differences are not great for all categories, they remain, they are consistent in direction, and for most categories they are very large.

Though party and regional differences cannot be explained away by controlling for constituency, the conclusion should not be reached that constituency characteristics are unimportant. Rather, what the analysis suggests is that, in the House at least, district traits have an impact, but one that is quite limited in scope and one that is filtered through the political context of party and section.[77] If Table 5 is re-examined, for instance, it may be seen that urbanism and larger numbers of non-white constituents are associated among Northeast and Border Republicans with libertarian voting on the Juvenile Court bill. The urban-rural difference is important on the *Mallory*–D.C. Crime composite. Among Republicans from the Midwest and West, the effect of district characteristics is less apparent. The only conclusion that seems warranted is that a minority group population in a non-metropolitian setting is the circumstance least conducive to libertarian voting.

Among Southern Democrats in the House, by contrast, district char-

77. Since all of the tables are composed of descriptive statistics, no tests of significance have been applied. Inferences should be read with great caution, especially in the present discussion, which centers on district characteristics, because both the absolute numbers and the percentage differences are small.

acteristics seem to have significant bearing. On the Juvenile Court bill urbanism is clearly associated with a more libertarian response. The proportion of the non-white population is inversely but importantly related to voting libertarian. Thus, in the South the congressmen from rural districts with a large non-white population were almost completely non-libertarian, but two-thirds of the congressmen from urban districts with relatively small non-white populations voted libertarian.

The Border and Rocky Mountain area Democrats in some ways resemble the Southern Democrats. Table 8 indicates that urban representatives are more likely to vote libertarian than rural representatives, and among rural representatives non-white population and libertarian voting are inversely related (except in the instance of the Juvenile Court bill on which no difference appeared). The voting behavior of the urban congressmen is erratic, perhaps for political reasons, or perhaps because the numbers are too small to permit a smooth pattern to emerge.

Among the other urban Democrats—those from the Northeast, Midwest, and Pacific Coast areas—a sizable minority group in the constituency seems to encourage libertarian leanings. In rural areas no clear pattern is evident. A positive association between libertarian voting and non-white population is evident in 1958, but rests on a small number of cases. At any rate, the difference lessens and disappears through time. Urban congressmen are consistently but not greatly more libertarian than their rural counterparts.

To the extent that Table 2 is adequate for such comparisons, the indications are that the large and heterogeneous constituencies of senators, who also enjoy a long term of office, have little explanatory power for criminal procedure roll calls.[78] Intra-party differences are neither large nor consistent.

Discussion

Essentially the same party and section voting pattern holds on all of the roll calls examined above. This is to say, the Juvenile Court

78. See the arguments advanced by Thomas R. Dye, "A Comparison of Constituency Influences in the Upper and Lower Chambers of a State Legislature," *Western Political Quarterly*, XIV (June, 1961), 473-481; and Donald R. Matthews, *U.S. Senators and Their World* (Chapel Hill, 1960), pp. 230-239.

bill and the abolition of capital punishment for the District of Columbia produced basically the same voting pattern as the *Mallory* and D.C. Crime bills. Thus, voting responses did not seem to depend on whether or not a Supreme Court decision was at issue. Nor did responses seem to depend on whether the issue was methods of police investigation or punishment vs. rehabilitation. The findings above, then, do raise a number of questions, the most important of which is why on a range of issues criminal procedure conflict seems to derive more from party and section than from constituency traits.

The differences both between and within the parties suggest that the impact of constituency characteristics is mediated by political tradition.[79] Democratic and Republican officeholders differ in predisposition, in group identification, and in kinds of active supporters. Similar differences distinguish Southern and Northern Democrats. Party and sectional differences may very well, then, be differences over whose civil liberties are to be protected and promoted, rather than the protection and promotion of civil liberties in general.[80] The now classic study of party leaders and followers by Herbert McClosky and others pointed out:

Republican and Democratic leaders stand furthest apart on the issues that grow out of their group identification and support—out of the managerial, proprietary, and high-status connections of the one, and the labor, minority, low-status, and intellectual connections of the other.[81]

Southern Democrats may not have quite as strong or as uniform an identification with propertied groups—whose stake in "law and order" is considerable—as Republicans, but Southern Democratic ties to minority groups and intellectuals are the weakest of any bloc in Congress. And, very much to the point here, minority group ties have

79. The discussion below was greatly influenced by Frank Munger and James Blackhurst, "Factionalism in the National Convention, 1940-1960: An Analysis of Ideological Consistency in State Delegation Voting," *Journal of Politics*, XXVII (May, 1965), 375-394; and George Robert Boynton, "Southern Conservatism: Constituency Opinion and Congressional Voting," *Public Opinion Quarterly*, XXIX (Summer, 1965), 259-269.

80. It might be noted that Senator Ervin, who was one of the most concerned critics of the Mallory decision and the Court's emphasis on the accused's rights, has emerged as a staunch defender of the privacy and other rights of government workers.

81. "Issue Conflict and Consensus among Party Leaders and Followers," *American Political Science Review*, LIV (June, 1960), 426. Party officials, it should be added, have not displayed opposing civil liberties tendencies on national security and First Amendment questions. See Samuel A. Stouffer, *Communism, Conformity and Civil Liberties* (Garden City, N. Y., 1955), pp. 26-54; and Thomas A. Flinn and Frederick M. Wirt, "Local Party Leaders: Groups of Like Minded Men," *Midwest Journal of Political Science*, IX (Feb., 1965), 84-94.

been the most important and persistent source of conflict within the Democratic party.

On criminal procedure questions, if connections with minority groups and intellectuals serve to reinforce libertarian tendencies and if connections with high status and especially propertied groups serve to attenuate such leanings, then the voting patterns described above may be explained. Democrats from the metropolitan areas of the Northeast, the Midwest, and the Pacific Coast are the most libertarian bloc in Congress, and it is they who have had the closest ties to minority groups and intellectuals. Border and Rocky Mountain Democrats draw support from both the more propertied element and from groups who are traditionally antipathetic or indifferent toward non-whites. And at the same time, these Democrats are influenced by the liberal/ low-status/minorities coalition, which is associated with the Roosevelt presidency. Presumably, then, cross-pressures are at work, particularly in the urban areas. In rural areas, where organization of and political activity by minority groups are least developed, libertarian leanings are not encouraged. Further, when the minority group members are numerous enough to keep traditional antipathies salient, criminal procedure libertarianism is especially unlikely to appear.

In the South, modest libertarian tendencies are more apparent in urban than rural areas, in part perhaps because Southern Democrats in cities are more likely to draw support and establish ties somewhat resembling those of their Northern party colleagues. Also minority groups are generally better organized and more effective politically in cities. At the same time, in both urban and rural areas, a large minority population seems to make the racial aspects of criminal procedure stand out to whites and inhibit libertarian voting. Minority sympathies are dependent not only upon encouragement from the minority groups but also upon the absence of overt hostility on the part of the majority. White antipathy appears to be most pronounced when the non-white population is large, a pattern first noted by V. O. Key some twenty years ago.

Pressures from whites counter to non-white sympathies are not restricted to the South. Since the dramatization of the crime issue in the 1964 presidential campaign and the spread of civil unrest and disorder in ghettos, Democrats seem especially susceptible to a "backlash" effect. In the first place, the small upsurge of libertarian voting among Southern Democrats in 1963 did not survive the events of 1964. Even more significant is what has happened among Northern Democrats. On the *Mallory* and D.C. Crime bills the proportion of Northern Democrats voting libertarian increased steadily from 1958 through 1963, reaching 80 per cent in the latter year (see Table 1). In 1965 on the recommittal roll call the libertarian proportion decreased only slightly, but on the roll call for final passage the libertarian vote fell back to the 1958 level, as fewer than two-thirds opposed the bill.[82] While the decline of libertarian voting occurred in all categories, Democrats from districts with an intermediate proportion of non-white residents seemed to feel the backlash most strongly. While more than three-fourths opposed the 1963 Crime bill, opposition that held up fairly well on the 1965 recommittal motion, fewer than three-fifths voted against the passage of the 1965 Crime bill. Thus, a re-examination of the figures in Table 8 shows that representatives from districts intermediate in proportion of non-white population became the least libertarian category of Northern Democrats on the final vote.[83] Where non-whites are numerous enough to arouse white fears but not numerous enough to constitute a large voting bloc, equivocation on and retreat from a libertarian stand is a likely occurrence.

While Republicans generally have closer connections with the more propertied groups than with those who are poor and discriminated against, Northeast and Border Republicans have established ties with minority groups and do possess a somewhat heterogeneous base of support. These minority group ties (and presumably ties with intellectuals as well) are more important among urban than rural representatives. Indications are, however, that even in rural areas minority group ties are of significance, for libertarian voting increases as non-white population increases. By contrast, the presence of non-white constituents seems to elicit little libertarian sympathy among Republicans from the Midwest and West. In rural areas non-white population may even have an adverse effect on libertarian voting. Over-all, just as in the case of Democratic sectional cleavage, Midwestern and Western Republicans are distinguished from their Northeastern and Border

82. By contrast, the 1959 recommittal and final passage votes were almost identical. See Table 1.

83. The proportions of Northern Democrats voting libertarian were as follows: representatives from districts 0-2.9 per cent non-white—65 per cent; from districts 3-19.9 per cent non-white—57 per cent; from districts 20 per cent and above non-white—87 per cent.

state party colleagues not by the type of constituency from which they come but by the nature of their relationship with minority groups and others who might have libertarian preferences.

Conclusion

Congressional debate pointed to at least four aspects of criminal procedure controversy: the civil liberties question of how to balance individual rights with public security and order, the class issue of whether or not lower status and especially racial minority groups receive equitable treatment by law enforcement agencies, the cultural clash over the causes and prevention of criminal behavior, and the institutional question of what is the proper role of courts, especially the Supreme Court. The roll calls examined did not indicate that these conflicts were separable in the Congress. Such a finding is not difficult to explain. Both the debate and the voting patterns suggest that, in the area of criminal procedure, civil liberties attitudes and class issues may be closely linked by means of group identifications. Furthermore, for a full generation now the Supreme Court has been more attentive to the rights of individuals who have suffered economic and social deprivation than to those who are prestigious and propertied. That attitudes toward the Court and toward judicial activism are influenced by group identification is not a new discovery. The cultural clash, too, is related to the group and class divisions of the nation. An emphasis upon punishment, discipline, and personal accountability is tied in with a set of values most closely associated with an entrepreneurial middle class. It is not surprising, then, that some conservative spokesmen see welfare "hand-outs" to the poor and "coddling" criminals as two facets of the same decline in morality. Contrariwise, the argument that criminal behavior is a consequence of poverty and prejudice or the argument that rehabilitation is the humane and civilized response to criminality may be expected to receive ready acceptance among representatives who identify with the lower strata of society.

By no means should the conclusion be reached that controversy over criminal procedure is a unidimensional conflict. Rather, what has been suggested here is that in the Congress differing group identifications along party and sectional lines and resulting differences in group access have had great impact on both the debate and the voting. Congressmen do not fall into one ideological camp or another—gradations of views are much in evidence and these can be related systematically to (but not explained completely by) group identifications and group access.

Relationships are not static. Racial considerations, of consequence from the beginning, appear to have become more important in the mid-sixties. Race therefore varies in significance not only geographically but over the course of time and events as well. Democrats whose ties to racial minorities have been strong are nonetheless subject to counter-pressures—real, imagined, or both—when race is both salient and threatening to whites. At a time when the nation is struggling with the problems of poverty and discrimination, controversy over criminal procedure may be both unfortunate and unavoidable.

Table 1. *Criminal Procedure Issues and the Conservative Coalition (proportion voting libertarian)*

	Southern Democrats[a]		Republicans		Northern Democrats	
House of Representatives						
1958 Mallory bill	1%	'87)[b]	3%	(178)	64%	(126)
1959 Mallory bill, recommit	1%	(96)	12%	(142)	72%	(177)
1959 Mallory bill, passage	2%	(94)	11%	(142)	72%	(176)
1961 Mallory bill	1%	(93)	8%	(159)	74%	(160)
1962 D.C. Juvenile Court bill	24%	(90)	49%	(153)	95%	(141)
1963 D.C. Crime bill	8%	(91)	9%	(152)	80%	(158)
1965 D.C. Crime bill, recommit	3%	(86)	19%	(124)	77%	(198)
1965 D.C. Crime bill, passage	3%	(85)	12%	(123)	64%	(194)
Senate						
1958 Mallory bill, "reasonable" amendment	16%	(19)	45%	(42)	88%	(25)
1958 Mallory bill, Ervin amendment	20%	(20)	83%	(42)	100%	(26)
1958 Mallory bill, Morse amendment	7%	(16)	10%	(39)	36%	(22)
1958 Mallory bill, passage	0%	(16)	12%	(41)	36%	(22)
1962 abolition of capital punishment in D.C.	0%	(20)	17%	(29)	43%	(35)
1965 D.C. crime bill, delete Mallory modification	0%	(18)	10%	(31)	52%	(44)
1967 D.C. crime bill, delete Mallory modification	0%	(15)	17%	(24)	41%	(39)

[a]South is defined here as the eleven states that comprised the Confederacy.
[b]In this and other tables the N's are in parentheses.

Table 2. *Party Comparisons in the Senate by Selected State Characteristics*[a] *(proportion voting libertarian)*

	urban[b]		rural		0-2.9% non-white		3% and above non-white	
1958 Mallory bill, "reasonable" amendment								
Democrats	100%	(12)	77%	(13)	89%	(9)	87%	(16)
Republicans	47%	(19)	43%	(23)	35%	(17)	52%	(25)
1958 Mallory bill, Ervin amendment								
Democrats	100%	(12)	100%	(14)	100%	(8)	100%	(18)
Republicans	90%	(20)	82%	(22)	93%	(16)	81%	(26)
1958 Mallory bill, Morse amendment								
Democrats	40%	(10)	33%	(12)	63%	(8)	21%	(14)
Republicans	6%	(18)	14%	(21)	7%	(15)	13%	(24)
1958 Mallory bill, passage								
Democrats	30%	(10)	42%	(12)	50%	(8)	29%	(14)
Republicans	16%	(19)	9%	(22)	7%	(16)	16%	(25)
1962 abolition of capital punishment in D.C.								
Democrats	37%	(16)	47%	(19)	58%	(12)	35%	(23)
Republicans	9%	(11)	18%	(17)	23%	(13)	13%	(15)
1965 D.C. Crime bill, delete Mallory modification								
Democrats	64%	(22)	41%	(22)	75%	(12)	44%	(32)
Republicans	14%	(14)	7%	(15)	0%	(13)	19%	(16)
1967 D.C. Crime bill, delete Mallory modification								
Democrats	41%	(17)	41%	(22)	42%	(12)	41%	(27)
Republicans	27%	(11)	8%	(12)	18%	(11)	17%	(12)

[a]Southern Republicans as well as Southern Democrats have been excluded from all computations here and below.
[b]In this and all other Senate tabulations, an urban state is one in which more than half the population is contained in urbanized areas as defined by the Census Bureau—that is, in central cities of 50,000 or more and the surrounding urban fringes. A rural state is one in which more than half the population lives outside urbanized areas.

Table 3. *Party Comparisons in the House of Representatives by Selected District Characteristics (proportion voting libertarian)*

| | 0-2.9% non-white | | intermediate percentage non-white[a] | |
	urban[b]	rural	urban	rural
1958 Mallory bill				
Democrats	59% (17)	46% (24)	78% (41)	33% (18)
Republicans	4% (23)	3% (68)	6% (54)	0% (26)
1959 Mallory bill, recommit				
Democrats	75% (24)	70% (43)	81% (52)	43% (28)
Republicans	18% (17)	10% (51)	19% (46)	0% (22)
1959 Mallory bill, passage				
Democrats	71% (24)	69% (42)	81% (52)	46% (28)
Republicans	17% (18)	10% (51)	18% (45)	0% (22)
1961 Mallory bill				
Democrats	74% (23)	63% (27)	88% (52)	41% (27)
Republicans	16% (19)	7% (67)	10% (40)	4% (26)
1962 D.C. Juvenile Court bill				
Democrats	100% (21)	88% (25)	98% (46)	86% (21)
Republicans	61% (18)	43% (65)	63% (40)	48% (23)
1963 D.C. Crime bill				
Democrats	85% (20)	75% (24)	91% (56)	44% (27)
Republicans	13% (23)	5% (61)	15% (34)	8% (24)
1965 D.C. Crime bill, recommit				
Democrats	83% (24)	67% (40)	90% (70)	41% (32)
Republicans	28% (21)	15% (41)	26% (27)	20% (20)
1965 D.C. Crime bill, passage				
Democrats	75% (24)	58% (38)	69% (68)	31% (32)
Republicans	24% (21)	5% (41)	19% (26)	15% (20)

[a]An intermediate percentage non-white is 3 per cent or more but less than 20 per cent for Democrats. No top limit was set for Republicans, but their districts very rarely contained a percentage higher than the teens and never higher than the twenties.

[b]An urban district is one in which more than half the population is contained in an urbanized area.

Table 4. *Sectional Cleavage Outside the South (proportion voting libertarian)*

	Border[a] and Rocky Mountain[b] Democrats		other Democrats		Northeast[c] and Border Republicans		other Republicans	
House of Representatives								
1958 Mallory bill	26%	(31)	77%	(95)	7%	(70)	1%	(101)
1959 Mallory bill, recommit	34%	(41)	84%	(136)	27%	(55)	2%	(81)
1959 Mallory bill, passage	37%	(41)	82%	(135)	28%	(54)	1%	(82)
1961 Mallory bill	41%	(41)	85%	(119)	13%	(56)	6%	(96)
1962 D.C. Juvenile Court bill	83%	(35)	99%	(106)	72%	(58)	37%	(88)
1963 D.C. Crime bill	50%	(38)	90%	(120)	17%	(48)	6%	(94)
1965 D.C. Crime bill, recommit	47%	(40)	85%	(158)	41%	(41)	9%	(69)
1965 D.C. Crime bill, passage	33%	(40)	72%	(154)	32%	(41)	3%	(68)
Senate								
1958 Mallory bill, "reasonable" amendment	83%	(12)	92%	(13)	67%	(18)	29%	(24)
1958 Mallory bill, Ervin amendment	100%	(14)	100%	(12)	94%	(17)	80%	(25)
1958 Mallory bill, Morse amendment	0%	(10)	67%	(12)	20%	(15)	4%	(24)
1958 Mallory bill, passage	0%	(10)	67%	(12)	24%	(17)	4%	(24)
1962 abolition of capital punishment in D.C.	14%	(14)	62%	(21)	36%	(14)	0%	(14)
1965 D.C. Crime bill, delete Mallory modification	31%	(16)	64%	(28)	25%	(12)	0%	(17)
1967 D.C. Crime bill, delete Mallory modification	17%	(18)	62%	(21)	50%	(6)	6%	(17)

[a]Border states are Delaware, Maryland, West Virginia, Kentucky, Missouri, and Oklahoma.

[b]Rocky Mountain states are Montana, Idaho, Nevada, Utah, Wyoming, Colorado, Arizona, and New Mexico.

[c]Northeastern states are the six New England states plus New York, New Jersey, and Pennsylvania.

Table 5. *Regional Comparisons Among Republicans in the House of Representatives by Selected District Characteristics (proportion voting libertarian)*

	1962 D.C. Juvenile Court bill	Mallory and D.C Crime bill composite[a]
Urban, 0-2.9% non-white		
Border and Northeast	80% (10)	29% (17)
Other Republicans	37% (8)	7% (15)
Urban, 3% and above non-white		
Border and Northeast	94% (17)	28% (43)
Other Republicans	39% (23)	11% (37)
Rural, 0-2.9% non-white		
Border and Northeast	50% (24)	15% (40)
Other Republicans	39% (41)	7% (81)
Rural, 3% and above non-white		
Border and Northeast	86% (7)	18% (11)
Other Republicans	31% (16)	3% (33)

[a]The composite is based upon the four Mallory bill votes and three D.C. Crime bill votes. The libertarian proportion includes congressmen voting libertarian on any one of the seven roll calls even if their records include some non-libertarian votes.

Table 6. *Regional Comparisons Among Democrats in the House of Representatives by Selected District Characteristics (proportion voting libertarian)*

	1958 Mallory bill	1965 D.C. Crime bill, passage
Urban, 3-19.9% non-white[a]		
Border and Rocky Mountain	20% (5)	60% (10)
Other Democrats	86% (36)	71% (58)
Urban, 20% and above non-white		
Border and Rocky Mountain	60% (5)	25% (4)
Other Democrats	90% (21)	96% (25)
Rural, 0-2.9% non-white		
Border and Rocky Mountain	37% (8)	57% (7)
Other Democrats	50% (16)	58% (31)
Rural, 3-19.9% non-white		
Border and Rocky Mountain	8% (12)	6% (17)
Other Democrats	83% (6)	60% (15)

[a]Rural districts with a 20 per cent or more non-white population and urban districts with 0-2.9 per cent non-white population are not entered because N's of 0, 1, or 2 make comparisons impossible or not meaningful.

Table 7. *Selected District Characteristic Comparisons among Southern Democrats on the D.C. Juvenile Court Bill (proportion voting libertarian)*

urban, 0–19.9% non–white	urban, 20% and above non–white	rural, 0–19.9% non–white	rural, 20% and above non–white
67% (9)	42% (12)	22% (27)	8% (63)

Table 8. *Selected District Characteristic Comparisons Among Democrats in the House of Representatives by Sectional Grouping (proportion voting libertarian)*

	Border and Rocky Mountain Democrats		other Democrats	
	urban	rural	urban	rural
1958 Mallory bill				
0–2.9% non–white	—[a]	37% (8)	63% (16)	50% (16)
3–19.9% non–white	20% (5)	8% (12)	86% (36)	83% (6)
20% and above non–white	60% (5)	—	90% (21)	—
1959 Mallory bill, recommit				
0–2.9% non–white	—	67% (9)	82% (22)	71% (34)
3–19.9% non–white	25% (8)	14% (16)	91% (44)	83% (12)
20% and above non–white	80% (5)	—	96% (23)	—
1959 Mallory bill, passage				
0–2.9% non–white	—	67% (9)	77% (22)	70% (33)
3–19.9% non–white	25% (8)	23% (16)	91% (44)	83% (12)
20% and above non–white	80% (5)	—	91% (23)	—
1961 Mallory bill				
0–2.9% non–white	—	60% (10)	81% (21)	65% (17)
3–19.9% non–white	63% (8)	19% (16)	93% (44)	73% (11)
20% and above non–white	75% (4)	—	92% (25)	—
1962 D.C. Juvenile Court bill				
0–2.9% non–white	—	75% (8)	100% (19)	94% (17)
3–19.9% non–white	87% (8)	75% (12)	100% (38)	100% (9)
20% and above non–white	100% (4)	—	100% (22)	—
1963 D.C. Crime bill				
0–2.9% non–white	—	57% (7)	85% (20)	82% (17)
3–19.9% non–white	89% (9)	24% (17)	91% (47)	80% (10)
20% and above non–white	50% (4)	—	100% (25)	—
1965 D.C. Crime bill, recommit				
0–2.9% non–white	—	71% (7)	87% (23)	67% (33)
3–19.9% non–white	70% (10)	18% (17)	93% (60)	67% (15)
20% and above non–white	75% (4)	—	100% (25)	—
1965 D.C. Crime bill, passage				
0–2.9% non–white	—	57% (7)	78% (23)	58% (31)
3–19.9% non–white	60% (10)	6% (17)	71% (58)	60% (15)
20% and above non–white	25% (4)	—	96% (25)	—

[a]Not included when *N*'s are 0, 1, or 2.

Spencer R. Gervin / . . . And Kids Have Rights Too

I

Extra-constitutional procedures for a juvenile offender are "for the salvation of such a child," averred the Pennsylvania Supreme Court in 1905, upholding the commitment of a fourteen-year-old boy to the House of Corrections for larceny. In vain did defense counsel remonstrate that the boy had been taken into custody by procedures flouting established process for arrest and that the boy's immurement had been effected without jury trial.[1]

Substance of the court's opinion was that, concerning children, the state is an alternate parent, charged with the discipline of the child whenever the natural parent is unable or unwilling to perform this function. Such natural parent

needs no process to temporarily deprive his child of its liberty by confining it in his own home, to save it and to shield it from the consequences of persistence in a career of waywardness, nor is the state, when compelled, as parens patriae, to take the place of the father for the same purpose, required to adopt any process as a means of placing its hands upon the child to lead it into one of its courts.

As precedent for the power of the state to ignore due process in juvenile cases, the Pennsylvania court cited an eighteenth-century English case.[2] Therein, noted the court, the rule was laid down "that the court are to judge upon the circumstances of the particular case, and to give their directions accordingly." That case concerned, however, a father seeking to recover custody of his daughter who had by agreement exchanged her apprenticeship for a more personal relationship with another. Refusing the paternal petition, the English court upon noting that the girl had received ill usage from her father refused to restore her to her father's authority.

1. *Commonwealth* v. *Fisher*, 213 Pa. St. 48 (1905), affirming 27 Pa. Super. Ct. 175 (1905).
2. *Rex* v. *Sir Francis-Blake Delaval, William Bates, and John Fraine*, 97 *English Reports—Full Reprint* (3 Burrow) 913 (1763).

Thus by a curious mixture of the inapplicable *parens patriae* concept and the inherent power of the state to protect minors from abuse and mistreatment by their natural parents, the Pennsylvania court wrought a new doctrine. Under this new doctrine, as *parens patriae* the state could deprive any minor of his liberty without the due process of law appropriate for adults.

It was this deprivation that the U.S. Supreme Court called in question in the 1967 *Gault* case.[3] While the Court's opinion therein does not purport to grant to juveniles the full range of due process available to adults, a beginning was made toward modification of juvenile court procedures—procedures which have substituted extra-constitutional proceedings for that increasingly immaculate due process which the Court has been of late imposing upon state criminal procedure.

Most significantly, the Court in the *Gault* opinion put an end to the *parens patriae* buncombe and redirected juvenile court procedure toward the more venerable *doli capax* concept in dealing with the young who are accused of violation of law.[4]

II

The common law avoided the problem of special handling of semi-adult offenders. Either a defendant was adult or he was not. If not, there could be no guilt on his part. If so, he was treated in court procedure as an adult and was punished as such. The distinction between adulthood and childhood swivelled around the Latin *dolus*, which may be translated craft or trickery or malice. One not capable of malice, that is *doli incapax*, was not amenable to criminal prosecution.

In effectuating this distinction the common law[5] resorted to presumptions. The first was that a child who had not yet reached his seventh year was incapable of harboring the criminal intent necessary for commission of crime, whether the offense was one at common law

3. *In re Gault et al.*, 387 U.S. 1 (1967).
4. Though commonly translated "malice," the Latin *dolus* tends to connote deliberate deceit and dissimulation. See, for example, Vergil's reference (*Aeneid*, II, l.252) to the "Myrmidonumque dolos" and Caesar's refusal (*De Bello Gallico*, IV, 13, l.3) to negotiate with a tribe that had sought peace "per dolum atque insidias."
5. See, for example, A.W.G. Kean, "The History of the Criminal Liability of Children," *Law Quarterly Review*, LIII (1937), 364, and Fredrick Woodbridge, "Physical and Mental Infancy in the Criminal Law," *University of Pennsylvania Law Review*, LXXXVII (1939), 426.

or one created by statute. No evidence might be adduced to show that such a child through precocity was in fact *doli capax*.

Second, between his seventh birthday and his fourteenth, the child was presumed at common law not yet to be capable of committing a crime. But this presumption, in contrast to the rule prevailing for those under seven, might be rebutted. The burden of rebuttal was on the state.

In an illustrative case, the Supreme Court of Illinois[6] reviewed the manslaughter conviction of an eleven-year-old boy. Citing the ancient rule that one under fourteen was presumed incapable of criminal deed, the court reversed the conviction with the finding that

the rule required evidence strong and clear beyond all doubt and contradiction, that he was capable of discerning between good and evil; and the legal presumption being that he was incapable of committing the crime, for want of such knowledge, it devolved on the People to make the strong and clear proof of capacity, before they could be entitled to a conviction. The record may be searched in vain to find any such proof. There was no witness examined on that question, nor did any one refer to it. There is simply evidence as to his age. For aught that appears, he may have been dull, weak, and wholly incapable of knowing good from evil. . . .

Godfrey (a slave) v. *The State*,[7] as a further illustration, involved an eleven-year old boy who had been found guilty of killing a four-year-old child. Correctness of the bench's charge to the trial jury respecting the boy's legal capability was the issue before the appeal court. The charge was the

defendant, being between seven and fourteen years of age, was prima facie incapable of committing crime; that to overturn the intendment in favor of his incapacity to commit crime, the jury must be convinced, from the evidence, beyond a reasonable doubt, . . . that he knew fully the nature of the act done, and its consequences; and that he showed plainly intelligent design and malice in the execution of the act.

Upholding this charge and the jury's finding of capacity, resulting in conviction and execution, the Supreme Court of Alabama explained:

An infant, above seven, but under fourteen years of age, is presumed not to have such knowledge and discretion, as would make him accountable for a felony committed during that period. But if that presumption is met by evidence clearly proving the existence of that knowledge and

6. *Angelo* v. *The People of the State of Illinois*, 96 Ill. 209 (1880).
7. 31 Ala. 323 (1858).

discretion deemed requisite to a legal accountability, the reason for allowing an immunity from punishment ceases. . . . There are many cases where children between those ages, being shown to have been cognizant of the criminal nature of the act done, have been punished under the criminal law. A girl, thirteen years of age, was executed for killing her mistress. Two boys, one nine, and the other ten years of age, were convicted of murder, because one of them hid himself, and another hid the dead body: thus manifesting, as was supposed, a consciousness of guilt, and a discretion to discern between good and evil. A boy of eight years of age, who had malice, revenge, and cunning, was hanged for firing two barns. A boy ten years old, who showed a mischevious discretion, was convicted of murdering his bed-fellow (4 Bla. Com. 23-24).

Finally, once the child had reached his fourteenth birthday, the common law treated him as an adult. At that moment he was presumed to be fully responsible for his crimes and completely capable of committing them, just as any other adult. The presumption of *dolus* was rebuttable of course, as with any other person, but only by strong and clear evidence.

III

It was not objection to these rules of common law which principally orbited the movement for juvenile courts and a special, extra-constitutional process for the recipient juvenile. Rather the juvenile court movement followed almost absent-mindedly in the wake of efforts to protect the juvenile from imprisonment with adult confinees.

Among the literature criticizing the common confinement of juveniles and adults, none more clearly expresses distaste for such admixture and at the same time jumps to the assumption that a special court for juveniles is required to prevent this objectionable practice than a 1910 work by the President of the Prison Association of New York.[8] The author states:

The Common Law methods of dealing with delinquent children as if they were adults are extremely harmful; in the case of adults those methods are execrable, but when applied to children they are infinitely worse.

8. Smith, "Criminal Law in the United States," I, 77-78, of Henderson, ed., *Correction and Prevention* (4 vols.; New York, 1910). See also Almy, "Juvenile Courts in Buffalo," *Annals of the American Academy*, XX (1902) 279; Beitler, "The Juvenile Court in Philadelphia," *ibid.*, p. 271; Kelsey, "The Juvenile Court of Chicago and Its Work," *ibid.*, XVII (1901), 298; and Williamson, "Probation and Juvenile Court," *ibid.*, XX (1902), 259.

Especially, the system of confining the children in the common jail while awaiting trial and, after conviction, of herding them with old and confirmed criminals in a punitive prison, is inevitably one of education in vice and crime. The vile infection of the place acts upon the receptive mind of the child with poisonous effect; he comes out of the prison branded with the name of criminal and yet made proud of the name. It is only in exceptional cases that such an experience fails to corrupt and pervert the child's aspirations and ideals; his whole moral nature has been deformed.

Then the writer points out that the "first radically effective measure" for correction of "such evils" was an 1899 act of the Illinois legislature creating a juvenile court.

Actually the thrust of the Illinois statute of 1899[9] was to establish special arrangements for punishment of the juvenile upon conviction. The already established circuit and county courts of the state were given jurisdiction of juvenile delinquencies. Delinquency was defined *inter alia* as violation by "one under the age of sixteen (16) years" of "any law of this State or any city or village ordinance. . . ." Upon being found delinquent the child might be sentenced to a state reformatory. If sentenced to an institution in which adult convicts were confined, the child was to be completely sequestered from such adult offenders.

Following the Illinois act of 1899, the movement for special handling of juvenile offenders was rapidly reflected in statutory enactments of other states. Despite differences in detail among the states, early laws were generally similar in their definition of "delinquency" as "an infraction of law." The procedural safeguards accorded adults accused of crime were not, however, expressly abrogated. This development was accomplished by court practice.

The subtle shift from special procedures for juvenile confinement to special extra-constitutional trial procedures arose out of this definition of "delinquency." A juvenile who had committed a crime was not prosecuted for the crime. Instead he was brought before the "court" for delinquency, defined as commission of a crime by a juvenile. Once this substitution of terms had been accomplished, the dilution of procedural due process was facilitated. The 1905 Pennsylvania case, cited

9. Hurd, *Revised Statutes of Illinois 1901*, chap. 23, ss. 169-189. This act was followed with one establishing a home for delinquent boys and another establishing a home for juvenile female offenders (Hurd, *Revised Statutes 1903*, chap. 23, ss. 191-244).

above,[10] is illustrative. One contention of defense in the case was that the Pennsylvania act of April 13, 1903, was unconstitutional, because of the absence of trial by jury for the accused juvenile. The constitutional guarantee that "the right of trial by jury shall remain inviolate" was found by the Pennsylvania Supreme Court to be inapplicable in this case. There was no criminal trial here; in fact, the purpose of the law was "to prevent a trial." The statute indeed was intended mercifully to spare the child the ordeal of a trial "if the child's own good and the best interests of the state justify such salvation." How could the child be denied the right of trial by jury when in fact the child was not being tried for anything?

The statute, further argued the court, set up a purely statutory proceeding and not one in accordance with the common law. "Every statute which is designed to give protection, care and training to children as a needed substitute for parental authority and performance of parental duty, is but a recognition of the duty of the state, as the legitimate guardian and protector of children where other guardianship fails." As for the possibility that, without the protection of due process, the child might be improperly put away, the court assured that "there is no probability, in the proper administration of the law, of the child's liberty being unduly invaded."

IV

Hence the concept has been established that a juvenile committing an offense, which if done by an adult would be a crime, has not perpetrated a crime at all but is a delinquent. Statutes classifying juveniles as such for this purpose are not criminal or penal at all; they are "progressive" and "humanitarian," "benevolent," "paternal," and "for reformation."[11]

As such "salvation" procedure took form with respect to juveniles, despite some variations the process followed much this form: (1) The juvenile was apprehended without necessity of warrant or other sworn complaint or of personal knowledge of the arresting official. (2) The

10. See n.1. This case has been cited more frequently than any other in challenges to the constitutional sufficiency of extra-constitutional juvenile court procedure.

11. As authority for the proposition that juvenile court proceedings are not criminal in nature, see *In the Matter of Hazel Sharp*, 15 Ida. 120 (1908); *The State* v. *Tincher*, 258 Mo. 1 (1914); *State* v. *Eisen*, 53 Ore. 297 (1909); and the cases listed in Appendix A to *Pee* v. *United States*, 274 F. 2d 556 (1959), at 561-562.

juvenile was not brought before a committing magistrate who should decide existence of reasonable cause to hold the juvenile and if so to set and receive a bail bond; instead, in the discretion of the juvenile "judge," the child was held in some public institution or released in someone's custody. (3) Indictment by grand jury, with its purpose of determining reasonable cause for bringing the juvenile to trial, was omitted. (4) Trial by petit jury was denied to the juvenile. (5) An attorney at the hearing was sometimes permitted, sometimes not; but cross-examination and rules of evidence were disregarded. (6) The privilege of self-incrimination was not observed. (7) Though appeals were permitted by statute in certain instances, no right of appeal was permitted unless specifically authorized by statute.

V

Such was the status of juvenile court procedure when the Supreme Court decided the *Gault* case in 1967.[12] The legal profession was, however, not unaware that under the guise of juvenile salvation an extra-constitutional system had evolved, a system which could not be reconciled with constitutional provisions and which was yielding some undesirable results.[13] The Supreme Court itself in the *Haley*[14] case had overturned a juvenile conviction based upon an involuntary confession, with the pronouncement that "[n]either man nor child can be allowed to stand condemned by methods which flout constitutional requirements of due process of law."

Reviewing in the *Gault* case the history of juvenile court process, the Court observed that the objective thereof was that "[t]he child was to be 'treated' and 'rehabilitated' and the procedures, from apprehension through institutionalization, were to be 'clinical' rather than punitive."

Questions of constitutional due process, as interference with this approach, were evaded by insisting that the "State was proceeding as *parens patriae*." Continued the Court:

12. See n. 3.
13. See, for example, Dvorak and Dvorak, "Commitment as Delinquent," *Journal of Criminal Law*, XIII (1922), 258; Wekstein, "Denial of Constitutional Safeguards to Juvenile Delinquents," *Cornell Law Quarterly*, XVIII (1933), 442; and the materials cited in n. 23 of the *Gault* opinion. Note also the revision of New York's juvenile procedure in 1962 to incorporate more due process: "Family Court Act of 1962," *Laws of New York*, 185th Sess., 1962, III, Chap. 686.
14. *Haley* v. *Ohio*, 332 U.S. 596 (1948).

The Latin phrase proved to be a great help to those who sought to rationalize the exclusion of juveniles from the constitutional scheme; but its meaning is murky and its historic credentials are of dubious relevance. The phrase was taken from chancery practice, where, however, it was used to describe the power of the State to act *in loco parentis* for the purpose of protecting the property interests and the person of the child. But there is no trace of the doctrine in the history of criminal jurisprudence.

The *Gault* case involved a fifteen-year-old boy, whose fault was that, based upon the oral complaint of a neighbor, he had allegedly made an obscene telephone call to her. The boy was apprehended by Gila County, Arizona, sheriff, confined for a while, released, then summoned to juvenile court. The apprehension was made without warrant or without personal knowledge of the offense by the arresting officer. No written specification of the charges against the boy was made, such as would have been necessary for arraignment or indictment. When time for hearing arrived, the parents were notified to bring the boy thereto by means of an informal note sent them by a probation officer. At the hearing the child was not represented by counsel. The complaining neighbor did not appear and testify in the presence of the accused juvenile. No transcript or summary notes of the proceedings were kept. The boy was not advised of his right not to testify against himself. In this connection, it is worth noting that, in the absence of testimony of the complaining neighbor, the only evidence against the boy was that which he gave himself in response to the judge's questioning. Had the boy been allowed to claim the privilege against self-incrimination, there would have been no evidence whatsoever against him.

The judge, in deciding what disposition to make of the boy, admittedly took into consideration that fact that the boy was already on probation for being in the presence of another boy who had stolen a wallet from a lady's purse. He also admitted that in his mind was a "referral" in which the boy was supposed to have stolen a baseball glove from another boy and lied to the police department about it. Although there was no accusation and no hearing on this latter offense, "because of lack of material foundation," the judge cited this incident in partial support of his conclusion that the boy was "habitually involved in immoral matters."

The boy was adjudged delinquent under Arizona law providing

that one under eighteen "who has violated a law of the state or an ordinance or regulation of a political subdivision thereof" is a juvenile delinquent. The boy was committed to the State Industrial School until he should reach his majority. As the Supreme Court noted, for the actual criminal offense an adult could upon conviction receive a fine of $5 to $50 and/or be imprisoned for not more than two months. In this case the juvenile received imprisonment for six years.

Turning then to the specific respects in which the *Gault* "trial" violated due process, the Court considered first the adequacy of the notice of charges. "Notice, to comply with due process requirements, must be given sufficiently in advance of scheduled court proceedings so that reasonable opportunity to prepare will be afforded, and it must 'set forth the alleged misconduct with particularity.' " In the context of juvenile procedure, the Court fell short of insisting upon arraignment and indictment but did specify that substantively "due process of law requires . . . notice which would be deemed constitutionally adequate in civil or criminal proceedings."

With respect to right of counsel, the Court found the proceedings against *Gault* invalid "because the court did not advise Gerald or his parents of their right to counsel, and proceeded with the hearing, the adjudication of delinquency and the order of commitment in the absence of counsel for the child and his parents or an express waiver of the right thereto." A proceeding where the child may be found a delinquent and confined for a number of years is "comparable in seriousness to a felony prosecution." The Court indicated it would permit no difference between adult and juvenile proceedings in this regard. In adult proceedings, the Court reminded that acceptance of any contention permitting absence of counsel had "been foreclosed by decisions of this Court.

With regard to confrontation by adverse witnesses, and opportunity to cross-examine them, the Court held the same standards had to be applied in juvenile proceedings as are applicable for adults. "It would be entirely unrealistic to carve out of the Fifth Amendment all statements by juveniles on the ground that these cannot lead to 'criminal' involvement," for evidently such incriminatory statements could lead to loss of liberty by the juvenile. In over half the states, noted the Court, the juvenile is not even assured of such confinement away from adults. Whatever deceptive label might be placed upon such confinement regarding a juvenile, "[i]t is incarceration against one's will, whether it is called 'criminal' or 'civil.'" That no person shall be compelled to be a witness against himself when his continued liberty is at stake, "our Constitution guarantees."

With regard to the issue of provision for appellate review of a juvenile court conviction and for creation of a record on which such review might be made, the Court found it unnecessary to reach this question in view of the manifest defects already noted. The Court, however, did note that absence of a record greatly complicates habeas corpus hearings, for without a record it is necessary to reconstruct trial court proceedings. As an indirect significance of this observation, the Court has clearly given precedent that habeas corpus may issue from federal courts when non-frivolous allegations are made that juvenile court procedure has transgressed constitutional restraints of due process.

VI

What then is the Court seeking to communicate in the *Gault* opinion? Certainly the Court is not hinting that special judicial procedures for juveniles must be discarded *in toto*. It would appear the Court is specifically approving such special procedures when these are of advantage to the juvenile and when the juvenile thereby receives greater consideration than ordinary due process affords. For example, observing the high rate of recidivism among juveniles, the Court assured it did "not mean by this [observation] to denigrate the juvenile court process or to suggest that there are not aspects of the juvenile system relating to offenders which are valuable." Again, referring to the "fatherly" proceedings in the informal juvenile court atmosphere, in which the judge touches the heart and conscience of the erring youth, the Court agreed that the "goodwill and compassion" are admirable.

When this informality, however, runs counter to prescriptions of due process, as with respect to self-incrimination, the Court would only grudge its appreciation "that special problems may arise with respect to waiver of the privilege by or on behalf of children." While differences in "techniques" may occur in juvenile procedure, the Court took care to admonish that these differences must be "not in principle."

Of pivotal importance in the *Gault* opinion is the Court's firm discarding of the *parens patriae* doctrine with respect to juvenile criminal procedure. It is possible that the Court is hereby moving in the direction of a return to the common law *dolus* doctrine. As this latter concept relates to juvenile procedure, it might permit informal hearings at which the judge privately determines the extent of the malice harbored by the juvenile miscreant. If his finding is that malice is not present or that the child's immaturity renders the malice less than a degree justifying criminal prosecution, juvenile procedures can then be used to reprove and chide the juvenile. The juvenile may even be restricted as to movement as in the case of a curfew from nocturnal activities. This approach appears substantively very close to the presumption that for the post-infant, pre-adult individual *doli incapax* is presumed and that before punishment in a criminal sense may be inflicted this presumption must be overcome.[15]

Once, however, as a result of these private, informal juvenile procedures, it is established that "malice makes up for lack of age," so that criminal sanctions like confinement may be imposed, due process in its most protective sense must be assured the accused.

The failure of the Court in Gault's case to take up the question of the defective arrest, the Court's reluctance while specifying adequate notice of charges to require formal indictment or similar procedure, the absence of mention of trial by jury, the non-specification of the necessity for a record—these indicate the Court is reorienting juvenile court process toward more venerable concepts without requiring that the question of *doli capax* be determined in the formalized courtroom by a jury. "The problem is to ascertain the precise impact of the due process requirement upon such proceedings."

Hence *Gault* is not the final case but is rather the first of a series of cases in which the Court must make more precise what due process requires when juvenile procedures have determined, in preliminary form at least, that the juvenile is *doli capax*. In such future cases such questions as indictment, trial by jury, public trial, maintenance of a record, and appellate review must be determined. Gault's case would hence appear to be an invitation for future trial and error by the states, under the Court's surveillance.

15. That the determination of maturity is itself a matter for which some due process is required, the Court suggested in *Kent* v. *United States*, 382 U.S. 541 (1966), although this case turned essentially upon construction of a statute.

Joseph L. Bernd / Equal Protection of Voting Rights: The Logic of "One Person, One Vote"[1]

"One person, One vote"

Gray v. Sanders, 372 U.S. 368, 381 (1963)

The burden of this article is that a logical application of the "equal protection" clause of the Fourteenth Amendment requires reform of the winner-take-all election model used in this country.

I. Experience Versus Logic

Preliminary to the application of logic to the "equal protection" provision, it is helpful to suggest that Mr. Justice Holmes uttered only a half-truth when he said: "Experience and not logic is the life of the law." It would be surprising indeed if either logic or experience in the pure form were to be found in judicial literature, in political theory, or for that matter in any other field of non-formal serious intellectual activity. Mathematics is uniquely the one wholly abstract realm in which experience is excluded in the formal sense. Yet even in mathematics it is hardly likely that the mathematician, either in learning extant math, or in creating (or demonstrating) new ideas, is free of the fruits of experience.

On the other hand, experience, even of a very simple sort, is ordinarily understood and explained in terms which relate disparate parts in ways not found in mundane experience. And the evidence of such worldly experience is never sufficient to account for relationships without the aid of inference.

The advantages of experience, in law and elsewhere, are the advantages of the factual as distinguished from the hypothetical, the potential, or the formal. The use of experience in problem-solving implies empirical verification. But to proceed with verification, infer-

1. Michael A. Weinstein, my colleague at Virginia Tech, read an early draft of the paper and offered valuable critical commentary.

ence is required. The temporal span of experience (in recorded history) unduly limits variability. In the words of the authors of *The American Voter*:

> But the inadequacy of "natural" data has to do also with what might be called the problem of limited variation. We return to the idea that theory consists of statements of the interrelationships of variables. It is evident variables of great importance in human affairs may exhibit little or no change in a given historical period. As a result, the investigator whose work falls in this period may not see the significance of these variables and may fail to incorporate them in his theoretical statements. And, even if he does perceive their importance, the absence of variation will prevent a proper test of hypotheses that state the relation of these factors to other variables of his theory.[2]

A logical deductive model is not limited to "natural" historical data. At least in the speculative sense, it can include any variable of any dimension. This is the unanswerable advantage of a logical deductive model over a model based on experience, although empirical testing is, in principle, eventually required. Whether this advantage, relevant to the scientific endeavor, is appropriate to the policy-oriented functions of courts of law is itself a policy question of some importance.

An examination of the arguments used regarding desegregation and reapportionment in "equal protection" cases reveals that experience and logic, respectively, are conspicuously evident. In the desegregation cases the use of experience takes the usual forms: (1) debate over the intent of the framers and ratifiers, (2) citations of precedents, and (3) social science evidence, itself a form of interpreted experience, some of it experimental. But the conclusions that under certain conditions of graduate education—racial separation is incompatible with "equal protection"—*Missouri ex rel Gaines* v. *Canada, Sweatt* v. *Painter, McLaurin* v. *Oklahoma State Regents*, or that in public education racial segregation is inevitably unequal, *Brown* v. *Board of Education of Topeka*—cannot be supported by experience alone. If we define experience "as perceptions of facts and values which have been encountered in isolation or in patterns," our difficulty is evident. Perceptions are subjective. Patterns where they are the results of subjective perceptions are clearly subjective also and are relative to the individual

2. Angus Campbell, Phillip Converse, Warren Miller, and Donald Stokes, *The American Voter* (New York, 1960), pp. 9-10.

perceiver. Facts may be unambivalent in an existential sense but they are related to values in the eye of individuals who perceive them. The ordering of values is thoroughly subjective and depends on the value judgments of the one who does the ordering. Facts, values, and patterns do not tell their own story or form unambiguous relationships. On the other hand, the opinions which are evident in the graduate school cases and the *Brown* case take what appear to be a logical form. This can be readily demonstrated in the following syllogisms:

1. Graduate School Cases (*Sweatt* v. *Painter, McLaurin* v. *Oklahoma*)

> *Major Premise*: A deepened understanding of constitutional equal protection requires that there be equality both of tangible and of intangible factors in education, as between persons of different races.
>
> *Minor Premise*: In Oklahoma and Texas the intangible factors of education were not equal.
>
> *Conclusion*: A denial of equal protection.

2. Public School Cases (*Brown* v. *Board of Education of Topeka*)

> *Major Premise*: Constitutional equal protection in education requires equality both in tangible and intangible factors (including factors of mental health and ability to learn).
>
> *Minor Premise*: Racial segregation by its very nature adversely affects the mental health and opportunity to learn of students.
>
> *Conclusion*: Racial segregation by its very nature is a denial of equal protection.

Obviously facts and experience in a very narrow sense played a part in these cases. Whether the cases were decided rightly and whether the facts were right or rightly interpreted is not at issue here. The point is merely that the circumstances of the desegregation cases are consistent with an explanation which includes the use of logic. Cases 1 and 2 above are simple syllogisms which are consistent with a gross consideration of the court opinions in these cases. It is evident that Holmes's remark does not accurately characterize these cases.

Of course the Holmesian comment is quite correct if viewed as a description of the evolution of experience, rather than as a statement concerning the methods, techniques, and tools of courts. For instance, as an example of the former explanation consider the electoral college. If its "logic" is equated with its formal provisions as controlling the choice of a president, then clearly it is an example that experience is the life of the law and not "logic." Consider also the Volstead act or other inoperative rules.

When we turn to consider the tools used by the Court in the reapportionment cases, the importance of logic is overwhelmingly evident. Entering what Mr. Justice Frankfurter had called the "political thicket," the Court began to frame new policy variables of judicially required reapportionment. In *Reynolds* v. *Sims*, Chief Justice Warren successfully used logic where it ran directly contrary to experience in many states: "Legislators represent people not trees or acres. Legislators are elected by votes, not farms or cities or economic interests."[3] Mr. Justice Harlan, dissenting in these cases—*Baker* v. *Carr, Gray* v. *Sanders, Wesberry* v. *Sanders*, as well as in *Reynolds*—cites the arguments from experience: intent of framers, precedents against entering the thicket, institutional evidence of the so-called "rational" concept of representation whereby considerations other than strictly statistical equality were permitted to influence apportionment."

It is true that in the *Wesberry* case, Mr. Justice Black for the majority narrated a history lesson concerning the framers of the Constitution at the Philadelphia Convention, but Mr. Justice Harlan's historical evidence on the other side, regarding Article I, Sec. 2, may be as good as that of Black.

The syllogism for the reapportionment decisions might look like this:

> *Major Premise*: A deepening understanding of equal protection (or one person, one vote) means equality in the ratio of constituency (or district) populations and representations. (For instance, if the average congressional district has a population of 460,000, one person has a representation weight of 1/460,000.) Every person should have the same representation weight.

---

3. *Reynolds* v. *Sims*, 377 U.S. 533, 562 (1964). The Chief Justice's statement was aimed at the Alabama apportionment system (see pp. 537-554 of the opinion) which clearly gave weight to slices of real estate and other considerations as distinguished from the mere number of voters in any given district. By contrast, see the opinion of Justice Frankfurter in *Baker* v. *Carr*, 369 U.S. 186, 266 ff. (1962); and see that of Justice Harlan in *Wesberry* v. *Sanders*, 376 U.S. 1, 20 ff. (1964).

Minor Premise: The legislative and congressional districts considered in *Baker* v. *Carr*, *Reynolds* v. *Sims*, and *Wesberry* v. *Sanders* are unequal in the ratio of district populations and representations.

Conclusion: The legislative and congressional districts in question failed to afford equal protection standards.

II. The Problems and Their Solutions

The Court's early efforts to achieve "equal protection" in the field of reapportionment (*Baker* v. *Carr*, *Gray* v. *Sanders*, *Wesberry* v. *Sanders*, *Reynolds* v. *Sims* et al.), in the opinion of this observer, have been responsible for progress, however crude and incomplete it may be in terms of achieving "logical" equal protection. But this advance makes it difficult to ignore the crude deficiencies of the standards which the Court has accepted with its reforms. Speaking for the majority in the Reynolds case, Mr. Chief Justice Warren says regarding state legislatures, "Mathematical exactness or precision is hardly a workable constitutional requirement."[4] In *Reynolds* the Court went on to suggest that legislative apportionment be only "based substantially" rather than exactly on population. It is assumed the principle of equal protection will not be diluted in any significant way. The Court in *Reynolds* makes additional concessions: "So long as the divergencies from a strict population standard are based on legitimate considerations incident to the effectuation of a rational state policy, some deviations from the equal protection principle are constitutionally permissible . . . ," and "a consideration that appears to be of more substance [than representing sparsely settled areas] in justifying some deviations from population-based representation . . . is that of insuring some voice to political subdivisions, as political subdivisions."[5]

In the same case the Court limited and logically weakened its new standard in still another respect. "In substance," said Warren, "we do not regard the Equal Protection Clause as requiring daily, monthly, annual or biennial reapportionment, so long as a State has a reasonably conceived plan for periodic readjustment of legislative representation. And we do not mean to intimate that more frequent reapportionment would not be constitutionally permissible or practically desirable.[6]

4. *Reynolds* v. *Sims*, 533, 577.   5. *Ibid.*, 580.
6. *Ibid.*, 583-584.

The two basic deficiencies of the model verbalized by the Court in the *Reynolds* case are: (1) as long as rough equality within limits permitting a variance of, say, 20 per cent is permitted, it remains possible to elect a legislative majority representing only a minority of population and a legislative minority representing a majority of population. This is statistical fact. The frequency with which, on the basis of probability statistics, laws with only minority support will actually be passed is a function of factors including the extent of the departure from population in the districting, the accidents of election, the volume of legislation, the closeness of legislative voting, the legislative rules, the use or non-use of the gubernatorial veto, and other variables. The only completely efficient solution to the requirement of "one person, one vote" is mathematical exactitude. In the age of the transistor it is wasteful and troublesome to fuss ad infinitum with the endlessly difficult problem of adjusting district lines when precision can be achieved by weighted voting. If, for instance, one district contains .9 per cent of population and another has 1.2 per cent, let the occupants of the district seats cast .9 and 1.2 votes respectively.

The second obvious deficiency of the present apportionment scheme, insofar as logical equality is concerned, is the result of constant population changes. Births, deaths, movements of persons occur and population figures are inaccurate the day, as well as the day after, the census-taker makes his rounds. It is a data processing problem, but it need not be a difficult one to reduce the dimensions of error in population records to negligible dimensions.

Formal and efficient records of births and deaths are already required by law and the data could be computerized at small expense. Records of personal movement are accumulated more slowly and less accurately. Prompt and highly accurate recording of such records may be expensive, but governmental and private groups (boards of development and chambers of commerce) currently make acceptable estimates. If these estimates were to be subjected to annual correction based on public records of taxes, licenses, etc., extremely reliable population estimates could be obtained with probable error reduced to a fraction of 1 per cent.

Weighted voting in legislatures coupled with computerized data processing can reduce the problems to negligible dimensions in percentage terms.

A more significant problem is that of "vote reversal."[7] Most efforts at "equal protection reform" have been aimed at prevention of vote dilution, discount, or debasement which occur when, as a result of malapportionment, fraud, or some electoral rule, a vote does not count at full value. Vote reversal occurs when a ballot, in fact or in effect, is counted for a candidate other than the candidate for whom the voter cast it. Vote reversal can be the result of fraud, but its most common occurrence in the American electoral system takes place as a result of the winner-take-all majoritarian (or plurality) single member district election which in effect translates a vote for a losing candidate into a vote for the winner. Logically this effect constitutes a proportionately more severe denial of equal protection than most malapportionment because the person casting a ballot which is effectively reversed loses 100 per cent of his vote.

The denial of equal protection which results from vote reversal is illustrated dramatically in Tables 1 and 2. In Table 1 party B has almost three times the popular strength of party A, but only equality in terms of offices won. Note that this denial of the "one person, one vote" standard occurs even though the size of the populations in the two districts and the size of the popular vote in each district are held even.

Table 2, Column A, like Table 1, illustrates the frustration of a popular majority even when all districts are assumed to be equal in

7. The concept of "vote reversal" was used by attorney Morris B. Abram in a 1952 brief attacking the Georgia County Unit System.

Gordon Tullock, *Towards a Mathematics of Politics* (Nov. 27, 1967), pp. 144-157 mistakenly suggests that he is the first to combine weighted voting and proportional representation. Actually, I touched on this possibility in July, 1964, three and one-half years before Tullock's publication. The two elements were identified in a published report of my lecture in The Dallas *Times Herald*, July 22, 1964, p. 32A. The idea was discussed on a number of occasions with colleagues and students at Southern Methodist University and later at Virginia Tech between 1964 and 1967. Another version of my model was published on November 3, 1967, in an article entitled "Some Problems of the Theory of Political Coalitions," *Virginia Tech Pamphlet I* (Blacksburg), p. 14, co-authored with Michael A. Weinstein.

Actually, the elements in these "inventions" are not new or novel. Proportional representation is an old idea and the system is widely used in Europe and elsewhere. A plan of weighted voting was used in New Jersey prior to 1964. Supreme Court decisions on apportionment and the development of computers have encouraged the concept. In 1964 C. Russell Phelps of the National Science Foundation called my attention to his research on the problem. The only agency required was to combine weighting and P. R. The basic conditions we should expect to find for an invention are evident: (1) a problem exists and (2) an advance in technology (the computer) permits a new solution. It is surprising that the "invention" did not occur sooner. We may discover that someone else said it before July, 1964. Both Tullock and Bernd should be prepared to take a back seat when a prior claimant appears, provided his proofs are in order.

population, and vote totals in each district are assumed to be equal. The choices of a popular majority are thwarted if the majority carries a small number of districts or seats each by a top-heavy margin, while losing a large number of districts or seats each by a thin margin.

Table 2, Column B, illustrates how the winner-take-all majoritarian system may leave a minority of 45 per cent completely unrepresented in terms of seats won.

Table 1. *Illustration of the Denial of Equal Protection by Vote Reversal (assume 100,000 population in District I and District II, below)*

	District I	District II	popular totals	offices won
Party A	5,090	100	5,190	1
Party B	4,910	9,900	14,810	1

Of course, a remedy for vote reversal, as we have defined it, is proportional representation—a scheme which enjoyed some popularity among American political reformers earlier in this century and which has been incorporated into the basic parliamentary electoral systems of many countries. In the United States earlier P.R. schemes lost their appeal to the voters when it appeared that the reform would encourage a multitude of minority parties and thus imperil the two-party basis of our national politics. It may be appropriate to speculate that a renewed attack on the winner-take-all majoritarian single member district basis of most legislative and congressional voting in the United States would receive little serious policy consideration in the foreseeable future unless the reform were to incorporate safeguards to protect the two-party system.

Aside from P.R., attacks on the majoritarian basis of election decisions have, at least in the United States, been designed to protect minority interests by requiring a proportion of voters greater than a simple numerical majority as a basis for an electoral decision. Examples are John C. Calhoun's notion of the concurrent majority and the idea of consensus for constitutional change advanced by Buchanan and Tullock in *The Calculus of Consent*. The objection to schemes of this type is that they would permit a minority, often a very small minority, to block majority action. Granted that the prevention of

Table 2. *Contests Between Party X and Party Y (all districts and district votes are assumed to be of equal size)*

A: Minority wins seats: majority vote is reversed				B: Majority wins seats: minority is unrepresented		
	popular vote	seats			popular vote	seats
majority	55%	2		majority	55%	10
minority	45%	8		minority	45%	0
	x = 90%	District 1			x	51
	y = 10%				y	49
	x = 96%	District 2			x	52
	y = 4%				y	48
	x = 49%	District 3			x	53
	y = 51%				y	47
	x = 48%	District 4			x	54
	y = 52%				y	46
	x = 47%	District 5			x	55
	y = 53%				y	45
	x = 46%	District 6			x	55
	y = 54%				y	45
	x = 45%	District 7			x	56
	y = 55%				y	44
	x = 44%	District 8			x	57
	y = 56%				y	43
	x = 43%	District 9			x	58
	y = 57%				y	42
	x = 42%	District 10			x	59
	y = 58%				y	41

majority tyranny is a legitimate concern of normative political science, the answer is not to be found in the creation of minority tyranny.

The solution offered here is not to offer minority control as a substitute for majoritarian winner-take-all decision-making, but to devise a scheme for postponing the winner-take-all effect in order that it might be deferred to the legislature where majority and minority party interests may be represented in proportion to their strengths.

The solution is simply to combine the P.R. principle with computerized weighted voting, as noted above. For instance, if candidate

A received 48.3 per cent of the votes and candidate B received 51.7 per cent, then both A and B are elected to the legislature with weights of 48.3 and 51.7, respectively. If A and B are chosen from a district with a population weight other than unity (1), the appropriate adjustment may be made by multiplying the population weight (1.2 for instance) by 48.3 and 51.7, respectively.

In order to refute the criticisms often levied against various P.R. schemes in the past, devices to protect the two-party system may be employed: (1) A cut-off point may be employed, say at 20 or 25 per cent, to deny legislative election to any candidate winning a percentage of popular votes below this figure. (2) The system might provide that no more than three or even two candidates are to be elected from any single district. Otherwise, even with a 20 per cent cut-off rule it would still be statistically possible to elect four or even five candidates from a single district. (3) The use of monetary deposits for candidacies and the forfeiture of the deposits if a candidate fails to poll a designated percentage (say 20 per cent) is another means of discouraging excessive fragmentation of voting consequent to a multitude of minor candidacies. Of course, a run-off is another means of narrowing the field.

What precisely are the advantages of the electoral model suggested here? At the risk of repetition, here is a brief summary. Representation, except for minor candidacies, becomes exact, not crude. Vote reversal as well as vote dilution is terminated. The formula, "one person, one vote," becomes a constitutional reality; again excepting minor candidacies, and the votes cast for them, there are no losing candidates in general elections to fill legislative seats. At least two candidates in each district cast ballots which are weighted in the legislature according to the number of votes received in the general election and the population of the district.

The model is an open-ended one and the problem is fully solved only if a run-off is held or if no more than two candidates are involved. On the other hand, if safeguards for the two-party system permit minor candidates to be eliminated because they did not receive a certain level of support, then vote reversal or dilution is *reduced* but not totally eliminated. If the system permits more than two persons from a district to be sent to the legislature from votes in a single contest, the legislature may become unwieldy, or the two-party system may be in jeopardy.

Whatever may be the respective merits of logically, as opposed to historically, conditioned judicial interpretations in general, the logical view of the "one person, one vote" standard serves at least to clarify one issue: Without some such model as is proposed here, the idea of equal protection as applied to elections and representation is a fiction. In the words of Robert J. Harris, "In law, to question a fiction is to kill it."[8]

III. The Problems of Implementation

The aim in this paper has been to identify a model capable of effectively and logically implementing the notion of equal protection as embodied in the idea of "one person, one vote." It is beyond the scope of this paper to suggest how, when, by whom, or even whether the model will be made logically effective in the United States.

It may seem to most students of American government that the effectuation of such a reform by judicial action in the foreseeable future is utterly inconceivable. Yet could not the same have been said a generation ago, regarding the judicially achieved reforms of the fifties and sixties in the fields of desegregation and reapportionment, to say nothing of first amendment prayer cases and rights of accused persons in criminal cases? If equal protection in any real sense is to be achieved in terms of electoral reform, it is likely to require judicial initiative.

Unlike congressmen and/or presidents, the members of the federal judiciary do not stand for re-election, or have limited tenure. Judicial reformers, unlike legislative reformers, do not have to contend with conservative institutions like the seniority system, the House Rules Committee, the rules permitting unlimited debate in the Senate, the interest group influences back home. Regarding the election reform proposed above, moreover, it is clear that membership in almost any American legislative body is prima facie evidence that one is a beneficiary of the winner-take-all majoritarian system. It would not appear to be realistic to expect these beneficiaries to initiate a reform which would require sharing the fruits of victory with the electoral foe. For

8. Robert J. Harris, *The Quest for Equality* (Baton Rouge, 1960), p. 131.

this reason, as well as because of the sheer inertia and the many obstruc-
tions of the legislative process, judicial initiation of reform is much
easier.

Our age has become aware that constitutional decisions are based
on something besides the intent of framer and ratifier, and/or precedents. So commonplace has it become to view the judicial branch
in terms of its political policy role and function that one scholar has
labeled this view of courts and judges as "conventional."

In a critical analysis directed toward the use of the intent of the
framers concept for interpreting equal protection in regard to the
racial segregation question, Robert J. Harris has noted the difficulty
of distinguishing between the subjective motivation of individual members of Congress and the ratifying legislatures and the objective intent
of a legislative body considered as a corporate entity. He perceives a
significant variety of motives ranging from the sordid aim of establishing and maintaining Republican party control of the South to the
noble and idealistic achievement of human equality and liberty.
Finally, says Harris, there were undoubtedly some who neither understood nor cared about what they were doing so long as they did not
run afoul of the radical leadership or risk political defeat in their
own constituencies.[9] Harris, of course, is talking about cases involving questions in which the intent of the framers is beclouded or uncertain. Is their intent controlling when policies are at issue which
clearly exceed anything anticipated by the framers and ratifiers?

Justice John Marshall Harlan (the younger) poses this issue squarely in his dissenting opinion in *Reynolds* v. *Sims* (at 590). The basic
elements of Harlan's reasoning are traditional criteria—"historical"
interpretation of language and meaning:

Today's holding is that the Equal Protection Clause of the Fourteenth
Amendment requires every state to structure its legislature so that all the
members of each house represent substantially the same number of people;
other factors may be given play only to the extent that they do not significantly encroach on this basic "population" principle. Whatever may be
thought of this holding as a piece of political ideology—and even on that
score the political history and practices of this country from its earliest
beginnings leave wide room for debate (see the dissenting opinion of
Frankfurter, J., in *Baker v. Carr*, 369 U.S. 186, 266, 301-323)—I think it

9. Harris, pp. 145-147.

demonstrable that the Fourteenth Amendment does not impose this political tenet on the States or authorize this Court to do so.

The Court's constitutional discussion, found in its opinion in the Alabama cases (nos. 23, 27, 41, ante, p. 533) and more particularly at pages 561-568 thereof, is remarkable (as, indeed, is that found in the separate opinions of my Brothers Stewart and Clark, ante, pp. 588, 587) for its failure to address itself at all to the Fourteenth Amendment as a whole or to the legislative history of the Amendment pertinent to the matter at hand. Stripped of aphorisms, the Court's argument boils down to the assertion that appellees' right to vote has been invidiously "debased" or "diluted" by systems of apportionment which entitle them to vote for fewer legislators than other voters, an assertion which is tied to the Equal Protection Clause only by the constitutionally frail tautology that "equal" means "equal."

Had the Court paused to probe more deeply into the matter, it would have found that the Equal Protection Clause was never intended to inhibit the States in choosing any democratic method they pleased for the apportionment of their legislatures. This is shown by the language of the Fourteenth Amendment taken as a whole, by the understanding of those who proposed and ratified it, and by the political practices of the States at the time the Amendment was adopted. It is confirmed by numerous state and congressional actions since the adoption of the Fourteenth Amendment, and by the common understanding of the Amendment as evidenced by subsequent constitutional amendments and decisions of this Court before *Baker v. Carr*, supra, made an abrupt break with the past in 1962.

The failure of the Court to consider any of these matters cannot be excused or explained by any concept of "developing" constitutionalism. It is meaningless to speak of constitutional "development" when both the language and history of the controlling provisions of the Constitution are wholly ignored. Since it can, I think, be shown beyond doubt that state legislative apportionments, as such, are wholly free of constitutional limitations, save such as may be imposed by the Republican Form of Government Clause (Const., Art. IV § 4), the Court's action now bringing them within the purview of the Fourteenth Amendment amounts to nothing less than an exercise of the amending power by this Court.

So far as the Federal Constitution is concerned, the complaints in these cases should all have been dismissed below for failure to state a cause of action, because what has been alleged or proved shows no violation of any constitutional right. . . .[10]

The basic argument against basing constitutional interpretation on historical grounds, as Harlan would have us do, is, of course, the desire to avoid the confines of an understanding which belonged to a

10. *Reynolds* v. *Sims*, 590.

past age, unfamiliar with the problems of our day. This does not mean that interpretation is merely relative to who is on the Court to interpret. Limits remain, but these limits are logical extensions of language rather than historically conditioned motives imputed to dead statesmen. To construe an idea such as equal protection in its logical sense avoids the narrow limits of a strictly historical interpretation. To understand equal protection in harmony with Myrdal's explanation of the American Creed tends to broaden the meaning of the clause rather than to restrict it, while clothing it in the dress of ideas associated with the heritage of the nation.

In a passage cited above (see footnote 9), Robert J. Harris has identified some of the inherent difficulties of interpreting the intent of the framers and ratifiers of the equal protection clause of the Fourteenth Amendment. His argument suggests to this observer the utter futility of attempting to muster historical evidence as a basis for a highly refined and complex contemporary judicial interpretation of the clause. The equal protection clause, like other controversial provisions, is couched in brief and general language. If we may agree with Harris that it arose from a variety of motives and interests, it seems highly likely that it held different meanings for different men. Perhaps we are warranted in assuming that the most intelligent, or wisest, members of the framers' Congress were aware of this inherent ambiguity in the clause.

The wise, or wisest, framers and founders possibly believed in "equal protection" fully. Perhaps they realized the precise applications of the concept in ages to come could not be foreseen, and they did not desire to limit the concept merely to usages they could foresee. If they had, they would have written in limitations which, in fact, they carefully omitted. It follows that a broadly logical interpretation is possibly the one which most nearly corresponds with the intent of the wisest framers. It is as if the latter anticipated that future generations would see things more completely and the language employed in constitution drafting would be capable of expansion to fit the idea of more complete equality of protection. Instead of a new constitution for each new generation, as Jefferson advocated in one of his famous letters, the wisest framers wrote down basic norms and left the ultimate interpretation to the inevitable decision-makers—the policy-makers of future ages.

Morris B. Abram, a distinguished trial lawyer, sees a continuing American revolution occurring in the courts of the land. In effect, law changes logically as the Constitution is interpreted in the light of the original purposes of the revolution which began in 1775. Equality is increasingly realized. Abram says:

This country is experiencing a great spiritual, legal and social change. This has been too long delayed. Much of it originated in the work of the United States Supreme Court of the last two decades. Today that court is not a body of encrusted legal technicians but a vital third branch of the government, interpreting and defending the constitution and moralizing through law to other courts, public officials and private citizens on the principles of our political heritage.[11]

Other scholars see a vacuum concept explaining judicial policy-making. The Court is uniquely equipped by its composition and its constitutional status to reform when the "political" branches of government cannot or will not act. Though the Court holds neither the purse nor the sword, it has other assets for policy formulation.

For racial justice, as well as for reapportionment, the Warren Court appears to have been operating under a vacuum theory of judicial functions in the American political system. Contrary to Robert A. Dahl's argument in 1957 that the Supreme Court can direct the course of national policy only as part of dominant lawmaking coalitions, the most aggressive uses of judicial power in the last decade have occurred precisely where political processes were stalemated or atrophied. Filling power vacuums by judicial action may have been motivated less by theory than appears. The weaponry used also has ranged from the "passive virtues" to the "blunderbuss."[12]

11. Morris B. Abram, "The Challenge of the Courtroom—Reflections on the Adversary System," *The Law School Record* (Autumn, 1963), p. 6. Abram is now president of Brandeis University.

12. Woodford Howard and Cornelius Bushoven, "The Screws Case Revisited," *Journal of Politics*, XXIX (Aug., 1967), 617-636; cf. Dahl, "The Supreme Court as a National Policy-Maker," *Journal of Public Law*, VI (1957), 279-295.

John A. Morgan, Jr. / From *Maxwell* to *Duncan*— Progress or Regression?

In the first year of this century the United States Supreme Court held in *Maxwell* v. *Dow* that the Fourteenth Amendment did not guarantee in state criminal proceedings the Sixth Amendment right to trial by jury.[1] Sixty-eight years later, precisely the opposite became the law. In *Duncan* v. *Louisiana* the Court held that "the Fourteenth Amendment guarantees a right of jury trial in all criminal cases which—were they to be tried in a federal court—would come within the Sixth Amendment's guarantee."[2] The view of the Fourteenth Amendment reflected in that decision is, to many, one of the principal justifications for characterizing the present Court as "liberal." But it does not necessarily follow from the "incorporation" rulings of the last few years that there will result a net gain for individual freedom from governmental oppression.

In the face of the oft-repeated insistence that "one of the chief objects that the provisions of the Amendment's first section . . . were intended to accomplish was to make the Bill of Rights applicable to the States,"[3] until very recently the Court steadfastly refused to equate the procedural limitations imposed by the Fourteenth Amendment with those spelled out in the Bill of Rights. Despite the Court's dictum as early as 1925 that freedom of speech and press were protected by the Fourteenth Amendment[4] and its subsequent "incorporation" of First Amendment freedoms,[5] as late as 1960 Glendon Schubert's textbook, *Constitutional Politics*, titled a chapter subdivision "The Second-Class Rights of Criminal Defendants."[6] Indeed, applying two criteria for measuring whether a right should be recognized as having been "nationalized,"[7] Schubert asserted that "*only* the First Amend-

1. 176 U.S. 581 (1900). 2. 391 U.S. 145, 149 (1968).
3. Justice Black, dissenting, in *Adamson* v. *California*, 332 U.S. 46, 71-72 (1947).
4. *Gitlow* v. *New York*, 268 U.S. 652 (1925).
5. *Fiske* v. *Kansas*, 274 U.S. 380 (1927), speech; *Near* v. *Minnesota*, 283 U.S. 697 (1931), press; *DeJonge* v. *Oregon*, 299 U.S. 353 (1937), peaceable assembly; *Cantwell* v. *Connecticut*, 310 U.S. 296 (1940), religion.
6. New York, 1960, p. 593.
7. "There are two criteria that ought to be met before one recognizes a right as

ment has been nationalized by marriage with the due-process clause
of the Fourteenth."⁸ Yet, the very next year marked the beginning of
a series of decisions which in rapid succession have at long last applied
to the states one after another of the safeguards included in the Fourth,
Fifth, Sixth, and Eighth Amendments.

Since declaring in *Mapp* v. *Ohio* that the Fourth Amendment's
right of privacy was enforceable against the states by the same sanction
of exclusion as used against the federal government,⁹ the Court has
added each year to the list of Bill of Rights guarantees applied to
state criminal proceedings. In 1962 the Eighth Amendment's protection against cruel and unusual punishment was declared binding on
the states.¹⁰ In 1963 *Gideon* v. *Wainwright* laid to rest the special
circumstances doctrine and made fully applicable to the states the Sixth
Amendment's guarantee of the assistance of counsel.¹¹ Later the same
year the Court held that the Fourth Amendment standard of legality
of searches without a warrant would be applied in determining the admissibility of evidence in state proceedings.¹² In 1964 the Fifth
Amendment right against self-incrimination was secured against state
invasion¹³ and the standard of reasonableness for obtaining a search
warrant was held to be the same under the Fourth and Fourteenth
Amendments.¹⁴ The Sixth Amendment right of confrontation was applied to the states in 1965,¹⁵ and the right to an "impartial" jury—if a
jury were used—the following year.¹⁶ That same amendment's guarantees of speedy trial¹⁷ and compulsory process for obtaining wit-
nesses¹⁸ were held to be required by the Fourteenth Amendment in
1967. And in 1968, the Fourteenth Amendment's absorption of the

---

having been nationalized: (1) the Court should consider its precedents to be inter-
changeable, citing cases decided directly under a different section of the Constitution as
authority for a subsequent decision under one of the due-process clauses; and (2) the
Court should discuss, in its opinions in cases arising under a due-process clause, the
right that has been 'nationalized' as though the relevant substantive clause bore directly
upon the case being decided" (*ibid.*, p. 529).

8. *Ibid.* Emphasis added.   9. 367 U.S. 643 (1961).
10. *Robinson* v. *California,* 370 U.S. 660 (1962).
11. 372 U.S. 335 (1963).
12. *Ker* v. *California,* 374 U.S. 230 (1963).
13. *Malloy* v. *Hogan,* 378 U.S. 1 (1964). See also *Murphy* v. *Waterfront Commission,*
378 U.S. 52 (1964), and *Griffin* v. *California,* 380 U.S. 609 (1965).
14. *Aguilar* v. *Texas,* 378 U.S. 108 (1964).
15. *Pointer* v. *Texas,* 380 U.S. 400 (1965). See also *Douglas* v. *Alabama,* 380 U.S.
415 (1965).
16. *Parker* v. *Gladden,* 385 U.S. 363 (1966).
17. *Klopfer* v. *North Carolina,* 386 U.S. 213 (1967).
18. *Washington* v. *Texas,* 388 U.S. 14 (1967).

guarantees of the Sixth was completed with the decision of the *Duncan* case.[19]

In case after case the language of the Court, as well as the frequent dissenting opinions of Mr. Justice Harlan, suggested that Schubert's criteria of nationalization had been met.[20] And therein lies a potential danger. In respect to the incorporation of the First Amendment, Schubert observed that "There is no particular extension of human liberty if the Court admits that the states must recognize freedom of speech to the same extent as the national government—and then concludes that neither must give too much recognition to the right of freedom of speech when anything of political importance is being discussed."[21] Just so with respect to the rights of defendants now held to apply to the states. It would be a pyrrhic victory, indeed, if the determinations that state courts are bound by the same procedural strictures as the federal courts were followed by a relaxation of the federal standards. And because it is in large measure true that "the Court proposes, but politics disposes,"[22] there is reason to fear that such a relaxation might occur.

While the Court has often been fiercely assailed for rulings directed solely at federal law enforcement practices, its vulnerability to successful attack is almost certainly increased when restrictions are imposed on local police practices. In a day of public anxiety over rapidly rising crime rates, student riots, and burning and looting in the cities, an intense reaction against measures allegedly hampering those bearing primary responsibility for law enforcement is all but inevitable. One can agree with *The New Republic* that "The tendency in some quarters to blame crime on the 'coddling' of criminals by soft-headed civil libertarians . . . is, of course, nonsense."[23] Nonsense or not, however, widespread popular opposition to judicial rulings which appear to have the effect of reversing convictions where guilt is "clear" on the basis of "mere technicalities" is to be expected. The Omnibus Crime Control and Safe Streets Act's provisions regarding wiretapping and the admissibility of confessions and eyewitness identifications are likely

19. The guarantee of a "public" trial was held required by the Fourteenth Amendment in *In Re Oliver*, 333 U.S. 257 (1948).
20. See n. 7, above.   21. *Constitutional Politics*, p. 530.
22. C. Herman Pritchett, "Equal Protection and the Urban Majority," *American Political Science Review*, LVIII (Dec., 1964), 875.
23. CLVIII, No. 26 (June 29, 1968), p. 5.

to be but opening salvos in a continuing legislative attack.[24] More remarkable than the act's passage was the deletion of the Senate Judiciary Committee's provisions which would have deprived the Supreme Court of jurisdiction to review the admissibility in evidence of confessions and eyewitness identifications in state criminal proceedings.[25] But this deletion merely underscores a predictably ironic side-effect of the nationalizing trend.

The Senate Judiciary Committee's report, as well as the wording of Title II as passed, suggest clearly what was indeed the case—that while the Court's *Mallory*[26] and *Wade*[27] rulings were objectionable in many quarters, it was *Escobedo* v. *Illinois*[28] and *Miranda* v. *Arizona*[29] that provoked the storm. Because of their more obvious impact on the law enforcement problems that concern the ordinary citizen, rulings directed at state courts are potent sources of the sustained antagonism ordinarily necessary for successful legislative attacks. But the attacks themselves, as the Omnibus Crime Control Act so clearly evinces, are likely to sweep more broadly, encompassing procedures in federal courts as well. And especially is this the case when the Court insists in ruling after ruling that the same standards apply whether the proceeding is federal or state. Thus, extending the procedural guarantees of the Bill of Rights to state court proceedings increases the prospect of successful attacks on the standards of justice in the federal courts. Put slightly differently, departure from the oft-criticized "watered-down" approach to Fourteenth Amendment rights carries with it the danger of watering down the Bill of Rights guarantees themselves.

There are, of course, limits to the effectiveness of legislative action. It remains to be seen whether the Crime Control Act's provisions will survive the test of constitutionality in the courts. And, in any event, efforts to revise decisions when it can be plausibly argued that the Court has expressly called for legislative action (as was the case with

24. Public Law 351, 90th Cong., 2d Sess.; approved June 19, 1968. U.S., *Statutes at Large,* LXXXII, 197.

25. See sections 3502 and 3503 of Title II as reported by the Committee, Senate Report No. 1097 (90th Cong., 2d Sess.), p. 10.

26. *Mallory* v. *United States,* 354 U.S. 449 (1957).

27. *United States* v. *Wade,* 388 U.S. 318 (1967).

28. 378 U.S. 478 (1964).   29. 384 U.S. 436 (1966).

30. Chief Justice Warren's opinion for the Court included the following passage: "It is possible for us to foresee the potential alternatives for protecting the privilege which might be devised by Congress or the States in the exercise of their creative rule-making capacities. Therefore we cannot say that the Constitution necessarily requires adherence

Miranda)[30] succeed more easily than do attempts to overturn rulings which are unequivocally stated as constitutional commands. There remains, however, a more subtle threat to federal procedural standards —relaxation by the judiciary itself.

In the face of widespread resentment of controversial decisions coupled with attempts, not only to reverse the offensive rulings, but to restrict the power of the Court, judicial back-tracking is always a distinct possibility. Despite the defeat of the provisions which would have restricted the Court's power to review state court decisions, Title II of the Omnibus Crime Control Act constitutes a greater legislative success than the Court's critics were able to achieve during the great battles of the thirties and fifties. Still, the "nine old men" remained seated when *West Coast Hotel Co.* v. *Parrish*[31] and *NLRB* v. *Jones & Laughlin Steel Corp.*[32] were decided; and *Nelson,*[33] *Watkins,*[34] and *Sweezy*[35] were followed by *Barenblatt*[36] and *Uphaus.*[37] Should continuing political pressure be similarly reflected in the Court's subsequent procedural rights rulings, its "incorporation" decisions could produce an anomalous result. For any leniency permitted at the state level would be a precedent for the federal courts as well.

Even if the threat of reprisals is totally ineffective, however, the

---

to any particular solution for the inherent compulsions of the interrogation process as it is presently conducted. Our decision in no way creates a constitutional straitjacket which will handicap sound efforts at reform, nor is it intended to have this effect. We encourage Congress and the States to continue their laudable search for increasingly effective ways of protecting the rights of the individual while promoting efficient enforcement of our criminal laws" (384 U.S. 436, 467).

It seems clear, as the Judiciary Committee minority pointed out (see Senate Report No. 1097, 90th Cong., 2d Sess., pp. 149-150), that the *Miranda* holding was firmly grounded on a constitutional basis and that the invitation to legislatures was merely to adopt alternative means for protecting suspects' constitutional rights which would be at least as effective as, and hopefully an improvement upon, the safeguards imposed by the Court. Nonetheless, critics of the decision could assert with some persuasiveness that "The Supreme Court itself suggests that Congress is free to enact legislation in this field. The Court's invitation for Congress to act could stem from a wide-spread notion that Congress is better able to cope with the problem of confessions than is the Court" (*ibid.*, 46).

In this respect the committee's reliance on a memorandum prepared by the American Law Division of the Legislative Reference Service is also worthy of note. A major facet of its conclusion was that "it is constitutionally permissible for Congress to formulate a test of admissibility different from that adopted by the Court, inasmuch as the adoption does not follow upon any attempt to change constitutional theory but rather upon a qualifying of the factual basis of the effectuation of that policy" (*ibid.*, 63).

31. 300 U.S. 379 (1937).   32. 301 U.S. 1 (1937).
33. *Pennsylvania* v. *Nelson*, 350 U.S. 497 (1956).
34. *Watkins* v. *United States*, 354 U.S. 178 (1957).
35. *Sweezy* v. *New Hampshire*, 354 U.S. 234 (1957).
36. *Barenblatt* v. *United States*, 360 U.S. 109 (1959).
37. *Uphaus* v. *Wyman*, 360 U.S. 72 (1959).

Court might well adjust its rulings in the direction sought by its critics in response to a different kind of pressure. By way of answering the charge that its *Miranda* ruling would unduly burden law enforcement officials, the Court pointed to "the exemplary record of effective law enforcement" compiled by the Federal Bureau of Investigation while adhering to practices "consistent with the procedure which we delineate today."[38] But local police departments are not the FBI, and the problems faced at these different levels are not necessarily the same. Certainly the difficulties accompanying the full range of crime prevention and detection activities carried on at the local level are more obtrusive than are those attending the relatively narrow law enforcement activities of the national government. Unless one assumes that the inadequacies of present efforts against crime are wholly subject to financial cure and that the necessary funds will quickly become available, practical considerations of local law enforcement effectiveness will almost certainly have a growing influence on the Court's decisions.

Discussing the power of lower courts to check the Supreme Court, Walter Murphy observed that "The Supreme Court typically formulates general policy. Lower courts apply that policy, and working in its interstices, inferior judges may materially modify the High Court's determinations."[39] Using the aftermath of the *Mallory* decision as an example of the power of inferior judges to reshape legal doctrine expounded by the Supreme Court, Murphy characterized the difference in viewpoint between the two levels as follows: "Where the Supreme Court had been viewing the conflict as between a defendant's constitutional rights and police administration, the lower courts saw the clash as between an individual's rights to technical procedures and the public's right to basic protections."[40] That state courts applying the Supreme Court's rulings on the rights of defendants will display a similar sensitivity to considerations of public safety can hardly be doubted. In this regard it is instructive to consider a recent comment by Chief Justice Joseph Weintraub of the Supreme Court of New Jersey. Speaking of the rule excluding from evidence the fruits of an unreasonable search and seizure, he said:

38. 384 U.S. 436, 483-484 (1966).
39. "Lower Court Checks on Supreme Court Power," *American Political Science Review*, LIII (Dec., 1959), 1018.
40. *Ibid.*, p. 1025.

We should be mindful that while the judge-made sanction supports the right of the individual to be free from wrongful invasion by the State, it tends to deny him protection from grievous invasion by the criminal. For unless we can assume that offenders set free by suppression of patent proof of their guilt will not resume a criminal course, we must recognize that the pain of the sanction of suppression will be felt, not by some abstraction called the "police" or "society," but by tomorrow's victims, by the innocent who more likely than not will be the poor, the most exposed and the least protected among us. Nor can we fail to note that while the sanction supports the high value inherent in freedom from unwarranted search, yet in another aspect it works against public morality because the suppression of the truth must tend to breed contempt for the long arm of the law. Such are the stakes, *and it is in their light that the unreasonableness of a search must be measured.*[41]

Thus, attempting to work within Murphy's interstices, state court judges can be expected to present the High Court with numerous opportunities to review its procedural rulings in light of their view of local exigencies. It would be surprising indeed if those views failed to have an impact.

The potential effect of adjustments to local exigencies in the wake of the incorporation decisions can be seen clearly by contrasting the Court's opinions in *Breithaupt* v. *Abram*[42] and *Schmerber* v. *California*.[43] In both cases the Court affirmed convictions based on the results of an involuntary blood test. But there the similarity ends.

In *Breithaupt*, claims that the defendant had been deprived of due process because the withdrawal of blood and the admission in evidence of the test result violated the Fourth and Fifth Amendments were summarily rejected. Relying on its earlier rulings that the Fourteenth Amendment did not embrace the Fifth Amendment privilege against self-incrimination[44] nor require in state prosecutions the exclusion of evidence obtained in violation of the Fourth Amendment,[45] the Court rested its decision solely on the conclusion that there had been no conduct so offensive to justice as to constitute a denial of due process. Whether the use of an involuntary blood test was consistent with the strictures of the Fourth and Fifth Amendments remained undecided.

In *Schmerber* the result was predictably different. With its intervening rulings in *Mapp* v. *Ohio* and *Malloy* v. *Hogan*, the Court

41. *State* v. *Davis*, 231 A.2d 793, 796-797 (1967). Emphasis added.
42. 352 U.S. 432 (1957). 43. 384 U.S. 757 (1966).
44. *Twining* v. *New Jersey*, 211 U.S. 78 (1908).
45. *Wolf* v. *Colorado*, 338 U.S. 25 (1949).

could no longer find that combating the increasing slaughter on the highways justified a state's using a compulsory blood test without holding the same technique constitutionally permissible at the federal level. Since the privilege against self-incrimination and the exclusionary rule were now applicable to the states, a compulsory blood test could not be employed if it violated the Fourth or Fifth Amendment. Not surprisingly, the Court found that it did not. Speaking to the Fifth Amendment claim, the Court held that "the privilege protects an accused only from being compelled to testify against himself, or otherwise provide the State with evidence of a testimonial or communicative nature, and . . . the withdrawal of blood and use of the analysis in question in this case did not involve compulsion to these ends."[46] As for the Fourth, "Such testing procedures plainly constitute searches of 'persons,' and depend antecedently upon seizures of 'persons' within the meaning of that Amendment."[47] However, the Fourth Amendment does not constrain against all intrusions into the human body, only against those "which are not justified in the circumstances, or which are made in an improper manner."[48] Finding that there was probable cause for the arrest, that the attempt to secure evidence of blood-alcohol content was an appropriate incident to the arrest, and that the test chosen was a reasonable one performed in a reasonable manner, the Court concluded that Schmerber's Fourth Amendment rights had not been violated. Thus, it appears that the *Breithaupt* approval of compulsory blood tests has been expanded to include the possibility of their use in federal proceedings.

Since the Fourth Amendment's protection is against "unreasonable" searches and seizures, it is here that federal standards would appear to be most vulnerable to modification in response to local considerations. Indeed, Justice Harlan issued a warning as to this possibility in *Ker* v. *California*. Casting the sole vote against applying to the states the federal standard of reasonableness of searches without a warrant,[49] he wrote:

46. 384 U.S. 757, 761.
47. *Ibid.*, 767.   48. *Ibid.*, 768.
49. Finding, however, that the search and seizure at issue did not offend "established Fourteenth Amendment concepts of fundamental fairness," Justice Harlan cast the crucial vote to form a narrow majority affirming the conviction. While his eight colleagues were agreed that the federal standard applied, they split evenly on whether it had been violated in this case.

The rule is unwise because the States, with their differing law enforcement problems, should not be put in a constitutional strait jacket. . . . And if the Court is prepared to relax Fourth Amendment standards in order to avoid unduly fettering the States, this would be in derogation of law enforcement standards in the federal system—unless the Fourth Amendment is to mean one thing for the States and something else for the Federal Government.[50]

A year later, in *Aguilar* v. *Texas,* Justice Harlan reiterated the concern he had expressed in *Ker.* In explanation of his grudging vote with the majority, he said:

But for *Ker* v. *California* . . . I would have voted to affirm the judgment of the Texas court. Given *Ker,* I cannot escape the conclusion that to do so would tend to "relax Fourth Amendment standards . . . in derogation of law enforcement standards in the *federal* system. . . ." Being unwilling to relax those standards for federal prosecutions, I concur in the opinion of the Court.[51]

Despite his vote in *Aguilar,* however, Justice Harlan was with the majority in two later decisions which, at the very least, represent a tendency in the direction he warned against.

Less than three months prior to its holding in *Aguilar,* the Court had overturned a conviction for conspiracy to rob a federally insured bank on the grounds that the warrantless search of a car had offended constitutional standards. Justice Black, writing for a unanimous Court in *Preston* v. *United States,* concluded that: "Once an accused is under arrest and in custody, then a search made at another place, without a warrant, is simply not incident to the arrest. . . . Therefore, . . . the search of the car without a warrant failed to meet the test of reasonableness under the Fourth Amendment, rendering the evidence as a result of the search inadmissible."[52]

Three years later, essentially the same issue was presented in a case involving a state conviction for a narcotics violation. In *Cooper* v. *California,*[53] as in *Preston,* the conviction rested in part on evidence which the police had seized in a warrantless search of a car some time after the defendant had been arrested. Again, Justice Black wrote for the Court, but this time for a bare majority. *Preston* was distinguished and the search and seizure declared reasonable on the grounds that:

50. 374 U.S. 23, 45-46.
52. 376 U.S. 364, 367-368 (1964).

51. 378 U.S. 108, 116.
53. 386 U.S. 58 (1967).

Here the officers seized petitioner's car because they were required to do so by state law. They seized it because of the crime for which they arrested petitioner. They seized it to impound it and they had to keep it until forfeiture proceedings were concluded. Their subsequent search of the car—whether the State had "legal title" to it or not—was closely related to the reason petitioner was arrested, the reason his car had been impounded, and the reason it was being retained.[54]

Despite Justice Black's efforts, however, it is difficult to escape the minority's conclusion that *Cooper* was on all fours with *Preston*, save for the fact that one was a state case and the other federal.[55]

Warden v. *Hayden*,[56] decided three months later with only Justice Douglas dissenting,[57] involved a more significant departure from earlier Fourth Amendment rulings. As the Court phrased it, the issue was

the validity of the proposition that there is under the Fourth Amendment a "distinction between merely evidentiary materials, on the one hand, which may not be seized either under the authority of a search warrant or during the course of a search incident to arrest, and on the other hand, those objects which may validly be seized including the instrumentalities and means by which a crime is committed, the fruits of crime such as stolen property, weapons by which escape of the person arrested might be effected, and property the possession of which is a crime."[58]

Concluding that nothing in the language of the Fourth Amendment supported the distinction, the Court thereby discarded the so-called "mere evidence" rule dating from 1886.[59] That considerations of primarily local moment influenced the Court's holding is suggested both by the fact situation which produced it and by the majority opinion. As partial explanation of the slow development of pressure to test the "discredited premise" underlying the distinction, Justice Brennan commented that "*Mapp* v. *Ohio* . . . only recently made the 'mere evidence' rule a problem in the state courts."[60] And it is noteworthy that the Court's characterization of the distinction as "based on premises no longer accepted as rules governing the application of the

54. *Ibid.*, 61.
55. Dissenting opinion of Justice Douglas, joined by Chief Justice Warren and Justices Brennan and Fortas (386 U.S. 58, 62; see esp. 65).
56. 387 U.S. 294 (1967).
57. Justice Fortas, in a concurring opinion joined by Chief Justice Warren, did express reservations, however, arguing that the ruling should have been more narrowly drawn (387 U.S. 294, 310; see esp. 312).
58. 387 U.S. 294, 295-296.
59. *Boyd* v. *United States*, 116 U.S. 616 (1886).
60. 387 U.S. 294, 309.

Fourth Amendment" was footnoted as follows: "This Court has approved the seizure and introduction of items having only evidential value, without, however, considering the validity of the distinction rejected today. See *Schmerber* v. *California*, 384 U.S. 757; *Cooper* v. *California*, 386 U.S. 58."[61] Both *Schmerber* and *Cooper* were, of course, post-*Mapp* and involved *state* proceedings.

It has often been argued that the victory of the incorporation theory would have the salutary effect of raising the standard of justice in the state courts to the level of the federal; *Schmerber, Cooper*, and *Hayden* suggest that the result might well be just the opposite. That the procedural standards of the Bill of Rights should be threatened by expanding their application seems curiously incongruous; but as Justice Holmes observed, "The life of the law has not been logic; it has been experience."[62] The question is—should the experience with the daily problems of local law enforcement be allowed to govern the life of the law in federal courts?

Despite the justified and laudable concern over police practices at the local level, the very size and resulting detached impersonality of the present-day national government give to law enforcement activities at that level an infinitely greater potential for repression. As Justice Frankfurter said, "The public opinion of a community can far more effectively be exerted against oppressive conduct on the part of police directly responsible to the community itself than can local opinion, sporadically aroused, be brought to bear upon remote authority pervasively exerted throughout the country."[63] In a day when growing popular concern over rapidly increasing crime rates combines with overstrained local financial resources to make increasing federal involvement in law enforcement activities all but inevitable, any relaxation of procedural standards affecting police practices at that level ought to be viewed with special alarm.

It is to be hoped that if the tendency to adjust constitutional standards to local practicalities is to continue, the High Court will mitigate the "reverse incorporation" effect on law enforcement practices at the national level by vigorously exercising its supervisory powers over the federal courts. Or better yet, the Court might obviate the temptation

61. *Ibid.*, 301, n. 8.
62. *The Common Law* (Boston, 1881; edited by Mark DeWolfe Howe and reissued, 1963), p. 5.
63. *Wolf* v. *Colorado*, 338 U.S. 25, 29 (1949).

to alter earlier rulings by adopting a less aggressive attitude toward state court determinations of harmless error.[64]

64. For examples of the Court's present stance, see especially *Fahy* v. *Connecticut,* 375 U.S. 85 (1963); Justice Harlan's separate opinion in *Stoner* v. *California,* 376 U.S. 483, 490 (1964); and *Chapman* v. *California,* 386 U.S. 18 (1967).

Albert L. Sturm / Bills of Rights in New State Constitutions

"A constitution states or ought to state not rules for the passing hour but principles for an expanding future."[1] This characterization of the fundamental law by Mr. Justice Cardozo is probably more applicable to the bill of rights in most American state constitutions than to other parts of these documents. Most provisions of state declarations of rights have long been regarded as fundamental and therefore have been subjected to less change than the contents of other articles. Nevertheless, bills of rights also reflect changing popular demands for guarantees against governmental encroachment.

This analysis examines the bills of rights in eleven American constitutions drafted since World War II to determine the nature of their contents, the extent of recent changes, and probable future trends. Of the eleven constitutions, six are in operation, three were rejected by the voters, one had not been submitted to the electorate at the time this was written, and one is a model document.[2] Collectively, these instruments provide a substantial cross-section of the thinking of state constitution-makers about the contents appropriate for a bill of rights in the second half of the twentieth century.

General Nature and Significance

Professor Robert S. Rankin, in whose honor this and other parts of this volume are written, has summarized the reason for inclusion of a bill of rights in all American constitutions as follows:

1. Benjamin N. Cardozo, *The Nature of the Judicial Process* (New Haven, 1921), p. 24.
2. The documents selected for this analysis are as follows: six American constitutions written or revised by constitutional conventions and ratified by the people during the period from 1947 to 1968, namely, those of New Jersey (effective in 1947), the Commonwealth of Puerto Rico (1952), Alaska (1959), Hawaii (1959), Michigan (1964), and Connecticut (1965); three proposed state constitutions prepared by constitutional conventions that were rejected by the voters in the referenda—New York (1967), Rhode Island (1968), and Maryland (1968); a proposed new constitution for Florida, which was drafted by a constitutional commission, presented to the Florida Legislature in 1967, and was scheduled for final legislative action before submission to the voters in

Man's struggle for constitutional government is centuries old and has been demanding in material and human sacrifice. Where he has been successful the symbol of his victory is civil liberty or right—the constitutional protection of the individual against arbitrary or tyrannical treatment by his government. Realizing the difficulty in securing and holding these rights we have stated them in the most prominent position among our constitutional principles.[3]

A bill of rights lists the guarantees of freedom from governmental encroachment considered by constitution-makers to be of sufficient fundamental importance to warrant inclusion in the basic law. All American state constitutions contain such declarations. They include traditional rights of persons and property won through centuries of struggle against arbitrary and tyrannical governmental action, as well as newer provisions that reflect modern problems and conditions. In setting bounds to governmental power and in specifying those freedoms believed to be necessary for human welfare and happiness, the bill of rights, as well as other parts of the fundamental law, expresses the basic ideals and faith of the people.[4]

One of the most persistent problems of political democracy is to maintain the optimum balance between human liberty and public authority. Constitutional bills of rights are the principal bulwark of individual freedom in an era of ever-expanding governmental functions and activities. The growing complexity of the social order and the consequent danger of improper use of public authority enhance the importance of the bill of rights, which, with few exceptions, is the lead article in state constitutions. Today, few if any areas of public law are the basis for more legal actions than the bill of rights in the federal and state constitutions.[5]

1968; and the sixth edition of the *Model State Constitution*, prepared under the auspices of the National Municipal League and issued in 1963.

3. *State Constitutions: The Bill of Rights*, State Constitutional Studies Project, No. 5 of a series of background studies (New York, 1960), p. 1; see also, by the same author, "The Bill of Rights," in *Major Problems in State Constitutional Revision*, ed. W. Brooke Graves (Chicago, 1960).

4. "Like other expressions of public policy, a state constitution cannot help but express the problems, interests, and concern of its people, even those which outsiders might not rank as important or enduring." Robert B. Dishman, *State Constitutions: The Shape of the Document*, State Constitutional Studies Project, No. 1 of a series of background studies (rev. ed.; New York, 1968), p. 28.

5. Public Administration Service, "Civil Rights and Liberties," Constitutional Studies Prepared on behalf of the Alaska Statehood Committee for the Alaska Constitutional Convention, 1955, I, Second Paper, 4.

Relationship to Federal Bill of Rights

State bills of rights commonly repeat most of the same guarantees listed in the first eight amendments to the Constitution of the United States. They also reiterate other restrictions on state action stated in the original national Constitution.[6] For many years the federal Bill of Rights was interpreted as limiting the national government only, imposing no restriction on state action.[7] But, after the Fourteenth Amendment was adopted, judicial interpretation gradually led to the incorporation of some of the fundamental guarantees of the federal Bill of Rights into the due process clause of the Fourteenth Amendment, which forbids any state to "deprive any person of life, liberty, or property without due process of law."[8] As interpreted and applied by the United States Supreme Court, the Fourteenth Amendment prohibits the states from abridging only those rights guaranteed in the first eight amendments that are "implicit in the concept of ordered liberty."[9] Since 1937, however, the United States Supreme Court has enforced a growing number of federal Bill of Rights guarantees against the states, thereby overruling earlier decisions to the contrary.[10] Recent judicial decisions have moved the national and state governments toward a single standard of civil rights, particularly in the area of procedure applicable to accused persons. Nevertheless, the Constitution

6. See Art. I, Sec. 10.

7. *Barron* v. *Baltimore*, 7 Peters 243 (1833).

8. See George W. Spicer, *The Supreme Court and Fundamental Freedoms* (2nd ed.; New York, 1967), chap. ii.

9. *Palko* v. *Connecticut*, 302 U.S. 319, 325 (1937).

10. Provisions of the federal Bill of Rights that have been applied to the states through the Fourteenth Amendment and the pertinent leading cases include the following:

First Amendment—establishment of religion, *Everson* v. *Board of Education*, 330 U.S. 1 (1947); freedom of religion, *Cantwell* v. *Connecticut*, 310 U.S. 296 (1940); speech and press, *Gitlow* v. *New York*, 268 U.S. 652 (1925); assembly, *DeJonge* v. *Oregon*, 299 U.S. 353 (1937).

Fourth Amendment—unreasonable searches and seizures, *Mapp* v. *Ohio*, 367 U.S. 643 (1961).

Fifth Amendment—self-incrimination, *Malloy* v. *Hogan*, 378 U.S. 1 (1964).

Sixth Amendment—confrontation of witnesses, *Pointer* v. *Texas*, 380 U.S. 400 (1965); compulsory process to obtain witnesses, *Washington* v. *Texas*, 388 U.S. 14 (1967); counsel, *Gideon* v. *Wainwright*, 372 U.S. 335 (1963); speedy and public trial, *Klopfer* v. *North Carolina*, 386 U.S. 213 (1967); and jury trial (felonies), *Duncan* v. *Louisiana*, 88 S. Ct. Rep. 1444 (May 20, 1968).

Eighth Amendment—cruel and unusual punishment, *Robinson* v. *California*, 370 U.S. 660 (1962).

In 1964, in *Malloy* v. *Hogan*, the U.S. Supreme Court pointed out that, at one time or another, ten justices of that body have supported the view that the Fourteenth Amendment has made applicable to state action all provisions of the first eight amendments to the Constitution of the United States (378 U.S. 1, 4 [1964]).

of the United States affords federal protection against state action only
for the guarantees contained in the original document and those rights
listed in the federal Bill of Rights that the United States Supreme
Court considers basic and essential to a "scheme of ordered liberty."

Although, since the nation was established, a minority has questioned the necessity for including a bill of rights in state constitutions,[11] these documents all contain such an enumeration. The principal reasons for their inclusion are: first, as explained above, not all
traditional rights that the people desire to be protected are safeguarded
under the national Constitution; second, many states wish to include
more detailed guarantees than those stated in the national document,
or additional rights deemed necessary because of local conditions;
third, some constitutional problems growing out of industrialization,
urbanization, and expanding governmental activity can be met more
effectively by the states, which have the primary responsibility for
exercising the general police power to protect persons and property
through the definition and enforcement of criminal law; and, finally,
continuing emphasis on state responsibility to safeguard fundamental
human liberties may aid in revitalizing state government and thus
impede the disturbing trend toward centralization noted by some
writers.[12]

Contents of State Bills of Rights

For purposes of analysis, provisions of state bills of rights may be
classified under the following headings: (1) political theory, (2) substantive personal and property rights, (3) rights of persons accused of
crime, (4) other procedural guarantees, and (5) miscellaneous provisions.[13] These categories are not exclusive; for example, due process
clauses have both substantive and procedural aspects, and by their
terms they relate to both persons and property. Any classification

11. See, for example, No. 84 of *The Federalist* in which Alexander Hamilton, defending the proposed Constitution of the United States against the charge that it contained
no declaration of basic rights, declared that "in strictness the people surrendered
nothing; and as they retain everything they have no need for particular reservations."

12. See Rankin, *State Constitutions: The Bill of Rights*, pp. 4-5. Writing more than
a decade ago, James P. Hart declared: "If the states cannot protect their citizens'
fundamental liberties, or are careless about such protection, then obviously the basic
fundamental vitality of state governments is immeasurably weakened." "The Bill of
Rights: Safeguard of Individual Liberty," *Texas Law Review*, XXXV (Oct., 1957), 924.

13. Generally, this classification follows that used by Professor Robert S. Rankin in
the sources cited above.

therefore reflects the selective and arbitrary judgment of the classifier. The accompanying table groups the major common provisions of the bills of rights in the eleven constitutions that comprise the sample for this analysis into four groups corresponding to the first four headings stated above.

Political Theory

Most state bills of rights contain provisions that affirm basic principles of American constitutionalism. Some of these are vague declarations of fundamental political philosophy that have little functional utility in a list of guarantees generally intended to be enforceable in the courts. Although there is usually general agreement with the principles expressed, it would appear that, if these statements are to be retained in the constitution, their expression would be more appropriate for the preamble.

The accompanying table identifies five common statements of political theory appearing in the bills of rights of eight recent constitutions. Of these, the most common is provision for subordination of the military to the civil power, which is stated in eight documents, including all those now operative in the sample. Seven of the eleven documents expressly state the principle of popular sovereignty in words identical or similar to those of New Jersey (Art. I, Sec. 2): "All political power is inherent in the people." Three documents assert the right of the people to alter their government; four state the purposes for which government is instituted; and five declare, in effect, that all persons have certain inherent rights. Illustrative of statements of inherent rights is the language of the Hawaii Bill of Rights (Art. I, Sec. 2):

All persons are free by nature and are equal in their inherent and inalienable rights. Among these rights are the enjoyment of life, liberty, and the pursuit of happiness, and the acquiring and possessing of property. These rights cannot endure unless the people recognize their corresponding obligations and responsibilities.

Significantly, the proposed constitutions of New York and Maryland omit all general and unenforceable statements of political philosophy from their bills of rights, as does the sixth edition of the *Model State Constitution*.[14] The Maryland document includes in its preamble

14. The National Municipal League has published six editions of the *Model State*

Common Provisions of Bills of Rights (Selected Constitutions, 1947-1968)

Provision	New Jersey (1947)	Puerto Rico (1952)	Alaska (1959)	Hawaii (1959)	Michigan (1964)	Connecticut (1965)	New York (proposed) (1967)	Rhode Island (proposed) (1968)	Maryland (proposed) (1968)	Florida (proposed) (1968)	Model State Constitution (6th ed., 1963)
A. Statements of Political Theory											
Popular sovereignty	x		x	x	x	x		x		x	
Right to alter government	x		x		x	x		x			
Purposes of government	x	x	x		x			x			
Subordination of military to civil power	x		x	x	x	x		x		x	
Inherent or basic rights	x	x	x	x	x	x	x	x	x	x	
B. Substantive Personal and Property Rights											
Religion											
Establishment	x	x	x	x	x	x	x	x	x	x	x
Free exercise	x	x	x	x	x	x	x	x	x	x	x
Freedom of expression											
Speech	x	x	x	x	x	x	x	x	x	x	x
Press	x	x	x	x	x	x	x	x	x	x	x
Petition	x	x	x	x	x	x	x	x	x	x	x
Assembly	x	x	x	x	x	x	x	x	x	x	x
Responsibility for abuse	x							x		x	
Truth as defense											
Due process of law	x	x	x	x	x	x	x	x	x	x	x
Equal protection		x	x	x	x	x	x	x	x	x	x
Antidiscrimination	x	x	x	x	x	x	x	x	x	x	x
Legal equality		x	x	x	x	x	x	x	x	x	x
Bear arms	x		x	x	x		x	x	x	x	
Just compensation (eminent domain)	x	x					x	x	x	x	
Organize	x	x	x				x				
Bargain collectively	x	x	x							x	x
Reserved rights (savings clause)	x	x	x	x	x	x		x	x	x	x
Prohibitions against:											
Slavery and involuntary servitude		x	x	x	x	x	x	x	x	x	
Impairment of contract obligations		x			x		x	x	x	x	
Quartering of soldiers	x		x	x	x	x		x		x	

Provision	New Jersey (1947)	Puerto Rico (1952)	Alaska (1959)	Hawaii (1959)	Michigan (1964)	Connecticut (1965)	New York (proposed) (1967)	Rhode Island (proposed) (1968)	Maryland (proposed) (1968)	Florida (proposed) (1968)	Model State Constitution (6th ed., 1963)
Irrevocable grants of special privileges or immunities	x					x					
Hereditary emoluments	x	x	x	x	x	x					
C. Rights of Accused Persons											
Habeas corpus	x	x	x	x	x	x	x	x	x	x	
Indictment by grand jury	x	x	x	x		x	x	x	x	x	x
Bail	x	x	x	x	x	x	x	x	x	x	x
Speedy and public trial	x	x	x	x	x	x	x	x	x	x	x
Trial by impartial jury	x	x	x	x	x	x	x	x	x	x	x
Counsel	x	x	x	x	x	x	x	x	x	x	x
Information on nature of accusation	x	x	x	x	x	x	x	x	x	x	x
Confrontation of witnesses	x	x	x	x	x	x	x	x	x	x	x
Compulsory process to obtain witnesses	x	x	x	x	x	x	x	x	x	x	x
Change of venue	x	x			x	x	x	x	x	x	x
Prohibition against:											
Unreasonable searches and seizures	x	x	x	x	x	x	x	x	x	x	x
Wiretapping or other electronic surveillance											
Excessive bail	x	x	x	x	x	x	x	x	x	x	x
Excessive fines	x	x	x	x	x	x	x	x	x	x	x
Cruel and unusual punishment	x	x	x	x	x	x	x	x	x	x	x
Self-incrimination	x	x	x	x	x	x	x	x	x	x	x
Double jeopardy	x	x	x	x	x	x	x	x	x	x	x
Bills of attainder			x	x	x	x	x	x	x	x	x
Corruption of blood											
Forfeiture of estate											
Ex post facto laws	x	x	x	x	x		x	x	x	x	
Imprisonment for debt	x	x	x	x	x			x	x	x	
Treason (defined)	x	x	x				x				
D. Other Procedural Guarantees											
Legal remedy—courts open	x		x	x	x	x	x	x	x	x	
Jury trial in civil cases						x	x	x	x		
Unreasonable detention of witnesses (prohibited)					x				x	x	
Fair treatment in investigations	x	x	x	x	x				x	x	

statements of popular sovereignty and the purposes of government. The Maryland Constitutional Convention Commission, which prepared a draft constitution for consideration by the recent Maryland Constitutional Convention, summarized its view on appropriate contents of a bill of rights as follows:

> The Commission is of the opinion that the solemnity of a new constitution would be enhanced by a more concise statement of the rights secured to the people. Moreover, the Commission recommends the omission of unenforceable statement of principle so that the mandatory nature of the guaranteed rights will be unquestioned. In this, the Commission takes as its model the Bill of Rights of the United States Constitution.[15]

This appears to be the view of many writers of new and recently revised state constitutions. The newer declarations contain fewer abstract statements and "constitutional sermons," which were common in the older documents.[16]

Substantive Personal and Property Rights

Religion, expression, and due process. Among the most fundamental guarantees in every state constitution are the substantive rights protecting the individual in his thoughts, expression, and action. These include the basic freedoms of religion, speech, press, assembly, and petition, which generally duplicate the contents of the First Amendment to the Constitution of the United States. These substantive guarantees and the procedural rights of accused persons are the most common protections provided in state constitutions, as the table indicates.

Every recent state constitution guarantees freedom of religion, prohibiting any constraint on its free exercise, and eight documents covered in the table forbid enactment of laws respecting an establishment of religion.[17] Other clauses relating to religion included in some documents prohibit religious tests (New Jersey and Rhode Island),

---

Constitution, the last appearing in 1963. The various editions of the *Model,* the first of which was published in 1921, incorporate the collective judgment of distinguished groups of practitioners and scholars on the proper contents of a state constitution.

15. Maryland, *Report of the Constitutional Convention Commission,* Aug. 25, 1967, p. 98.

16. See Dishman, pp. 47-49.

17. "In the words of Jefferson, the clause against establishment of religion by law was intended to erect a 'wall of separation between church and State.'" *Everson* v. *Board of Education,* 330 U.S. 1, 16 (1947).

public aid for religious purposes (Alaska and Florida), and religious preference (New Jersey, Michigan, and Rhode Island). Typically, however, recent constitutions follow the federal example in focusing attention on the "free exercise of religion" and "establishment" in the religion provision.

All eleven state bills of rights in the sample of recent constitutions guarantee all forms of freedom of expression specified in the First Amendment to the national Constitution with the single exception of the proposed Rhode Island instrument, which omitted explicit reference to freedom of speech. Five documents specify individual responsibility for abuse of freedom of expression, and five specifically provide for truth as defense in libel or defamation actions.

Of broader and more general character among the positive substantive guarantees in state bills of rights are the "due process," "equal protection," "antidiscrimination," and "legal equality" clauses. The table indicates that ten recent documents contain a provision forbidding any person to be deprived of life, liberty, or property without due process of law; eight prohibit denial of the equal protection of the laws; ten constitutions include antidiscrimination provisions, all except three of which also contain "equal protection" guarantees; in addition, three constitutions provide expressly for "legal equality." Due process and equal protection guarantees, like the basic freedoms of the First Amendment, are generally recognized as of fundamental importance, and there is little dissent from their inclusion in state bills of rights. Antidiscrimination and legal equality clauses, however, are relatively new provisions.

Equal Treatment. The controversy over segregation and the 1954 decision of the United States Supreme Court[18] stimulated new interest in the problem of discrimination and led to demands for inclusion of specific "equal treatment" statements in bills of rights.[19] Although protection now exists under the national Constitution, most new state constitutions incorporate a specific "equal treatment" or "antidiscrimination" guarantee in the bill of rights. The proposed Constitution of New York, which was rejected by the voters in 1967, contained the most comprehensive such provision. Article I, Section 3(b) provided:

18. *Brown* v. *Board of Education,* 347 U.S. 483 (1954).
19. W. Brooke Graves, "A New Bill of Rights," *National Municipal Review,* XLVI (May, 1957), 238-244, and "State Constitutional Law: A Twenty-Five Year Summary," *William and Mary Law Review,* VIII (Fall, 1966), 17-21.

No person shall, because of race, color, creed, religion, national origin, sex or physical or mental handicap, be subjected to any discrimination in his civil rights by the state or any subdivision, agency or instrumentality thereof or by any person, corporation or unincorporated association, public or private. The legislature shall provide that no public money shall be given or loaned to or invested with any person or entity, public or private, violating this provision.

This provision would have applied to both public and private entities, and its areas of protection were more extensive than those stated in any counterpart provision of other state instruments. The only additional area of protection specified in other documents is ancestry. More typical of such provisions is the Maryland guarantee against "discrimination by the State because of race, color, religion, or national origin" (Sec. 1.03).

Traditional substantive guarantees. With the exception of recent "equal treatment" guarantees, the rights discussed above are generally regarded as traditional in most state bills of rights. Other positive personal and property rights that may be so classified are the right to bear arms, included in six of the documents of the sample, and the requirement of just compensation for property taken for public use, stated in eight bills of rights covered in the table. Like some other constitutional rights, the eminent domain provision is located elsewhere than in the bill of rights in the Michigan Constitution and the proposed Florida document. Eight of the eleven recent state constitutions contain a "savings clause" providing, in effect, that the enumeration of rights in the constitution shall not be construed to impair, disparage, or deny others retained by the people.

With the exception of the proposed New York document and the *Model State Constitution,* all documents covered in this analysis contain one or more substantive prohibitions, most of which are stated in the Constitution of the United States. Three constitutions included in the sample of recent documents forbid slavery and involuntary servitude; six, the impairment of contract obligations; six, the quartering of soldiers; three prohibit irrevocable grants of special privileges or immunities; and two forbid hereditary emoluments.

Social and economic rights. The rights of labor to organize and to bargain collectively are among the new guarantees in some recently formulated constitutions. These rights appear in four of the documents covered in the table. Excluding the Constitution of the Commonwealth of Puerto Rico, the New York provision is the most comprehensive, and is stated in the context of a general declaration of state policy to support and protect rights of labor. Article I, Section 10(a) provides:

It shall be the policy of the state to foster and promote the general welfare and to establish a firm basis of economic security for the people of the state. Labor of human beings is not a commodity nor an article of commerce and shall never be so considered or construed. The state shall secure the right of employees to organize and to bargain collectively through representatives of their own choosing. No person shall be denied employment or the right to join a labor organization of his choice on the grounds of race, color, creed, or national origin.

The Hawaii and Florida provisions both extend the guarantees to public employees, but the latter expressly forbids them the right to strike. The Florida document is the only one of the eleven constitutions that contains a "right to work" provision; in effect, this forbids closed shop and union shop agreements between labor and management.[20]

These are controversial issues and there is considerable difference of opinion about the propriety of their inclusion in a constitution. Advocates of the rights of organization and collective bargaining declare that there is sufficient general recognition of their fundamental nature to merit specific protection in the basic law; opponents of inclusion believe that these matters are still so much involved in controversy that they had better be left to legislative determination.[21]

Of more dubious suitability for inclusion in a constitutional bill of rights are guarantees of various social rights and services. Some services, well established and generally acknowledged to be proper functions of the state, are believed by some persons to have reached the stage of development to merit express constitutional recognition. Education, health, and welfare are illustrative. Some state constitutions provide for these and similar services, but not usually in the bill of

20. Art. I, Sec. 6. "Right to work" proposals were debated in the Michigan Constitutional Convention, but the issue was so highly controversial that delegates voted to exclude any such provision from the constitution. See Albert L. Sturm, *Constitution-Making in Michigan, 1961-1962* (Ann Arbor, 1963), p. 164.

21. See Graves, "A New Bill of Rights?"; Rankin, *State Constitutions: The Bill of Rights*, p. 13; and Milton Greenberg, "Civil Liberties," in John P. Wheeler, ed., *Salient Issues of Constitutional Revision* (New York, 1961), pp. 18-19.

rights. The Constitution of Puerto Rico and the recently proposed New York document are major exceptions. The Puerto Rican Bill of Rights expressly recognizes the right to a free elementary and secondary education, to obtain work, to a proper standard of living, and to various other stated social services.[22] New ground is broken by the proposed New York Bill of Rights, which would have expressly authorized the legislature to provide a system of workmen's compensation, unemployment and disability insurance, and protection against the loss or inadequacy of income and employment opportunities; in addition, the lawmaking body would have been required to implement provision for the protection and education of the people against "unfair, inequitable or dishonest sales, marketing and financing practices."[23]

Although the welfare state is an established fact in American government, a majority of constitution-makers appear to believe that such services have not yet reached the point, in most states, that they are equated with the traditional guarantees in the American heritage of liberty.[24] These social and economic services are not restraints on government, they are rarely judicially enforceable, and they are generally regarded as matters more appropriate for legislative action.

Rights of Persons Accused of Crime

Among the most basic and traditional of all guarantees in American bills of rights are those particularly applicable to accused persons. Their purpose is to afford protection against arbitrary police action and to insure fair procedure in any official action that may result in loss of liberty or property. Although some of these guarantees have substantive aspects, they are predominantly procedural in character. The importance of procedural rights was well summarized by Mr. Justice Frankfurter in his comment: "The history of American freedom is, in no small measure, the history of procedure."[25]

Criminal procedure. The recent constitutions listed in the table contain both affirmative procedural guarantees and prohibitions, most of which are included in the national Constitution as amended. Affir-

22. See esp. Art. II, Secs. 5, 16, and 20.   23. Art. I, Secs. 10(b) and 12.
24. See the commentary in the *Model State Constitution* (6th ed.; New York, 1963), pp. 25 ff., and Greenberg, pp. 18-19.
25. *Malinski* v. *New York*, 324 U.S. 401, 419 (1945).

mative rights of accused persons stated in these documents include: indictment by grand jury, the right to bail, to a speedy, public trial by an impartial jury, provision for counsel, the right to be informed of the nature of the accusation, provision for confrontation of witnesses against the accused, compulsory process to obtain witnesses, right to a change of venue to secure a fair trial, and other miscellaneous requirements of just procedure. Most of these documents prohibit unreasonable searches and seizures, excessive bail, excessive fines, cruel and unusual punishment, self-incrimination, double jeopardy, bills of attainder, ex post facto laws, and imprisonment for debt. A minority of the eleven documents forbid corruption of blood and forfeiture of estate; four define treason.

Although there is little sentiment for altering most of these procedural rights, many states, including some listed in the table, have modified traditional common law procedures in modernizing their systems for administering justice. Exemplifying the innovations stated in recent constitutional bills of rights are: authorization to use the information,[26] as well as presentment or indictment by grand jury, in formally accusing a person of crime; waiver of jury trial if desired by the accused; and, in jury trial for non-capital offenses, conviction by less than a unanimous vote of the jurors.

All eleven constitutions in the selected sample assert the venerable privilege of the writ of habeas corpus. With the exception of Maryland, which does not authorize suspension under any circumstances, this privilege may usually be suspended when in cases of rebellion or invasion the public safety requires it. Four constitutions vest the suspending authority specifically in the legislative body.[27] This basic right and most other protections to insure fair procedure for persons accused of crime are strongly asserted in all new and revised constitutions. Moreover, the trend of federal court decisions in recent years is toward applying the procedural guarantees of the federal Bill of Rights to the states.[28] Present emphasis on both national and state levels of government obviously is very heavy to extend maximum protection to accused persons. Exemplifying this concern is the applica-

26. A written accusation by a prosecuting officer under oath.
27. Puerto Rico (II, 13), Hawaii (I, 13), Connecticut (I, 12), and the proposed Rhode Island document (I, 9).
28. See the cases cited above in n. 10; see also *Individual Liberties: The Administration of Justice*, prepared by the New York Temporary State Commission on the Constitution, March 16, 1967, pp. 147-148.

tion of the right of counsel to proceedings and stages other than the criminal trial.[29]

Notwithstanding the libertarian emphasis on the rights of the individual who is accused of crime, there is also growing demand for strengthening the hands of law enforcement authorities. Reflected to some extent in the modification of traditional common law procedural guarantees in recent state bills of rights, this demand is likely to become greater in the aftermath of extensive civil disorders during the last few years. In no constitutional provision is the basic problem of finding the optimum equilibrium between human liberties and public order brought in sharper focus than in the searches and seizures provision.

Searches, wiretapping, and privacy. All recent constitutions contain a prohibition against unreasonable searches and seizures, following the standard of the Fourth Amendment to the national Constitution. Six of the eleven documents covered in this analysis, in varying terms, also forbid unreasonable interception of private communications or other invasion of privacy. Puerto Rico prohibits wiretapping; typically, however, the provisions that mention electronic surveillance authorize interception of private communications for reasonable cause. The searches and seizures provision of the proposed Maryland document (Section 1.05) is as follows:

The right of the people to be secure in their persons, houses, papers, and effects against unreasonable searches, seizures, interception of their communications, or other invasion of their privacy, shall not be violated, and no warrants shall issue, but upon probable cause, supported by oath or affirmation, and particularly describing the place to be searched and the persons or things to be seized, or the communications sought to be intercepted.

The proposed New York document and the *Model State Constitution* have similar provisions on the subject. The New York provision would prohibit unreasonable searches and seizures and unreasonable interception of telephone and other communications, except that

29. *Ibid.*, pp. 162-174; *Escobedo* v. *Illinois*, 378 U.S. 478 (1964); *Miranda* v. *Arizona*, 384 U.S. 436 (1966); and *Douglas* v. *California*, 372 U.S. 353 (1963). The President's Commission on Law Enforcement and Administration of Justice, in its 1967 report, declared that legal assistance should be provided "in all legal processes that threaten the respondent with a substantial loss of liberty." *The Challenge of Crime in a Free Society* (Washington, 1967), p. 150.

statutes may permit the interception of such communications upon court orders under specified conditions. Evidence obtained in violation of the provision would be inadmissible in judicial, legislative, and administrative proceedings.[30] The proposed New York searches and seizures and interceptions provision would vest responsibility for supervision of police practices in the judiciary; it would also incorporate the exclusionary rule prohibiting use of evidence unlawfully obtained by the police.[31]

There is much difference of opinion concerning "legalized" wiretapping and electronic surveillance. Those who oppose these methods believe them to be an unjustifiable invasion of privacy; on the other hand, police officers assert that effective law enforcement and protection of life and property sometimes require the use of such methods in coping with criminals. Some people believe that ample protection of individual rights exists in the prohibition against unreasonable searches and seizures; they point also to judicial assertion that police methods offensive to human dignity are covered by the due process clause of the Fourteenth Amendment.[32] New emphasis on improving criminal law enforcement and continuing interest in protecting personal liberty and privacy present a persistent problem, not only to judges and legislators but to constitution-makers as well.

Other Procedural Guarantees

State bills of rights contain fewer provisions relating to civil procedure than to criminal proceedings. Three of the recently drafted bills of rights include a general guarantee that the courts shall be open and a legal remedy available to any person who suffers injury.[33] Nine of the eleven selected documents in this analysis provide for jury trial in civil cases. The Michigan and Florida constitutions forbid unreasonable detention of witnesses, and three documents assert a new right to fair treatment in investigations.

30. Art. I, Sec. 4. See Sec. 1.03 of the *Model*. The Michigan Constitution provides that the section on searches and seizures should not be construed to bar from evidence in any criminal proceeding any narcotic drug, firearm, bomb, explosive or other dangerous weapon seized by a peace officer outside the curtilage of any dwelling house in the state (Art. I, Sec. 11).

31. The exclusionary rule was applied to the states under the due process clause of the Fourteenth Amendment in 1961 in *Mapp* v. *Ohio*, 367 U.S. 643.

32. *Rochin* v. *California*, 342 U.S. 165 (1952).

33. Connecticut (I, 10), Rhode Island (Proposed, I, 5), and Florida (Proposed, I, 21).

Jury trial (civil cases). Only the Puerto Rico and the *Model* documents omit a guarantee of jury trial in civil cases. The Connecticut Constitution and the proposed instruments of Rhode Island and Florida expressly apply the jury trial provision to all types of cases. In most recent constitutions, however, the provision for jury trial authorizes waiver; some such provisions specify minimum dollar amounts required for the guarantee to become mandatory. In the new constitutions, the trend in drafting provisions on jury trial in civil cases is toward greater flexibility—in the amount of money involved, the size of the jury, and the requirement for a verdict. The Alaska provision (Art. I, Sec. 16) exemplifies modification of the common law requirements to meet modern needs:

In civil cases where the amount in controversy exceeds two hundred fifty dollars, the right of trial by a jury of twelve is preserved to the same extent as it existed at common law. The legislature may make provision for a verdict by not less than three-fourths of the jury and, in courts not of record, may provide for a jury of not less than six nor more than twelve.

Fair treatment in investigations. The growing concern for protection of individuals in the course of legislative investigations and administrative procedures is reflected in new provisions in three recently drafted constitutions. The constitutions of Alaska and Michigan apply the new guarantee specifically to legislative and administrative investigations;[34] the proposed Maryland document would have made it applicable to all governmental organs.[35] The power of lawmaking bodies to collect information as a basis for policy-making is inherent in the legislative process, but a strong case exists also for protection against abusive attacks on personal honor, reputation, and private life.

Administrative practices and procedures also may encroach upon the rights of the individual. Although the principle of separation of powers and due process requirements afford protection, a number of states have enacted administrative procedure acts to provide specific safeguards against erosion of fundamental rights.[36] New constitutional

34. Alaska (I, 7) and Michigan (I, 17).
35. The Maryland provision is as follows: "No person shall be denied the right to fair and just treatment in any investigation conducted by the State or by any of their departments or agencies" (Art. I, Sec. 1.04). The Puerto Rican Bill of Rights provides: "Every person has the right to the protection of law against abusive attacks on his honor, reputation and private or family life" (Art. II, Sec. 8).
36. Ferrel Heady, "The New Reform Movement in Regulatory Administration," *Public Administration Review*, XIX (Spring, 1959), 89-100; Rankin, *State Constitutions: The Bill of Rights*, pp. 9-12.

provisions on this subject appear to indicate a trend to give these guarantees a stronger base.

Miscellaneous Rights

Most of the guarantees discussed above appear in at least a number of state bills of rights. No attempt has been made to classify or to include in this analysis those provisions that have few, if any, counterparts in other documents. Some recognition, however, is probably desirable for new guarantees that appear likely to emerge in future revisions.[37]

The *Model State Constitution* forbids political tests for public office, and states the oath or affirmation required of all officeholders (Sec. 1.07). Hawaii expressly precludes disqualification of persons to serve as jurors because of sex (Art. I, Sec. 12). In Puerto Rico, incarceration before trial may not exceed six months (Art. II, Sec. 11), and suspension of civil rights, including the right to vote, ceases upon completion of a term of imprisonment (Art. II, Sec. 12). The Rhode Island Bill of Rights declares that "every man being presumed innocent until he is pronounced guilty by the law, no act of severity which is not necessary to secure an accused person shall be permitted" (Art. I, Sec. 14).

Penal administration in Alaska is required to be "based on the principle of reformation and upon the need for protecting the public" (Art. I, Sec. 12); furthermore, the power of Alaskan "grand juries to investigate and make recommendations concerning the public welfare or safety shall never be suspended" (Art. I, Sec. 8). The proposed Florida document expressly forbids administrative penalties except as provided by law and declares that "no person charged with crime shall be compelled to pay costs before a judgment of conviction has become final" (Art. I. Secs. 18 and 19).

Two new provisions of the 1967 proposed New York Bill of Rights merit the attention of constitution-makers: the first authorizes citizens' suits to restrain unconstitutional acts or expenditures; the second asserts the right to inspect the records of the state, local governments, and public authorities, in the manner provided by law.[38] Finally, the

37. Excluded are those provisions that stem from purely local conditions, such as the "rights of fishery," declared in Art. I, Sec. 17, of the proposed Rhode Island document.
38. Art. I, Secs. 2 and 11, respectively.

proposed Maryland document excepts from the general prohibition
against suspending constitutional provisions the power of the general
assembly to provide for temporary suspension of specific provisions
during an emergency caused by disaster or enemy attack (Sec. 1.17).

Trends and Issues

From the preceding survey of major common provisions of state
bills of rights in recent American constitutions, some trends are clearly
discernible, especially if the newer documents are compared with the
instruments they were designed to replace. Excepting the *Model State
Constitution*, few, if any, of the new constitutions formulated to serve
as operating basic instruments of government incorporate all of the
emerging features of modern constitution-making. Tradition and difficulty in altering established modes of conduct notwithstanding, the
new bills of rights indicate substantial improvements over their earlier
counterparts.

They are shorter, and their contents more clearly, precisely, and
accurately stated. They contain far less extraneous matter, such as
abstract statements of general political theory that are unenforceable
and have no proper place in a list of rights intended to be mandatory.
Collection of guarantees formerly scattered throughout other parts of
the constitution and more logical organization are additional features
of most new bills of rights. The drafting of these documents, with
some exceptions, is definitely superior to that of earlier declarations of
rights.

Besides editorial improvements, the bills of rights in new and revised constitutions show some tendency to omit guarantees that no
longer have much meaning in modern American life. They contain
fewer traditional prohibitions, such as those concerning quartering of
soldiers in private residences in peacetime, corruption of blood, forfeiture of estate, titles of nobility, and hereditary emoluments. Most
recently drafted declarations of rights repeat the prohibitions of the
Constitution of the United States against bills of attainder, ex post
facto laws, and impairment of contractual obligations, but a few avoid
this duplication. Practically all recent declarations incorporate the
basic guarantees of the Fourteenth Amendment, which apply to the
states, relate to both substantive and procedural matters, and are con-

sidered to be of such fundamental importance as to merit duplication in state constitutions.

The preceding content analysis has identified the major substantive changes in state bills of rights. They include some omissions, updating of traditional provisions, and addition of new guarantees. These changes evidence not only a desire for greater clarity and precision of statement in the fundamental law, but also an effort by constitution-makers to express both new and traditional rights in flexible terms that permit adaptation to rapidly changing conditions and needs. Flexibility is a hallmark of excellence in a constitution; rigidity of expression necessitates frequent amendments which soon clutter up the document.

The issues of constitution-making emerge from the pressures and needs of the environment in which a constitution operates. This is exemplified in the recent and current emphasis on protection of the rights of minorities and the disadvantaged, which is reflected in anti-discrimination provisions and refinement of procedural guarantees to accused persons. National civil rights legislation during the period of this analysis undoubtedly will have an impact on future development of individual rights protected by state constitutions.[39] The continuing problem of balancing human liberties against requirements for maintaining public order will not diminish. Constitution-makers, for example, will have to evaluate the arguments for and against the addition to the basic law of a "right of privacy."[40] The growing complexity of the social order will necessitate re-evaluation and extension of traditional guarantees. For example, what additional modifications are needed to adapt the grand jury, a common law institution, to modern requirements? Does the present provision for bail continue to serve its originally intended purpose? Would it be desirable to introduce a constitutional right to pre-trial release in the absence of a showing that an accused person presents a substantial risk that he will not

39. This legislation includes the Civil Rights Acts of 1957 (P.L. 85-315), 1960 (P.L. 86-449), and 1964 (P.L. 88-352), the Voting Rights Act of 1965 (P.L. 89-110), and the Civil Rights Act of 1968 (H.R. 2516).

40. See Alan F. Westin, "Science, Privacy, and Freedom: Issues and Proposals for the 1970's," *Columbia Law Review*, LXVI, Part I ("The Current Impact of Surveillance on Privacy") in No. 6 (June, 1966), 1003-1050; and Part II ("Balancing the Conflicting Demands of Privacy, Disclosure, and Surveillance") in No. 7 (Nov., 1966), 1205-1253; and Robert B. McKay, "The Right of Privacy: Emanations and Intimations," *Michigan Law Review*, XLIV No. 2 (Dec., 1965), 259-282.

appear on the return date?[41] Should a constitution prescribe standards and purposes of criminal punishment?[42] What emerging rights have achieved sufficient public acceptance and recognition to merit inclusion in a constitution? These questions exemplify the types of issues, both procedural and substantive, that will confront state constitution-makers of the future.

41. See New York Temporary State Commission on the Constitutional Convention, p. 33; also the President's Commission on Law Enforcement and Administration of Justice, p. 131.

42. Expressing his views and those of three other Supreme Court justices, Chief Justice Warren, in 1958, wrote: "This Court has had little occasion to give precise content to the Eighth Amendment [cruel and unusual punishment], and, in an enlightened democracy such as ours, this is not surprising. . . . The Amendment must draw its meaning from the evolving standards of decency that mark the progress of a maturing society" (*Trop* v. *Dulles*, 356 U.S. 86, 101 [1958]).

Fred R. Dallmayr / Equality and Social Change*

Equality has become a fighting word again. After decades of relative neglect, the issue of equal treatment has moved again into the limelight of contemporary social reality and social thought. To some, the issue is a source of hope and inspiration, to others it is a cause of dismay; few remain unaffected. In the United States, the civil rights movement has reasserted human equality and the need for mutual interracial respect in a great variety of areas, including education, transportation, and employment. At the same time, decisions of American federal courts have stipulated an egalitarian standard—one man, one vote—as guidepost for political representation and the apportionment of legislative bodies. On the international level observers are agreed that one of the chief problems faced by developing nations resides in the advancement of emancipation and self-determination against the background of social fragmentation and inequality.

Despite its impact and political relevance, however, the concept of equality is a somewhat elusive, if not alien ingredient in contemporary social and political research. As it seems, there are certain practical connotations in the term which militate against its full absorption into the framework and vocabulary of scientific analysis. To be sure, equality receives its fair share of scholarly homage and tribute; however, within the prevailing framework of analysis, the term tends to be either redundant or extraneous. There is something peculiar about a scholarly framework or perspective which renders a key issue of social reality either irrelevant or enigmatic.

Elements of a Theory

Contemporary social and political science exhibits a multitude of focal concerns and interests; units of analysis and investigation range from the individual over groups to the social and political system. However, despite the seeming variety of focal preferences, there is a dominant outlook or perspective which, to a large extent, pervades

* This essay is part of a larger projected study of the role of equality in the modernization of Western societies.

and links current research: briefly, this perspective is marked by its fervor for abstraction and by its reliance on social stability and integration. These features can be detected in several socio-psychological and group approaches; they are particularly evident in structural-functional and systems analysis. While it can reasonably be claimed that generalization is endemic to scientific procedure and a useful instrument of investigation, abstraction in contemporary approaches appears frequently as an end in itself, a haven not to be disturbed by the impurities of social experience. The term "system" itself is a high-level abstraction with tenuous foundation in observable social reality. Pursued as a single-minded endeavor, the focal concern of this approach, with its claim of explaining social phenomena in terms of "systemic" qualities, easily turns into a quixotic attempt to illuminate the knowable by the unknown, social experience by its shadow. The focus on system also has implications for the problem of social change. Clearly, on the level of "system" as such nothing very significant can occur. Whatever process or change takes place is either presupposed by definition or, more commonly, happens *to* the system through the operation or intervention of an enigmatic *deus ex machina*. Quite apart from these and other defects, the sketched approach is not very hospitable to the issue of equality; in fact, the concept appears irrelevant in a dual sense. As a corollary of the quest for abstraction, equality tends to be reduced to mathematical equation or tautology; in this sense, of course, equality could never have been a matter of social dispute. On the other hand, empirical reality can easily be shown to be a realm of diversity and differentiation. Thus, whatever social impact equality possesses is bound to dissipate again into an extraneous or enigmatic force.

Since the following pages intend to focus on equality and its implications for social change, it seemed advisable to select a theoretical framework more hospitable to this undertaking. The perspective chosen for present purposes may be described as a conflict model of society based upon human action or practice. The selection of this framework does not involve a complete suppression of prevailing categories; it is neither necessary nor expedient, for instance, to neglect entirely the terminology or findings of systems analysis. The present paper simply aims to give greater weight or emphasis to conflict and human action than is customary in much of contemporary social (and especially political) science. To be sure, the perspective adopted here is by no means without precedent or support. The action framework, after all, is prominently associated with the writings of Max Weber and his followers. Nevertheless, in the hands of some of its recent adherents, the action framework itself has been transformed into a relatively abstract and static scheme—a scheme easily amalgamated with structural-functional and systems analysis.[1] In contrast to this formal scheme, the present essay tries to grasp human action as a concrete occurrence or event in social and political reality. Viewed in this manner, the action focus is bound to inject a dynamic quality into social research, human action being embedded in a time dimension ranging from past preconditions to future projections. In addition, the action focus is likely to accord greater weight to human purpose and responsibility than is customary in prevailing models. To be sure, contemporary social science does not as a rule ignore human aspirations and preferences; the relevance of such factors, however, tends to be reduced by their segregation in an internal "cultural" domain whose existence is presupposed and whose genesis remains again largely obscure.

The focus on human action has as a major corollary the emphasis on counteraction. While there are occasions and incentives for human collaboration, there are always abundant motives for conflict and disagreement. The reason for this state of affairs is not hard to detect. "To act" is a summary or shorthand expression which tends to conceal the objectives as well as the empirical constraints of human endeavor. Action commonly involves an element of human choice; such choice, however, is rarely between untarnished good and unmitigated evil, but has frequently to be effected between complex alternatives in special historical and social circumstances. In this realm of ambiguity observers and participants are prone to differ on the relevance of empirical factors and on the means most suitable to the accomplishment of goals under given conditions. More frequently still, disagreement extends from empirical constraints and procedures to final goals and objectives. Even where widespread agreement on goals and objectives can be found, social harmony and tranquillity does not necessarily ensue. Some common values, it is true, are in abundant supply and

1. Compare Talcott Parsons, *The Structure of Social Action* (New York, 1937), and *The Social System* (Glencoe, Ill., 1951). For a criticism of abstract formalism, see Ralf Dahrendorf, "Out of Utopia," *American Journal of Sociology*, LXIV (1958), 115-127.

thus do not normally constitute a source of controversy. In the case of other goods, however, scarcity provides a powerful incentive for social conflict. The range of scarce values has not always been uniform; in different historical periods, land, capital, skills, and prestige have served as basic yardsticks of social ambition and status. In addition, political control and the ability to impose normative sanctions have at all times been among the most vigorously contested scarce commodities. Quite apart from any hypothetical drive for power, political control tends to be a crucial factor for human behavior because its exercise may facilitate or obstruct moral self-determination and the implementation of choices in a variety of fields. Scarcity implies that the desired goods cannot be broadly allocated or universally shared by all at the same time. Even where efforts at equitable distribution are made, universal acceptance of the effected arrangement cannot be taken for granted. As Wilbert Moore observes, "the equity of any system of differential allocation of scarce values is subject to challenge as to both principles and results."[2] Equality and social conflict are thus intimately linked.

The emphasis on human action and conflict brings into view the chief sources of social and political change. This should not be taken to mean, however, that the transformation of social and political structures is a result of arbitrary or random impulses. Little would be gained, in fact, by the adoption of the conflict model if the explanation of social change were again dependent on chance factors or enigmatic forces. In reality, human action and counteraction occur within a concrete social and historical context; within this context available choices and social interests are not infinitely variable, nor are all desired goods infinitely divisible. From the distribution of desired (especially scarce) values and from the social constraints of human choice emerge configurations of groups which can be viewed as structural elements of society; the chief point of conflict theory is that such structural elements may contribute to the transformation and supersession of social and political systems. In the words of Ralf Dahrendorf, "the intent of a sociological theory of conflict is to overcome the predominantly arbitrary nature of unexplained historical events by deriving these events from elements of their social struc-

2. Wilbert E. Moore, "A Reconsideration of Theories of Social Change," *American Sociological Review*, XXV (1960), 815. See also his *Social Change* (Englewood Cliffs, N.J., 1963), pp. 83-84.

tures."[3] Among the sources of social conflict Dahrendorf emphasizes primarily political factors; as a result, the chief structural elements in his theory are social groups determined by their respective relationship to political control. As he points out, the minimum conditions of conflict theory are specified once the carriers of "positive and negative dominance roles" are seen as forming two quasi-groups with opposite latent interests. The bearers of these roles organize themselves into groups with manifest interests and proceed to battle with each other over the preservation or change of the status quo. "The conflict among interest groups in the sense of this model," Dahrendorf concludes, "leads to changes in the structure of their social relations, through changes in the dominance relations."

Conflict theory concentrates on differences of social interests and positions; this does not imply, however, that society cannot exhibit a certain degree of harmony or integration. The chief issue for social science is not so much integration itself, but the manner in which social balance is achieved and maintained: whether through a mechanism of nature or through human effort and design.[4] The assumption of a natural tendency toward equilibrium or homeostasis constitutes one of the most powerful predilections in contemporary social science; according to Harold Laski, the notion of a harmony of interests functions as "an inarticulate major premise" in much of Western social thought. The prevalence of this predilection is sometimes contested by social scientists; but protestations to this effect are frequently mere verbal exercises which are belied by the adopted theoretical framework.[5] The chief defect of the equilibrium model is its tendency to obfuscate major aspects of social reality and social change, including the contest for equality. As Gunnar Myrdal observes, the acceptance of the model tends "to move our practical and political conclusions in the direction of the idea that everything will come out to the satisfaction of all if the natural forces of the market are left

3. Ralf Dahrendorf, "Toward a Theory of Social Conflict," in A. Etzioni and E. Etzioni, eds., Social Change (New York and London, 1964), p. 100.

4. Maurice Duverger oversimplifies matters somewhat when he distinguishes between the two basic perspectives of conflict and integration: "According to one, politics is conflict, a struggle in which power allows those who possess it to ensure their hold on society and to profit by it. According to the other view, politics is an effort to bring about the rule of order and justice, in which power guarantees the general interest and the common good against the pressures of private interests." The Idea of Politics (Indianapolis, 1966), p. xii.

5. On this point, see Dahrendorf, "Toward a Theory of Social Conflict," p. 103, n. 7.

their free play—which, of course, also implies that it is more permissible to forget about the equality postulate." Conflict theory, in an effort to grasp the dynamic factors in social reality, starts from a radically different premise: the assumption that, at least in the realm of human relations, nature left to its own devices is prone to produce disequilibrium and disharmony. The assumption implies, in Myrdal's words, that there is no natural tendency "toward automatic self-stabilization in the social system. The system is by itself not moving toward any sort of balance between forces but is constantly on the move away from such a situation. In the normal case a change does not call forth countervailing changes but, instead, supporting changes, which move the system in the same direction as the first change but much further."[6]

Nature and Civilization

The assumption of equilibrating or homeostatic tendencies in society is derived through analogy from processes in physical nature. The underlying conception is that, in the absence of human interference, natural processes entail stability and order; the same benign plan is said to operate in human affairs. In the short run, to be sure, nature may be a stern taskmaster imposing severe deprivations on individuals or groups; in the long run, however, these deprivations are seen as part of a benevolent design leading society to ever-higher levels of harmony and happiness. In contrast to this pastoral image, the perspective presented here implies a certain rupture between nature and man, a certain alienation of human purpose from natural processes. Nature, in this view, may have its own designs, but they are at best indifferent to human welfare. Civilization is not a simple gift but a precarious acquisition wrested from an unco-operative, if not jealous, nature. From the viewpoint of man, nature appears more frequently malevolent than benign; in the realm of social relations in particular, things left to themselves (or to their natural proclivities) are prone to engender disharmony and chaos rather than universal happiness.

6. Gunnar Myrdal, *Rich Lands and Poor* (New York, 1957), pp. 13, 134. Myrdal also argues that the notion of stable equilibrium "has run through our whole economic and social speculation during the past two hundred years and has until this day determined the main concepts of all the social sciences, and not only economics" (p. 144). Cybernetic theory tries to account for disequilibrium chiefly through the concept of "positive feedback"; but apart from leaving the sources of the process largely unexplained, the feedback mechanism tends to be limited to abnormal events such as panics, runaway inflations, and the like.

Man's contest with nature is not a temporary interlude, but a constant task; against this background, much of social development can be viewed as a story of man's slow emancipation from natural bonds. Theories of social change frequently reflect this elementary contest, although they may be couched in more complex language or focus on selected aspects of development.[7] In pre-modern (or pre-industrial) society, for instance, it is commonly assumed that social relations were still very intimately linked with the processes and constraints of nature. Kinship and family bonds prevailed, while human activity centered on hunting and gathering or on the cultivation of the soil. The social fabric at this stage was still relatively uncomplicated or "homogeneous"; at the same time, chiefly due to the rudimentary form of division of labor, social organization retained a relatively "incoherent" character. The political, economic, and religious aspects of society were blended and mixed, with the result that social structures and institutions remained undifferentiated and functionally "diffuse." An important corollary of this situation was that natural conditions and distinctions were directly translated into legal forms, a process which led to the proliferation of parochial or "particularistic" norms and frequently to the growth of a social hierarchy of orders and estates, each with distinct (typically hereditary) privileges. The prevalence of these conditions made it virtually impossible to conceive the social fabric as a product of human design or interaction.

The beginning of the modern age saw far-flung explorations and the accumulation of precious metals under mercantilist auspices. Through these policies and the accumulation of wealth in private hands, the foundations were laid for a modern market economy and for modern advances in industry and technology. The emergence of the market economy, coupled with industrialization, heralded the decline of the influence of natural conditions and the growing mastery of man over nature. One effect of this change was the obliteration of internal legal barriers in society, especially of the hierarchical arrange-

7. According to Herbert Spencer, the basic movement of society is from "incoherent homogeneity" to "coherent heterogeneity." Talcott Parsons' theory of "pattern variables" suggests that society moves from a stage characterized primarily by particularism (local or ethnic customs), ascription (assigned status), diffuseness (of social roles and functions), and affectivity to a stage marked by universalism, achievement, specificity, and affective neutrality. For some of these concepts and theories and for Parsons' later "differentiation model" see Parsons, *The Social System*, p. 67; Etzioni and Etzioni, eds., pp. 10-14, 83-97.

ment of estates and hereditary privileges. The removal of "ascribed" status positions encouraged a freer competition among individuals for wealth, social prestige, and power, a competition guided by a spreading "achievement" motivation. With competition and a growing division of labor, the social fabric tended to become more diversified and "heterogeneous." To some extent, this development was manifested in the differentiation (for limited purposes) of the economic, political, and religious aspects of society and in the increased functional "specificity" of social structures and institutions. At the same time, the decline of natural barriers and the growth of economic enterprise had the result that, for the first time, social relations could be conceived, at least potentially, as the result of human interaction and purpose.

The sketched story of human emancipation, however, should not be viewed as a simple linear development; nor can progress in this direction be taken for granted. The obstacles to civilization are like the rock of Sisyphus, always ready to crush and undo the fruits of man's labor. At every step, nature seems bent on reclaiming the territory wrested from her by human effort. Thus it happens that with the passage of time, human institutions and practices tend to congeal into conventional objects and constraints, through a process which may be described as the "naturalization" or "reification" of human design. This phenomenon is of special relevance to the problem of equality. Social modernization and development have been described as a movement toward greater heterogeneity and specificity; the story of civilization, in this sense, is the story of a growing social diversity and differentiation. At the same time, however, social development throughout many centuries has involved the progressive emancipation of man from nature (and from all bonds claimed to be natural). In pre-modern times, only a limited number of individuals could be considered emancipated or free in this sense; in successive centuries, as a result of major social and political struggles, emancipation spread to other social segments or groups. This progress of emancipation, however, amounts to an expansion of equality among the members of society.[8] Civilization thus involves an apparent paradox: its progress

8. For the argument that social development involves a movement toward both differentiation and equality, see Lucian W. Pye, *Aspects of Political Development* (Boston and Toronto, 1966), pp. 45-48 ("development syndrome"; a third factor listed is capacity); James S. Coleman, ed., *Education and Political Development* (Princeton,

is intimately linked with increasing diversification and differentiation (a differentiation which, at every step, tends to congeal into harsh inequality due to the process of "naturalization"); at the same time, civilization means a struggle for emancipation and equality. How can this dilemma be resolved?

The Puzzle of Equality

The paradox of civilization revolves largely around the postulate of equality; that this notion contains a riddle is undeniable. On the one hand, equality may refer in a strictly logical sense to a mathematical equation, in which case the concept tends to merge with identity or tautology. On this level, however, it becomes difficult if not impossible to envisage different empirical individuals between whom equality is supposed to obtain; the entire empirical universe tends to disappear behind a static, transcendental sameness. On the other hand, equality involves a relationship of comparability between different empirical individuals. Attention to individuality, however, is bound to reveal subtle differences in almost every empirical detail; to this extent, equality as a basis of comparison tends to submerge in a flood of empirical diversity. Equality thus seems to involve both more and less than identity or diversity; in effect, a dialectical tension seems to operate between the aspects or ingredients of the concept. The existence of this tension is by no means a novel or even modern discovery. At least since classical antiquity discussions of equality have centered on the complexity and heterogeneous ingredients of the concept. Aristotle established an important precedent in this respect by distinguishing between different types or forms of equality: especially between strict or "arithmetic" equality (involving the principle of mathematical equation) and proportional or "geometrical" equality (involving the distribution of values in accordance with unequal merit or achievement).

Contemporary philosophical literature is by no means unfamiliar with the puzzle of equality; most writers who discuss the concept are quick to note its diverse shades and connotations. Bernard Williams, for instance, speaks with some amazement of the "spectacle of the

---

1965), p. 15. Compare also Lloyd Fallers, "Equality, Modernity, and Democracy in the New States," in Clifford Geertz, ed., *Old Societies and New States* (New York, 1963), pp. 158-219.

various elements of the idea of equality pulling in . . . different directions." As he points out, the concept seems to be torn between the
"extremes of absurdity and of triviality," between the extreme of
identical treatment of all persons in all respects and the alternative of
similar treatment only in similar circumstances (where "circumstances"
might conceivably include every empirical difference among individuals).[9] Williams is not alone in this assessment; others have noted
the same tension and have used different terms to label the basic ingredients of the riddle. Thus, Richard Wollheim distinguishes between "quantitative" and "proportional" equality, while William
Frankena elaborates on the "egalitarian" and the "meritarian" (or
distributive) aspects of the concept. In an essay directed against equality understood as a levelling device, another writer juxtaposes "equality
of respect" (involving the principle of universal humanity) to "formal
equality" (involving the principle of universality of rules).[10] It would
not be difficult, though exceedingly tedious, to expand this list of
terms used in discussions of equality in contemporary literature.

Given the disparate ingredients of the riddle, the question arises
how its pieces can be fitted together or correlated. Again, the problem
of this relationship is no recent discovery. Jean Bodin displayed awareness of the problem when, after discussing the principles of strict and
distributive equality, he added a third principle, the idea of "harmonic
justice," as a unifying link between the two elements.[11] In contemporary literature the problem is by no means ignored, although suggested
solutions tend to be somewhat abstract or elusive. Bernard Williams
shows his preference for a conciliatory settlement when he writes that
"we should not throw one set of claims out of the window; but should
rather seek, in each situation, the best way of eating and having as
much cake as possible." Unfortunately, he does not disclose how this
feat is to be accomplished. Isaiah Berlin, in an effort at conceptual
mediation, suggests that the modern idea of justice requires the equal

9. Bernard Williams, "The Idea of Equality," in P. Laslett and W. G. Runciman,
eds., *Philosophy, Politics and Society* (2nd Series; Oxford, 1962), pp. 111, 130.

10. See Richard Wollheim, "Equality and Equal Rights," in Frederick A. Olafson, ed.,
Justice and Social Policy (Englewood Cliffs, N.J., 1961), p. 113; William K. Frankena,
"The Concept of Social Justice," in Richard B. Brandt, ed., *Social Justice* (Englewood
Cliffs, N.J., 1962), p. 12; J. R. Lucas, "Against Equality," *Philosophy*, XL (1965), 296-307.
In a similar vein R. W. Baldwin presents "equality" and (distributive) "equity" as the
two main principles of justice; *Social Justice* (Oxford, 1966). Compare also my "Func-
tionalism, Justice, and Equality," *Ethics*, LXXVIII (1967), 1-16.

11. Jean Bodin, *Six Books on the Commonwealth* (1576), trans. M. J. Tooley (Oxford,
n.d.), Book VI, chap. vi, p. 204.

treatment of all individuals unless there are good reasons for depart-
ing from this practice; but this seems to be more a way of stating
than of resolving the problem. The same could probably be said
about other recent formulations. Frankena advances the proposition
that "justice is treating persons equally, except as unequal treatment
is required by just-making considerations . . . of substantial weight in
the circumstances"; according to Wollheim, the principle of equality
condemns all special rights which are not consequential upon general
rights.[12] No doubt, there is considerable merit in these and similar
formulations as guides to conceptual orientation; the drawback lies in
their tendency to obfuscate the reality of the equality-diversity dilemma. The issue is not only how the puzzle of equality can be mentally
dissolved, but how the contest of disparate elements can be grasped
and overcome in social reality.

Equality and Social Dynamics

On a merely conceptual level, the equality riddle almost invites
tautological subterfuge. Moreover, as has previously been observed,
the problem itself does not properly come into view in an abstract and
static perspective: if the focus is centered on strict equality, distinct
individual objects tend to disappear; if attention is shifted to these
objects, comparability begins to vanish. In juxtaposition, the elements
of the puzzle are more likely to cancel each other than to produce a
synthesis. As it seems, equality as a problem of social reality emerges
only in a dynamic context, in the dimension of time. This dimension
may be seen as the missing link of the riddle. Equality, thus, appears
intimately tied to development and social change. Social development,
however, implies the process of diversification and heterogeneity; at
the same time, it is only in this context that equality can meaningfully
assert itself as a concrete postulate. From this perspective the dilemma
of equality and of civilization might be formulated in these terms:
growing diversification constitutes an advance in civilization only to

12. Williams, p. 131; Isaiah Berlin, "Equality as an Ideal," in Olafson, ed., p. 129;
Frankena, p. 10; Wollheim, p. 118. According to John Rawls, justice conceived as fairness or fair practice involves two basic principles: first, that each person participating
in the practice has an equal right to the most extensive liberty compatible with a like
liberty for all; and second, that inequalities are arbitrary unless it is reasonable to
expect that they will work out for everyone's advantage. See "Justice as Fairness," in
Olafson, ed., p. 81.

the extent that it is accompanied or paralleled by an expansion of emancipation and moral self-determination, by a growing respect for the principle of "universal humanity" among wider segments of society or mankind.

The interrelation between empirical diversity and self-determination can be illustrated by reference to individual experience (although, of course, no claim is made as to a complete correspondence between individual and social development). From his earliest life, the individual finds himself enmeshed in a great diversity of empirical factors, many of which are not matters of his choice. He is born at a certain time and place, from parents with a certain social status and with certain national or ethnic features. His physical attributes make him tall or short, corpulent or slender, robust or frail. He grows up in a certain environment, receives different forms of education and acquires certain habits and talents; subsequently he takes an occupation in accordance with his capacities and inclinations. We may assume for purposes of argument that initially or up to a certain point, these diverse factors combine into a meaningful or tolerable fabric, permitting the individual to conduct his life as a unique and purposive agent. With time (and progressing "naturalization"), however, many of these factors may congeal into hard limitations, into an inert mass of random "facticity." The diversity which previously was his nurture and shelter, may now turn into his prison. At this point man is faced with the alternative of becoming a passive object of his past or of recovering his quality as responsible agent. In the terminology of Jean-Paul Sartre, man can be defined as "a flight out of the present into the future," a flight effected through active design and projection in the dimension of time. The first step on this road is an act of negation of positive or random facticity. Man gains a distance from the surrounding world and from himself as part of this world; by transcending his past and his present, he turns into pure and abstract consciousness. At this level, however, man loses his distinct individuality; he becomes equal to all other men in a formal, mathematical identity. In order to regain his individuality, he must project himself into the future, by inserting his choice and design into the web of concrete human relations. In this manner, human practice can be seen as an act of surpassing a given condition in the direction of a new purposive synthesis of concrete experience.[13]

Human experience, however, does not take place in isolation; it regularly occurs in a social context. In examining the significance of equality in the process of social development, one may start from a hypothetical (and highly untypical) situation: the situation of a society whose elements are more or less balanced or equitably arranged. Even under favorable conditions, this harmonious situation is unlikely to persist in reality for very long. Inadequate training and individual dispositions are prone to introduce fluctuations in established structural patterns; the hazards of recruitment to vacant positions may add further dislocations. More important, tensions or strains are apt to result from the prolonged imposition of normative patterns and from the differential allocation of scarce values, including the unequal distribution of rewards for social positions. New discoveries and needs may emerge in society and with these changes an emphasis on new types of scarce resources and on new elite structures. In addition, change-producing tensions may derive from the proliferation and multiplication of existing inequalities or, in Melvin Tumin's phrase, from "the tendency for any inequality to increase over time and to diffuse to other situations, unless otherwise restrained."[14] Due to these and other factors, the social rank order which previously may have been relatively balanced degenerates progressively into a random arrangement of factual super- and subordination. With this development, however, the legitimacy of the normative order declines and society is embarked on the course of social conflict.

In a situation of tension and conflict, different positions in society are prone to entail different practical theories or belief patterns. Privileged elite groups may wish to justify their position through a variety of arguments—arguments which sometimes include an appeal to a distributive version of equality. In this version the established

13. For some of the ideas and terminology used above see Jean-Paul Sartre, *Being and Nothingness*, trans. H. E. Barnes (New York, 1956); *Critique de la raison dialectique, précédé de Question de méthode*, Vol. I (Paris, 1960); *The Transcendence of the Ego*, trans. F. Williams and R. Kirkpatrick (New York, 1957); and "Materialism and Revolution," in W. Barrett and H. D. Aiken, *Philosophy in the Twentieth Century*, II (New York, 1962), 387-429. Compare also Herbert Spiegelberg, "Equality in Existentialism," in J. Roland Pennock and John W. Chapman, eds., *Equality* (Nomos IX; New York, 1967), pp. 193-213.

14. Melvin M. Tumin, "On Inequality," *American Sociological Review*, XXVIII (1963), 24-25; see also his *Social Stratification: The Forms and Functions of Inequality* (Englewood Cliffs, N.J., 1967).

rank order is defended as corresponding to different inherent "virtues" or qualities of social layers and groups; equality, it is asserted, requires at best the equal treatment of peers, but "nature" has not established such equality among all men. In a more forthright and unadorned formulation it may be claimed that the privileged status of dominant groups is necessarily equitable because nature, if unobstructed, entitles the strong and "fit" individuals to prevail over others. While designed to appeal to the entire society, however, such justifications will regularly be acceptable only to privileged groups and their allies. In reaction against theories of natural selection and superiority, underprivileged groups will tend to elaborate their own goals and belief patterns. In a context of moderate conflict, the demands of such groups may simply aim at a share in available rights and privileges, at a more complete "integration" within the existing normative structure. The implementation of this goal frequently involves attempts to secure equal treatment to different social layers in certain "essential" respects or key domains, such as education, voting, or employment. At a more advanced stage of social disintegration, however, underprivileged groups may be dissatisfied with this solution and may drift into a more or less complete alienation from society, into a state of withdrawal or "retreatism."[15] At this stage, their value patterns tend to take the form of negative beliefs, expressing a radical rejection of all dominant structures and practices. The rejection regularly includes the social rank order and most forms of differential treatment; but insistence on uniformity or identity of treatment is likely to render this perspective somewhat abstract and utopian. In order to transform social reality, alienated groups have to project their own purpose into the concrete fabric of social conflict and pursue a policy of active reorganization—that is, a policy aiming at the restructuring of social relations in accordance with the equal humanity of all members or at least larger segments of society.

At this point, a few additional comments should perhaps be added on "nature" and "natural"—terms which, throughout history, have figured prominently in discussions of equality. In the process of social change, "nature" assumes a bewildering variety of shades and connota-

15. On withdrawal and retreatism see Robert K. Merton, *Social Theory and Social Structure* (rev. ed.; Glencoe, Ill., 1957), pp. 153 ff. and 187 ff.; Everett E. Hagen, *On the Theory of Social Change* (Homewood, Ill., 1962), pp. 185-236. Compare also Sartre's use of the term "disengagement" in "Materialism and Revolution," p. 426.

tions. One way of seeking a path through this wilderness is to explore the interaction between nature and its counterterm, man. At a relatively primitive stage, man was still fully embraced or engulfed by the realm of nature; human life and the physical environment were still inseparable. It was the slow development of civilization which introduced tension and conflict into this intimate relationship. The linkage was ruptured once man succeeded in developing tools and methods to perfect his mastery over nature, thereby demoting the latter term to a synonym for the physical environment.[16] As previously observed, however, the development of civilization is not a linear progress; at every point, nature tries to reclaim the territory wrested from her by man. An integral part of social development is diversification and growing heterogeneity; as a result, civilization entails tension and conflict not only between man and nature, but also between man and man. The process of "naturalization" signifies that social diversity tends to congeal into harsh inequality; the same process also gives rise to social theories and justifications formulated in terms of physical criteria. There are several ways in which the terms "nature" and "natural" can be invoked at this point. It may be asserted that established social rank orders are justified because they reflect different human "natures," each endowed with different virtues and capacities. In this view, empirical variety is immediately linked with moral values and normative standards. According to a less idealistic version of this view, empirical inequalities are claimed to be "natural" simply because nature, left to its own devices, encourages the stronger and abler individuals to prevail over others. In this argument—where the "fittest" appears as the best and might seems to make right—the term "nature" designates a principle or standard which is supposed to govern the natural universe.[17]

16. As Lynn White, Jr., comments on the invention of the heavy plow in the Middle Ages: "No more fundamental change in the idea of man's relation to the soil can be imagined: once man had been part of nature; now he became her exploiter. . . . Man and nature are now two things, and man is master." *Medieval Technology and Social Change* (Oxford, 1962), p. 57.

17. Some of the implications of this argument are stated by Simon Greenberg: "Hence when governments permitted 'nature' to take its own course and interfered as little as possible with the activities of their citizens, it was inevitable that new social inequalities should at once develop which were in many ways as evil as those they had previously removed. . . . Nature when left to its own devices is not concerned with equality or any other human value." See "Comment," in Lyman Bryson, ed., *Aspects of Human Equality*, 15th Symposium of the Conference on Science, Philosophy and Religion (New York, 1956), p. 108.

The "fitness" argument and similar physical analogies can be challenged through several counterarguments; for different purposes, these arguments may in turn resort to the terms "nature" and "natural." Thus, the proposition may be advanced that existing inequalities are artificial, man-made or socially conditioned devices, while nature favors equality. The proposition requires brief elaboration. "Nature" in this case tends to refer to certain basic features which all men share in common: they all are born and die, are able to kill and be killed, and require vital nourishment to live. These and similar features belong to all men as part of the human species, and can be invoked as weapons against arbitrary social distinctions.[18] By appealing to the "species" of man, of course, the argument easily shifts to a somewhat abstract, conceptual level; in rationalistic language, equality may be claimed to prevail in a pristine "state of nature" entirely unpolluted by empirical or social accident. In general terms, the proposition of natural equality seems to be characteristic of the "retreatism" stage; in some formulations, the term "natural" actually denotes a "negative" or anti-positive element, implying a rejection of all empirical differences between men. The conception of natural equality, however, remains rarely satisfied with negation; commonly it is coupled with the demand that society be reorganized so as to reflect the common humanity of its members. In this manner, "nature" receives again a more constructive connotation: it comes to designate a practical imperative or a postulate of civilization; as such, the term definitely does not denote what is empirically "natural" or what "comes naturally."[19]

Conceptions of Equality: A Typology

The preceding sketch of the process of social change suggests the possibility of identifying a limited set of major, recurrent conceptions

18. In Sartre's words: "The declaration that 'we too are men' is at the bottom of any revolution. And the revolutionary means by this that his oppressors are men. . . . It is, above all, an absorption and an assimilation of the oppressing class by the oppressed. . . . The unity into which he wants to merge himself and his fellows is not that of the human kingdom, but of the human species." See "Materialism and Revolution," p. 412.

19. As Sartre continues: "But his attitude toward the *natural* is obviously ambivalent. In a way, he plunges into Nature, dragging his masters with him. But, on the other hand, he proclaims that he wants to substitute a rational adjustment of human relationships for what has been produced blindly by Nature. This order will be produced only by obeying the prescriptions of Nature. But the fact is that this order must *be conceived* within a Nature that denies it. . . . In short, transition to antiphysis means the replacement of the society of laws by the community of ends" (*ibid.*, pp. 413-414).

of equality. Attempts at developing a classification of such conceptions have not been lacking. Relying on a somewhat broad dichotomy, one writer distinguished between a "liberal" and a "socialist" perspective, involving respectively a moderate-proportional and a strict version of equality.[20] However, apart from the ambiguity of the term "liberal," this classification oversimplifies matters greatly by identifying socialism with a rigid egalitarianism, an identificaton which is not supported by the historical record. In a more ambitious analysis, Sanford Lakoff recently expounded three different "concepts of equality" which, as he claimed, were present in their essential features throughout history: a "conservative" concept, reflecting a pessimistic view of human nature; a "liberal" concept, aiming at equal liberty and melioristic in character; and a "socialist" concept, optimistic in tendency and aspiring toward complete equality, chiefly through collectivist means. This analysis likewise suffers from oversimplification, especially in regard to the combination of socialism and egalitarianism. Moreover, the "conservative" perspective does not seem to involve a separate "concept of equality." As presented by Lakoff, the perspective is based on the "identification of equality with depravity in human nature and mass dictatorship in society" and on the "belief that the demand for equality was inspired by envy and appetite rather than a sense of justice." In this manner the conservative view constitutes merely a rejection of equality; at best it coincides with the radical or socialist view, though with a negative prefix.[21]

The following discussion is an attempt to correlate conceptual categories more closely with social change and social conflict. In the process of social change, there is a strong probability that, at different stages, different versions of equality will be invoked for different purposes by the various groups or structural elements of society. Obviously, the categories which are presented below have to be viewed as broad benchmarks or "ideal types" of value and belief patterns; in actual historical situations, these benchmarks will only be approximated to

20. W. B. Gallie, "Liberal Morality and Socialist Morality," in Peter Laslett, ed., *Philosophy, Politics and Society* (1st Series; Oxford, 1956), p. 123.
21. Compare Sanford A. Lakoff, *Equality in Political Philosophy* (Cambridge, Mass., 1964), pp. 9-10. At many points, the attempt to substantiate the three concepts in history becomes a procrustean scheme. On the "conservative" side, the study lists Calvin, Hobbes (?), Rousseau (?), Tocqueville, Kierkegaard, Stirner, Nietzsche, and Freud; on the "liberal" side, Luther, the Levellers, Hooker, Locke, Condorcet, Mill, and Spencer; on the "socialist" side, Müntzer, Winstanley, Mably, Morelly, Babeuf, the young Hegel (?), and Marx.

a greater or lesser degree. It should also be noted that, as ingredients of the process of social change, the discussed categories stand at the crossroads of the present and the future; with varying emphasis, they all reflect the linkage between the assessment of what "is" and the judgment of what "should be," between passive contemplation and human action.

In the course of social change, conflict arises over existing normative patterns and the distribution of scarce values. The process of "naturalization" entails the possibility that established social arrangements and normative patterns are defended as part of the order of nature.[22] There are several ways in which, at this point, equality can be invoked in defense of existing privileges. One type of argument claims that the diverse ranks or layers of society are justified by virtue of special inherent qualities of the respective individuals or groups. The postulate of equality, it is asserted, involves merely the equal treatment of those endowed with equal or similar qualities or placed in similar circumstances. This view which focuses entirely on proportional or distributive criteria (to the virtual neglect of the principle of common humanity) can be described as the *social hierarchy* conception of equality.[23] The conception is primarily contemplative in character, relying on the observation of empirical differences and natural inequalities of ability or strength. These differences, however, are not only observed but also approved; normative significance is directly ascribed to observed factors of reality and equity is assumed to emerge from empirical diversity.

The defense of established arrangements does not necessarily rest, however, on such a close amalgamation of equity and social reality. The justification may also take the form of an appeal to a comparatively abstract conception of natural order. Nature, it is admitted, may not always be gentle or equitable in empirical details; but harmony and happiness are bound to result, in the long run, from the operation of her basic principles or "laws." In this perspective the postulate

22. For the "ascriptive" freezing of status aspirations and symbols by elites, compare S. N. Eisenstadt, "Breakdowns of Modernization," in Jason L. Finkle and Richard W. Gable, eds., *Political Development and Social Change* (New York, 1966), p. 586.

23. "Order is the harmonious arrangement of classes and functions which guards justice and gives willing consent to law and ensures that we shall all be safe together. Order also signifies the honor or dignity of a rank in society, and it signifies those established usages which deserve veneration." Russell Kirk, "Segments of Political Science Not Amenable to Behavioristic Treatment," in James C. Charlesworth, ed., *The Limits of Behavioralism in Political Science* (Philadelphia, 1962), p. 57.

of equality coincides essentially with the observance of a general and relatively invariant "rule" or "law." For this reason, the view may be called the *abstract* or *formal law* conception of equality.[24] As will be noted, the conception is also primarily passive or contemplative; but normative approval in this case is ostensibly extended only to the general framework of "laws" while the realm of concrete empirical detail is disregarded (or treated as indifferent). The focus on an abstract framework leaves room for spontaneous initiative and encourages a relatively unrestrained and unmitigated scramble for social position and privilege, a scramble in which natural prowess and agility are at a premium. Despite its relative aloofness, the neglect of empirical reality thus amounts in effect to an endorsement of whatever rank order happens to prevail or emerge in society.

Apart from its employment in defense of established social arrangements, the postulate of equality can be invoked in a variety of ways for purposes of social change. At a relatively moderate stage of social conflict, less privileged or underprivileged groups may simply desire to be accepted into the normative structure, to share more fully in the rights and privileges of dominant groups. In this situation, the postulate of equality is likely to assume a dual meaning: it involves, first of all, the maintenance (though more equitable application) of a general "rule of law"; at the same time, the postulate penetrates into the realm of social diversity at least to the extent of demanding a broader recognition of equal rights and equal treatment of different social layers in certain key domains. The view might be designated as *moderate reform* or *integration* version of equality. As can readily be seen, the perspective reflects a precarious blending of contemplative acquiescence and human design. The existing normative structure is reviewed and found relatively tolerable; but moral acquiescence extends only tentatively to the operation of the "rule of law." By the same token, instead of remaining aloof of empirical problems, the perspective advocates at least gradual social adjustments for the purpose of bringing equitable relief to disadvantaged groups and of effecting a closer interaction between the rule of law and social reality.

At a more advanced stage of social discord, underprivileged groups may despair of the possibility of reform within the established norma-

24. For comments on the formal rule conception of justice and equality, see Chaim Perelman, "La Règle de Justice," *Dialectica*, XIV (1960), 231; Berlin, pp. 132-137.

tive structure; as a result, they may be attracted to the view that all established inequalities and privileges are arbitrary and should be removed as completely and as rapidly as possible. This view, which corresponds chiefly to a stage of disengagement or "retreatism," might be described as *radical* or *identity* version of equality. The existing social structure has been examined and scrutinized, but found wanting; only a major change, it is felt, can remove existing inequities. Insistence on identity, however, is likely to leave this version suspended between the present and the future. The neglect of empirical diversity may be a suitable weapon of destruction, but is insufficient for constructive innovation. In order to implement their goals, underprivileged groups have to engage in constructive action in the face of a multitude of empirical problems and obstacles. The perspective which emerges at this point may be designated as the *social reconstruction* version of equality. This version regularly includes a strong emphasis on equal humanity as a standard of social relations; insistence on this standard, however, tends to be coupled with a continued attention to developing social and individual needs. The perspective thus involves a combination of equity with concrete social factors, commonly on the basis of a revolutionary principle of social organization.

As previously mentioned, the discussed conceptions should be viewed as broad benchmarks which are only approximated by actual belief patterns in concrete situations. The relative independence of these benchmarks is reflected in the fact that, depending on historical circumstances, the pursuit of similar social or political goals may involve a shift in type; the promotion of individual initiative, for instance, may change from a policy of moderate reform to a defense of established privilege. There is also the possibility of multiple combinations and mixtures between the discussed conceptions. Thus, the reconstructionist type frequently includes aspects of the identity version and vice versa; some elements of the identity view may be contained in the hierarchical conception (for instance, when all members of a certain rank or social layer are expected to receive strictly equal treatment). With the spreading emphasis in modern times on equality of rights, a combination of identity and abstract rule criteria has become prominent. This version starts from a hypothetical equivalence of all members of society and proceeds, on this basis, to construct a complex framework of abstract principles and rules—a framework whose operation in the real world is bound to render the initial equivalence purely fictional. A merger of radical premises and contemplative conclusions, the sketched outlook might be described as *ambivalent radicalism*. Another combination, weighted more toward contemplative acquiescence, has been a similarly recurrent feature in the process of social change. Though attracted by the assumed simplicity of traditional social relations, this view is repelled by the harsher features of social inequality as they have developed over the years; at the same time, the view rejects the evils of unbridled competition which may attend the complete destruction of ascriptive hierarchy arrangements. Due to its peculiar mixture of ingredients the perspective may be termed an *eclectic* conception of equality.[25] One should also keep in mind that not every social theory is necessarily linked with a commitment to some version of equality. As is well known, some doctrines reject the very notion of equity and insist on the absolute uniqueness of social arrangements. Frequently, such doctrines place the guiding principle of society in an inspired leader or in completely unpredictable or spontaneous action. The perspective is sometimes connected with a despotic regime, sometimes with anarchist movements; *random* view of society is probably an adequate description.[26]

Equality and Personality Profiles

The discussed conceptions of equality permit a further development: the elaboration of corresponding personality profiles or personality types. This possibility can only be indicated briefly in the present context. As with conceptions of equality, recent decades have witnessed numerous attempts to identify personality types which are characteristic of recurrent social or political attitudes and dispositions. One of the most prominent fruits of such efforts is Harold Lasswell's delineation of

25. According to Richard Lowenthal, the common characteristic of an "eclectic" (or populist) position "is the search for a synthesis between the basic values on which the traditional culture of the society in question was founded and the need for modernization." See "The Points of the Compass," in John H. Kautsky, ed., *Political Change in Underdeveloped Countries* (New York, 1962), p. 343. Kautsky refers to "anti-aristocratic yet anti-industrialist views" and gives as examples the Narodniks and Social Revolutionaries in Imperial Russia and agrarian socialists in general ("An Essay in the Politics of Development," *ibid.*, p. 54).

26. Isaiah Berlin mentions the position of those who "object to all rules as such and desire a society, whether this is practicable or not, governed in an unsystematic manner by the will of an inspired leader, or by the unpredictable movement of the Volksgeist, or the 'spirit' of a race, a party, a church." He describes this position as "romantic irrationalism" (pp. 136, 148).

the "political man." As Lasswell recognized, however, this construct provides only the broadest outlines of a design whose features should be refined and differentiated in accordance with varying political contexts and individual social positions. When employed in a careless or indiscriminate manner, the design easily deteriorates into stereotype, the stereotype of a more or less pathological power-seeker and power-wielder. On a more limited scale, similar comments could be made (and have been made) on the "authoritarian" and "conservative" personality types.[27] To be sure, any classification of social and political dispositions encounters terminological difficulties; the following attempt is no exception. The terms "conservative," "liberal," and "socialist" have been avoided as general labels, chiefly because of the diversity of attitudes covered by each of these terms. It should be emphasized that the subsequent typology does not rest on fixed or static personality structures; rather, attitudes are assumed to emerge from the interaction of psychological dispositions and social conditions. Thus, it is quite possible that, under the impact of social and historical experiences, individuals or groups may shift from one attitudinal category to another.

The personality type corresponding to the hierarchical conception of equality may be described as the *traditionalist,* or *particularist.* Observing the range of established social diversity and inequality around him, the particularist concludes that, for all practical purposes, such diversity and inequality reflects a wise design of nature and should therefore be maintained. Loathing uniformity and monotony, he uses this sentiment as a weapon to oppose measures granting greater social and political equality, although such measures might allow others to develop their own individuality to a greater extent. He is likely to be an idealist at least in a certain sense; he stresses the importance of inherited higher values and is repelled by crude materialism and scientific standardization. He is able to discover harmony and order in social arrangements where others might only see accident and domination. From another perspective he may be considered a realist. He studies and observes existing reality with great care and patience; every

27. Compare Harold D. Lasswell, *Psychopathology and Politics* (Chicago, 1930), *Power and Personality* (New York, 1948); Theodore W. Adorno *et al., The Authoritarian Personality* (New York, 1950); Richard Christie and Marie Jahoda, eds., *Studies in the Scope and Method of "The Authoritarian Personality"* (Glencoe, Ill., 1954); Herbert McClosky, "Conservatism and Personality," *American Political Science Review,* LII (1958), 27-45. See also Robert E. Lane, "Political Character and Political Analysis," *Psychiatry,* XVI (1953), 387-398.

empirical detail is dear to him and it pains him to see it altered or removed.[28]

It is somewhat more difficult to find an adequate label for the attitude underlying the absolute rule conception of equality; the term *physiocrat* seems to have fewer disadvantages than other labels. The physiocrat finds social relations definitely governed by the order of nature; however, this order is claimed to be relatively indifferent to concrete detail or individual welfare in the short run and to reside chiefly in the operation of broad general principles. Equality to the physiocrat means at best that all human beings are somehow ultimately subject to the same laws of nature; but from this circumstance no claim can be derived regarding equalization of social conditions in any sense whatever. Like the particularist, the physiocrat thus accepts social rank orders in principle; but he is less inclined to endow partic- ular layers with inherent "virtues" or qualities. He keeps his gaze fixed at long-range destiny and is prone to be distracted or annoyed by human complaints about injustice or inequality. In contrast to the particularist, the physiocrat is not averse to natural science and quan- tification. In his view, physical analogies impose order on empirical diversity without disturbing nature's design; they also remove the un- certainty of moral discourse. Although an idealist of sorts (by stressing nature's teleology), the physiocrat does not commonly talk in terms of spiritual values. Unlike the particularist, he likes to hide his prefer- ences under the bushel of scientific neutrality and to conceal his values under the guise of invariant natural laws.[29]

In literal translation, of course, the term *physiocrat* could apply both to the particularist and the defender of natural laws, since both rely to some extent on the "rule of nature." The more restrictive use of the term, however, seems justified in view of the historical circum- stance that the "physiocratic school" was concerned chiefly with the observance of general economic laws rather than the preservation of

28. For comments on the "realism of conservatism" see Myrdal, pp. 133-136. For a distinction between the personality types of the "realist" (who is inclined "to deduce what should be from what was and what is") and the "utopian" (who tends "to ignore what was and what is in contemplation of what should be"), compare E. H. Carr, *The Twenty Years' Crisis* (London, 1949), pp. 11-21.

29. According to Sartre, the philosophy of ruling groups is prone "to conceal its pragmatic character; as it is aimed not at changing the world, but at maintaining it, it claims to *contemplate* the world as it *is*. It regards society and nature from the viewpoint of pure knowledge, without admitting to itself that this attitude tends to perpetuate the present state of the universe by implying that the universe can be known rather than changed" ("Materialism and Revolution," p. 409).

traditional rank orders. To enhance the distinction, the label *formalist*
might be employed to designate a particularly strong preoccupation
with abstract rules or principles. It should be noted, incidentally, that
physiocracy, as used here, is not necessarily limited to the defense of
unregulated or free enterprise. The term comprises the possibility of
human intervention and regulation, provided that such intervention
is designed to strengthen the reign of natural laws and to hasten the
emergence of a truly "scientific" social order. There is no deep gulf,
after all, between Herbert Spencer's doctrine of natural selection and
harmony and Lester Ward's vision of "sociocracy." Depending on
circumstances, the physiocrat thus may turn out to be a "sociocrat"
and even a "technocrat."

The *moderate reformer* shares some of the physiocrat's dispositions.
Like the latter, he tends to support the existing social order at least
in its basic principles or general framework; he also places some confidence in the spontaneous operations occurring within this framework.
However, his acceptance of social change is not entirely limited to
natural processes and technical innovations; unlike the physiocrat, he
remains concerned with human experience and is willing to modify
social arrangements at least to the extent of reducing blatant inequity
and discrimination. In contrast to the reformer, the *radical* has abandoned the hope of accomplishing his goals within the established order.
Examining social arrangements around him, he concludes that only
a complete change of course can reassert man's relevance in the midst
of blind factuality; existing society by contrast appears to him as an
oppressive burden, a senseless ballast. To escape suffocation under
this ballast, the radical retreats into the solitude of bold negation and
uncompromising independence; his conduct is likely to alternate between complete (though deceptive) apathy and sudden outbursts of
agitation.[30] If there is idealism in the radical's position, it tends to be
a subdued and somewhat contorted kind; harassed by justifications of
the existing order, he is wary of high-sounding ideals and intent on
formulating his own tenets. His aim is not to be elevated to the level
of his oppressors; rather he is content with pulling both himself and
his oppressors down to the level of a common human species. On this
level, the radical is not averse to the language of natural science and

30. On this combination of passive acquiescence and uncompromising assertion of
demands, see Eisenstadt, pp. 584-585.

quantification, thus invading the physiocrat's domain. However, while the physiocrat tends to be a positivist, the radical is prone to stress the contingency of nature: the aspect that existence in all its forms is at best possible, not necessary.[31]

Favoring a reconstructionist version of equality, the *social architect* has a design or a blueprint for a new society at least in its major outlines, projected against the background of the diversity of empirical obstacles and contingencies. Commonly the design places great emphasis on the equal humanity of all members or larger sectors of society; at the same time, however, recognition is given to the diversity of individual performance and individual needs. In general terms, the social architect is not greatly preoccupied with maintaining rigid social uniformity, but rather with providing the basis for the emancipation and development of human capacities at the broadest scale. The remaining personality profiles can briefly be outlined. The *ambivalent radical* starts from the assertion of strict human equivalence, but submerges this premise in an abstract design of rules compatible with the physiocrat's outlook. The *eclectic*, or *populist*, is distressed by the harshness of existing inequalities and the prevalence of social injustice; however, he does not place much confidence in programs of social innovation or in bold individual protest. In an effort to mollify existing practices, he is likely to appeal to traditional moral obligations of ruling elites or to propose the re-establishment of simple, harmonious community relations patterned after the model of the extended family. Using the term in its popular, not its historical or technical meaning, the *romanticist* supports absolute spontaneity and a random conception of society.

The sketched attitude profiles and personality types have been offered merely as guideposts and possible avenues of research; they await to be verified and tested in historical studies and empirical investigations.[32] Even in this preliminary form, however, the preceding

31. "If the universe exists, its development and the succession of its states can be regulated by laws. But it is not *necessary* that the universe exist, nor is it necessary that being in general, exist, and the continguency of the universe is communicated through all the links, even the most rigorous, to each particular fact" (Sartre, "Materialism and Revolution," p. 412). Compare also E. Victor Wolfenstein, *The Revolutionary Personality: Lenin, Trotsky, Gandhi* (Princeton, 1967).

32. For some current explorations of the relationship of personality and society or politics, compare, e.g., Gordon J. Di Renzo, *Personality, Power, and Politics* (Notre Dame, Ind., 1967); M. Brewster Smith, Jerome Bruner, and Robert White, *Opinion and Personality* (New York, 1965); Arnold A. Rogow and Harold D. Lasswell, *Power,*

discussion of equality in the context of social change should reveal the great diversity of politically relevant personality patterns and the over-simplification implicit in the reduction of "political man" to a pathological exercise of power. As Max Weber was careful to observe, social and political life comprises acts both of commission and omission; even recondite and seemingly esoteric attitudes are bound to have direct or remote repercussions on the maintenance or transformation of social and political conditions. This view does not disparage the integrity of esoteric pursuits; it simply lends credence to the old adage that man, although perhaps not "by nature" civil or fit for social concord, is inevitably a political animal—through his complicity in the fortunes or misfortunes of his fellow men and through his inability to disclaim the consequences of his actions.

Corruption, and Rectitude (Englewood Cliffs, N.J., 1963); James Davies, *Human Nature in Politics* (New York, 1963); Fred I. Greenstein, "The Impact of Personality on Politics: An Attempt to Clear Away Underbrush," *American Political Science Review*, LXI (1967), 629-641; "The Need for Systematic Inquiry into Personality and Politics: Introduction and Overview," *Journal of Social Issues*, XXIV (1968), 1-14; Harold D. Lasswell, "A Note on 'Types' of Political Personality," *ibid.*, pp. 81-91; M. Brewster Smith, "A Map for the Analysis of Personality and Politics," *ibid.*, pp. 15-28; Rufus P. Browning and Herbert Jacob, "Power Motivation and the Political Personality," *Public Opinion Quarterly*, XXVIII (1964), 75-90.

Philip B. Secor / Academic Freedom in Political Context: The North Carolina Speaker-Ban Law[1]

I

During the closing hours of the 1963 session of the North Carolina General Assembly, the House of Representatives suddenly voted to suspend regular parliamentary procedure; within four minutes the House passed Bill 1395. Less than an hour later the President of the Senate gaveled down the opposition of a few startled members of the upper house and ruled that a voice vote in that chamber had adopted House Bill 1395. Thus was enacted into law—there is no gubernatorial veto in North Carolina—one of the most controversial pieces of state legislation enacted in recent years, Chapter 1207 of the Session Laws of the North Carolina Legislature for 1963: An Act to Regulate Visiting Speakers at State Supported Colleges and Universities.

The story of how so politically volatile and constitutionally questionable a law ever got onto the North Carolina statute books may reveal something of the relationship between politics and constitutional law. The story may also help put into focus an important constitutional problem in our era, namely, the relationship between academic freedom and state power.

The 1963 session of the General Assembly of North Carolina was enough to try the patience of any Southern moderate. The most difficult problem confronting the legislators was how to find a way, consistent with maintaining their own seats, of conforming to recent Supreme Court decisions requiring legislative redistricting according to population. As if that were not enough to fray the nerves of a state's-rights oriented legislator, he had also to deal with a number of proposals by the dynamic, liberal Democratic Governor, Terry Sanford,

1. Parts of this chapter appeared previously in the *Kentucky Law Journal*, LV (1966-1967), No. 2, under the title "The North Carolina Speaker Ban Law: A Study in Context." The preparation of that article was a joint effort by this writer and several other members of the Davidson College Chapter of the American Association of University Professors. The author gratefully acknowledges his indebtedness to his colleagues in this earlier endeavor: Mr. William Bondurant and Professors Richard Gift, Louise Nelson, Brown Patterson, and Locke White.

a friend and supporter of President Kennedy. Sanford was an aggressive advocate of his programs for higher education, secondary schools, increase in the minimum wage, compulsory motor vehicle inspection, etc. As the session drew to a close in mid-June, Governor Sanford issued another of his several threats to call a special session of the Legislature if redistricting was not accomplished before adjournment.

Not only was the Legislature having difficulty with redistricting—a problem seen by many legislators as forced upon them by an over-reaching U.S. Supreme Court in alliance with a liberal President and Governor—but this same Court and President seemed to be presenting other unwanted problems to the body. The summer of 1963 was one of the worst of the "long hot summers" of racial conflict in the United States. As a preface, President Kennedy had announced his far-reaching civil rights legislative program. During this same summer, the Supreme Court handed down its decisions outlawing the compulsory reading of the Bible in the public schools.

Between them the President and the Supreme Court had cut three wide, but ragged, swaths through the traditions of most North Carolina legislators. The President had made clear his ambitious intentions in the area of civil liberties for the Negro; the Court had told state legislators that they would have to reorganize their sovereign legislative bodies; and the Court had said that there could be no more Bible reading in the schools supported by the public funds of a "Bible-belt" state.

In an atmosphere charged with opposition to the Supreme Court it is not surprising that the state House of Representatives voted in mid-June in favor of a constitutional amendment which would create a Super Supreme Court of the United States. The proposed court would be composed of the fifty state chief judges with the power to review all decisions of the U.S. Supreme Court. This resolution passed the North Carolina House of Representatives by a vote of 64 to 51. A few days later, on June 20, the North Carolina Senate defeated the House measure. Although the Senate vote was overwhelmingly opposed to the Super Court, 28 to 12, it is noteworthy that the Senate reached its conclusion over the strong objections of its President, Clarence Stone.

Stone had used his extensive powers on behalf of the House bill calling for the Super Court. The Charlotte *Observer*'s Raleigh bureau,

in reporting Stone's behavior while he presided over Senate delibera-
tion on this bill, quoted Stone as saying, "It's a good bill." Later
he commented that the U.S. Supreme Court "was a disgrace to any
civilized people." Still later, in response to a request from the floor
to speak on the bill, after Stone had attempted to force the resolution
through without discussion by including it with routine matters, the
Senate President remarked sarcastically to his colleague, "I thought
you would [want to speak], Daniel Webster." Then during the debate
when a speaker asked the membership of the Senate in a rhetorical
manner what rights Americans still had, Stone, speaking from the presiding officer's chair, said, "None." When another legislator remarked
that everyone, after all, had disagreed with the Supreme Court at one
time or another, Stone said from the chair, "Vote with us then."[2]

But despite Stone's strong efforts in behalf of the Super Court bill
it was defeated in the Senate. This occurrence, however, indicates
something of the strained conditions under which the 1963 Legislature
was operating as it drew to the close of its session, and it also suggests
something about the attitudes of the President of the Senate.

On the last scheduled day of the legislative session, June 21, the
Legislature approved the creation of the State School for the Performing Arts, and the Senate yielded to a House proposal permitting
electrical co-operatives of North Carolina to build generating facilities
without the approval of the Utilities Commission.[3] Since the legislature had still not solved the most difficult problem of the session,
legislative redistricting, President Stone of the Senate and the Speaker
of the House, Clifton Blue, agreed not to adjourn on June 21, but to
allow several more days for a last effort to pass suitable redistricting
legislation. June 25 was designated as the final adjournment date. In
the June 25 issue of the Charlotte *Observer*, the editors began to wrap
up the legislative session with articles listing the merits and demerits
of the session. As yet there was no mention of any Speaker-Ban Law.

While the public was reading the June 25 newspaper wrap-ups of
the legislative session, Representative Phil Godwin of Gates County
was on his feet in the House of Representatives, under suspension of
rules, introducing what was to become the Speaker-Ban Law. After a

2. Charlotte *Observer* (June 21, 1963), p. 3-C.
3. This was the climax of a long struggle between the private power companies and
the rural co-operatives in North Carolina, resolving the matter temporarily in favor
of the co-operatives.

quick voice vote, Speaker Clifton Blue ruled the bill to have passed
the House. It was then transmitted at once to the Senate, read by
President Stone, put to voice vote and declared to have received a
majority. Charlotte *Observer* reporter, J. Jenkins stated: "In the Senate galleries the vote sounded extremely close, but Stone's ruling prohibited a nose count. He left the dais shortly after with his hand
clasped to his forehead." Stone, reporter Jenkins continued, "ignored
several protesting colleagues" as he declared that the bill had "been
enacted into law." Some of the senators were left standing at their
seats in a vain effort to get recognition when Stone, on the final voice
vote, shouted, "The ayes have it." Senator Luther Hamilton of Car-
teret County protested that he had not been recognized before the
vote, although he had been trying to get the chair's attention. Stone
said, "I didn't see you." Hamilton replied, "Sometimes we see what
we want to see" and then added that the "bill is not worthy of the
Senate of North Carolina." Stone then "threw down his gavel and
turned to glower at Hamilton" and, "in a voice shaken with emotion,"
said, "Do you want to overrule me?"[4]

On the next, and what was to be the last day of the session, Senator
Hamilton, a former Superior Court Judge, was joined by several of
his colleagues in an effort to have the Senate resolution recalled. Their
motion to recall was defeated by a vote of 25 to 19.

Thus was enacted Chapter 1207 of the Session Laws of the General
Assembly of North Carolina (Codified as 6.S. 116-199 and 116-200):

AN ACT TO REGULATE VISITING SPEAKERS AT STATE SUPPORTED
COLLEGES AND UNIVERSITIES.

116-199. No college or university, which receives any State funds in
support thereof, shall permit any person to use the facilities of such college
or university for speaking purposes, who:

(A) Is a known member of the Communist Party;

(B) Is known to advocate the overthrow of the Constitution of the
United States or the State of North Carolina;

(C) Has pleaded the Fifth Amendment of the Constitution of the
United States in refusing to answer any question, with respect to Communist or subversive connections, or activities, before any duly constituted
legislative committee, any judicial tribunal, or any executive or administrative board of the United States or any state.

4. Charlotte *Observer* (June 25, 1963), p. 1-A.

116-200. This act shall be enforced by the Board of Trustees, or other governing authority, of such college or university, or by such administrative personnel as may be appointed therefor by the Board of Trustees or other governing authority of such college or university.[5]

Just why such a bill was introduced and passed at this time may never be fully known. The national political climate, tensions in the state Legislature, the views of particular and powerful legislators, all played a role. Also important was the fact that the University of North Carolina was supposed by many North Carolinians to be supporting overly "liberal" ideas which had been so troublesome and frustrating for Southerners in recent years and for the North Carolina Legislature in particular during its present session. Whether fair or not, the impression was widely held in North Carolina that the University was the kind of place where the values and traditions of Tar Heel moderates were too easily sacrificed and where the causes of national-liberal "eggheads" were propagated. It was widely believed that state sovereignty and religion were being attacked and national civil rights espoused within the state's most prestigious higher educational citadel. Here, many felt, youngsters' heads were being filled with dangerous notions, antithetical to the best traditions of North Carolina.

Another suggested cause of the introduction and passage of the bill was the appearance of some Negro demonstrators at the Sir Walter Hotel in Raleigh during the last week of the session. Representative Phil Godwin, who introduced the bill, denied all such explanations and further insisted that he had no political intent in the timing of the bill's introduction at the end of the session. He persisted that his intention was only to provide a national security measure as a guard against communism. Representative Godwin expressed surprise that the bill was controversial.[6]

5. N.C. Gen. Stat., Chapter 1207: 116-199, 200.
6. Rep. Godwin's assertion that his intention was to add to the national security by restricting certain kinds of speech in North Carolina is credible in light of activity in recent years in a number of states along the same lines. Similar laws and administrative regulations have been put into effect or seriously considered in many states. A speaker-ban law was enacted in California in 1953. Several bills were introduced but not passed in Ohio in 1963, New Hampshire and Virginia in 1964, and Alabama in 1965. There were lengthy discussions in the legislatures of Kentucky, Michigan, and South Carolina about such legislation in the mid-sixties. Administrative bans on Communist speakers have existed in recent years at the University of Illinois, Ohio State University, Indiana University, the University of Washington and the State University of New York at Buffalo. For comments on these cases and reviews of the constitutional issues involved, see Robert Van Alstyne, "Political Speakers at State Universities: Some Constitutional Considerations," *University of Pennsylvania Law Review*, CXI (1963),

But, whether its author was surprised or not, the law was certainly to become one of the most controversial pieces of legislation ever enacted by the North Carolina General Assembly. Almost immediately following adjournment of the Legislature on June 26, newspapers and educators throughout the state began to protest the Speaker-Ban Law. On June 27 the Charlotte *Observer* in its lead editorial, attacked the law on several grounds, calling it "a questionable breach of parliamentary procedure and legislative fairness." On the same day North Carolina Attorney-General Wade Bruton announced his opinion, later elaborated in a lengthy statement by his deputy, Ralph Moody, that the law was consistent with the federal and state constitutions.

On June 29 the presidents of Davidson, Meredith, and East Carolina Colleges joined UNC President William Friday in public opposition to the bill. In the weeks and months which followed, educators, newspapers, and various organizations throughout the state worked to show the objectionable features of the law to the general public.

Most of the objections to the Speaker-Ban Law focused on the question of academic freedom. Almost without exception educators' responses to the law were that it represented a most serious threat to freedom of inquiry at the University of North Carolina and, as an unfortunate by-product, a threat to the prestige of the University and therefore to the state itself. While unrestricted access to the rostrums of higher educational institutions was rarely advocated, it was usually urged that the decision as to who might and might not use such platforms should be left to the decision-making bodies of each individual institution and not be a matter of general legislative prescription.

Paragraph C of the first section of the law was objected to by educators on the grounds that it was morally wrong, if not unconstitutional, to penalize any person for having exercised a clear constitutional right by pleading the Fifth Amendment before a legislative committee or administrative tribunal.

It was also frequently urged that far from enhancing national security, the law actually encouraged the spread of communism, mak-

---

328; Pollitt, "Campus Censorship: Statute Banning Speakers from State Educational Institutions," *North Carolina Law Review*, XLII (1963), 179; Van Alstyne, "Memorandum on the North Carolina Speaker Ban Law" (hearing before Speaker Ban Study Commission, State Legislative Building, Raleigh, N. C., in North Carolina Collection, Louis Round Wilson Library, University of North Carolina at Chapel Hill).

ing it more difficult to combat by tending to force the movement underground. Those ideas which are prohibited often become unnecessarily appealing to young minds, it was said; also there is no evidence that communism as an ideology has found a fertile seedbed among American college youth.

There were several specific instances of the deleterious effects of the act upon the educational health of North Carolina in the years immediately following the passage of the law. Some professional organizations decided not to hold their meetings on the campuses of state institutions, sometimes as a specific protest to the law. Notable among these organizations was the Southern Political Science Association.

A number of scholars declined invitations to speak on the campuses of state institutions. The most widely publicized instance involved a famous British geneticist, the late J. B. S. Haldane. Professor Haldane had accepted an invitation to speak at the University at Chapel Hill but then refused to answer questions submitted to him under the requirements of the Speaker-Ban Law. Thus the invitation was cancelled. In 1964 he wrote an article entitled, "Perspectives in Biology and Medicine," in which he included a footnote noting that the University of North Carolina had withdrawn an invitation to him after he had lectured elsewhere throughout the United States.

There were undoubtedly many other instances which will never be documented because they involved invitations not extended. One example which is known involved a sociologist, from an Eastern European nation, who had a key role in drafting a new constitution for his country. He was visiting the United States under the auspices of the State Department, studying the nature of the American system of government. The sociologist was not invited to speak at the University specifically because of the feeling that to do so would be in violation of the provisions of the Speaker-Ban Law. That same distinguished individual did speak at other universities in the United States. Also invitations to noted communist scholars in fields as diverse as the dramatic arts and applied mathematics were not extended specifically because of the law.

An American scientist at one of the state universities was advised not to apply for participation in a USA-USSR Exchange Program as it was doubtful that a scientist working at an American university which could not reciprocate by extending an invitation to his counter-part from the Soviet Union would be eligible for an exchange pro-gram. There was also an instance where an American lecturer was not invited to speak at one of the North Carolina state institutions on the grounds that he had at one time pleaded the Fifth Amendment before the House Committee on Un-American Activities.

Another serious effect of the law, which is similarly difficult to document, was its effect upon faculty recruitment on the state cam-puses. There does, however, seem to be evidence that the law had damaging effects in this regard. A statement unanimously adopted by the Faculty Council at the University of North Carolina at Chapel Hill in October, 1963, stated that in the eyes of most university teachers in the United States any governmental restriction of free expression on a college campus was a black mark against that institution.

II

Since the North Carolina General Assembly meets only every other year, it was not until 1965 that the question of amending or appeal-ing the Speaker-Ban Law could be considered by the legislators. In the interim between the two sessions, North Carolina experienced an intense struggle within the Democratic party for the gubernatorial nomination. The candidates were a former federal judge, L. Richard-son Preyer, a former state Superior Court judge, Dan K. Moore, and an attorney, R. Beverly Lake.

The Speaker-Ban Law was not the central issue in the primary election, although it was an important one. Dr. Lake, who spoke for the conservative wing of the party, openly supported the law; Judge Preyer, regarded as the liberal candidate, equivocated on the issue, although some who studied his record and were friendly to his candi-dacy were certain that he shared Governor Sanford's opposition to the law; Judge Moore gingerly supported the law.

The rather decisive defeat of Preyer in a primary run-off with Moore was interpreted widely as a popular endorsement of the Speaker-Ban Law. The later endorsement of the law by the American Legion and the Veterans of Foreign Wars strengthened the general impres-sion of popular support for the law.

Throughout the 1965 session efforts were made by some legislators and many educational groups in the state to develop an effective movement either for repeal or amendment. Amendment proposals, which were seriously discussed, focused on removing the Fifth Amendment provision, eliminating restrictions on non-political speakers, and giving the administrations of particular state universities discretionary powers in deciding when to prohibit speakers.

Those groups and individuals calling for amendment or repeal of the law tended more and more, as the 1965 session wore on, to see their principal hope in some leadership from Governor Moore. The Governor had stated on a number of occasions that he would not oppose and might even support certain modifications in the law; but he had never pursued this possibility with any vigor.

In May, only a few weeks before the end of the 1965 session, the movement to change the law was given a boost by a wire to Governor Moore from the major higher educational accrediting agency for North Carolina, namely, the Southern Association of Colleges and Schools. The association's statement, which was made public, was delivered after intensive investigation of the Speaker-Ban Law situation and said in effect that if the North Carolina Speaker-Ban Law remained it might adversely affect the association's decision on accreditation of North Carolina universities and colleges.

About a week later, on May 28, 175 members of the faculty of the University of North Carolina at Chapel Hill issued a statement criticizing political interference in the affairs of the University and stating that they "would feel compelled to seek positions and settings conducive to our academic pursuits" if such interference did not cease. A few days later, on June 11, 113 members of the faculty of the University of North Carolina at Greensboro issued a statement declaring that they would resign if the accreditation of the University were withdrawn. Professors at the University branch in Charlotte also expressed strong feelings against the law. The thinly veiled threats of mass faculty resignations throughout the state were apparent in all of these statements.

On June 1, Governor Moore issued a statement in which he said that he did "not believe it would be in the best interests of higher education for the General Assembly to consider the repeal of the Speaker-Ban Law at this time." The Governor went on to say, "the Speaker-Ban Law has become a symbol of resistance to Communism in North Carolina. The General Assembly would not be receptive to any move to repeal this law or substantially amend it." The Governor then recommended the creation of a nine-member commission to be composed of five persons appointed by himself and two each by the House and Senate to study the Speaker-Ban Law question at length and to formulate recommendations. Before it adjourned in mid-June, the Legislature approved Moore's proposal and established the study commission.

The commission held hearings on August 11-12, and September 8-9, 1965. In addition to certain legislators, representatives of the American Legion and Veterans of Foreign Wars spoke in favor of the law. Among those speaking for repeal or amendment were Watts Hill, Jr., chairman of the North Carolina Board of Higher Education, Emmett B. Fields, chairman of the Commission on Colleges of the Southern Association of Colleges and Schools, John P. Dawson, first vice-president of the American Association of University Professors, and representatives from the American Association of University Women, the League of Women Voters, Phi Beta Kappa, and various chapters of the American Association of University Professors in the state. Also Dr. William C. Friday, president of the Consolidated University of North Carolina, joined by the chancellors of the branches of the university and presidents of the state colleges, spoke against the law.

On November 5 the study commission handed its report to Governor Moore. The two-fold recommendation was that: (1) trustees of each educational institution in the state should have the authority and responsibility to adopt and publish speaker policies, and (2) that a general statement on speaker policy (contained in the commission report) should first be adopted by all of the institutional trustees before any amendment of the law should take place. By November 12 the trustees of all of the state-supported institutions had adopted the commission's recommended speaker policy, and in November the General Assembly was called into special session by the Governor for consideration of the study commission's report.[7]

The speaker policy, recommended by the commission and approved by the trustees of the state-supported institutions before the special

7. For a full statement of the Commission's recommendations, including its recommended Speaker Policy, see *Dickson et al.* v. *Sitterson et al.*, United States District Court for the Middle District of North Carolina, Order No. C-59-6-66, Feb. 19, 1968, 5, 6.

session of the General Assembly began, affirmed the responsibility of the trustees of each state institution to maintain a strongly anti-communist viewpoint and a willingness to assure that their educational institutions would not serve "the purposes of the enemies of our free society." On the other hand, the speaker policy affirmed the importance of free speech within an educational environment because "An essential part of the education of each student . . . is the opportunity to hear diverse viewpoints expressed by speakers," because "It is highly desirable that students have the opportunity to question, review and discuss the opinions of speakers representing a wide range of viewpoints," and because "It is vital to our success in supporting our free society against all forms of totalitarianism that institutions remain free to examine these ideologies to any extent that will serve the educational purpose of our institutions and not serve the purposes of the enemies of our free society."

The recommended speaker policy also said that those speakers who visit a campus in order to advocate "any ideology or form of government which is wholly alien to our basic democratic institutions" should be invited only infrequently and when it would "clearly serve the advantage of education." The policy left it to the discretion of the trustees when such speakers might appropriately be invited and affirmed that "the administration of the Institution shall be responsible and accountable for visiting speakers on our campuses." Furthermore, the recommendation stated that each administration "will adopt rules and precautionary measures consistent with the policy herein set forth regarding the invitations to and appearance of visiting speakers."[8]

There was never much doubt that the General Assembly in special session would approve the proposal of the study commission. By this time the opponents of the law were numerous and prestigious.[9] In September the Charlotte *Observer* published a newspaper poll showing that a majority of the legislators in both Houses would probably

8. *Ibid.* Moore, on February 11, 1966, interpreted this policy to mean that each prospective speaker should be judged by the administration on each state campus by four principles: (1) The frequency of this type of speaker on the campus should be considered. (2) The appearance must clearly show the advantages to education. (3) When permission is granted, there should be care exercised by the institution. (4) Campuses should not be exploited as convenient outlets of discord or strife (Charlotte *Observer* [Feb. 11, 1966]).

9. Senator Barry Goldwater, for instance, made a public statement generally construed to be in opposition to the North Carolina Speaker-Ban Law of 1963.

accept the commission's proposal. The special session met for only two and one-half days and on November 17 adjourned after amending the 1963 law in the manner recommended in the study commission report.

During its brief session the Legislature voted down quickly several other proposals designed to save the original act. One of these would have referred the commission report to the people in a public referendum. This effort and others failed in large measure because of Governor Moore's political efforts, which were now completely supportive of the commission's recommendations. The Governor made his support quite clear in a speech before the joint session during its first day on November 15.

During the debate, several other amendments were introduced by proponents of the original law. One proposal introduced by Senator Robert Morgan would have required that the administration of each state college and university publish a monthly list, reporting all proposed speakers to its board of trustees. Former North Carolina Governor Luther Hodges entered the fray at this point and is reported to have directly urged several legislators on Tuesday evening and again on Wednesday morning to reject this amendment and to accept the commission report in toto.

The amended law as adopted stated, in part:

The board of trustees of each college or university which receives any state funds in support thereof, shall adopt and publish regulations governing the use of facilities of such college or university for speaking purposes by any person who:
(1) Is a known member of the Communist Party;
(2) Is known to advocate the overthrow of the Constitution of the United States or the State of North Carolina;
(3) Has pleaded the Fifth Amendment of the Constitution of the United States in refusing to answer any question, with respect to Communist or subversive connections, or activities, before any duly constituted legislative committee, any judicial tribunal, or any executive or administrative board of the United States or any state.[10]

The major difference between the amended law and the original act was that now the trustees of each institution would be responsible for developing the specific regulations concerning speakers falling within the three prohibited categories, instead of having a legislative

10. *Dickson* v. *Sitterson*, 6, 7.

ruling automatically prohibiting all such speakers from ever appearing on the university and college campuses of the state.[11]

Although one can argue the case for the wisdom of this amendment on the grounds of better protection for academic freedom, the basic reasons for the amendment were nevertheless political. There are two important political reasons why the law was amended. The first was the massive and successful effort made by many organizations and individuals to sway public opinion through persistent and organized attacks on the law and through constant pressure on legislators.

The second, and I think decisive factor, in the amendment of the law was Governor Moore's decision to put the political power of his office behind the commission's recommendations. Without the Governor's support, which had been lacking in all previous attempts to amend or repeal, it is doubtful that the crucial moderate wing of the Legislature would have supported the commission report. Although it is risky to assess motives of high public officials, it seems likely that an important factor was the Governor's need to support the recommendations of a commission which he himself had appointed. The North Carolina Speaker-Ban controversy, like all difficult political issues, descended from the lofty regions of moral debate and entered the arena of political gamesmanship. One of the rules of the game in American state politics is that effective chief executives do not lose initiative to their legislatures on important issues.

Another practical reason for the expeditious legislative approval of the report was that the chairman of the commission, who presented

11. The regulations adopted by the Executive Committee of the Board of Trustees of the University of North Carolina on January 14, 1966, were as follows (*ibid.*, 8):

1. All statutes of the State relating to speakers and the use of facilities for speaking purposes are to be obeyed.

2. Only recognized student, faculty and University organizations are authorized to invite speakers.

3. Non-University organizations authorized through official channels (*e.g.* Extension Division) to meet on the campus are to be routinely informed that the use of facilities must conform to State laws.

4. Student attendance at campuswide occasions is not compulsory.

5. The appearance of speakers on campus does not imply approval or disapproval of them or what is said by the speaker.

6. As a further precaution and to assure free and open discussion as essential to the safeguarding of free institutions, each Chancellor, when he considers it appropriate, will require any or all of the following:

    a. That a meeting be chaired by an officer of the University or a ranking member of the faculty;

    b. That speakers at the meeting be subject to questions from the audience;

    c. That the opportunity be provided at the meeting or later to present speakers of different points of view.

the recommendations to the Legislature, was also the Speaker-Elect of the House. This was a fact which a politically astute governor like Dan K. Moore had not overlooked in appointing his commission chairman. The fact that Representative Britt would, as House Speaker, wield great power over legislative committee assignments certainly added important political force to his moral defense of the commission's recommendations.

The 1965 amended legislation represented a compromise. Neither proponents nor opponents of the original law were satisfied. There remained a Speaker-Ban Law under which the administrations at state colleges and universities were required to formulate policies for visiting speakers and to submit them for approval to their boards of trustees. On the other hand, the politically sensitive state Legislature could no longer formulate and pass judgment on the speaker policies of state schools. Nevertheless, since trustees in North Carolina are selected by the Legislature, that body still maintained an indirect control over matters touching academic freedom.

III

Very soon after new speaker regulations were adopted by the trustees of the University of North Carolina under the authority of the amended Speaker-Ban Law, these regulations were put to the test. Students at the University of North Carolina at Chapel Hill invited Herbert Aptheker, director of the Institute of Marxist Studies, and Frank Wilkinson, head of the Committee Seeking to Abolish the House Un-American Activities Committee, to speak on their campus. The executive committee of the board of trustees voted 8 to 3 on February 7, 1966, to rescind the invitation under the authority of the North Carolina Speaker-Ban Law.[12]

On March 2, Wilkinson made two off-campus speeches at Chapel Hill, one from a sidewalk adjacent to the campus and one in a re-

12. Wilkinson had originally been invited on January 14 by Roy James McCorkel, Jr., president of Students for a Democratic Society on the Chapel Hill campus. Aptheker was invited on or about February 1 by Paul Dickson, III, president of the student government at Chapel Hill, Ernest S. McCrary, editor of the student newspaper, *The Daily Tar Heel*, and George Nicholson, III, student chairman of the Carolina Forum. The invitation to Aptheker was endorsed by the faculty, the president, and the chancellor of the University. Subsequent to the negative decision by the executive committee of the board of trustees, Chancellor Sharp called their decision an "unfortunate action."

ligious meetinghouse near the campus. Following this, Acting Chancellor J. Carlyle Sitterson, who had replaced Chancellor Sharp, ruled that a tape-recording of Wilkinson's speech could not be played on the campus and that his speech could not be read by someone else on the campus. On March 9, Herbert Aptheker, following a speech on the Duke University campus, spoke to approximately two thousand students across a stone wall dividing the campus from the town of Chapel Hill. This performance was viewed by millions of Americans on network television.[13]

Following rapidly upon the Aptheker-Wilkinson incidents, invitations were issued by student and faculty groups, with the approval of Acting Chancellor Sitterson on the Chapel Hill campus and Chancellor John T. Caldwell of the North Carolina State University at Raleigh, to a number of communist scholars. United States Communist party chairman Gus Hall and North Carolina Ku Klux Klan Grand Dragon J. Robert Jones, both of whom had pleaded the Fifth Amendment before congressional committees, were invited to speak at the Raleigh campus. Neither accepted the invitation, however.

On March 31, 1966, fourteen plaintiffs filed a suit in the U.S. District Court in Greensboro, North Carolina, seeking to enjoin the University trustees and administrations from enforcing the amended Speaker-Ban Law as it had been applied to Wilkinson and Aptheker and to have the law declared unconstitutional. Joining Wilkinson and Aptheker as plaintiffs in the suit were the president and the president-elect of the student body of the University of North Carolina at Chapel Hill, the editor of the student paper, *The Daily Tar Heel*, and several other leaders of student organizations.

There were several arguments presented against the law. It was urged that the amended statute and regulations made pursuant thereto were unconstitutional because they prohibited speakers who had only used their constitutionally protected right to plead the Fifth Amendment. Also it was argued that the law represented an infringement of the First Amendment protections of free speech as applied to state action by the Fourteenth Amendment. By changing the 1963 law so as to transfer to the boards of trustees responsibility for enforcing

13. Student Government President Dickson attempted unsuccessfully to defy Chancellor Sitterson's orders by arranging large audiences for both Wilkinson and Aptheker on the University campus. In each case police officers prevented the meetings and the students and speakers then moved to off-campus property. *Ibid.*, 15-18.

regulations requiring limitations on speech, the state government had not freed itself from the prohibitions of the First Amendment.

Although it is clear that free speech is not an absolute right—I will not recite the well-known cases here—it is also clear that some criminal conduct must be associated with speech before it may be prohibited. What criminal act may result from speech is of course difficult to determine in advance. One standard used by the U.S. Supreme Court would suggest that in the balancing of public interest against private free-speech rights, it must be decided whether the "gravity of the evil, discounted by its probability, justifies such invasion of free speech as is necessary to avoid the danger."[14] If one attempts to apply this standard to the Speaker-Ban Law, he should recall that this act denied a forum for speech not because the would-be speaker had advocated a dangerous or undesirable position but only because he is "known to be" a communist or to have pleaded the Fifth Amendment.

This sort of prohibition was alleged by plaintiffs to be untenable because it would be impossible to predict what evil might flow from a speech which had not yet been given. The law represented, therefore, a prior restraint upon free speech.[15] Also the Supreme Court had recently ruled that convictions on the basis of mere membership in organizations without any proof that the defendant himself intends to accomplish the aims of the organization by use of violence will not stand.[16]

It was argued, of course, that the First Amendment was not violated by the Speaker-Ban Law because persons prohibited from speaking on the property of tax-supported educational institutions were free to speak elsewhere. The difficulty with this argument is that it groups all types of public property into a single category and fails to recognize that a university is, for instance, unlike a jailhouse alley. A university is a place that has been publicly dedicated to the pursuit of truth and the free expression of various conceptions thereof.

One of the other important arguments of the plaintiffs in the

14. *Dennis* v. *United States,* 341 U.S. 494, 499 (1951).
15. *Near* v. *Minnesota,* 283 U.S. 697 (1931).
16. *Noto* v. *United States,* 367 U.S. 290 (1961). In January, 1967, the Supreme Court invalidated portions of the New York Educational and Civil Service Laws which required dismissal of public employees who were members of certain Communist organizations on the grounds that the sections were too vague. *Keyishian* v. *Board of Regents of the Univ. of the State of N.Y.,* 385 U.S. 589 (1967).

case went to the vagueness of the statute. The Fifth and Fourteenth Amendments provide due process guarantees which are violated when a statute is not sufficiently clear in meaning so that persons of average intelligence can know whether their activities are prohibited by the law.[17] In the debates surrounding the act, the legislation was described, defended, attacked, and analyzed in so many different ways that it was clear in advance that reasonable men differed as to its meaning and application. Such phrases as "known members of the Communist Party" raised the question, "known to whom?"

For almost two years this case was pending in the United States District Court in Greensboro. Finally, on February 19, 1968, the three-judge court unanimously declared the North Carolina Speaker-Ban Law and the regulations made pursuant thereto unconstitutional on the grounds that they violated the Fourteenth Amendment because they were too vague. In support of its decision the court cited numerous Supreme Court cases which have held that statutory vagueness, especially where the free speech protections of the First Amendment are involved, is ample justification for striking down a state law.[18]

Although the court struck down the Speaker-Ban Law, it did not settle the major constitutional questions and problems which this law presented. If the North Carolina Legislature were subsequently to draw a statute limiting speech on state-supported campuses in such a way as to remove the ambiguity in the present statute, it is entirely possible that the court would uphold such a statute.

In expressing its opinions on matters not immediately germane to the question of statutory vagueness, the court stressed the threat of a "Communist conspiracy" which "is dedicated to the destruction of freedom" and which attempts to accomplish its aims by "the use of college campuses" in order to have "an optimum chance of reaching and influencing a maximum number of young people." The court also chastised a policy of bringing to a college campus speakers who are invited merely because they are controversial and therefore able to satisfy the "whimsical curiosity" of students. When students invite speakers, the court warned, "the pressure of audience appeal

17. *Lanzatta* v. *New Jersey*, 306 U.S. 451, 453 (1939). *Keyishian* v. *Board of Regents.*
18. The Court cited *Connally* v. *General Construction Company*, 269 U.S. 385, 391 (1926); *N.A.A.C.P.* v. *Button*, 371 U.S. 415 (1963); *Smith* v. *California*, 361 U.S. 147 (1959); *Small Company* v. *American Sugar Refining Co.*, 267 U.S. 233 (1925); *Elfbrandt* v. *Russell*, 384 U.S. 11 (1966); *Baggett* v. *Bullit*, 377 U.S. 360 (1964); *Whitehall* v. *Elkins*, 389 U.S. 54 (1967); *Keyishian* v. *Board of Regents.*

may entail them to so prefer sensationalism as to neglect academic responsibility." Indeed, the court suggests, such factors "apparently motivated the plaintiff students in the Spring of 1966."[19]

Throughout its decision the court stressed the right of the state to protect its people from the Communist threat and the corollary right of the state to limit speech on campus in order to guard against what the court saw as the danger of irresponsible speech. In fact, the court seemed to be issuing a warning that if university and college speaker programs were not "more balanced" and less filled with "extremists," another "legislative response" might be expected.[20]

Advocates of a generous constitutional definition of free speech on college and university campuses and a correspondingly restrictive definition of state power to limit such speech will find little comfort in the present judicial settlement of the North Carolina Speaker-Ban Law controversy. Although the specific law in question is now invalidated, most of the substantive principles of the supporters of this law remain unscathed. Insofar as courts ever do settle such matters, the basic right of state governments to influence significantly the content of the educational process at public higher educational institutions has been affirmed. National security interests are held to be valid determinants of when to limit speech on state-supported campuses.

But such matters as these are not settled by a single court decision. The process of defining the limits both of free speech and of state power is a continuous process. The question of where to draw the line between community protection and academic freedom will, in fact, be exacerbated by the rapid growth in our society of state-supported colleges and universities. We are now only in the early stages of what will be an increasingly urgent need to define the nature and scope of free speech in higher education.

As with all such social needs, we will find the answer to this in temporary and proximate accommodations of conflicting values and interests. The courts will play the important but limited role of temporarily promulgating feasible "solutions" within the ample framework of constitutional law. But the courts are only part of a broader political process which continuously tests their decisions and presents new problems and alternative solutions. This process will bring into

19. *Dickson* v. *Sitterson*, 22-23.   20. *Ibid.*

dynamic interrelationship the differing values and interests of college students, professors, academic administrators, legislators, professional politicians, and many other groups and individuals with a stake in the constant and creative conflict between the values of the public welfare and academic freedom.

Alfred O. Canon / A Negro Candidate for Mayor in the Urban South

I. Political Background of "Memphis Down in Dixie"

October 5, 1967, marked a significant turning point in Memphis political history in several important aspects: (1) the city was shifting from a Commission form of government to a Mayor-Council plan; (2) the new mayor and council were being elected for the first time under a run-off provision established by an act of the Tennessee Legislature; (3) a Negro attorney, A. W. Willis, who had been a two-term member of the Tennessee House of Representatives, and one of ten Negro political leaders in the United States featured in *Life* magazine (October 13, 1967), was one of seven candidates for mayor.

In spite of an active campaign in the white community and a Negro voter registration of 80,033, Willis finished *fourth*, polling 17,744 votes or 12.2 per cent of the total vote. Obviously, he did not receive any substantial percentage of the Negro vote. What conclusions may one draw from the results as they relate to the potential threat of the Southern Negro to break the white hold on local government in this region?

Memphis has a population of 600,000, of whom 37 per cent are Negroes. It is located at the junction of three states and is the economic and cultural center of a predominantly agricultural region composed of western Tennessee, northern Mississippi, eastern Arkansas, and southeastern Missouri. Until recent years when manufacturing plants and distribution centers or sales offices were moved to Memphis from Eastern or Midwestern cities, the population was largely drawn from the "Deep South" and consequently reflected the racial attitudes of the area. Although the Negro only slowly achieved social equality in Memphis after the basic court decisions of 1954 and subsequent years, 1967 found not merely token but de facto integration of city schools, libraries, hotels, restaurants, golf courses, theaters, parks, city transportation, and other public and private facilities.

Fortunately, the Negro had never encountered the problem of

being denied the right to register or to vote in Memphis. This political freedom was, of course, due at least in part to the methods employed by the Crump machine during its forty-four-year rule.

E. H. Crump was easily the dominant political figure in Memphis and, to a lesser degree, Tennessee politics from 1910, when he was elected mayor, until his death in 1954. His power was first challenged and then broken on the state level in 1948 with the successful race of Estes Kefauver for the U.S. Senate. A group of Memphis business and professional men, led by a hardware company executive, Edmund Orgill, opposed Crump in the 1948 senatorial race and then went on to elect Orgill mayor in 1955, shortly after Crump's death.

During Crump's regime it was customary for Negroes in the city and county to be registered and voted as part of the machine's strength at the polls. Some observers estimate that no more than 10,000 Negroes were ever registered prior to the first challenge to Crump in 1948. A prime benefit to the Negro, therefore, was the clearly established precedent that he was entitled to register and to vote. There were no legal obstacles in his path, although it was necessary to register periodically and to pay a poll tax. These requirements were enforced against *white and Negro*, however, and there seems to have been no systematic campaign to prevent Negro registration or voting.

In 1948, prior to the Kefauver campaign, there were an estimated seven thousand registered Negro voters in Memphis. During an intensive Negro registration drive, as many as 18,500 were probably registered. By 1955, well before Negro voter registrations were taking place under court order in parts of the deep South, more than 35,000 Negroes, or 25 per cent of the city's total registration, were qualified to vote. As a result of the introduction of a permanent registration system in 1949, and the virtual abolition of the poll tax, the Negro once registered could continue to qualify as a voter unless he stayed away from the polls for four years. By 1959 the number of registered Negro voters had increased to more than 50,000, and in the summer of 1967 the total had risen to 78,655 as compared with 152,562 registered white voters. It was on the potential of this voting group that the New York *Times* could predict on August 9, 1967, that "with a heavy Negro bloc vote, Mr. Willis could lead the field in the October 5th election."

II. Negro Candidates in Recent Past Elections

Willis' campaign for the mayor's post was to a degree the culmination of efforts which Negro candidates had been making for more than a decade in the Memphis political arena. In the 1955 municipal election, a Negro Baptist minister fell six thousand votes short of election to one of the four seats on the school board. In 1958, a Negro attorney polled 26,266 votes in an unsuccessful race for the state Legislature.

By 1959, the Negro community was ready to make its strongest bid for elective office with a slate of candidates running for the school board, tax assessor, juvenile court judge, and the city commission. One of the candidates, Russell Sugarmon, Jr., native Memphian and graduate of Harvard Law School, had practiced law in Memphis since 1956. At the age of thirty he entered the 1959 race for commissioner of public works with one partner, Ben L. Hooks, running for juvenile court judge, and a third partner, Willis, serving as a campaign manager for both candidates.

As the Negro campaigns, especially the Sugarmon effort, mounted in intensity, there was great pressure during the summer in the white community to force some of the five white candidates to withdraw. One of the stronger white candidates did pull out (although his name remained on the ballot), and the successful candidate, William Farris, attorney and city personnel director, had the endorsement of both newspapers and many, although not all, of the "good government" or civic groups. Farris polled a total of 58,925 votes, and Sugarmon came in second with 35,348 votes. The white candidate in third place, John Ford Canale, had 19,297 votes. The 1959 election was of such intense interest, largely because of the racial overtones, that 129,870 ballots were cast—well over the previous high of 86,370 in the 1955 city election.

Hooks, Negro attorney and Baptist minister, was defeated in his juvenile court race but was later appointed by Governor Frank Clement to the Shelby County Criminal Court, the highest judicial position ever attained by a Negro in Tennessee. In August, 1966, Hooks was unopposed in his first bid for election to the judgeship.

In 1960 a Negro was elected to the Shelby County Democratic

Executive Committee and became the first Negro to hold an *elective* office in Shelby County since the Reconstruction period. It was in this 1960 general election that A. W. Willis ran unsuccessfully for the Shelby County Quarterly Court in his first bid for a major elective office. The thirty-six-year-old attorney was born in Birmingham, but had lived in Memphis since he was two. He was a product of the Memphis public schools, graduated from Talladega College, and obtained his law degree from the University of Wisconsin. After a period in the armed forces from 1943 to 1946, and his college education, Willis returned to Memphis to practice law in what became the first integrated law firm in Memphis. His business interests led him to become co-founder and president of a savings and loan association with assets of more than $2 million, and the president of a realty and mortgage company.

In July, 1961, Willis became the subject of a bitter controversy in the city commission when Mayor Henry Loeb successfully blocked his appointment to the Memphis Transit Authority and prevailed upon the commission to accept another Negro appointee who was presumably more acceptable to the conservative or segregationist elements of the city.

By 1964, Willis was ready to make his first successful political race. In the August 6 Democratic primary, he defeated three opponents in a race for the Tennessee House of Representatives, polling 24,726 votes to a combined total of 39,038 for the three white candidates (who received 19,799, 17,680, and 7,559, respectively). In November, 1964, Willis went on to edge out a white Republican candidate by a vote of 97,373 to 94,668 and thus became the first Negro to serve in the Legislature from Shelby County since Reconstruction.

He had the distinction in 1965 of being the only Negro member of the Tennessee Legislature, where he was a member of the Legislative council and served on several key committees. As a first-term Democratic representative, he voted for a bill to strengthen milk price controls, a mental health "bill of rights" act, a bill to extend truck length limits, minimum wage legislation, a driver re-examination bill, and a measure which gave Republicans control of the election commission in thirty-seven of the state's ninety-five counties. During his tenure in the Legislature, Willis became chairman of the Governor's

Committee on Human Relations and was vice-president of the Shelby Democratic Club.

When Willis came up for re-election in November, 1966, he ran unopposed for one of the sixteen newly created state legislative districts and received 8,140 votes. Two other Negroes, J. O. Patterson and Russell B. Sugarmon, were also elected to the Legislature at that time.

III. The 1967 Municipal Election

It was in 1966 that Willis served as vice-chairman and director of the Program of Progress Committee, which recommended the mayor-council form of government. Although the incumbent mayor, William B. Ingram, Jr., vigorously fought the change, the voters approved the new government charter amendment on November 8, 1966, by the wide margin of 56,808 to 39,211. The new mayor and the thirteen-member council were to be elected on October 5, 1967, with a run-off taking place, if needed, on November 2.

As the campaign for mayor began, Willis cast his hat in the ring along with those of six other candidates. His white opponents included Mayor Ingram, former Mayor Loeb, two incumbent city commissioners, Hunter Lane and Pete Sisson, County Sheriff William N. Morris, and Mrs. O. E. Oxley, operator of a small downtown airport.

Willis announced a platform which called for revision of the tax structure and a possible increase in revenue, promotion of higher wages, establishment of a Small Business Administration and a Commercial and Industrial Commission, upgrading of educational and recreational facilities, elimination of substandard housing, a step-up in the anti-poverty program, an end to racial discrimination, and the creation of a civilian review board for police.

In talks to Negro voters, Willis challenged them to "shake off 100 years of fear and inferiority because you're black. This is a crusade that will lead to democracy and freedom." Representative John Conyers, liberal Negro congressman from Michigan, came to Memphis to campaign for Willis because of his "desire to see Memphis break the cotton curtain and be the first major city in America to elect a Negro mayor."

From the beginning of his campaign Willis apparently assumed that he would (*a*) get a significant portion of the Negro vote, and (*b*) that he would have to obtain 10,000 to 15,000 white votes in order to win. His campaign managers, Mrs. Russell Sugarmon (wife of his law partner) and Dr. Darrell J. Doughty, professor of Bible at Southwestern College, concentrated their efforts in organizing support in the white suburban areas of East Memphis. The intent was to convince both white and Negro voters that Willis could and would pick up white votes. To a certain extent Willis appealed to the conscience of the white liberal to show that a Negro had a chance to "prove himself" and his race as the top elected official of a Southern city: "I'm running to give the white folks the opportunity to free themselves of guilt, 100 to 200 years of guilt and hypocrisy."

The real problem, which became more apparent as the campaign neared the final stages, was to prevent Negro voters from swinging to Mayor Ingram, who was working day and night in the Negro community. Some Negroes joined the mayor's campaign because of past and promised favors from the mayor. A good many Negroes probably resented the fact that Willis represented the successful and wealthy Negro group and thought that he had forgotten them. Others questioned the possibility that any Negro candidate could win and wanted to cast their lot with a winner—even a white candidate—at Willis' expense. As Willis put it,

This campaign is raising for the first time the real problem of racial inferiority. The Negro has been taught to be inferior. He thinks the white man's ice is colder, his sugar is sweeter, his medicine is better. When I step out and say I want to be Mayor of the town, that's way ahead of most Negroes' thinking. They've first got to believe in themselves, they've got to believe that a Negro is capable of running the city.

Willis repeatedly stressed his campaign platform (better educational opportunities, such as a junior college, a system of kindergartens, an expanded anti-poverty program, open housing legislation, etc.) and told his Negro audiences, "Forget about I'm black and vote on that (i.e., the platform) and that alone."

Negro supporters of Mayor Ingram continued to press the theme that it was "impossible for you [Willis], or any Negro to become mayor of our city at this time." In a letter circulated by the Union Baptist Churches Association, which apparently represented ten Negro churches, two Negro ministers repeated a rumor which Willis continued to deny without complete success: "We are not saying that you have been paid $35,000 to divide the Negro vote as has been rumored on every corner and in the newspaper. We want to think that no member of our race would stoop to such a level as to use his own people to further his own selfish purposes."

As the election results were tabulated on the night of October 5, 1967, it was obvious that the Negro vote was a big factor in the election—but not in the way anticipated by some observers. The two run-off spots were won by Loeb with 47,778 votes and Ingram who polled 36,074. Sheriff Morris, endorsed by the *Commercial Appeal*, was in third place with 30,979; and Willis finished fourth with 17,744. Commissioners Lane (endorsed by the *Press Scimitar*) and Sisson finished fifth and sixth with totals of 8,795 and 3,262. Mrs. Oxley trailed the field with 256 votes.

In an interesting sidelight to the mayor's race, three Negroes were elected to the thirteen-man city council. Two of the councilmen, J. O. Patterson, Jr., and Rev. James L. Netters, were chosen to represent districts having a predominantly Negro population. The third council member, Fred L. Davis, librarian in the County Registrar's Office, was elected by a vote of 9,934 to 8,718, defeating a white candidate in a district which was the nearest to being evenly divided between white and Negro registered voters, with 18,189 white and 16,309 Negroes.

It was obvious that the turnout of Negro voters was light despite the fact that a Negro candidate was in the mayor's race and that several others were seeking council posts. Van Pritchartt, *Press Scimitar* city editor, commented on the fact that of the 80,033 Negroes registered, 53 per cent voted as compared with more than a 61 per cent turnout of voters in the election as a whole. In predominantly white ward 57, the turnout was 76.5 per cent.

The second key factor relative to the Negro vote was that Ingram received 54 per cent of the vote in the thirty-four predominantly Negro precincts, while Willis got only 37 per cent in the same area. As the *Commercial Appeal* commented on the day following the election:

Perhaps the most surprising element in the race was the magnitude of Mayor Ingram's victory in the Negro areas although there had been reports in the waning days of the campaign that the Mayor was forging ahead of Mr. Willis. The margin of the mayor's support in the Negro community had been considered the biggest unpredictable factor in the race.

Out of a total of 159 precincts, Loeb carried ninety-three; Ingram, fifty-six; Morris, seven; and Willis, three. Willis carried one predominantly Negro precinct and two in mixed racial areas but came in second in all other so-called Negro precincts. (In the November 2, 1967, run-off, Loeb, the winner, carried all of the white precincts, while Ingram swept all of the Negro precincts.)

One of the "major surprises," as the *Memphis Press Scimitar* put it in an editorial following the election, was the fact that Ingram got more of the Negro vote than did Willis: "The significant thing here is the destruction of the Negro bloc-voting myth. Individual Negro citizens obviously exerted their right of choice to a large degree."

How does one account for the relatively light Negro support which Willis received? There are several factors which can be cited:

1. Ingram ran a very well-financed campaign, concentrating on the Negro voters and stressing the jobs which he had given Negroes in his term as mayor.

2. Negro ministers supporting Ingram were apparently successful in persuading many of their people that Willis could not win and that he had been paid by Loeb to enter the race in an effort to undercut Ingram.

3. The rank-and-file Negro voters may have felt jealousy or resentment toward Willis and the NAACP leadership of which he was a part. Perhaps the "civil rights progress" of the past decade in Memphis actually had little effect on the Negro who still worked for "five dollars a day and car fare." The "average Negro" may have identified more with Ingram and his "common man" approach than with the more wealthy Willis. Ingram had successfully built up his image as a defender of Negroes in his tenure as city judge and in his battles with the police.

4. The Willis campaign was not as well financed, showing total expenditures of $12,382, and probably was not as effectively organized as those of Ingram and Loeb.

5. Willis and his managers may have erred in spending time and energy seeking white votes while failing to estimate correctly Ingram's appeal in the Negro areas. There was a zealous attempt on their part to persuade the white liberals to support the "best qualified candidate," but this idealistic approach may have ignored the more basic appeal

which Willis could have made to the Memphis Negroes to "stick by their own race."

Ironically, Willis may have suffered from a tendency on the part of the Negroes to think for themselves and to vote for the candidate who could do the most for them. In this instance, they apparently felt that Ingram would look after their interests more realistically than Willis. Whether or not this was a correct assumption, it seemed a significant factor in the failure to produce a Negro bloc vote. A large number of Negroes voted for a white candidate because he represented the type of leadership they wanted at city hall. In doing so they rejected one of their own race who was, at the same time, too radical for a great segment of the white community. Perhaps this was a sign of political maturity or it may have been an indication, as Willis put it after the election, "that the people who could most benefit, the Negro people, could not grasp the problems."

Lawrence E. Noble, Jr. / Some Reflections on Political Change

> "I cannot help wondering why God created Coloured people, seeing all the resultant difficulties caused thereby."
>
> Quoted from a letter in *Church Times* appearing in *New Statesman* (December 22, 1967), p. 872.

In Greene County, Tennessee, in 1899, the sentiments of the letter writer in the British *Church Times* sixty-eight years later would have had little immediate relevance. There were 29,027 white people in Greene County and only 1,569 Negroes, 5 per cent of the population. In Greeneville, where Robert Rankin lived as a boy, the "nigger" problem was not of first magnitude, if of any magnitude.

In 1900 in Tennessee there were 480,246 Negroes, in the South 7,922,969, and in the nation 8,833,994, 23.2 per cent of the population of Tennessee, 32.3 per cent of that of the South, and 11.6 per cent of that of the nation. The South held 98.6 per cent of the Negro population of the nation, and only 6 per cent of the Negroes of the South lived in Tennessee.[1] Jim Crow was very well entrenched in the nation, and the nation was rural; state governments were strong. The national government's revenues for 1900 were some $567 million, with a surplus over expenditures of $46 million. The national debt was $1.26 billion. There was no income tax amendment, there were no effective civil rights laws. The Civil War had been over for thirty-five years. An accommodation had been made to the end of slavery and to the inception of the new degrading position for the Negro. Certainly there was little surface likelihood that a Greene County lad would play a vital role in the revolution that was to begin in earnest when he was past fifty years of age.

The purpose of the following essay is to reflect on some aspects of the current revolution sweeping the world, and in particular in the

1. The statistics in this paragraph are from U.S. Bureau of the Census, *Historical Statistics of the United States, Colonial Times to 1957* (Washington, 1960).

United States, reaching as it does or will even the remote and unlikely place of Greene County.

Political change ordinarily comes very slowly in the United States. The decentralized nature of the system is a major cause of this key characteristic. Supreme Court decisions are pronounced, but slowly and sporadically enforced. Congress passes laws which are honored often only in the breach. The enforcement machinery is localized, and this is an effective roadblock to change. Emotional issues related to race, to religion, to patriotism are especially slow to succumb to change. Views on these matters are baked into the local society, and the enforcement of decisions and laws in these fields is primarily in the hands of local people, even though they include officers and employees of the national government.

The system is one of laws and not of men. The political leaders and opinion makers, especially in times of domestic strife, cry out over and over again for law and order, law and order. But this is too often the law and the order of the status quo in that community as seen by the local establishment, and perhaps most often reflects the views of a local majority. *Smith* v. *Allwright* outlawed the white primary in 1944. Twenty-one years later Congress had to pass a law to give the Negro the vote in all elections, a right that had existed in the United States Constitution since 1870. Most schools in the South were still segregated fifteen years after *Brown*. Six years after Bible reading and prayer in public schools were declared to be a denial of the freedom of religion guarantee of the Fourteenth Amendment, in many communities across the nation the illegal practices continued on a large scale.

Majority rule and minority rights are in special tension under such a government resting on a written basic instrument. What happens in effect is that there is no ultimate protection for the minority in the face of a determined majority. The positive law, and local practice, become a force for the flouting of the basic law in which are embodied the minority rights. The urging to respect the law becomes mockery when this exhortation turns out to mean that the majority obeys the law which best suits its interests of the moment. In fact, a major role of law has always been to lock in the status quo in the name of order. When injustice is present in the system, the law becomes a bulwark for the perpetuation of the injustice.

In the federal system presently in use in the United States these deplorable conditions with respect to individual rights are aggravated to an intolerable degree by twentieth-century shifts in some of the conditions of society and in the development of technology. The United States is decentralized to the state level, and the state is basically a rural concept. An urban nation so arranged cannot with realism recognize or relevantly attack its domestic problems. The states as presently constituted are in actuality obsolete. They cannot be improved enough to save them.[2] They must be laid to rest, and new concepts and institutions must replace them—those one-time effective entities, the present states.

Decentralization must be retained in such a sprawling and populous nation, but the decentralization must be to an urban institution. The old state lines must be erased, and new lines must be drawn around the large urban centers. Such a new arrangement will not mean less freedom and less popular control, but rather more of those cherished conditions. The rural fringes of each urban area will be properly and fairly represented in the decision-making councils. These rural interests have no genuine cause for alarm at such a change in federalism. Hopefully, after the bitter lessons taught by the rural forces for so many decades, the urban interests will not abuse their rural friends as they were formerly abused by those same citizens. The rural people may calm their feelings of alarm by observing a lesson taught by Southern blacks to Southern whites. Unless it is one of the many rationalizations for continued injustice, a strong force allegedly contributing to white reluctance to give elementary political rights to blacks has been the white fear that black political power would retaliate in anger against the whites for the decades and even centuries of white oppression. But where blacks in the South have finally come into positions of authority there has been no such abuse. The blacks in power respect the basic tenets of the political system. There is no evidence to suggest that rural forces would fare worse in urban hands than have white in black.

The political impediments in the way of a rational and relevant federal decentralization are formidable. There seems little hope that

2. One of many recent detailed proposals for improving the present system is in Committee for Economic Development, *A Fiscal Program for a Balanced Federalism* (New York, 1967).

formal measures of change on a large scale will take place in the foreseeable future, if ever. The goal must be sought by indirection and by
informal changes. Initiatives have already begun from the national
level. A needed element to hasten the coming of a viable federalism is
in the field of local political leadership. Urban political and governmental institutions have the opportunity and the responsibility to produce this vital leadership. The prospects, however, that such a haphazard, scattered, and undirected and unco-ordinated maze of urban
centers will respond favorably in a reasonable period of time are not
bright.

The inherent localism, the uneven and uncertain movement of the
political and governmental machinery to adopt the policy originally,
and to enforce it effectively once the decision is taken, and the rural
political basis of the urban nation, all combine with the uncertainty
of minority rights in the face of powerful majorities and with the
often perverted use of law for unjust ends to place in continued and
serious jeopardy many of the basic rights of common and uncommon
citizens alike. This is particularly true with regard to the weak and
timid members of the body politic, and these weak and timid include
at least the poor and the Negro, many of whom are one and the same.
Who speaks for these people? Who defends them and pursues their
rights and their deserts?

Why does not the ordinary black citizen speak? Why does he
need to speak for that which by right is his own? These questions
have many partial answers. Complex factors are at the base of the
failure to speak and the need to speak. One factor deserves attention
here. That factor is fear. The role of fear in the realm of politics is
a vital role of which European civilization has been aware for centuries. Fear of what? of whom? Physical fear? Fear of loss of what
status and security one has, however small or great that might be?
Fear forestalls from action those who need to act to assert their rights,
or to demand their rights. In turn, fear enters into the considerations
of those who have the power and often the responsibility to bestow
those deserved rights. Into this paradox of fear enters fear in two other
dimensions.

Long experience has shown that men with power will move politically to use that power when they are instilled with fear of the loss
of that power. They will move negatively or positively, but they will

move. That they may be paralyzed by fear is also a possible reaction, but that is a negative response often temporary in nature. Paralysis does occur. The United States may in the late 1960's be in such a state of paralysis on some domestic problems. Continued pressure will move the nation out of that state. Paralysis, spontaneous and temporary, is no doubt healthier for the body politic than willful and permanent indifference.

The motives of these power holders for movement in the face of fear will be mixed, but fear itself will be a prime mover. These men fear to share or lose their power, and they will bring into play a calculus of fear in their efforts to determine how far to move, how much to give up and yet to continue to retain that power and all of its benefits and sweet pleasures. But these men of power who have rights and favors to bestow must be confronted ultimately with fear if they are to move. Reason is not enough to overcome their fear of loss of power. Apparently the system itself has not the inherent rationality that will inform these leaders with reason and with prudence. They view appeals to compassion and justice as idealistic and academic, even naïve. It is fear that pushes them over the brink and into the vortex of meaningful decision.

Before they do in fact submit and determine to move positively toward justice and right, they will use another facet of fear. They will retaliate against those who make demands for a piece of power through the exercise of rights and privileges; they will threaten, hoping that fear thereby engendered will quiet the demands from below, either quiet them permanently, or at least postpone the day of action, perhaps into future generations when succeeding power holders will have to endure the agony and the tribulation of choosing to relinquish some power.

This last resort to fear against those below, this final detour through the mazes of postponement and injustice, will fail when the final confrontation of fear faces the power holders. This final confrontation must be presented from the fearful hosts below. These hosts are weak and inarticulate, so they must be led by extraordinary men, self-determined leaders inspired by the very tenets of the West which, twisted and contorted in the minds of the power holders, and poured now as a soothing pap, now as a sickening swill, into the mass mind through the education system and through the media of mass communication, undergird the intolerable status quo against which the hosts finally move. These needed leaders must have all the passion and compassion, the courage, the skill, and the rage, and even the madness by the standards of the mass middle, of unusual men in history in order to make effective the confrontation.

A number of problems of organization are very difficult of solution for the seekers after justice and right. In the vast United States there is the difficulty of uneven development. Shortages of dedicated and courageous leadership, lack of funds and the organization and material brought by such funds, including effective communications, the unsophisticated and undisciplined nature of the hosts, and the formidable nature of the status quo give the situation an inherent unevenness. Experience suggests however that the actual naked confrontation with fear in one community, vividly conveyed through the wonders of technology to the entire nation, occasionally produces fear from the resulting threat of confrontation that is as effective as an actual confrontation. This threat situation appears to be the exception, however, and not the rule, and it cannot be relied upon for the acquisition of the desired goals.

This fear which one engenders in order to produce favorable political action is almost always associated with physical violence, or the threat of violence. Traditionally the political system of the United States has been thought to have non-violent change as a hallmark, slow change, orderly non-violent change. The system has been explained in terms of its purpose as one which mitigates and resolves recurring conflicts.[3]

It can be persuasively argued that in the law and order system, the deliberate use of fear and its accompanying violence cannot be tolerated if the system is to endure. Few would probably dispute the assumption that an overwhelming majority of the people of the United States would disapprove of the use of violence as an instrument of policy through which to achieve the goals of the political system. However, when the non-violent avenues of the system are used decade after decade with no appreciable results, when "business as usual" is the attitude of the decision-makers and their followers except for occasional fits of action caused by momentary pangs of conscience or some

3. See Robert A. Dahl, *Pluralist Democracy in the United States: Conflict and Consent* (Chicago, 1967).

crisis, or by both, when "a long train of abuses and usurpations" leaves great hosts of citizens in despair and hopelessness as to the justice and utility of the system, when these and accompanying miseries build frustration into their lives, these people are forced to step outside the canons of the system in order to act. They do not have to wreck the system or clamor for an entirely new system. They can be accorded their just deserts through significant changes in the social and economic aspects of the present structure. But it must be admitted that significant changes are hard to extract under present conditions, for the status quo by its very nature discourages interest in change in itself in favor of interest in altogether different arrangements. In any case, regardless of the form of the results of change, acceptable change only can come for large segments of the society by their moving for a time outside, precipitating the confrontation, wresting the sought-after concessions, and then returning to whatever the new structure might be.

The resort to fear and violence as political strategy is not looked upon as a necessary or desirable permanent or institutionalized characteristic of a rejuvenated system. Rather this strategy is a desperate move wherein deliberately destructive and negative techniques are employed for constructive and positive ends. The aim is to bring the society to its senses, to return its conscience to it, not to establish chaos and anarchy. Not even the most radical rebel leader is able to make a home for himself on the razor's edge. The goals are social, economic, and political justice, the means are extreme, the most extreme, but the goals are honorable, and the strong conviction is that the ends justify the means. There is a willingness, a doggedness, to apply this extreme pressure until the goals are achieved, either piecemeal in rather substantial segments, or all at once. The system will have to accommodate itself to its own goals. The system cannot win the battle for the status quo and survive. Apparently it can learn this lesson only through undergoing some tragic experiences.

To alternative suggestions of stepped-up and more imaginative political activity through accepted channels by these frustrated people, or by others working in their behalf, the record to date returns gloomy and discouraging prospects. Pressure groups for Negroes have existed for decades, and these have gallantly and skilfully fought the battles. Surface victories have been won, many of them in many fields, but after the hurrahs resounded throughout the land, the old conditions continued in the most significant areas of daily living for the ordinary person. Victories have not even come in some of the most basic areas, such as housing and employment. But these pressure groups go on with perseverance, and they proliferate, all in the best national traditions. The system stymies them, slows them, and blunts and negates their most seemingly successful efforts, so that this avenue to change, while important as a necessary foundation for what must come, is by itself too gradual to be acceptable to those many "who have been down too long."

Political party activity as a road to justice is even less hopeful than pressure group action. History and the nature of the United States political system teach one clear lesson: they teach the Big Middle. The ponderous political mass in the center, ideological in its non-ideology and pragmatism, monopolizing the traditional sources and tools of power, and cleverly pulling into itself policy innovations from the near fringes, has forestalled effective radical political action. The extreme right and the extreme left have been kept off balance, fragmented, alienated, weak and ineffective. These groups through the years have come and gone, and made minor marks, but none has been able to become a permanent fixture from which a continuous and fruitful battle could be fought against the citadel of injustice, the Big Middle. Over the decades the major parties have tossed bones, but the constant postponement of more meaningful measures has finally brought a rejection of bones, and also a rage at the callousness of the Big Middle. There is no evidence that there is any change at hand or on the horizon, or over the horizon, that is likely to come about in this dismal political picture.

The blacks and the poor are those segments of contemporary United States society for whom the traditional ways are no longer acceptable. The poor are victimized by the economic system. The blacks are victimized by the matter of color. Since by its very nature the economic system as presently constituted cannot function without a bottom, a bilge, and since this least desirable of strata, the social and economic bilge, will hardly be sought out, the places at the base can most readily be filled by easily identifiable persons. The most obvious badge in this society is the badge of color. Hence the black is doubly victimized by the system. Color works against him at every level, and color in effect reserves for him a "natural" place in the bilge.

He is not alone in the bilge, however, and in fact is not in the majority there. The unplanned, wasteful, crazy-quilt, happenstance-like, socio-economic-determined educational system assures the black that the white poor will be there with him, in the segregated bilge. This is as it must be, for in fact there are not enough blacks to provide the necessary bottom for the economy. The present educational system is geared to produce the needed populace for the bilge. The nature of the economy will have to be changed before there is any motivation or necessity for radically changing the character of public education.

Economic changes that must be effected before the problems of the vast hordes of dispossessed can be mitigated and then eliminated are those that are associated with what has been termed a mixed economy. The public sector must be considerably enlarged, especially in the area of a broadly defined concept of public utility, in an expansion of the concept of social services, and in selected areas of heavy industry. A degree of planning through which the system can become more rationalized is a necessity. These and other changes will hopefully be accompanied by the policy of a guaranteed income. Until these or similar changes are effected, the masses of poor will remain on the outskirts of the nation's economy. An economic place of decency and respect must be made for the poor of all races. This can only be done in a mixed economy where the public sector is large enough to provide a place for the present poor, and especially for the black, for whom the private sector is incapable of developing and sustaining the proper interest and support.

The presence of the black in the white society provides the society with its greatest challenges and opportunities. The problem has been and continues to be that the challenges are met with antagonism and negativism, or with formal gestures and surface action which only build false hopes later unfulfilled, leaving the problem more difficult of solution than it was before the gestures were made. In the sixties the nation began to realize that the white South is not the sole culprit on the race issue. The Negro "problem" turned out to be a white problem of national scope. Experience in the United Kingdom and elsewhere suggests that this is an international white problem. In the future, of course, the roles are apt to be reversed, so that the minority whites will become the problem for the non-whites. At the present stage of this likely development, however, at least in the United States, the problem is one for whites. The whites brought the Negro here against his will, built a nation designed basically for Europeans and resting on European civilization. The United States is and always has been primarily European. People of color, whatever color, were not intended to have an equal role with Caucasians. History has confirmed this characteristic of the nation, confirmed it and clearly highlighted it. It is not always clear, however, just what status the whites had in mind for the people of color, other than an inferior status. The motives and reasons for this white attitude have also been unclear, or at least complex and varied. But these matters are well known to history.

The present puzzle for many observers, and no doubt for all or most of the people of color, is the continuation of the white attitude in the face of much strong evidence in contradiction. Individual blacks by the thousands over the decades have demonstrated through their lives that blacks are in fact members of the human race, that they are not some lower form of creature. These blacks have shown that they can in fact live and thrive successfully within European institutions. Such examples have been numerous enough to convince us that they were not products of accident or fortune. Yet whites continue to look upon this evidence as exceptions that prove the rule of general inferiority of the black mass. Hence the old institutions and traditions and attitudes are perpetuated virtually unchanged. One may point to court decisions and legislation, and "progress" in many areas of the life of the nation, and claim that we are moving slowly toward goals of justice and equality, but this "whistling in the dark" is simply a masquerade before the mounting and increasingly disturbing evidence to the contrary. The presently constituted institutions, public and private, are unable to accommodate the Negro as an equal. This situation is reinforced by a public education policy, by religious institutions, by a business community, and by a mythical attitude toward national history and destiny, all attractively and persuasively packaged and spread about by a remarkably effective set of communication media instruments, all of which form a protective jacket of seemingly impenetrable qualities. Working from within this elaborate network of social arrangements, and through the institutions of such a structure, one would hardly with reason expect to produce significant changes which would require basic alterations in some of the conditions for which the entire system was designed and has been developed to foster and protect.

It is therefore not surprising, only disappointing, that the nation has not adjusted itself to the presence of the Negro who has finally decided that he will no longer believe the white view of the Negro. Certainly the whites are to be congratulated on the efficiency with which they have been able to convince the Negro of black inferiority. The whites have been extremely clever in this matter, so much so that they have become complacent about it and have apparently outsmarted themselves in the process. It may well be that a white can never genuinely accept a black as truly worthy. Black may be too deeply rooted in the white man's mind as a symbol of baseness, of uncleanliness, of unsanitary conditions, of a condition somehow less virtuous or worthy than white, or brown or yellow or red. In any case, and for whatever complex reasons, crisis conditions have developed which seriously question the future of the society as it is presently structured. The black man has been forced to act outside the rules of the system in order to make the system respond. This situation is unprecedented. We have a long history of violence in the nation, but never have the seeds of violence been sown so heavily in terms of geographical spread and intensity or concentration. The present situation is also different from others of the past in that it is informed by similar developments on an international scale. It forms the United States share of the global clamor for justice for all peoples. The black people and the poor people now have friends and ideological support, and these people have justice on their side. Theirs is a moral cause based on the loftiest principles of European civilization. They are acquiring leadership of the character necessary to take them before the seats of power, and they are developing tactics and strategies of action borrowed from fields of human activity other than politics.

The United States' political and governmental structure, its traditional blueprint of federalism; its ludicrous national legislature based on anachronistic localism; its pompous and sluggish judicial system whose decrees are enforced or not as executive and administrative officers see fit; its chief executive struggling abortively to lead within a framework conceived almost two centuries ago; its two political parties concerned with the solidification of the status quo and playing at being serious opponents; its incredibly productive economic system bent intently on just that, production; its superficial educational system prating the lessons of conformity and status quo; its communication media prostituted to the goddess profit; its social arrangements set up on the basis of quantity and not quality; its religious institutions hell-bent on a competition in irrelevancy; such a system has no time or place for the poor or for the black. There is no noticeable move toward effective voluntary action for change. The neglected people are thus forced to move on their own. They will demand what they deserve, what is theirs by right. They turn perceptively to the tactic and strategy of fear and violence, the ultimate resources after the conventional resources have been tried and been proved useless and barren of results, and even of hope.

In the course of a single lifetime, devoted as it has been to the study and praise and practice of the principles of a total constitutional, legal, and political system that rests heavily on classic concepts of individual rights and justice, the system has finally ground to a halt and is foundering from a stubborn refusal to apply its own revered concepts to all its own people. The dispossessed hosts, however, are not so lacking in faith in the fundamental but unused and neglected tenets of the system that they will allow the system to languish and die. Rousseau used a phrase in a different context that describes the next stage in the development of the system: the system will be "forced to be free." This approach, which means that the society will have to grapple with unfamiliar strategies and tactics in a very agonizing and frustrating and perhaps hysterical manner, hopefully will result eventually in the admission that change must come, and in substantial and even radical innovations in the economic, social, and political aspects of society. The efficacy of fear as a political tool, and the inherently absorbent character of the essentially accommodating system, can be the salvation of the system, and can raise it to a new level of compassion and justice. The future is in the hands of those who control the system. They and their supporters will finally determine whether the system will adjust and renew and become compassionate and creative, or whether it will be wrecked by their own narrowness and stubbornness.

Charles B. Hagan / Cigarettes and Public Policy: The Inauguration of a New Policy

I

Recent scientific findings demonstrate that cigarette smokers risk a higher probability of ill health and earlier death than do non-smokers. These findings have been announced officially by several governments; here the concern is with the announced findings of an agency of the U.S. government.

Research connecting cigarette smoking with specific illnesses has been under way for some time. The most damaging evidence began to appear in scientific and medical journals just prior to World War II, and since then additional findings have continued to accumulate. The result has been public pressure to eliminate the consequences that could be produced by cigarette smoking. Many private organizations involved in activities relating to such health problems as cancer, heart disease, and bronchial troubles have pressed in the same direction. The Kennedy administration responded in 1961 with the appointment of a committee to investigate and report the situation. The report was made in 1964, following a similar one in Great Britain.[1]

Before dealing with the findings of the American report,[2] it will be useful to examine the status of tobacco in the United States. Prior to these recent developments on the national scene, there had been some state legislation bearing on the sale of cigarettes. Before World War I their sale had been prohibited in a number of states, and the commerce clause of the national Constitution had been held not to be a barrier to state control of the sale of imported cigarettes. A cigarette manufacturer in North Carolina had sent cigarettes in an open container to a retailer in Tennessee, a state that prohibited their sale. The retailer would place the open container on his counters and make

1. Royal College of Physicians of London, *Smoking and Health: A Summary of a Report Prepared by the Royal College* (London, 1962).
2. *A Report of the Advisory Committee to the Surgeon General of the Public Health Service on Smoking and Health*, Public Health Service Publication No. 1103 (Washington, 1964).

sales from it. The obvious gambit was to take advantage of the immunity of interstate commerce from state regulation, a situation that had undermined state restraints in some cases. The ruling of the Supreme Court in this instance[3] allowed the state law to control the sales. The decision is interpreted as manifesting a public policy toward cigarettes prior to the immense popularity of cigarette smoking. Lingering evidence of this public attitude toward cigarettes exists in the legislation in many states that prohibits their sale to minors—legislation that would presumably be upheld against constitutional challenges under the due process clause of the Fourteenth Amendment. The rationale would have rested, prior to recent findings, in that general catchall of state authority, the police power, i.e., the authority of the states to provide for the welfare of its citizens. The findings of the report are clearly of sufficient stature to support regulatory legislation grounded in protecting the public health.

The popularity of cigarettes is usually traced to the enormous increase in sales during and subsequent to World War I. They were mainly sold to males, but in the late twenties, advertising by cigarette companies began tentatively to open up the market to women. Constant expansion of cigarette sales in the intervening years has been the pattern. Simultaneously with this increase in the use of cigarettes, there has been a decline in the use of smoking tobacco for pipes and in the sales of cigars. This enormous change in the tobacco marketing pattern has its ironic aspect, as will be seen later in the findings of the 1964 report.

Elaborate sales organizations developed to market the raw tobacco output to cigarette manufacturers, and with this marketing process came large expenditures in advertising, an important feature in the competition between the companies in brand names. The raw material of the finished product, tobacco leaf, is produced in many states, and the crop involves heavy labor expenditures in time and effort. It is often said in tobacco-growing regions that it takes thirteen months to grow tobacco. It is often grown in small patches and sometimes is the main source of cash for its growers. In some areas the small farms are substantially self-sufficient, with the tobacco patch as the source of cash to purchase things that cannot be produced, such as clothing, household appliances, etc.

3. *Austin* v. *Tennessee*, 179 U.S. 343 (1900).

Tobacco was designated as a basic commodity in agricultural legislation in early New Deal days,[4] and it has retained that status to the present time. In many states the number of growers and the peculiar position of tobacco in the income of small farmers combined as a critical influence in the decision-making process in agricultural legislation. Overproduction has been a persistent problem, and controlled production the characteristic solution. Tobacco is also exported in substantial quantities and thereby has developed an independent importance in foreign trade—it is productive of foreign exchange. The excise tax on cigarettes has long contributed substantially to the revenues of the national government. A substantial portion of the retail price has always been the federal excise tax. In recent years the states and the cities have added their impositions, thus increasing the significance of cigarettes as a revenue item. These levies are often the bases for bond issues. Given the questionable moral status of cigarettes as evidenced in the state legislation cited earlier, it has been difficult to conduct public campaigns against the tax increases. Cigarette smoking was not essential and could obviously be considered a luxury by tax-imposing legislators. Moreover, advertising focused its appeals on the leisure facets of smoking. The fact that smoking became a habit not easily broken provided a certain market for the manufacturers and a stable source of income to the tax imposers.

Any set of proposals that envisaged a substantial limitation on the marketing of cigarettes obviously had a built-in set of interests that would restrain policy makers. The proponents of change would have to develop a base of attack that undercut the foundations of many existing practices. Moreover, the costs of the changes would be large: new sources of income for the farmers; new employment for members of labor unions; easy and profitable sales for manufacturers and retailers; and, last but not least, new sources of income for governments at all levels in the system.

It would not be accurate to label the economic and political situation of cigarettes as impregnable, but the operators of the existing system had many potential bases of support. Most segments of society (whether envisaged vertically or horizontally) had been embraced in one way or another, if not in more than one way, in the structure that

4. It was included in the 1933 legislation. Public Law No. 10, 73d Congress, May 12, 1933.

may be called the cigarette interest. The opposition to the cigarette in some measure could be located in the sentiments that tied its use to immorality, but since more than a majority of the adult population was entwined, and many were quite obviously moral individuals, that route to the imposition of restraints was foreclosed. If the cigarette was to be restricted, a source of support had to be found that would cut across all segments of society and that would have an impeccable moral base. That base, it will be argued here, is the maintenance of the health of the population, and the supporting evidence is located in scientific findings, each of which has prestige in contemporary society. The remainder of this essay recounts the stages in the controversy in the United States to the present date.

II

One of the earliest studies to suggest the damages that can be traced to cigarettes appeared in 1939. Intermittent articles in various medical and scientific journals are to be found in subsequent years.[5] The first major appearance of such findings in a popular journal is an article in *Reader's Digest* in 1954 with a follow-up piece a year later. The many health organizations, with their varied specialties, began making judgments in the fifties. International exchanges began also, i.e., research studies dealing with the correlations between cigarette smoking and various diseases and/or bad conditions in the physiology of smokers. New reports have continued to appear in scientific and learned journals. The first governmental report which directly challenged the use of cigarettes is the British report published in 1962. Prior to this date a demand for public action in the United States had been made to President Kennedy, who did not directly respond. However, the Surgeon General, the head of the Public Health Service in the Department of Health, Education, and Welfare, became active. Steps were taken that led to the appointment of a committee to appraise the findings connecting cigarette smoking with the health problems of those who smoked. The process of selecting the committee created unique problems. The report was finally made in 1964, and it marks a distinct stage in the public policy situation. A variety of govern-

5. Each of the subject matter chapters in the report has a bibliography. Public Health Service Publication No. 1124 (1963) is a *Bibliography on Smoking and Health, 1958-1963*.

mental and private activities thereby gained enough impetus to induce changes in the marketing situation with regard to cigarettes. Each of these activities merits some description as part of the new status quo of cigarettes.

The British report of 1962 was made to the Royal College of Physicians by a committee that had been appointed in 1959. The committee's assignment had been, "To report on the question of smoking and atmospheric pollution in relation to carcinoma of the lung and other illnesses." Not all of its conclusions will be summarized here but the following may be cited:

> The benefits of smoking are almost entirely psychological and social. It may help some people to avoid obesity. There is no reason to suppose that smoking prevents neurosis.
>
> Cigarette smoking is a cause of lung cancer and bronchitis, and probably contributes to the development of coronary heart disease and various other less common diseases. It delays healing of gastric and duodenal ulcers.[6]

It is not the intention to examine the British report in any detail, but only to point to its ideological relation to the United States report of 1964. An examination of the two reports will show a close connection in the types and character of findings.

Events that preceded the appointment of the committee in 1961 threw some light on the context in which the U.S. report was made. In 1954 the cigarette manufacturing industry formed a research committee (the Tobacco Industry Research Committee, subsequently renamed the Council for Tobacco Research—U.S.A.) to conduct investigations and to enable it to evaluate the findings in the many studies already made and the new ones that were being published. The council "supports research through a program of grants-in-aid." It has a scientific advisory board headed by a director who is an eminent scientist. The reports of the director include summaries of the findings of independent scientists subsidized with the substantial funds that have been made available for their researches.

In the fifties long-standing organizations devoted to the study of human physiology and diseases, e.g., cancer, heart, and bronchial troubles; medical societies; and the institutes of health in the Department of Health, Education, and Welfare made grants for studies that

6. Royal College of Physicians, *Smoking and Health.*

related to cigarette smoking. Parent-teacher associations and private health organizations began to take policy positions that warned of the dangers of smoking cigarettes.

The general burden was that cigarette smoking was linked in some manner to all these ills. The findings are always quantitative and correlative. There has not yet appeared a theory that connects smoking to disease in a cause-effect relationship of a simple character. The complexities of the variables and the variations in findings enable the opponents of control always to suggest that further research and testing is necessary to establish the base for a public policy. Some of these features will be examined below. Two conceded findings make trouble for the proponents of a change in policy toward cigarettes. First, not all cigarette smokers develop the illnesses that are asserted to be connected with cigarettes, although a high proportion of those who have certain illnesses do smoke. However, some who do not smoke have the illnesses. The second problem emerges from the differences in the quantities of illnesses in female and male smokers; usually fewer females are affected. There are many hypotheses advanced to explain the variations, but they exist as an area of doubt for opponents.

The difficulties of interpreting evidence correctly do not exhaust the case of the opponents of change. They argue, and often the leaders of change agree, that it is not the government's responsibility to decide for the individual whether he should smoke. The opponents of change make the proposition: even though it is the case that smoking cigarettes will probably shorten life and increase markedly the prospect of illnesses, the individual should still make the decision. Obviously this line of reasoning postulates a range of discretion in individuals that appeals to many who do not smoke. In none of the materials surveyed in the preparation of this paper has the reply been made that adults who continue smoking and become ill are costly to the society. The costs would appear in the form of failures to report for work, with the consequent loss in total outputs, in smaller outputs traceable to physical weaknesses that coincide with the habit of cigarette smoking, and in the less tangible but nontheless greater demand that is made on hospital and physician's time and skills—time and skills that may otherwise be devoted to illnesses that are not so firmly associated with individual behaviors that have predictable probable results. The obvious counterargument would be that the social and personality consequences of smoking are worth the risks involved. The answers to these equations are not simple, and not merely because smoking is a habit that is difficult to overcome.

The economic base of cigarettes ramifies in a number of directions in the economy. Mr. Bowman Gray, who was chairman of the board of R. J. Reynolds, appeared on behalf of his company and associated cigarette manufacturers before the Committee on Interstate and Foreign Commerce of the House of Representatives. He made the following statement:

The tobacco business is this country's oldest industry, and millions of persons depend, directly or indirectly, upon tobacco for their livelihood. In 1964, some 500,000 farms—approximately 700,000 farm families—produced tobacco which had a cash value of over $1.3 billion. The importance of tobacco to our foreign commerce and to our balance of trade has been pointed out frequently. Exports of leaf tobacco and tobacco products totaled more than $544 million in 1964. Indeed, the value of tobacco exports is equal to almost one-fifth of this country's balance-of-payments deficit. Federal, State and local governments derived about $3.3 billion in tax revenues from cigarettes in fiscal 1964. The tobacco industry is clearly a vital sector in this country's economy.[7]

He did not point out that another program of the national government provided for control of the growth of tobacco as a basic commodity. The controls date from the early New Deal and have been continued with greater regularity than for most of the "basics." Twenty-one states have some connection with the growth of tobacco. In some of the same states manufacture of cigarettes is an important industry which, through the manufacturing process, relates organized labor to the output of cigarettes. The marketing of the product coincides with the geographical area of the nation. The making of a political base for the industry is obvious.

No state or locality is solely concerned with tobacco production and the subsequent stages of its processing. Moreover, the same communities whose economic livelihood is closely related to tobacco have members who fear the widespread habit of smoking. Not least among these are the parents of the youngsters whose future health is forecast in the medical findings.

There is then the advertising angle. The press in all its forms has

7. U.S. Congress, House Committee on Interstate and Foreign Commerce, *Hearings on H.R. 2248,* 89th Congress, 1st Session, 1965, p. 283.

gained income from cigarette advertisements. Granted that advertising cannot persuade a population to do something that it does not wish to do, the techniques can turn a potential desire into action. Magazines and newspapers gained revenues from cigarette manufacturers who were anxious to attract the customers of their competitors. The appearance of radio and later television has been accompanied by increased expenditures for advertising, and more and more there has been a tendency to shift the burden of expenditures to television. Operators of broadcast stations were then faced with the ethical issue of timing the appearance of such advertisements. The National Association of Broadcasters became concerned with its "moral responsibility," or at least the president of the association voiced such a view. Should cigarette advertisements be offered at the times when young people were watchers? Should the Federal Communications Commission in its role as the responsible governmental agency seek to wield its authority so as to lessen the attractions of the cigarette by specifying the times at which such advertisements appeared?

The Federal Communications Commission has also become involved through the application of its "fairness doctrine." The stations broadcasting advertisements for cigarettes have been asked to grant time for materials countering the assertions about cigarettes. Some stations have occasionally done this, but the legal standing of the doctrine has been challenged so that the practice is not universal. Several advertising practices have been discontinued, such as the featuring of athletes and very young people in conjunction with smoking cigarettes. These developments may more properly be tied to the code discussed below.

III

It was in such a context that the Surgeon General appointed an advisory committee in 1961. Its report, as has been said before, was three years in the making. In his foreword, the Surgeon General said, in part:

Few medical questions have stirred such public interest or created more scientific debate than the tobacco-health controversy. The interrelationships of smoking and health undoubtedly are complex. The subject does not lend itself to easy answers. Nevertheless it has been increasingly apparent that answers must be found.

As the principal Federal agency concerned broadly with the health of the American people, the Public Health Service has been conscious of its deep responsibility for seeking these answers. As steps in that direction it has seemed necessary to determine, as precisely as possible, the direction of scientific evidence and to act in accordance with that evidence for the benefit of the people of the United States. In 1959, the Public Health Service assessed the then available evidence linking smoking with health and made its findings known to the professions and the public. The Service's review of the evidence and its statement at that time was largely focused on the relationship of cigarette smoking to lung cancer. Since 1959 much additional data has accumulated on the whole subject.

Accordingly, I appointed a committee drawn from all the pertinent disciplines, to review and evaluate both this new and older data and, if possible, to reach some definitive conclusions on the relationship between smoking and health in general. The results of the Committee's study and evaluation are contained in this Report.[8]

Since this is a study of the policy-making process and the significance of scientific findings to that process, the background of the selection of the committee is of some concern. It has been indicated that studies linking cigarettes with lung cancer existed, and the Public Health Service had shared in the development of the information. The creation of another committee had further implications for future developments in public policy, and if that policy restricted the marketing of cigarettes it was obvious that the operators of the political system of the United States would be drawn into the process, for they would play a significant role in the formation of any new rules.

The major operators of the American political system are many, but for a significant change in national policy the president and the Congress will almost certainly become involved in any one of several ways. The proponents of change in policy toward cigarettes obviously were aware of many of the rules of that game. In 1961 the presidents of the American Cancer Society, the American Public Health Association, the American Heart Association, and the National Tuberculosis Association sent a letter to the newly elected President, John F. Kennedy, urging "the formation of a Presidential commission to study the widespread implications of the tobacco problem."

While no action was taken by the President, representatives of the

8. *Surgeon General's Report,* p. v.

organization met with the Surgeon General. The Surgeon General "shortly thereafter proposed to the Secretary of H.E.W. the formation of an advisory committee composed of outstanding experts who would assess available knowledge in this area (smoking vs. health) and make appropriate recommendations. . . ." A few days later (June 7), the Surgeon General stated that he was going to establish "an expert committee to undertake a comprehensive review of all data on smoking and health." The President later in the same day at his press conference acknowledged the Surgeon General's action and approved it. A couple of weeks later the Surgeon General met with several organizations (some of those listed above) with the notable addition of the Tobacco Institute, the Federal Trade Commission, and the President's Office of Science and Technology. In this meeting several matters were agreed upon: (1) the committee's work would be divided into two stages, one to be an assessment of the evidence and the second to be recommendations, and (2) it was agreed that the second stage went beyond expert findings and would involve other governmental agencies.

A few days later a list of 150 names was compiled of persons qualified to perform the tasks assigned. Later this list was pared by the organizations, any one of which was allowed to "veto any of the names on the list, no reasons being required. Particular care was taken to eliminate the names of any persons who had taken a public position on the questions at issue." From the refined list of the Surgeon General were selected the persons to execute the first step in the evaluation. Eleven persons were associated with the first phase of the work, with the Surgeon General as chairman. The various members were selected with certain competencies in view. The second phase was to follow upon the report of this first group.[9]

Several comments are relevant. The considerations and the tensions that accompanied this selection process made it obvious that the findings would carry considerable significance for future policy. And the interested parties or organizations were granted important roles in the selection process. Those persons who had engaged in the research that developed the challenging findings were eliminated from participation in the evaluation of the evidence. Finally, the President was reluctant to become the direct sponsor of the undertaking. The political system was operating in a typical manner.

9. *Ibid.*, pp. 7-8.

The report elaborates the meanings to be attached to the concept of *cause*. However, that will not be discussed here, except to note that there inheres in the varying conceptions enough ambiguity to allow the proponents of restrictions to argue that cigarettes caused illnesses and premature deaths, while the opponents of restraint could assert equally that no causal connections had been shown. The report's summary rests with the following definition:

The word *cause* is the one in general use in connection with matters in this study, and it is capable of conveying the notion of significant, effectual, relationship between an agent and an associated disorder or disease in the host.

Among the other findings are the following:

In view of the continuing and mounting evidence from many sources, it is the judgment of the Committee that cigarette smoking contributes substantially to mortality from certain specific diseases and to the overall death rate.

Cigarette smoking is causally related to lung cancer in men; the magnitude of the effect of cigarette smoking far outweighs all other factors. The data for women, though less extensive, point in the same direction.

Cigarette smoking is the most important of the causes of chronic bronchitis in the United States, and increases the risk of dying from chronic bronchitis and emphysema. A relationship exists between cigarette smoking and emphysema but it has not been established that the relationship is causal. . . .

It is established that male cigarette smokers have a higher death rate from coronary artery disease than non-smoking males. Although the causative role of cigarettes in deaths from coronary disease is not proven, the Committee considers it more prudent from the public health viewpoint to assume that the established association has causative meaning than to suspend judgment until no uncertainty remains. . . .

The habitual use of tobacco is related primarily to psychological and social drives, reinforced and perpetuated by the pharmacological actions of nicotine. . . .

Social stimulation appears to play a major role in a young person's early and first experiments with smoking. . . .

These statements do not include all of the findings of the commission, but the others only expand or modify them. The over-all general conclusion is conveyed in the following judgment: *Cigarette smoking is a health hazard of sufficient importance in the United States to warrant appropriate remedial action.*[10]

10. *Ibid.*, pp. 31-33.

The solomonic character of that remark does not destroy its assertion that some kind of remedial action is necessary, but the character
and elements of that action are not indicated. The range of possibilities for remedial actions is immense, beginning with the distribution of learned reports such as this one and moving to the other
extreme of heavy criminal penalties for the marketing of cigarettes.
Congressional and state legislative responses are obviously possible, and
there are actions by the administrative agencies that could affect the
distribution of cigarettes in many ways.

The irony, suggested earlier, rests in the finding that while illness
is found more frequently in pipe and cigar smokers than in non-
smokers, neither form of smoking even closely attains the harmful
effects of cigarettes. The original smoking devices are less harmful in
substantial measure than the most recent device, and that is the case
with or without the wide use of the filter.

The response to the report has been manifold. The industry continued and expanded its grants for research. The manufacturers of
cigarettes adopted a code governing the contents of advertisements for
cigarettes and appointed Robert B. Meyner, former governor of New
Jersey, as the administrator with a five-year contract at a fixed salary
and funds for a staff. The code specifies in considerable detail rules
about the contents of advertisements. Governor Meyner has complete
authority to approve or disapprove advertising messages. The rules in
the code compel the cigarette manufacturing firms to discontinue certain messages, notably those aimed at persons below the age of twenty-
one, those involving free distribution of cigarettes to students, and
those designed to make smoking seem attractive to minors. Advertisements had to be submitted to the administrator prior to being used.
The jurisdiction of his agency, as stated by Meyner, "includes labelling,
it includes practically all promotional efforts."[11]

The National Association of Broadcasters modified its code to accomplish substantially the same results. However, the code of the NAB
could not compel compliance with its terms by the member stations
and firms. The changes introduced by the tobacco industry in creating the code altered the conditions of cigarette advertising in a substantial manner. The modifications could in part be traced to the

11. U.S. Congress, Senate Committee on Commerce, *Hearings on S.559 and S.547*, 1st
Session, 89th Cong., 1965, Part I, p. 563.

potential entry of the Federal Trade Commission into the field. That body's activities will be recounted below.

The total response of the cigarette firms was not incorporated in the code. The Tobacco Institute and the trade association of the manufacturers challenged the findings of the report and, on behalf of the industry, gave funds to the *Council for Tobacco Research—U.S.A.* The council in turn made grants for research to many different organizations and individuals, the American Medical Association for one. The grantees were in control of the research undertakings financed by the grants; the results belonged to the researchers, and no effort was made to control the results. Thus, the Tobacco Institute and its members prepared papers and made speeches that usually attempted to counter the propositions and proposals of the groups that were supporting developments in public policy to restrict the use and marketing of cigarettes.

The governmental response to the report took many directions. Programs for informing school children were developed by health agencies in co-operation with school agencies. A few states, including New York, enacted legislation imposing restrictions on the marketing of cigarettes; but, as will be related later, congressional legislation voided such enactments, at least those dealing with adults. It is assumed here that state legislation prohibiting sales to minors remained effective. The expansion in the use of vending machines to sell cigarettes facilitated the acquisition of cigarettes by minors, even though sales to them were prohibited by state laws. Some vendors agreed to locate their machines where minors were unlikely to congregate, but that obviously did not completely meet the problem. The posting of warning signs on machines was another means of coping with the situation. Nonetheless, parents often gave cigarettes to their children in any case, and the children could purchase cigarettes for their parents.

Many agencies of the national government had connections with cigarettes in one way or another, but their positions demonstrated considerable ambiguity. The agencies with ties to the production and distribution of cigarettes were the Department of Commerce and Agriculture: the former simply as the general exponent of the views of management and ownership, and the latter as the exponent of the tobacco growers. In rather general terms, each responded as might have been expected.

It has been pointed out that President Kennedy did not directly sponsor the creation of the committee in 1961, although he gave it support in a later press conference. By the time the report was made (1964), President Johnson was in office, and has rarely referred to the matter in his public statements and speeches. In fact, he sent a health message to Congress on February 10, 1964, in which there was no mention of the report. In a press conference on March 8 he responded to an inquiry by pointing out that the report had not been made a government report, by which he seems to have meant that the results had not been governmentally approved.[12] The President's office has never opposed legislation to control the marketing of cigarettes, and the incumbent did sign the legislation enacted by Congress in 1965.

The report has been adopted by HEW as stating proper findings, and it has become the base for a number of activities in a variety of agencies. Not unexpectedly the subdivisions of HEW have been greatly influenced. The Public Health Service has been a vigorous proponent of action on behalf of a number of governmental activities, and the Surgeon General has played an active role as a speechmaker. Conferences have been sponsored in which conclusions and recommendations have been made, and when Congress began to consider legislation PHS provided useful witnesses in favor of some kind of control. PHS has also been associated with a large number of private and governmental agencies in the National Interagency Council on Smoking and Health, organizations of people engaged in public school and college health work, cancer and heart groups, the Children's Bureau, and others. The council has been active in pressing for additional research and publicizing the findings.

Other departments in the executive branch responded to the situation in different ways. The Department of Agriculture, in some ways a representative of tobacco growers, sponsored increases in appropriations that would provide for research in the varieties of tobacco and the leaf properties that might decrease the potential harmfulness of tobacco. The Department of Commerce submitted an equivocal letter in response to the request of a congressional committee for its views. The department conceded the existence of an important report, but at the same time it seemed to say that existing agencies were proceeding in proper fashion and were doing an entirely adequate job.

12. *Science* (March 27, 1964), p. 1418.

The Federal Trade Commission, which generally supervises competitive practices and advertising claims, has tangled with cigarette advertisers in various ways. It had succeeded in stopping the so-called tar and nicotine contests in which advertisers claimed decreased quantities of both in their cigarettes. The report provided findings and conclusions that became the basis for renewed activity on the part of the FTC, which issued an order restricting "positive" claims in the advertising of cigarettes and for the first time required assertions about the dangers of cigarette smoking in advertisements and on cigarette containers. The commission issued an elaborate justification of the legality of this novel warning device, ordered effective as of July 1, 1965. Since Congress had legislation under consideration in early 1965, the chairman of the Senate committee requested postponement of the effective date of the order. The FTC agreed, and subsequent legislation prohibited the commission from taking action before 1969. Congress, however, has engaged in activities related to the report. The major result has been the legislation of 1965, which will be discussed below.

Members of Congress have responded in ways which parallel the situation among the public at large. Some of them have rejected the findings on much the same bases as those suggested earlier, and in some instances the response correlates with the tobacco interests of the constituency. Some congressmen, especially former Senator Neuberger (D. Ore.), have been active proponents of legislation to restrict cigarette sales. Since Congress enacted the legislation, it is obvious that more of its members favored "restraints" than opposed them. But the contents of the legislation display a number of compromises. It is not amiss to predict that more restrictions are likely in the near future if the research findings continue to support them.

Several members of each of the houses introduced bills to develop a public policy that seemed inherent in the report's conclusions. Each house conducted hearings—in the Senate by the Committee on Commerce, chaired by Senator Magnuson (D. Wash.), and in the House by the Committee on Interstate and Foreign Commerce chaired by Oren Harris (D. Okla.). Each committee made a report favoring legislation, and the enacted legislation was the outcome of a conference between the two houses. There were differences of considerable import in the different enactments, but the concern here is with the final enactment.

IV

The new law is called the "Federal Cigarette Labeling and Advertising Act."[13] The establishment of "a comprehensive Federal program to deal with cigarette labeling and advertising with respect to any relationship between smoking and health" is the goal, and the means to that end is to be achieved by warning the public "that cigarette smoking may be hazardous to health by inclusion of a warning to that effect on each package of cigarettes." A second goal was to protect the national economy by prohibiting "diverse, nonuniform, and confusing cigarette labeling and advertising regulations with respect to any relationship between smoking and health." The latter provision obviously is intended to avoid the existence of a variety of regulations that might result from the exercise of the state's authority to protect the health and welfare of its citizens. It has been pointed out above that New York had already enacted legislation, and obviously other states might have followed the lead. As a result the manufacturers may have had to make containers for each. The congressional legislation is made applicable to all territories of the United States, but cigarettes intended for foreign sales are exempted from the packaging requirements. Imported cigarettes must comply with the statutory requirement.

The definition of cigarettes is comprehensive:

1. Any roll of tobacco wrapped in paper or in any substance not containing tobacco, and

2. any roll of tobacco wrapped in any substance containing tobacco which, because of its appearance, the type of tobacco used in the filler, or its packaging and labeling, is likely to be offered to, or purchased by, consumers as a cigarette described in the preceding clause.

The statute requires the following statement to be on all the packets of cigarettes offered for sale in the United States: "Caution: Cigarette Smoking May Be Hazardous to Your Health." The statement must be given a conspicuous location in legible type, contrasted by typography, layout, or color with printed matter on the package. The

13. P.L. 89-92, U.S., Statutes at Large, LXXIX, 282 (1965).

wording, its location, and other details were different in various drafts of the legislation, and the above is the agreed upon formula. The proponents of stronger legislation wished the statement to use the verb "is" rather than the milder version "may be." The verb has the burden of carrying the quality of the finding on which the legislation ultimately rests. It has been pointed out that the finding is a statistical one, and that all who smoke do not develop the illnesses which are conceived to be the grounds for informing the smoker. Other discussions related to the location of the statement on the container. At different times the statement was to appear on the larger side of the containers, but the final version did not in fact specify this, with the result that the formula is now carried on one of the narrow sides.

There are also provisions that relate this legislation to other agencies and their policies. These provisions prohibit the requirement of any other statement on the package, and in addition the law reads, "No statement relating to smoking and health shall be required in the advertising of any cigarettes the packages of which are labeled in conformity with the provisions of this Act." These clauses are designed to restrain the Federal Trade Commission from pursuing its projected plan of controlling the advertising of cigarettes. In the course of developing the legislation the possibility emerged that the control of cigarettes might become an assignment of the Office of Public Health in connection with its administration of food and drug legislation. One of the statutes administered by that subdivision of the Department of Health, Education and Welfare is the Hazardous Substances Labeling Act. The potential implications of such a situation must have had its terrors for the tobacco industry. But Congress eventually withdrew that possibility in favor of the above controls.

The possibility of Federal Trade Commission activity in the exercise of its authority over advertising is also controlled in the legislation. The statute prevents the requirement of any statement about smoking and health in advertising if the container has the required statement. The act does not limit the authority of the FTC "with respect to unfair or deceptive acts or practices in the advertising of cigarettes . . . ," and it also explicitly denies that it makes a decision as to the authority of the Commission "to require an affirmative statement in any cigarette advertisement." The authority of the commission to issue positive requirements in advertisements generally is broader than the immediate issue of cigarettes, and the matter is not resolved.

The two agencies, the Department of Health, Education and Welfare and the Federal Trade Commission, are required to make reports to Congress on developments in knowledge about the effects of cigarettes and the practices in advertising and marketing of cigarettes. It is difficult to avoid the inference that Congress was unwilling to resolve some implicit problems by these two provisions.

It is also probable that the required statement on the container solves another problem for cigarette manufacturers. There has been litigation instituted by smokers against manufacturers, assigning responsibility to the manufacturers for failure to inform cigarette consumers of the dangers inherent in smoking. The liability is to be found in the common law of negligence, if it exists. It would seem that the statement on the containers would remove any liability thereafter for such manufacturers. Purchasers are advised of the dangers involved in smoking, and therefore they make the decision to engage in the act after information has been made available.

One of the common remarks appearing in the discussion of restrictions on the sale of cigarettes is the unwillingness of the lawmakers to deny persons the privilege of smoking. The inference is that the consumer is entitled to make the decision as to his future health chances. On first sight that seems to be a satisfactory resolution of the ethical problem, but does this situation differ from the use of other materials dangerous to users and where prohibition is the usual policy? For example, it is difficult to see the difference between smoking cigarettes made of tobacco and those made of marijuana, especially since recent findings show that the latter may not have unhealthy consequences.

The enforcement of the new policy on cigarettes is lodged with the attorney general acting through the district attorneys. Violation of the statute is made a misdemeanor, and private injunctions are available in some situations. The reports that are required of the two agencies make it certain that the issues will be raised again in 1969. Already, members of Congress have introduced additional measures to extend controls. It is evident that the status of cigarette smoking is not yet fixed for the future. Already the "tar derby" is under way again. The Federal Trade Commission has now developed a smoking machine that permits it to measure precisely the quantities of tar and nicotine in cigarettes, and the cigarette companies are permitted to quote these quantities in their advertisements. Undoubtedly other developments are yet to come.

V

There are many tribulations in forming public policy, even in less complicated areas than tobacco. In other areas the economic interests at stake are neither so huge nor so diverse and the scientific findings are more precise, i.e., more acceptable to those who have to interpret their implications for public controls. In the instance of cigarette smoking, the findings are complex and difficult to follow. The statistical base may be excellent; certainly most experts in the medical fields involved are persuaded that the quantitive evidence is too overwhelming to go unheeded. Opponents urge a simpler theory of causation and rely on the incapacity of statistical findings to do the work of an adequate closed system.

The political process has been geared closely into the operations of the private industry by allowing those who are affected in various ways to participate in the ongoing stages of working out compromises. The political parties have not played a distinctive role, but there has emerged a fairly cohesive aggregation of those who gain financial benefits by the manufacture and sale of cigarettes. There is also a differently structured aggregation that operates in opposition. The legislative outcome can be viewed as the manifestation of the temporary weighting of the respective strengths of the participants. The next stage may be different, and more extensive controls may be confidently predicted. Scientific findings in the areas of public health may work slowly, but they seem the likely victors.

Robert E. Clute / Fundamental Rights in the African Commonwealth

In a study such as this there is a temptation to treat in detail the specific provisions of the African constitutions and the resultant case law. However, numerous legal studies have been published on these developments and a replication of such research would seem to be of little value. The purpose of this work is rather to examine the operational environment and the political structures of those former British territories which now make up the African Commonwealth in an exploratory search for possible causal factors molding such developments. Individual events under survey are not considered to be exhaustive descriptions of the political scene in sub-Saharan Africa, but are related as being illustrative of the major trends and realities effecting the growth of fundamental rights and constitutionalism in the African Commonwealth.

Developmental Problems

Sub-Saharan Africa, unlike developing areas with more advanced indigenous cultures and a longer history of statehood,[1] must undergo a rather drastic and complete transformation of society which will subject the inhabitants to considerable social strain for some time. This is particularly true since in the African Commonwealth the process of nation building and modernization occur simultaneously under a forced rate of acceleration, rather than in the more leisurely fashion experienced by the Western world. The initial stage, i.e., the movement from a primitive to a transitional society, necessitates the submission or replacement of diverse, primitive subcultures, at least in matters affecting political power, through a new, more unified national culture. This stage is therefore marked by considerable stress and possible threats of violence. The primitive subcultures undergoing transformation will of course affect the new conglomerate culture, but the

1. See Guy Hunter, "Some Comparisons Between Tropical Africa and South-East Asia," *International Affairs*, XL (1964) 47-59.

resultant product will be *sui generis*. The process of ongoing action by which development occurs is, in the main, an interaction between the centrifugal forces of diversity emerging from the primitive sub-cultures and the centripetal forces of uniformity which receive impetus from nationalism and the innovative, modernizing elements of the new transitional societies. Not infrequently the drive of the latter toward unity may be carried out with considerable disregard of fundamental rights and existant constitutional instruments.

In the case of the developing nations the Western world has been rather taken aback that independence from colonial rule was not accompanied by the emergence of full-fledged Western-style democracies in which fundamental rights are inviolable. Perhaps the emergent nations of the British Commonwealth have been the greatest source of disappointment because of the myth of Mother England raising a host of colonies to democratic statehood in the Westminster tradition.

Although Britain probably did a better job of fostering self-develop-ment and self-government than any other colonial power, her efforts until World War II were directed mostly toward the white or so-called "old Commonwealth" countries and scarcely at all toward sub-Saharan Africa. British Africa attained freedom with practically none of the prerequisites of democracy. The British impact did not begin until late in the nineteenth century, and the total period of colonial tutelage in most of Commonwealth Africa was slightly over a half-century. Colonial influence was also mainly concentrated in coastal areas or large cities and rarely affected the so-called bush or up-country areas. Sub-Saharan Africa on attainment of independence was one of the most underdeveloped areas of the world. The indigenous population was in the main poor, illiterate, divided by tribalism, and had practically no experience of participating in or being directly ruled by a mod-ern government.

In addition to the above mentioned problems, the political systems of the African Commonwealth are being subjected to considerable con-stitutional strain by the adoption of new structures and institutions which were designed, not for the African scene, but to meet the needs of more advanced, homogenous, alien cultures. Great demands are being placed on the adaptive and integrative functions in these systems at a time when the pattern-maintenance functions are dependent on ill-fitting, often untested institutions and constitutions. The latter must either change rapidly to meet the demands or the regimes will not be able to survive, as has been illustrated by the number of coups which have occurred in this area. Furthermore, the operation of such institutions has been made exceedingly difficult by the dearth of an active citizenry, organized pressure groups, communications, skilled governmental personnel or other desired roles, human resources, and natural resources essential to the proper functioning of such systems.

At first, the momentum of the old colonial order and the thrill of newly gained freedom were sufficient to maintain stability within the framework of the constitutions which had been created under British auspices as a precondition to independence. However, as the Commonwealth systems began to create a stable concept of nationhood and to prepare the economic infrastructures necessary for modernization, it became apparent that the powers needed by the central governments could only be attained at the expense of the tribal cultures. Had the political systems been able to create expectancy in the form of material improvements for a larger portion of their populations, the process of the transfer of power would probably have been less painful. However, the masses were still removed from both the modern economy and the political institutions. Private entrepreneurs were lacking. Economic developments were slow and mostly in the area of state enterprises which personally touched only a small portion of the population. Outside of the bureaucracy few functional interest groups emerged. Rather than operating as a broker of interest groups as in the West, the institutions of the African Commonwealth countries were often forced to operate through tribal, ethnic, or religious groups. Compromise was difficult as it often resulted in a loss of what were considered to be fundamental rights by the members of the various groups concerned.

Inputs, in the form of demands and support, were mainly forthcoming from the government personnel, the small urban population, and the elite of the tribe or tribes whose major interests were supported by the government. The feedback necessary to create further support from the general population often was not attained. The latter situation was due in part to the fact that the nations involved were still engaged in the creation of economic infrastructure,[2] such as edu-

2. See L. J. Fickett, Jr., ed., *Problems of Developing Nations* (1966), pp. 52-63; E. V. Hagen, *On the Theory of Social Change* (1962) p. 44.

cation, road-building, communications, improved health services, etc., which are necessary for industrialization, but do not in themselves result in increased standards of living. The major benefits to the common man have been in the form of a grade school education (which does not ordinarily prepare the recipients for a productive role in modern society but may actually increase stress[3] by creating expectancies and demands which neither the economy nor the political system can satisfy) or increased health standards which have created a population explosion. Thus the period of development necessary to provide the infrastructure for modernization may well be the most dangerous political stage in the process of economic development.

The lack of expectancy and support on the part of the masses and the accompanying incursions on their tribal and religious subcultures have called for increased central powers and controls in order to ensure pattern maintenance and goal attainment within the political systems. Governments are faced with the dilemma that influence can not be achieved through rewards, so they must resort to sanctions such as preventive detention acts, sedition acts, and press controls. In some cases the need for central power has necessitated formal constitutional amendment, in other cases a tacit ignoring of constitutional provisions. In extreme cases such as Ghana, Nigeria, Sierra Leone, and Uganda, events have led to government coups which resulted in outright suspension of the constitutions or portions thereof. The net result often has been a marked fluidity in constitutional developments.

The Environment

Cultural diversities lingered on in the African Commonwealth much longer than necessary due to the British utilization of indirect rule. In view of the lack of funds and manpower needed for the effective occupation of such vast land areas, direct rule was often confined to coastal areas, river mouths, or cities, whereas the bush or up-country was generally ruled through tribal chiefs or elders. The latter were given a relatively free hand within their own cultures so long as overall British policy toward the area was followed. Perhaps the most notorious example of this practice was Northern Nigeria where rule

3. See, for example, Archibald Calloway, "School Leavers and the Developing Economy of Nigeria," in *The Nigerian Political Scene* (1962), pp. 220 ff.

through the emirates left the local Moslem culture practically intact. Nigeria consequently was faced with an enormous if not insoluble problem of acculturation and politicization. British Africa was thus burdened with chieftancies varying in population from a few thousand to several million people. The complexity of the problem may be illustrated by the fact that Ghana has sixteen tribal groupings, tiny Gambia has six major tribes, and Tanganyika before becoming a part of Tanzania had more than 120 tribes. With independence, the newly created political entities containing such chieftancies were faced with a serious problem of creating national unity and loyalty out of a tradition of extreme parochialism in an area of many subcultures.

Perhaps the greatest challenge to constitutionalism in the African Commonwealth has been that of tribalism. However, the mere number of tribes in a given country is not indicative of the problem. In fact, a large number of smaller tribes within a country where no single tribe can gain hegemony over the others may well foster compromise and hasten the process of nation building. Africa's problems have in the main come from situations involving large tribes whose natural boundaries are dissected by national boundaries, from large tribes which cannot be assimilated by groupings of weaker tribes, or from situations where a few large tribes in a single country are too closely balanced in power to be able to effect compromises. These situations may be illustrated by the Somali in Kenya, the Buganda in Uganda, and the Ibo revolt in Nigeria, respectively. Sierra Leone was initially able to effect a compromise between the Mende and Temne tribes under the leadership of the Sierra Leone People's party. However, the military claimed that the last general elections in 1967 had brought on the threat of a tribal war between the two tribes. The first coup was presumably instigated to prevent such a war. Some quarters in Sierra Leone dispute the fact that any threat of tribal war existed at the time of the take-over.[4]

Tribalism presents a particularly difficult problem in the protection of fundamental rights. Many black Africans, whether modern or traditional in their views, tend to look to their tribe for protection of their personal and fundamental rights rather than to the national govern-

4. See *Report of the Dove-Edwin Commission of Inquiry into the Conduct of the 1967 General Elections in Sierra Leone*, Sierra Leone Government Printing Office (1967), pp. 2-3, 17.

ment. Tribal kinsmanship ties and authority are extremely strong even in the large urban centers of Africa, as is illustrated by the role of tribal associations which assist members and exert considerable influence over their tribal following.

Nigeria is an extreme illustration of the role of the tribe in protecting fundamental rights. The pogroms against the Ibo in Northern Nigeria were eventually answered by open Ibo revolt. Once civil war was under way it mattered little in other parts of Nigeria whether or not an Ibo supported Biafra. Ibos suffered interference with their basic rights all over Nigeria to such an extent that vast numbers migrated back to Iboland. Today in Nigeria an African with no tribal markings, a lighter skin, and European-style clothing may run considerable risk and discomfort outside of Biafra, as he may be mistaken for an Ibo unless he can prove the contrary to the satisfaction of his accosters. The fact that Nigerian universities outside of Biafra are now devoid of Ibo faculty is mute testimony that even professors could not escape such an onus.

Another ethnic dimension adding to diversity is that of non-Africans. East and South Africa, of course, have the problem of white settlers which fortunately is not the case in the West African Commonwealth. The problems of white domination of black Africans eventually caused the Republic of South Africa to leave the Commonwealth. With the advent of independence, the European influence declined considerably, but the large landholdings and commercial activities of Europeans still present problems in some areas where the term "colonialist" has been replaced by the term "expatriate."

The Asians (mostly Indians and Pakistani), the Lebanese, and to a lesser extent the Syrians have long been the merchants and traders of Commonwealth Africa. They have an unenviable position roughly analogous to the Jews of Europe before World War II and face considerable animosity due to their cultural and economic position. The laws of numerous African Commonwealth countries are designed to exclude or discriminate against such individuals, even though they have been born within these countries. Discriminatory legislation covers such matters as citizenship, voting, holding of office, ownership of real property, occupational licensing, and other rights. Table I is indicative of the extent of the problem of the non-African in Commonwealth Africa.

Table 1. *Selected Population Figures.*[5]

country	year	total population	African population	European population	Asian population	Arab population
Kenya	1962	8,636,263	8,365,942	55,759	176,616	34,048
Malawi	1961	2,890,000	2,867,230	8,750	10,630	
Sierra Leone	1963	2,180,355	2,172,848	4,030	278	3,201
Tanganyika	1962	8,788,466	8,665,336	20,598	76,536	19,700
Uganda	1959	6,536,616	6,449,558	10,866	71,833	1,946
Zambia	1963	3,581,760	3,410,000	74,540[a]	7,790a	
Zanzibar	1958	299,111	228,815	507	18,334	46,989

[a]In 1961.

At the moment both Tanzania and Kenya are carrying out policies which have resulted in considerable tension within their Asian populations. Although Asians were permitted to opt for citizenship on independence in both countries, many actually did not choose to do so. In Tanzania slightly more than half chose Tanzanian citizenship. In Kenya only about 20,000 applied for citizenship before the December, 1965, deadline, and only about 11,000 have actually been granted citizenship of Kenya to date.

Recent deportations of Asians from Tanzania have reportedly involved both citizens and non-citizens. First Vice-President Karume announced on January 29, 1968, that the Zanzibar Revolutionary Council had decided to expel parents who sent their children abroad to marry. This regulation was evidently aimed at Arabs who married in the Middle East and Asians who married in Pakistan and India. The following day the Zanzibar government announced that the parents of all students who had left the island after completing their high school studies would be expelled.[6]

Kenya with an Asian population in excess of 176,000, most of whom are not citizens but who have British passports, recently passed new laws imposing greater restrictions on the acquisition of trade, licensing, and work permits which affected many Indians and Pakistani. A mass exodus of Asians bound mostly for the United Kingdom began in late January, 1968. Government officials noted in February that about one hundred persons were leaving daily. Colin Legum reported that one

5. United Nations, *Demographic Yearbook* (1963), Table 9, pp. 302-306, except for the Sierra Leone data which is taken from *1963 Population Census of Sierra Leone*, Vol. II, *Social Characteristics* (Central Statistics Office, Sierra Leone, 1965), Table 6.

6. *Daily Nation* (Kenya) (Jan. 29, 30, 1968).

thousand immigrants arrived in the United Kingdom in a single week ending February 17. Although the Commonwealth Secretary, George Thomson, conferred with President Kenyatta on the matter, the latter was unwilling to slow up the Africanization of his economy under the above-mentioned laws.[7] The British government finally stopped the flow by an act of Parliament of March 2, 1968. However, administrative measures are to be made to issue 1,500 entrance permits annually to heads of families who are Asians from Kenya.[8]

Closely allied with tribalism is the problem of communications and mass media. Weak, inexperienced, poorly equipped national governments in Africa often lack the communications necessary to develop national identity and unity. Table 2 is illustrative of the tremendous problems in communications. Oral communication is hampered by the fact that with the exception of Swahili in Tanzania and Krio in Sierra Leone there is no indigenous language capable of being understood by the whole nation in any of the African Commonwealth countries, although English is the *lingua franca* of the elite. In Kenya, for example, Kikuyu is spoken by only 20.8 per cent of the population. Ghana is the most fortunate African Commonwealth entity in this respect, as almost two-thirds of the population speak Twi-Fanti.

High illiteracy rates are also a major stumbling block to written media. Zambia has an illiteracy rate of 58.6 per cent, with the remaining Commonwealth countries varying between 74.9 per cent in Uganda to 93.5 per cent in Malawi.

Wide dispersion of the population has also placed a great strain on communications. Urban areas tend to attract the elite and to serve as islands of politicization and acculturation for the system; however, the degree of urbanization in this area is very low.

The above-mentioned diversities are accentuated by a dearth of communications and mass media. As may be seen in Table 2 the number of newspapers, radio receivers, and available cinema seats is exceedingly low. The nationwide picture is worse than the figures

7. The Nationalist (Tanzania) (Feb. 5, 1968); *The Uganda Argus* (Feb. 7, 1968); *Daily Nation* (Feb. 8, 1968); *The Observer* (London) (Feb. 18, 1968).

8. *The Times* (London) (March 2, 1968). The passage of this act by the United Kingdom will have far-reaching effects on the Commonwealth and is already being discussed in Sierra Leone in connection with the Akar case. The latter case involves the legality of Constitutional Amendment No. 2 which deprived Sierra Leonean citizens of the right to sit in the House of Representatives unless their father and father's father were Negroes of African decent or they had been registered as citizens of Sierra Leone for at least twenty-five years.

Table 2. Selected Cultural and Communications Indicators.

country	percentage of dominant indigenous language[a]	percentage of illiteracy	percentage of population in capital cities or cities of over 100,000[b]	Percentage of population by religion[c]			daily newspaper circulation per 1,000 inhabitants[d]	radio receivers per 1,000 inhabitants[e]	annual cinema attendance per 1,000 inhabitants[f]
				Christian	Moslem	other or unknown			
Gambia	40 (Mandingo)		.089	14	5	81	7 (1963)	9 (1961)	1.6 (1961)
Ghana	61.6 (Twi-Fante)	80–85†	.079	11	4	85	31 (1963)	69 (1963)	.5 (1961)
Kenya	20.8 (Kikuyu)	75–80†	.049	33	9	58	9 (1963)	11 (1963)	.3 (1959)
Malawi		93.5 (1945)*	.005	6	34	60		.8 (1963)	.1 (1955)
Nigeria	33.7 (Hausa)	88.5 (1952-1953)*	.088	8	11	81	10 (1963)	11 (1963)	.2 (1961)
Sierra Leone	45 (Mende)	85–90†	.059	14	19	67	8 (1962)	4 (1962)	
Tanganyika	51.9 (Swahili)	90–95†							
Tanzania			.011				3 (1962)	36 (1962)	.5 (1960)
Uganda	50.1 (Luganda)x	74.9 (1959)*	.034	24	3	73	8 (1960)	14 (1963)	.3 (1959)
Zambia		58.6 (1963)*					7 (1959)	16 (1962)	

[a]Russett, pp. 108-110. Russett's data is based on the 1942 population. The figure for Gambia is for 1963 and comes from the United Nations, Demographic Yearbook (1964), Table 30, p. 681. That for Uganda is for 1959 and refers to the percentage of African population only, ibid. (1963), Table 10, p. 322.

[b]Ibid. (1964), Table 7, pp. 167-171.

[c]Gabriel Almond and James S. Coleman, eds., The Politics of Developing Areas (1961), p. 27.

[d]UNESCO, Statistical Yearbook (1964), Table 33, p. 436.

[e]Ibid. (1964) Table 40, pp. 492-493.

[f]Ibid. (1964) Table 40, pp. 492-493; Russett, op. cit., pp. 129-131 and UNESCO, op. cit. (1964), pp. 473-474.

[x]% of African population in 1959.

[†]Almond and Coleman, op. cit., p. 280.

[*]UNESCO, op. cit. (1964), Table 4, pp. 36-37. Figures are for African population only.

indicate, as in most countries such facilities are concentrated mainly in the cities. All three media face numerous problems because of language diversity which considerably hurts their range and effectiveness. This rather bleak communications picture is further hampered by the rather high degree of government control of and participation in communications.

The lack of private entrepreneurs has left newspapers principally in the hands of the government or foreign enterprises. The few locally owned private newspapers are at a considerable disadvantage as they are usually not able to subscribe to world news agency wire services. The first full-fledged school of journalism was established in 1962 at the University of Nigeria. Lack of capital will also discourage the growth of private newspapers for some time.[9]

The oversensitive governments have also been angered by what they consider to be a hostile coverage by the foreign and opposition press. Libel laws throughout the African Commonwealth are not clear and precise, which makes comments on political personalities a rather risky affair. Of course, some countries have engaged in outright censorship. Since the military coups in the West African Commonwealth a number of newspapers have disappeared, while those remaining seem to be little more than official organs of the military in power. In Freetown, Sierra Leone, for example, two major papers have survived, i.e., *Unity* and the *Daily Mail*. In effect, although privately owned, these newspapers are for all practical purposes organs of the National Reformation Council. Editorials as a rule either reinforce government policy or are previews of forthcoming government policy. On occasion, journalists who depart from this pattern and publish public news not favored by the government are subjected to governmental threats which result in printed apologies on the part of the editor.[10] The news on the government-owned Sierra Leone radio is often a dreary repetition of the morning paper, if not read from the newspaper verbatim.

One noted African editor has said that the most obvious trend in African journalism is the increasing evidence of state control.[11] Newspapers of party organs (which in one-party states is tantamount to a government organ) and government-owned newspapers have been in-

---

9. Emanuel Adagogo, "Problems of an African Editor," *Africa Report*, II (Jan. 1966), 40-42.
10. See for example, *Unity* (Sierra Leone) (Feb. 26, 1968).
11. Adagogo, p. 40.

creasing at a rapid rate. Government information services have increasingly been used as a public press to build government support. This is perhaps best explained by Mr. Mukupo of the Zambian Information Services who argues that the private press is principally a hostile institution serving the urban areas. In arguing for government newspapers he states in part: "When governments need to explain policy, transmit their decisions, instructions, wishes, suggestions, or laws, or discuss new ideas and projects with their electorate, they must have a forum which is not antagonistic to the overall goals of national policy."[12]

Finally, the outlook of the population toward civil rights is colored somewhat by religious orientation. Although this area has Christians, Hindus, Jews, Moslems, and Animists, the major conflict in religious values seems to arise between Christians and Moslems. This is due in part to the Moslem attitude toward law, the relation of religion to the state in the Moslem culture, and the status of women in Moslem regions. Table 2 is illustrative of problems in communication and cultural diversity.

The danger of ethnic, religious, and tribal diversity has long been raised as an argument for increasing the strength of national governments in the African Commonwealth and has in a number of instances been used as a basis for the disruption of the constitutional process and the suppression of fundamental rights. The Ashanti in Ghana were the first to feel the brunt of Nkrumah's preventive detention acts and extraconstitutional measures. The recent suppression of the Constitution in Uganda was obviously a challenge on the part of the national government to break the power of the Baganda, which make up about one-eighth of the population. There is little doubt that black African's impatience with Arab domination played a key role in the successful uprisings in Zanzibar. There is also little doubt that tribal rivalry was one of the principle factors in bringing on the coup which suspended the constitution of Nigeria. Tribal, ethnic, and religious diversities are key problems which must be solved before viable nation-states can be realized and constitutional stability can be achieved.

12. Titus Mukupo, "The Government and the Press," *Africa Report*, II (Jan., 1966), 39-40.

Fundamental Rights or Socioeconomic Stability?

The provisions for fundamental rights in the constitutions of the African Commonwealth countries did not grow out of the diversity of the African environment, but emerged rather suddenly in the new constitutions which Britain sponsored in each country as a precondition to the attainment of independent Commonwealth status. An African delegate to a commission created to study the drafting of constitutions for Basutoland (now Lesotho) and Swaziland noted rather sagely that as long as the British were in command of the situation no one heard of a bill of rights, whereas the latter became a prominent factor on the eve of British withdrawal.[13] The ambassador of Sierra Leone to the United States recently called attention to the fact that since there were no indigenous customs or conventions relative to the African constitutional context there was no choice but to turn to written constitutions.[14]

Carl Friedrich notes that since Roosevelt's Declaration of the Four Freedoms in 1941 and the United Nations Declaration on Human Rights, traditional civil liberties have been overshadowed in post-1945 constitutions by new freedoms of a social or economic character such as the right to social security, to education, and to an adequate standard of living.[15]

Denis Cowen does not find that Africa is an exception to this trend and notes that the African would usually define freedom to mean a minimum of social benefits covering poverty, illiteracy, health, and cruelty. Cowen finds that the fundamental difficulty of civil liberties championed in the nineteenth century, such as freedom of expression, freedom of assembly, etc., is that they all tend to challenge the power of the state, a luxury which many Africans in the process of nation building do not feel that they can afford at the moment.[16]

Perhaps this attitude was best expressed by an African delegate to

13. Denis W. Cowan, "Human Rights in Contemporary Africa," *Natural Law Forum*, IX (1964), 11.
14. G. B. O. Collier, "Human Rights in Sierra Leone," *Howard Law Journal*, II (1965), 503.
15. Carl J. Friedrich, "Rights, Liberties, Freedoms: A Reappraisal," *American Political Science Review*, LVII (1965), 841-854.
16. "Human Rights in Contemporary Africa," pp. 1-24 and "African Legal Studies—A Survey of the Field and the Role of the United States," *Law and Contemporary Problems*, XXVII (1965), 562-563.

the above-mentioned commission for Basutoland (Lesotho) and Swaziland who declared that limited government was a luxury for economically deprived African states and continued in part:

I would go further and say that we need strong government. I do not say tyrannical government; but it would be foolish for us to place such severe and vague limitations upon government that it may not be able to carry through plans for the provision of at least an adequate minimum of food, clothing and shelter. There can be no point in having freedom of speech, freedom of worship and all the other worthy classical freedoms if people are not at the same time free from hunger and ill health and illiteracy.[17]

One student of constitutional development in Tanganyika concluded from a study of government papers, parliamentary debates, and numerous speeches that the most important functions of a modern state are to maintain internal order, to promote continued economic development, to eliminate poverty and ignorance by government welfare services, and to create unity and nationhood out of tribal diversity.[18] This is no doubt rather representative of African aspirations if one adds the fact that self-determination would probably be placed ahead of personal rights in the order of preference of many of the African elite.

All African members of the Commonwealth of Nations attained written constitutions prior to the achievement of independence. All such constitutions except those of Ghana and Tanganyika broke with English tradition in that they contained detailed provisions for basic fundamental rights.[19]

The 1957 conference on the Nigerian Constitution revealed strong minority fears of domination by numerically predominant tribes. A Commission of Enquiry was formed which confirmed that such minorities feared cultural domination, inequitable award of scholarships, economic discrimination in public services such as roads and utilities,

17. "Human Rights in Contemporary Africa," p. 10.
18. J. P. W. B. McAuslan, "The Republican Constitution of Tanganyika," *International and Comparative Law Quarterly*, XIII (1964), 509.
19. G. K. J. Amachree, "Fundamental Rights in Nigeria," *Howard Law Journal*, II (1965), 463-499; T. Collier, pp. 500-507; T. O. Elias, "The New Nigerian Constitution," *Journal of the International Commission of Jurists*, II (1959-1960), 30-46; D. L. Grove, "The Sentinels of Liberty? The Nigerian Judiciary and Fundamental Rights," *Journal of African Law*, VII (1963), 152-171; M. K. Mwendwa, "Constitutional Contrasts in East African Territories," *East African Law Today* (1966), Commonwealth Law Series, No. 5, pp. 1-22; S. A. de Smith, "Fundamental Rights in the New Commonwealth," *International and Comparative Law Quarterly*, X (1961), 83-102, 215-237; Karel Vasak, "The European Convention on Human Rights Beyond the Frontiers of Europe," *ibid.*, XII (1963), 1206-1231.

in representation, and in the conduct of elections. Finally, there was apprehension as to the future of both local government councils and the position of the chiefs. Once again concern had centered to a great extent on social welfare factors. The minorities wanted to be protected against these real or imagined dangers by the creation of a large number of new states in Nigeria, but instead there was provided in the Constitution a Fundamental Rights provision. Although ethnic minorities had not requested the latter provisions, the church groups testifying before the commission had asked for guarantees for the rights of individuals.[20]

In the case of Nigeria, a detailed Chapter on Protection of Fundamental Rights and Freedoms of the Individual, modeled heavily on the European Convention on Human Rights and Fundamental Freedoms, was included. This was perhaps unfortunate as the United Kingdom was a signatory to the latter convention which made the instrument applicable to all African territories until they attained fully independent status in the community of nations. Perhaps the disparity between pre-independence practice and the letter of the convention was not such as to inspire much confidence on the part of Africans for its future success.[21] At any rate, the Nigerian Constitution served as a model for the constitutions of Gambia, Kenya, Malawi, Sierra Leone, Uganda, and Zambia.

The new constitutions, although they varied slightly, did for the most part conform to the Nigerian formula. The constitutions covered most of the conventional freedoms coveted by the democracies of the Western world, such as the right to life, property, protection from slavery, inhuman treatment, deprivation of property, equal protection of the law, freedom of conscience, expression, assembly or association, and discrimination on the grounds of race or creed.

It is true that such provisions were in some cases hedged by qualifications. For instance, the provisions regarding discrimination on the grounds of "race, tribe, place of origin, political opinions, colour or creed" do not apply to persons who are not citizens of Malawi, Zambia, Uganda, or Sierra Leone. The word "tribe" is conspicuously lacking in the latter phrase in the Kenyan Constitution. The phrase also does not apply to certain family or personal laws, such as adoption, marriage, divorce, burial, and inheritance. The anti-discrimination clause of

20. Amachree, pp. 469 ff.   21. Vasak, pp. 1216-1220.

Nigeria did not cover discrimination on the grounds of sex due to the position of women in the Moslem culture of the North. According to the Nigerian Constitution people from other parts of Nigeria could not own land in Northern Nigeria, although residents of the North could own land anywhere in Nigeria.[22] Despite these weaknesses the formal constitutional provisions were such that their observance in spirit would most probably have resulted in a very adequate level of respect for fundamental rights and freedoms. However, in many cases legal and extralegal influences have made great inroads on the original constitutional provisions.

The Governmental Structures

Another outstanding characteristic of the nations under study is the strong role of the executive. Perhaps this is necessitated in a transitional society by the need for a charismatic leader to capture the imagination, loyalty, and support of the more parochial subject-citizen produced by tribal societies.[23] Banks and Textor in their *Cross Polity Survey* found decidedly more leadership charisma in African political systems than elsewhere in the world, and the trend toward a strong executive has increased considerably since that study.[24] The executives are also strengthened in developing areas because they control external affairs which play such a key role in matters of technical, economic, and military assistance. By the first anniversary of their independence Kenya, Tanganyika, Uganda, and Zanzibar all abolished the monarchial form in favor of a republican form of government with a stronger executive.[25]

The position of the executive has also been strengthened by a lack of effective opposition parties and in some cases by constitutional pro-

22. See S. A. de Smith, *The New Commonwealth and Its Constitutions* (1964), *passim*. See, for example, the Constitution of Sierra Leone (1961), Chapter 2; the Constitution of Uganda (1962), Chapter 3; the Constitution of Malawi (1964), Chapter 2; and the Constitution of Zambia (1964), Chapter 3.
23. See, for example, W. T. Morrill, "The Ibo Traditional Cultures," *Comparative Studies in Society and History*, V (1962-1963), 427. Compare R. F. Gray, "Political Parties in New African Nations," *ibid.*, pp. 450-451, and Carl J. Friedrich, "Political Leadership and the Problem of Charismatic Power," *Journal of Politics*, XXIII (1961), 3-24.
24. See A. S. Banks and R. B. Textor, *A Cross-polity Survey*, (1963), 10/164M. See also Gabriel Almond and James Coleman, *The Politics of Developing Areas* (1960), pp. 566-567.
25. Mwendwa, p. 2.

visions which have stifled opposition by creating a one-party state. Kenya and Ghana legally became one-party states in 1964,[26] and Tanzania followed in 1965.[27] After the recent coups in Ghana, Nigeria, and Uganda, political parties were suspended. Prime Minister Albert Margai of Sierra Leone noted in February, 1966, that he had received a number of resolutions in support of a one-party state,[28] but the military coup which occurred the following year suspended all political parties. A one-party state need not necessarily threaten fundamental rights, as has been evidenced in India. However, Nkrumah of Ghana, who combined the strong executive with a one-party system, left a rather sad record regarding fundamental rights prior to his demise, which serves as a warning against personal leadership unrestrained by law. The resultant coups in Ghana, Nigeria, Sierra Leone, and Uganda have of course placed fundamental rights at the mercy of the executive or ruling junta, as the case may be.

Often leaders have demanded increased executive power in the name of nation building and have maintained that unity cannot be created out of diversity unless such powers are provided. This view was followed by Dr. Nyerere in 1962 when he noted in part, "The executive must have the power to carry out the functions of a modern state . . . especially in the circumstance of a new nation such as ours."[29] In the resultant Constitution of Tanganyika, Mr. Nyerere was given the power to dissolve Parliament at any time, to appoint, create, and remove ministers, the authority over the civil service, and "except as may be otherwise provided by law in the exercise of his functions the President shall act at his own discretion and shall not be obliged to follow advice tendered by any other person."[30] Later a presidential committee was appointed to make recommendations for the creation of a one-party state. The committee noted in part: "The Government believes that the rule of law is best preserved, not by formal guarantees in a Bill of Rights which invite conflict between the executive and the judiciary, but by independent judges administering justice free from political pressure."[31] This lofty statement sounds in the best of British

26. Chanan Singh, "The Republican Constitution of Kenya: Historical Background and Analysis," *International and Comparative Law Quarterly*, XIV (1965), 927-929; "Recent Developments in Ghana," *Bulletin of the International Commission of Jurists* (Dec., 1965), No. 24, pp. 20-27.
27. " 'Tanzania:' A One Party State," *ibid.* (Aug. 1965), No. 23, pp. 35-45.
28. McAuslan, p. 508.   29. *Ibid.*, p. 509.
30. *Ibid.*, p. 516.   31. *Ibid.*, p. 543.

tradition until one examines the unusual powers of the president who may undergo "no criminal proceedings whatsoever" while in office.[32] In all fairness it must be noted that President Nyerere has thus far seemed to support the rule of law, but he has created an executive framework which is subject to personal whim and could lead to tyranny as was the case in Ghana. Tanzania also provided for a very strong executive, as did Kenya where the former office of governor-general and prime minister have been combined into one office. The presidency of Uganda on the other hand is constitutionally a rather weak office with most power residing in the prime minister and cabinet, but the latter[33] nonetheless make up a strong executive.

The growth of the executive powers has been accompanied by a movement toward stronger, unitary governments, which have become the order of the day. Nigeria and Ghana both began with regional, semi-federal features. Nkrumah's impatience with the Ashanti and other recalcitrant groups soon caused the central government to effectively stifle any real federal features in Ghana. Regionalism lasted a good deal longer and was a more important factor in the Nigerian political system, but the high degree of hegemony demanded by the more backward Moslem culture of the Northern Region greatly hampered progress and eventually resulted in the military coups. Regionalism likewise failed in Uganda, Kenya, and the Federation of Rhodesia and Nyasaland.[34]

The centralism of the unitary state with a strong executive is reinforced by the lack of trained personnel to counterbalance the executive in lawmaking and law enforcement functions. The lack of an experienced bureaucracy has been a severe handicap. Existant high-ranking African civil servants also were often mistrusted by the new post-independence regimes because their careers were closely associated with the former colonial powers.

The Nigerian system is illustrative of the lack of trained indigenous personnel. Only twenty-six Nigerians had held senior civil service posts in 1938. By 1948 Nigerians held only about 7.7 per cent of the senior posts, and by 1954 they had progressed to only about 16 per cent of them. From 1958 to 1963 the Nigerianization of the senior civil service progressed from roughly 48 per cent to 87 per cent of the

32. *Ibid.*, p. 561.   33. Mwendwa, pp. 6-11.
34. *Ibid.*, p. 5; J. H. Proctor, Jr., "The Role of the Senate in the Kenyan Political System," *Parliamentary Affairs*, XVIII (1965), 389-415; Singh, p. 929.

total number of posts.[35] Prior to the end of World War II all senior
civil service officers in Kenya were European, the middle ranks contained Asians, some Europeans, and a few Africans, and the lower
ranks were mostly Africans. After World War II a few non-Europeans
were raised to senior rank, but it was not until independence became
imminent that non-Europeans began to enter the civil service in significant numbers.[36] Other African Commonwealth countries faced
similar problems. Consequently, after independence the Africanization of the civil service became one of the major aims of these entities.

The legislative experience of the indigenous population was likewise very slight. Most African Commonwealth countries succeeded to
highly centralized governments in which the governor and his council
had been all-powerful, while the legislature had been subservient to
the executive.[37] The appointment of Africans to the legislative councils was a development of World War II in British Africa. The first
African appointments to the legislative councils of Kenya and Uganda
were made in 1944 and 1945, respectively.[38] The legislative role was
developed rapidly and with little preparation. For instance, there
were no elected and only twenty-eight nominated Nigerians in the
Legislative Council of Nigeria prior to the elections of 1957/1958.
However, subsequent to the elections there were 320 elected Nigerians
in the House of Representatives.[39] In 1948 there had only been four
Africans on the Legislative Council of Kenya, but with free elections
and the dropping of color bars on independence, 163 Africans were
elected to the legislature of that country.

The rapid entrance of Africans into the legislatures could only be
accomplished by admitting grossly inexperienced people. For instance,
in the first Senate of Kenya two of the twenty-eight senators had served
on the Legislative Council and both had served on the latter body for
less than two years. There was a heavy reliance on former schoolteachers who composed almost half of the Senate in Kenya. Most of
the others had occupied small government posts. There were only
five businessmen in the Senate and only three senators had completed
a university education.[40]

35. L. F. Blitz, ed., *The Politics and Administration of Nigeria* (1965), pp. 219-221, 225.
36. Singh, pp. 902-915.
37. Aniruda Gupta, "The Zambian National Assembly: Study of an African Legislature," *Parliamentary Affairs*, XIX (1965-1966), 48.
38. Singh, pp. 902-905.   39. Blitz, p. 4.
40. Proctor, p. 397.

The first protectorate-wide elections in Uganda during 1961 produced a similar pattern, as sixty-seven of the 198 candidates were schoolteachers. The remainder of the candidates had the following occupations: thirty-four businessmen, twenty-two farmers, thirteen party officials, twelve lawyers, eleven traders, seven clerks, six union officials, three journalists, one physician, one author, and twenty-one from miscellaneous occupations.[41]

In the case of the Sierra Leone elections of 1957, eight of the thirty-nine legislators elected were former schoolteachers, four were trade union leaders, eight were active party workers or officials, seven were merchants, and only six came from professional backgrounds other than teaching. Of the thirty-nine members elected, sixteen had no government experience at all and only four had experience on a national ministerial level. The remaining nineteen had some experience on a local or municipal governmental level.[42]

The weakness of a representative body lacking in experience and leadership vis-à-vis a charismatic leader in a strong executive office is illustrated by the case of Kenya. Ronald Ngala, leader of the opposition KADU party in Kenya, had insisted at the constitutional conference in London that a Senate be charged with preserving the rights of the regions. However, debate in the Senate proved to be second-rate, few legislative amendments were advanced, and the examination of bills was brief and perfunctory. The first showdown occurred in December, 1963. Due to the Shift raids in the North Eastern Region, the government proclaimed a state of emergency which would lapse unless approved by 65 per cent of both houses of the legislature within seven days. It seemed that the Senate might not gain the necessary majority and Tom Mboya, minister for justice and constitutional affairs, in speaking to the body said in part:

Let nobody be deceived that if the motion is not passed there will be no state of emergency. Then you will have no one to blame but yourselves. The world will know that the people who first made it impossible for the Kenya Constitution to work were the Opposition and not the Government. My own view is that it is wrong to live outside of the Constitution, . . . but I also know that as a Government we have a responsibility to safeguard human lives and property and the integrity of this country's

41. Robert O. Byrd, "Characteristics of Candidates for Election in a Country Approaching Independence: The Case of Uganda," *Midwest Journal*, VII (1963), 1-27.
42. W. J. M. Mackenzie and Kenneth Robinson, *Five Elections in Africa* (1960), pp. 396-397.

boundaries and that responsibility is supreme. . . . This Government must act, and, I hope, Mr. Speaker, with full support of the Senate. . . .[43]

This veiled threat and the subsequent approval of the Senate was but a single event of a series of attempts to weaken that body. Mass media gave much poorer coverage to the Senate meetings than to House meetings and sometimes ignored the Senate altogether. At one period the Senate could not convene for some time because proper personnel were not available to record the proceedings. Although the proceedings of the House were printed within two weeks, there was great difficulty in publishing the Senate records which were sometimes published as much as five months after the meetings being reported. One opposition senator warned that the Senate was being made to appear nonexistent. However, the government was still not satisfied with a weakened Senate because entrenched provisions of the Constitution could be amended only by a Senate majority of 90 per cent and a House majority of 75 per cent. Finally, after considerable government pressure, the leader of the parliamentary opposition declared, "I have a full mandate to declare today that the official opposition is dissolved. KADU is joining the Government . . . and the opposition today will vote with the government for the new Constitution in the Senate." One-party rule had arrived in Kenya and the Senate no longer posed a threat. Any hopes of protecting regional rights within Kenya were thus greatly weakened.[44]

The judicial branches likewise have some rather serious weaknesses which keep them from being in a strong position to enforce any fundamental rights which the party in power would oppose. Not the least of these difficulties is to be found in the dearth of trained lawyers and a lack of contact between the judicial system and the people.

For instance, in 1959 Nyasaland had only one African who was a practicing barrister.[45] By 1961 Uganda had only 150 practicing advocates, of which there were twenty Africans, ten Europeans, and the rest Asians. Most advocates were concentrated in Kampala. Out of twenty resident magistrates in Uganda, only one was African.[46] In Kenya prior to independence the entire magistry and all professional

43. Proctor, p. 409.   44. *Ibid.*, pp. 389-415.
45. "Nyasaland and the Devlin Report," *Bulletin of the International Commission of Jurists* (Aug., 1959), No. 9, p. 52.
46. R. W. Cannon, "Law, Bench and Bar in the Protectorate of Uganda," *International and Comparative Law Quarterly*, X (1961), 879; Singh, p. 915.

officers of the judiciary department were Europeans.[47] Nigeria by 1960 had a thousand legal practitioners, who were concentrated mostly in Southern Nigeria and Lagos.[48] On attainment of independence in 1961, Tanganyika had only two African lawyers.[49] As of February 29, 1968, Sierra Leone had 44 registered, practicing barristers and solicitors.[50] Neither Kenya nor Uganda had jury trial for non-Europeans prior to their independence.[51]

Most lawyers in the African Commonwealth were and still are without any specialization in their practice, but carry on a general practice combining the role of the British barrister and solicitor. Those who have studied law are largely trained in the British tradition. As late as 1965, Justice Singh, of the High Court of Kenya, noted that there were no textbooks in Kenya law and that mostly English textbooks were in use.[52] This is an important factor since British lawyers have a much different attitude toward fundamental rights and are not accustomed to working with written constitutions. However, the African entities have begun to establish their own law schools which should eventually improve the situation. For instance, University College at Dar es Salaam admitted fourteen students in 1961 and seventy-five students in 1965. However, the increased enrolment has not alleviated shortages in private practice at the moment as most young African lawyers enter government service as soon as they are qualified to do so.[53] This is not surprising due to the lack of private entrepreneurs, the role of the government in business, and the fact that government service seems to offer the quickest avenue to high socioeconomic status.

Historically, Western-style justice was also divorced from the masses of British Africa by a dual system of superior courts applying a modified form of British law, and "native courts" applying indigenous law. Most justice in British Africa was meted out by the so-called native courts, which were generally manned by non-lawyers such as chiefs or tribal elders. They not only enforced native law but had the power

47. Singh, p. 915.
48. Sir Adetokunbo Ademola, "Personal Problems in the Administration of Justice in Nigeria," *Law and Contemporary Problems,* XXVII (1962), p. 580.
49. William Twinning, "Legal Education Within East Africa," in *East African Law Today,* p. 117.
50. Data obtained from list of registered barristers and solicitors made available to the author through the courtesy of Mr. Omrie Golley, Master and Registrar of the Supreme Court of Sierra Leone.
51. Cannon, p. 879; Singh, p. 915.   52. Singh, p. 924.
53. Twinning, p. 120.

to punish petty offenses under the Western-style penal codes. Except for serious offenses the non-European population had little to do with the superior courts.[54] The courts of Tanganyika are illustrative of the dual system. During 1953 the native courts of Tanganyika handled 66,000 criminal cases, whereas less than 39,000 criminal cases were heard by the High Court.[55]

Although some states such as Uganda have now done away with the dual court system, the masses are still divorced from the courts because of the traditional legal pattern, poor communications, high rates of illiteracy, the dearth of practitioners, and the fact that there is no effective system of legal aid or provision for supplying defense counsel for indigents. The depth of the problem is illustrated by the fact that in Uganda there is no legal aid at all for civil cases. Although legal aid is provided by the government of Uganda in the case of a murder charge, such aid is confined to the trial and is not provided to draft appeals or in appeal proceedings.[56] In the case of Nigeria it was suggested that civil rights might be better protected if cases could be taken to native or customary courts, but the Lancaster House Constitutional Conference in 1958 flatly rejected the proposal. Consequently, the High Court served as court of first instance and there was a right of appeal to the Federal Supreme Court of Nigeria. However, the High Court could assign counsel or arrange a "dock brief" only *after* the case had already been brought before it.[57] In effect, the legal aid necessary to enforce fundamental rights is a luxury which few Africans can financially afford.

African Commonwealth constitutions in general followed the British practice of an independent judiciary, but post-independence developments have made some inroads in this area. Under the 1960 Constitution of Ghana the president had the power to appoint judges of the Supreme Court or High Court, but such judges could be removed only by a two-thirds vote of members of Parliament. However, the president could withdraw the designation of chief justice from a Su-

54. *Ibid.*, p. 117. A third legal pattern to be found in many parts of Commonwealth Africa is that of Hindu and Moslem law, which, although affecting smaller numbers than native or Western law, adds to the problems of legal diversity.

55. J. H. Jeaney, "The Structure, Composition and Jurisdiction of Courts and Authorities Enforcing the Criminal Law in British African Territories," *International and Comparative Law Quarterly*, IX (1961), 409.

56. Cannon, p. 891.

57. T. O. Elias, "New Nigerian Constitution," *Journal of the International Commission of Jurists*, II (1959-1960), p. 41.

preme Court judge without resort to Parliament. The judiciary of Ghana suffered a severe blow in 1963 when Nkrumah became angered at the acquittal by the Supreme Court of three persons charged with treason in connection with an attempt to assassinate him. Early in the following year a clause was added to the Constitution that read: "the President may at any time, for reasons which to him appear sufficient, remove from office a Judge of the Supreme Court or a Judge of the High Court.[58] In March, 1964, three judges of the Supreme Court and one judge of the High Court were subsequently removed from office.[59]

The 1960 Constitution of Nigeria contained provisions on the appointment and removal of the judiciary which served as a model for a number of subsequent Commonwealth constitutions. The judges of all superior courts were to be appointed by the Judicial Service Commission and could be removed only by a tribunal composed of judges or former judges, to be followed if need be by submission to the Judicial Committee of the Privy Council. The Nigerian system was much admired, but when Nigeria became a republic in 1963 the Judicial Service Commission was abolished. The new constitutional provision provided for appointment by the president with the advice of the prime minister and removal by Parliament.[60] The constitutions of Malawi, Sierra Leone, Tanganyika, Uganda, and Zambia likewise contained provisions similar to those of the 1960 Nigerian Constitution which provided for executive appointment and removal on the advice of a Judicial Service Commission.[61] Sierra Leone undoubtedly has the strongest, independent judiciary in the West African Commonwealth and has managed to retain its independence to a remarkable degree even under the military rule of the National Reformation Council.

The trials in connection with the army mutiny in Tanganyika during January, 1964, were a bright spot in the independence of the judiciary. Five of the accused were found not guilty and others received prison sentences varying from five to fifteen years. *The Na-*

58. Leslie Rubin, *The Constitution and Government of Ghana* (1964), pp. 205-206, 269-270.
59. "Recent Developments in Ghana," p. 21.
60. Eme O. Awa, *Federal Government in Nigeria* (1964), pp. 178-180.
61. See, for example, the Constitution of Sierra Leone (1961), Secs. 75-86; the Constitution of Tanganyika (1961), Secs. 59-65; the Constitution of Uganda (1962), Secs. 90-98; the Constitution of Malawi (1964), Secs. 76-79; and the Constitution of Zambia (1964), Secs. 97-100.

tionalist, the newspaper of the ruling party, editorialized rather sharply that the courts had been too lenient. President Nyerere replied through the Government Information Service that any attempt to interfere with the sentences would abrogate the rule of law and continued: "The rule of law is the basis on which rests the freedom and equality of our citizens. It must remain the foundation of our State. We must not allow even our disgust with the mutineers to overcome our principles."[62]

The legal systems of the developing areas are in a particularly difficult position. They have not yet affected the lives of the traditionally oriented masses in sufficient intensity to build up their expectancy or gain their support. In fact, communications are so poor that it is highly doubtful that a significant portion of the traditionally oriented population would be adequately aware of their rights or inclined to initiate legal action to preserve such rights.

The portion of the population most familiar with modern legal institutions, most dependent on them in their daily lives, and most able to pay for such service are the governmental and urban elite. As a matter of fact, the future of the legal profession itself depends on the success of this portion of the society which will carry out the modernization process, for there could be little future for a Western-trained lawyer or judge in a society in which indigenous, tribal law dominated. Thus the lot of the legal profession more naturally lies with the elite of the political system than with the tribally oriented portions of the population. The courts are thus in a difficult position to take a strong stand against the elite leadership of the government.

Conclusions

During the initial stages of economic modernization and nation building in Commonwealth Africa the most significant factor in constitutional developments had been the struggle between the centralizing forces of the national governments to attain these goals and the forces of diversity emanating from tribal, religious, and ethnic groups which tend to foster the status quo.

In the ensuing conflict the trained elite, with English as their

62. "A Stand on the Rule of Law in Tanganyika," *Bulletin of the International Commission of Jurists* (Sept., 1964), No. 20, p. 49.

lingua franca, with a monopoly on modern technology, with control of the governmental apparatus, and with hegemony in communications, have had the decided advantage. In the process, constitutional instruments have been deeply affected and transformed by political and environmental realities. The latter process has been evidenced by the failure of federalism, the growth of the executive, the lack of effective restraints on the executives through the legislatures or courts, the movement to one-party systems, and the resort to extraconstitutional measures.

The above-mentioned developments, although harmful to fundamental rights, have in part been necessitated by too great a disparity between constitutional instruments and existent realities in the process of establishing new national cultures. The effects of the disparities would in fact probably have been greater had it not been for the feeling of affinity and favorable cognitive images which most African Commonwealth systems hold for the Western world. Many Commonwealth Africans still look to their tribal or religious groupings for protection of their civil rights. Such rights are often viewed as having been conferred rather than being inherent. The creation of a deep, indigenous commitment of the masses to basic fundamental rights may take considerable time and development.

In the past, fundamental rights and freedoms have on occasion been somewhat eclipsed by pressing problems of economic and political development. Despite the high moral tone of the United States Constitution, the American political system continued to condone the institution of slavery for generations, and civil rights cases did not attain great volume until this century. Even the Soviet Union, which has a rather sad history of constitutionalism and fundamental rights, seems to be improving slightly in that area now that Russian hegemony has been established, Communist institutions have achieved effective stability, and the process of modernization has been completed.

If the governments of Commonwealth Africa are able to effect policy decisions which offer compensatory rewards (in the form of pride of nationhood, improved social services, and higher standards of living) for the loss of cultural diversity, sufficient support may be forthcoming to maintain the systems without resorting to extreme authoritarian or totalitarian styles of government. The high priority which many Africans have given to economic and social factors in expressing their expectancies of the new constitutions would support the probable success with this type of reward. The role of factors outside of the system's internal environment in such matters as foreign, economic, technological, and military aid would, of course, play a key role in supplying the necessary incentives until economic "take-off" could be attained. Stability might also be achieved negatively through a heavy reliance on sanctions, but the danger of revolts and instability would be considerably greater.

The data examined reveal some of the prominent, common, causal factors in the constitutional development of the entities under examination. However, it is rather difficult, if not impossible, to predict what the outcome may be for such a large number of independent political systems. The position of these and other developing countries is rather *sui generis* in that history offers no examples of states at this level of development which have attempted to achieve nationhood and to modernize simultaneously at such an accelerated pace. Survey research results and data on which one could attempt reliable predictions as to the future of the individual states are also practically nonexistent. One might hypothesize that once these countries have successfully modernized and removed or minimized internal diversity, their constitutions would become realigned with those of the Western, democratic societies. This would seem to be a reasonable assumption as the political and social actualities being institutionalized by such constitutional instruments would bear more resemblance to the milieu from which Western constitutions emerged. However, the example of the Soviet Union has shown that democratic, constitutional developments are not necessarily an outgrowth of economic development or internal unity.

Fundamental rights do not suddenly emerge full-blown. The acquisition of a deep-seated commitment to such rights requires a developmental process similar to that of economic and political development in general before a period of "take-off" can be attained. That is not to say that the people of Commonwealth Africa will not arrive at proper responses to constitutional challenges and problems of fundamental rights. However, such solutions may be quite different from the original constitutional models, for they will to a great extent be molded by the varied circumstances, aspirations, and expectancies of the political entities concerned.

Enid Campbell / Civil Rights and the Australian Constitutional Tradition

I

Australia lacks a comprehensive bill of rights. Provisions entrenching individual rights and freedoms are completely absent from the Australian state constitutions and they play a very small part in the Australian federal Constitution. So far as they are legally recognized and protected, individual liberties in Australia depend principally upon ordinary statute law and decisional rules established and acted upon by the courts.

The decision not to include a bill of rights of the American type in the Australian federal Constitution was hardly surprising when one considers the course of constitutional development in the Australian colonies down to federation and the extent to which Australian constitutionalism had been influenced by British practices and traditions. But the decision cannot be regarded as inevitable, nor can it be explained simply as an expression of an unreasoned or uncritical bias against constitutional arrangements which had no counterpart in the legal system of the mother country. Australians already were familiar with the idea of a fundamental or superior law controlling legislative action. Furthermore, in framing a national constitution, they were not unwilling to take instruction from constitutions other than the British, notably from the United States Constitution. They relied heavily on it in the working out of a scheme for division of governmental authority between central and regional governments. None of the drafts for an Australian federal Constitution contained anything answering the description of a bill of rights, yet in the final draft presented for enactment as a statute of the British Parliament there were a few clauses affecting individual rights and liberties which clearly owed something to the American model. Why did the draftsmen go this far, but not so far as to propose an exhaustive or near exhaustive series of rights guarantees?

II

What goes into a country's constitution is largely determined by
its historical experience. Behind the adoption of a Bill of Rights for
the United States there lies a long history of tension and conflict, tension and conflict that encouraged a rather suspicious attitude toward
governmental authority and an unusual concern for the rights of the
individual. The circumstances which had led many men of conscience
to make their homes in North America were not easily forgotten. Nor
could Americans overlook the circumstances which had finally led
them to reject the authority of their imperial government and declare
their independence. It was little wonder, then, that having resolved
to unite under a federal form of government, they should have been
especially mindful of the risk of abuses of governmental power and
should have preferred a constitutional structure which concentrated
so heavily on the prevention of these abuses. It should be remembered
too that the constitution-making process took place at a time when
men fervently believed in the idea of natural rights, rights flowing
from a natural law superior to any human law and rights which man-
made law ought morally to respect. The federal Constitution was designed not simply as a basic law delineating the spheres of jurisdiction
of the parties to the federal arrangement. It was intended also to
express the aspirations of the American people, their convictions regarding the purposes of organized political society, and their commitment to the idea of fundamental human rights.

There are parallels between the American and Australian colonial
experiences, but there are also important differences which were bound
to produce rather different attitudes in regard to the proper scope and
function of a written constitution. The Australian colonial experience
was not one that generated heat, passion, or prejudice. Relative to
that of the United States, it was short and uneventful. Colonial statesmen, it is true, had to take the initiative in pressing for a relaxation of
imperial controls and for the granting of larger powers to local governments, but the transition from dependence to internal self-government
was accomplished quite amicably, in a relatively short time, and without the anguish that had accompanied the movement for independence in America. Clearly Great Britain had learned a great deal about

the art of administering colonies as a result of its dealings with the Americans, which lessons were not wasted on the newer colonies in the southwest Pacific.

The Australian colonies also reaped the benefits of a more sophisticated and conscious individual rights legal tradition. The first European settlement in Australia dates back no further than 1788. This was the age of Blackstone, a time for boasting about the liberties of Englishmen and the security which the laws of England gave to them. The main battles to produce this state of affairs had been fought and won. It was the good fortune of Australians to be able to take this kind of legal order as their starting point; and what is more important, they did not even have to fight to persuade their imperial rulers that the rights of Englishmen were theirs by right. Contrast their position with that of the several generations of Americans whose claim to share in the amelioration of English law liberties was, if not completely denied, frequently disputed. In the early years of American settlement, the imperial view was always that English law extended to the plantations only as a matter of royal grace and favor.[1] Why else, it was argued, should it have been necessary to make explicit provision in colonial charters to assure subjects resident in the plantations enjoyment of "all liberties, franchises and immunities . . . to all intents and purposes as if they had been abiding and born" in England? In fact, the grant theory of English law reception did not greatly impede the transplantation of principles of decisional law, which after all, were supposed to be declaratory of anterior law, but it did militate against automatic transmission of laws of statutory origin, among them laws for the better protection of individual liberty. The position taken by the British law authorities was that irrespective of whether a charter grant of English liberties imported a grant of antecedent statute law, no statute of the realm enacted after settlement should be deemed to apply within a plantation unless it had been expressed so as to apply either to the particular plantation or to plantations in general.[2] Post-

---

1. This doctrine was approved by the king's judges in *Calvin's Case*, 7 Co. Rep. 2a, 17b-18a (1608), but it was not new. The judges merely deduced law from the practice previously followed in regard to Ireland.

2. *Privy Council Memorandum*, 2 P.Wms. 75 (1722); opinion of Attorney-General Yorke (1729) in W. Forsyth, *Cases and Opinions on Constitutional Law* (London, 1865), 2; 25 Geo. II, c. 6, s. 10. Colonial acts adopting post-settlement English legislation were sometimes disallowed.

settlement statutes which could be regarded as bettering legal safe-guards of liberty were seldom so extended.

Compare the situation of the Australian colonies. By the time New South Wales was settled in 1788, it was generally accepted that when British subjects settled in newly discovered territories not previously under European rule, they took with them so much of the law of England then in force as was reasonably capable of being applied in their new environment.[3] This law was considered their "birthright and inheritance" in the sense that it could not be withheld from them save by proper legislative enactment. Legally, then, the Australian colonists could claim the benefit of such liberty regarding enactments as the Habeas Corpus Act, 1679, and applicable provisions of the Bill of Rights, 1689.[4] For a time, it is true, they had grounds for complaining that their rights were not as amply protected as those of Englishmen at home. Jury trial was not available as of right for some forty years after settlement, but only for the reason that in a penal colony it was thought unsuitable and unworkable. Grand juries were eliminated as part of the prosecution process for the same reason.

As in the American colonies, legislative enactments in the Australian colonies were subject to certain legal controls, most of them imperially administered. In each case there was the general requirement that colonial legislation be not repugnant to the fundamental laws of England. If colonial legislation was repugnant to these laws, the courts could hold it invalid or it could be disallowed by Order in Council. Few American colonial acts were struck down upon judicial review, but a large number were disallowed, many of them on account of non-conformity with the English law standard or breach of elementary canons of justice. Consistent veto of colonial acts on such grounds, if not always welcomed, must certainly have accustomed colonial lawyers and lawmakers to the idea of enforceable fundamental law limitations, and must have made the subsequent adoption of formal constitutional controls of legislative output all the easier. In the Australian colonies the scrutiny of local legislative acts to determine their conformity with

3. The development of the new doctrine can be traced through *Smith* v. *Brown*, 2 Salk. 666 (n.d.); *Dutton* v. *Howell*, Shower P.C. 24, 32 (1693); *Blankard* v. *Galdy*, 2 Salk. 411 (1694); *Privy Council Memorandum*, 2 P.Wms. 75 (1722); *Campbell* v. *Hall*, 1 Cowp. 208 (1774); *Freeman* v. *Fairlie*, 1 Moo. Ind. App. 305 (1828). See also 1 *Blackstone's Commentaries*, 107.

4. The application of the law of England was confirmed by 9 Geo. IV, c. 83, s. 24 (1828), which act also advanced the cut-off point of reception to 1828.

fundamental English law was more a task for the judiciary than for the Colonial Office. The royal prerogative of disallowance remained, but it tended to be used more sparingly than it had been during the American colonial era, possibly because of the existence of locally administered controls.

When provision was made in 1823 for a New South Wales legislature, the British Parliament made it a rule that no bill should be placed before the legislature unless it had been certified by the chief justice to be not repugnant to the laws of England, but consistent with them as far as the circumstances of the colony would allow.[5] In 1828 the scheme for mandatory judicial review was altered slightly. Henceforth a bill could pass the legislature without prior judicial veto, but within fourteen days of its enrolment, the judges of the Supreme Court could certify to the governor that the act was repugnant to English law. If such a certification were made, the governor was obliged to suspend the act's operation until the matter was considered by the legislature. The legislature was not obliged to accept the judges' advice and if it decided that the measure should be adhered to, the act was to "take effect and be binding" until His Majesty's pleasure was known.[6] This latter procedure was followed until the granting of responsible self-government in the 1850's, but even then there was still the possibility of judicial review upon proceedings *inter partes*.

On the whole, judicial review of colonial legislation on grounds of repugnancy to English law did not inspire confidence in the judiciary's ability to moderate legislative excesses without stultifying legislative initiative; if anything, it reinforced legislative demands for a minimum of judicial interference. From the outset there were conflicts between the judicial and legislative branches, and although they were not always concerned with civil liberties issues, they did create very grave doubts about the wisdom of requiring legislatures to conform to vague, open-ended legislative standards, the application of which in particular cases was likely to be controversial and always unpredictable.

The kind of difficulty that could arise is well illustrated by the disagreement which occurred in the 1820's between Chief Justice Forbes and Governor Darling over proposed legislation to regulate the press. Darling was deeply troubled by the ferocity of press criticism

5. 4 Geo. IV, c. 96, s. 29.　　　　　6. 9 Geo. IV, c. 83, s. 22.

of the colonial administration and formed the opinion that unless
some form of censorship were imposed, the colony could be faced with
civil disorder. The control measures he put forward were certainly
stringent ones, but their stringency was dictated by the fact that the
colony was still primarily a penal settlement and was being run something along the lines of an open jail. Penal discipline had to be
maintained at all costs. Following the example of the lieutenant governor of Van Diemen's Land, Governor Darling proposed that newspapers be published only under license and be subject to stamp duty.
Publication of a newspaper without license was to be a criminal offense.
Licenses were to be dispensed on an annual basis by the governor;
they were to be revocable at will and liable to forefeiture if the printer
or publisher were convicted of seditious or blasphemous libel. Chief
Justice Forbes, as it was his constitutional duty to do, reviewed the
bill before its presentation to the Legislative Council. His opinion
was that the licensing scheme would be repugnant to the laws of England. "By the laws of England," he wrote, "the liberty of the press
is regarded as a constitutional privilege, which liberty consists in exemption from previous restraint; by the proposed bill a preliminary
license is required which is to destroy the freedom of the press and
place it at the discretion of the Government. By the laws of England,"
he continued, "every man enjoys the right of being heard before he
can be condemned either in person or property." But under the proposed bill, "the Governor, with the advice of the Executive Council,
may revoke the license granted to any publisher at discretion, and
deprive the subject of his trade without his having the means of knowing what may be the charge against him, who may be his accuser,
upon what evidence he is to be tried, for what violation of the law
he is condemned." Moreover, the bill would make the governor and
his council judges in their own cause, "that cause one of political opposition to their own measures."[7]

Forbes, it should be added, did not assert that freedom of the press
was in any sense absolute, for he allowed that if the governor and his
council publicly declared "that they believe the safety of the Colony,
or its peace (in the legal sense) disturbed or hazarded by the licentious-
ness of the Press," then he would "certify that, assuming such to be

7. Forbes to Bathurst, May 1, 1827, *Historical Records of Australia*, series I, vol. 13,
293-294.

the true state of the colony, a bill for suspending the Press altogether, until such danger shall have passed away, is not repugnant to, but is consistent with, the spirit of the English law."[8] But no such declaration had been made and Forbes's own assessment of the situation was that the extreme measures proposed were not justified.

Inasmuch as the English law standard did admit qualifications and exceptions in favor of peculiar local circumstances, judges applying it were forced to make a judgment more political than legal, and being political, it was the kind of judgment about which there was likely to be disagreement. Even judges could disagree, as they did over an act of 1834 to suppress bushranging.[9] This was an act enlarging powers of arrest without warrant and putting on persons arrested under the act the onus of proving their innocence under pain of being held in custody until the requisite proof was forthcoming. On this occasion, Chief Justice Forbes and his fellow judge, Mr. Justice Dowling, felt that the end justified the means; Mr. Justice Burton, on the other hand, thought that the mischief could have been remedied "by a less sacrifice of the fundamental principles of the law."[10]

But what were the fundamental principles with which the colonial acts had to conform? Mr. Justice Boothby of the South Australian Supreme Court entertained some curious ideas on the subject, ideas which when put into practice threatened to block almost every legislative measure that had no exact British precedent. Boothby thought it incompetent for a colonial legislature to abolish or limit the operation of grand juries, to make felonies or misdemeanors triable summarily, or to empower an administrative officer to determine questions of land title preparatory to the issue of a certificate making the title so recorded indefeasible. To give that power, he argued, would be to take away the right to jury trial "in matters relating to the ownership of land, as provided by Magna Carta and the Bill of Rights."[11] Boothby's uncompromising and extreme stand on fundamental law questions precipitated something of a crisis in South Australian politics, and although his opinions were not generally shared by his brother judges

8. Forbes to Horton, May 27, 1827, *ibid.*, series IV, vol. 1, 727.

9. 5 Will. IV, No. 9 (New South Wales). The bushrangers were in some ways the equivalent of the American outlaws. They made their living by theft of sheep and cattle and highway robbery. See Russel Ward, *The Australian Legend* (Melbourne, 1958), chap. vi.

10. *Historical Records of Australia*, series I, vol. 17, 524 *et seq.*

11. *McEllister v. Fenn*, Gt. Brit., Parl. Pap. 1862, vol. 37, p. 113 *et seq.*

or by the British law officers, a time came when it was felt necessary to remove any further risk of judicial obstruction by abrogating the English law standard altogether. This final step was taken in 1865 when the Imperial Parliament declared simply that no colonial law was to "be deemed to have been void or inoperative on the ground of repugnancy to the law of England," saving only those cases where colonial laws were repugnant to British legislation extending to the colony by express words or necessary intendment.[12]

It is doubtful whether the Boothby episode greatly impaired the standing of the judiciary either in South Australia or elsewhere in Australia. But it did draw attention to the dangers of fundamental law limitations which gave too wide a scope for judicial interpolation and may have reinforced legislative bias against any form of judicial review which involved judges in the making of judgments depending on considerations other than strictly legal ones.

III

The constitutional model which appealed most to Australians in the nineteenth century was the British. When colonial statesmen urged the need for constitutional change, it was usually for change that would establish a form of government more akin to that operating in the mother country, government by sovereign legislatures and responsible parliamentary executives. The British constitution was something to be admired and something to be emulated. The Americans had not thought so, but their recollections of British type constitutionalism were not exactly those of nineteenth-century Whigs. As colonists, Americans had come to distrust omnicompetent parliaments as well as heads of state who were unamenable to popular will. The Australian colonists too had experienced government by a supreme imperial legislature and by constitutional monarchs and their agents, but their experiences had taught them only to desire for themselves much the same self-government as was enjoyed by Englishmen at home. The idea of parliamentary supremacy brought to mind historic episodes each marking yet another milestone in the quest for freedom

12. Colonial Laws Validity Act, 1865, s. 3. The circumstances giving rise to the act are discussed fully by D. B. Swinfen, "The Genesis of the Colonial Laws Validity Act" [1967], *Juridical Review*, 29. See also Enid Campbell, "Colonial Legislation and the Laws of England," *Tasmanian University Law Review*, II (1965), 148.

and democracy: battles between liberty-loving parliamentarians and liberty-disregarding monarchs, parliamentary successes in the struggle to contain prerogative power and to subject it to legal regulation, and the enactment of laws to secure individuals in the liberties that were their due. Nor could one overlook Parliament's more recent accomplishments in the reconstruction of the law to fit the needs of a new and dynamic society. Since the Reform Act, 1832, Parliament had responded well to public opinion, and though many problems still awaited its attention there were few who doubted its capacity to deal with them.

This much enthusiasm for the parliamentary institution was bound to rub off on the colonials. The Australians may not have held their politicians in high esteem, but their confidence in the power of legislative action to better the human condition was high. They had come to expect a good deal of their governments, for theirs was a hostile environment in which the individual labored at his peril. It was the function of government to insure the individual against failure in private enterprise and to supply the enterprise that the private sector would not or could not supply—in short, to play the part of pioneer. With expectations such as these, the emphasis was likely to be less on the limitation of governmental power than on its enlargement.

Nor was the emphasis changed when thought moved in the direction of federal union. Under the federal scheme, it is true, the state parliaments would not enjoy the amplitude of power they had enjoyed before federation, but between them the Commonwealth and state parliaments would have almost as much latitude as the British Parliament. Furthermore, so long as each kept within its jurisdiction, there would not be any questioning of legislative acts except in the forum of public opinion. The federal Constitution was not to be an instrument by which the Australian people would affirm their commitment to democratic values or make law out of political morality. It was to be simply a basic law defining and distributing powers between a national and regional governments and regulating relationships between them.

The decision not to include a comprehensive bill of rights in this Constitution flowed not only from a reluctance to impose greater restraints on legislative action than were necessary to give effect to the federal principle. The federating colonies were jealous of their sovereignty and their representatives would have construed any suggestion to incorporate a universally applicable bill of rights as an attempt to derogate from that sovereignty. On the other hand, guarantees of individual liberties binding only the federal government would not have made much sense. At the time the expectation was that the federal government would assume responsibility only for a few governmental functions and these functions were not ones which were likely to touch on questions of civil liberty. The potentialities of federal power were not then fully appreciated, but even if the delegates had been permitted a glimpse of the future, their attitude toward bills of rights probably would not have been very different. They were simply not the kind of men who would have set much store by general declarations of rights which they knew from experience had to be qualified. Many of them were lawyers who approached the task of drafting a constitution in the same spirit as they would approach the drafting of a deed or will. To them the language of a constitution needed to be exact and precise enough to indicate to those who were to be bound by it what they could and could not do. In this respect the United States Constitution was not altogether satisfactory, and although it could serve as a guide it was also an object lesson in the dangers of vagueness in language and was a document which ought to be improved upon.

The lawyers' criticisms of the American Bill of Rights went not only to the question of vagueness in expression, but to the question of necessity. Why, they seemed to ask, was it necessary to write guarantees of individual liberty into the Constitution when liberty was already legally recognized and protected? And given a political ordering that would make governments responsive to public opinion, was it likely that the Australian people would suffer their legislators to derogate from their liberties? These were the sorts of attitudes one would have expected of men schooled in English legal traditions, but as we shall see they were not always the attitudes that prevailed. Lawyers' cautions were not always heeded and their prejudices were sometimes overborne.

IV

In the draft Australian Constitution that came before the British Parliament in 1900 for enactment as an imperial statute, there were several clauses which Americans would immediately recognize as having been patterned after provisions in their Bill of Rights. Sec. 51 (xxxi) empowered the federal Parliament to make laws with respect to the acquisition of property, provided that the acquisition was on "just terms." Compare this with the Fifth Amendment's prohibition of the taking of private property for public use "without just compensation." Compare, too, s. 116 with the First Amendment. "The Commonwealth," s. 116 declared, "shall not make any law for establishing any religion, or for imposing any religious observance, or for prohibiting the free exercise of any religion, and no religious test shall be required as a qualification for any office or public trust under the Commonwealth." In s. 117 we see a much watered-down version of Article IV, s. 2, and the first part of the Fourteenth Amendment. Sec. 117 declared that: "A subject of the Queen resident in any State, shall not be subject in any other State to any disability or discrimination which would not be equally applicable to him if he were a subject of the Queen in another State." Consider also the resemblance between Article III, s. 3, and s. 80. The latter provided that: "The trial on indictment of any offence against any law of the Commonwealth shall be by jury, and every such trial shall be held in the State where the offence was committed, and if the offence was not committed within the State the trial shall be held at such place or places as the Parliament prescribes."

If the framers of the Constitution were not enthusiastic about bills of rights, how did these provisions come to be included in the Constitution and why these rather than others? Were the variations in language thought to be significant? Have they in fact made any difference to the manner in which the provisions have been interpreted?

When at the federal convention held in Melbourne in 1898 Edmund Barton moved the addition of a compulsory acquisition power, the question of controlling the exercise of that power was not even discussed. The power, Barton argued, was necessary because otherwise the Commonwealth could acquire only by contract, and purchase would prove more expensive than compulsory acquisition.[13] The states already had made legislative provision for expropriation but always so that private property owners should be compensated. In insisting that federal acquisitions should be on "just terms" the makers of the Constitution were therefore doing no more than giving constitutional expression to policies agreed upon by the states, and making sure that the same policy should apply to acquisitions of state property by the federal government. As it has been interpreted by the High Court of Australia, "just terms" is not exactly the same as the "just compensation" provided for under the Fifth Amendment. Compensation, according to the High Court, means payment of a full money equivalent. Although such payment satisfies the requirement of just terms, the requirement can be satisfied by something less.[14] The terms on which the Commonwealth acquires must be fair, but they need not be the fairest.[15] Their fairness is assessed not only with reference to the interests of property owners whose property is acquired, but with reference to the interests of the whole community.[16] Thus, in the High Court's estimation, it is not unfair to refuse owners payment for any appreciation in property values that may have resulted from the government's stimulus to demand[17] or for the expectation of profit on future sales.[18] There has been a division of opinion on whether just terms requires payment of interest between the time of acquisition and the time of payment. In the United States it has been held that the right secured by the Fifth Amendment does entail payment of interest, but it is doubtful whether s. 51 (xxxi) of the Australian federal Constitution would be read as requiring interest to be paid in all cases.[19]

The history of the freedom of religion guarantee in s. 116 is rather curious. It appears to have originated with Andrew Inglis Clarke, a Tasmanian delegate. Clarke was attorney-general for Tasmania and, as both his federal movement activities and later writings demonstrate,

13. *Official Record of the Debates of the Australasian Federal Convention*, Third Session, Melbourne, 1898, 151-154.
14. *Nelungaloo Pty. Ltd.* v. *The Commonwealth*, 75 C.L.R. 495, 569 (1948).
15. *Ibid.*
16. *Grace Bros. Pty. Ltd.* v. *The Commonwealth*, 72 C.L.R. 269, 291-292 (1946).
17. *Ibid.*, 269.
18. *Poulton* v. *The Commonwealth*, 89 C.L.R. 540 (1953).
19. See R. W. Baker, "The Compulsory Acquisition Powers of the Commonwealth," in R. Else-Mitchell, ed., *Essays on the Australian Constitution* (2nd ed.; Sydney, 1961), pp. 212-215.

his debts to American constitutional thought were not inconsiderable.[20] It was his model constitution that was used by the drafting committee of 1890 as the basis for the initial draft of a federal constitution. In this model of Clarke's there was a freedom of religion guarantee obviously drawn from the First Amendment and like the First Amendment it was expressed to bind all governments.[21] However, in its final form, the guarantee bound only the federal government. Before this stage was reached, Clarke's draft had been amended to cover only the states;[22] this change had been made on the theory that since the Commonwealth would not have power to legislate with respect to religion, a provision prohibiting it from interfering with religious freedom or establishing religion was unnecessary.[23] But then Henry Bourne Higgins, one of the Victorian delegates, made the point that federal power over religion might be inferred from certain words that were to appear in the Constitution's preamble, words referring to Almighty God. Therefore, he concluded, the Commonwealth's hands should be tied.[24] The suggestion that legislative authority might be inferred from the preamble was altogether fanciful and seems to have been recognized as such by the other delegates. Yet at this point they began to have second thoughts about the wisdom of having a clause directed against states and states only. Freedom of religion, it was thought, was already respected by state laws, and the proposed constitutional provision represented an unjustified and wholly unnecessary limitation on state power.[25] Undismayed by the defeat of his original motion, Higgins came forward with another clause, this time one expressed to bind only the Commonwealth and extending the prohibition to the imposition of religious tests for public office.[26] When put to the vote, Higgins' clause was carried by a majority of nine (25:16). Contrary to the assurances of other lawyers attending the conventions, the majority of delegates seems to have been persuaded by Higgins that without the prohibition the Commonwealth would have been in a position to regulate Sunday observance throughout Australia. This was a subject on

20. See J. Reynolds, "A. I. Clarke's American Sympathies and His Influence on Australian Federation," *Australian Law Journal*, XXXII (1958), 62.
21. The model constitution is reprinted as an appendix to Reynolds' article; see secs. 46 and 81.
22. Ch. V, cl. 16 of draft Bill of 1891.
23. *Official Records of the Debates of the Australasian Federal Convention*, Third Session, Melbourne, 1898, 661.
24. *Ibid.*, 654-656.   25. *Ibid.*, 659-661.
26. *Ibid.*, 1769.

which different political factions had very different views, and it was clear that the mere prospect, however remote, of a federal government legislating in this area was one which most state representatives desired to avoid.

No case has arisen in which the High Court has struck down federal legislation on the ground of infringement of s. 116. To begin with, the Court seemed to take a rather narrow view of the scope of the guarantee. Free exercise of religion, it was said, was not impaired unless what the law forbade or required constituted an interference with the individual's liberty to engage in religious practices or observances.[27] But more recently the Court has said that it will not presume to judge what beliefs are capable of being religious in character, and that the freedom guaranteed by s. 116 is not limited to religious practices or observances.[28] On the other hand, the Court has emphasized that the freedom guaranteed is not absolute. "It is consistent with the maintenance of religious liberty," Chief Justice Latham said, "for the State to restrain actions and courses of conduct which are inconsistent with the maintenance of civil government or prejudicial to the continued existence of the community. The Constitution protects religion within a community organized under a Constitution, so that the continuance of such protection necessarily assumes the continuance of the community so organized."[29]

The presence of s. 116, it should be noted, has not prevented the federal government from giving financial aid to children attending denominational schools or from making grants-in-aid to states on condition that the aid be paid to denominational schools. Although the legislation in question has not been tested in the courts, it seems unlikely that any legal challenge would succeed.

The attitude of the federal convention delegates to bills of rights is nowhere better illustrated than in the debates leading to the adoption of s. 117. The section arose from a clause in the Constitution Bill of 1891 (Chap. V, cl. 17) reading as follows: "A State shall not *make or enforce any law abridging any privilege or immunity of citizens of other States of the Commonwealth, nor shall a State* deny to any person within its jurisdiction the equal protection of the laws" (emphasis

27. *Krygger* v. *Willliams*, 15 C.L.R. 366 (1912).
28. *Adelaide Company of Jehovah's Witnesses, Inc.* v. *The Commonwealth*, 67 C.L.R. 116, 124 (1943).
29. *Ibid.*, 131-133.

supplied). At the federal convention in Melbourne in 1898 the clause encountered opposition. The bill as a whole had been referred to the colonial parliaments and some of them had queried this particular clause's meaning. The Legislative Assembly in New South Wales and the Legislative Council in Tasmania pointed out that legally there was no such thing as state citizenship and suggested that the words indicated by italics be deleted. The Tasmanian Legislative Assembly, possibly at the instigation of the attorney-general, Andrew Inglis Clarke, suggested an alternative clause as follows:

> The citizens of each State, and all other persons owing allegiance to the Queen and residing in any territory of the Commonwealth, shall be citizens of the Commonwealth, and shall be entitled to all the privileges and immunities of citizens of the Commonwealth in the several States, and a State shall not make or enforce any law abridging any privilege or immunity of citizens of the Commonwealth, nor shall a State deprive any person of life, liberty or property without due process of law, or deny to any person within its jurisdiction, equal protection of the laws.[30]

The move to incorporate this Fourteenth Amendment-type clause in the constitution met with a singularly unsympathetic response. The Victorian attorney-general, Isaac Isaacs, was especially critical of the proposed clause. It was, he said, vague and unnecessary, and it would interfere too much with state rights. The Fourteenth Amendment, he added, had been brought about by rather peculiar circumstances, had been carried only by force of arms, and had already given the Americans a great deal of trouble.[31] O'Connor, another lawyer delegate, was not persuaded that a due process clause was superfluous; in his opinion it might be needed to restrain unjust majorities.[32] Isaacs replied by saying that the idea that a supreme court "should control the legislatures of the States within their own jurisdiction" was positively "dangerous."[33] To Dr. Cockburn of South Australia, a due process clause was an "insult" to the legislators.[34] In the end, the Isaacs view prevailed, and references to due process and equal protection of the laws were deleted.[35] The question of how to prevent states

30. *Official Records of the Debates of the Australasian Federal Convention,* Third Session, Melbourne, 1898, 667.
31. *Ibid.,* 667-670. See also *ibid.,* 383-388.
32. *Ibid.,* 683, 688.   33. *Ibid.,* 683.
34. *Ibid.,* 688.   35. *Ibid.,* 691.

from discriminating against residents of other states was then dealt with as a matter of draftsmanship.[36]

The Constitution emerged without a due process clause but it did establish at least one minimum procedural requirement and, what is perhaps more important, established what many would regard as a prerequisite of due process: separation of judicial power from other governmental powers and the independence of the federal courts that were to exercise that power.[37] The procedural requirement related to jury trial, so often identified (whether rightly or wrongly) with vindication of individual liberty in the face of overwhelming public power. In the draft Constitution of 1891 it was proposed to make jury trial mandatory for all indictable offenses cognizable by courts established under the Constitution. At the Adelaide convention in 1897 and again at the Melbourne convention in 1898, Higgins moved to have the reference to jury trial omitted on the ground that the clause as framed would prevent Parliament from dispensing with juries in cases where they were inappropriate, notably in commercial cases. Higgins' motion to amend was lost, but only after delegates had been reassured by Isaacs that jury trial would be mandatory only if the offense charged was indictable and that the indictability of a federal offense depended solely on Parliament's will.[38] Isaacs pointed out that there was a significant difference between the Australian clause and its American counterpart, Article III, s. 2(3). The latter provided that the trial of *all crimes* should be by jury, whereas the former prescribed jury trial for indictable offenses only.[39] Subsequently, Edmund Barton suggested rewording of the clause to make it absolutely clear that trial by jury would be required only where the accused was proceeded against on indictment. If the original clause were allowed to stand, he reasoned, the result would be that if Parliament provided that an offense was punishable either on indictment or summarily, trial would always have to be by jury, regardless of the mode of prosecution. Isaacs dis-

36. The meaning of s. 117 remains cloudy. The importance of the section has been diminished by the High Court's ruling that it does not prevent states from discriminating on the basis of domicile: *Davies and Jones* v. *The State of Western Australia*, 2 C.L.R. 29 (1905).

37. See Constitution, Ch. III, and *The Queen* v. *Kirby; ex p. Boilermakers' Society of Australia*, 94 C.L.R. 254 (1956), 95 C.L.R. 529 (1957).

38. J. Quick and R. R. Garran, *The Annotated Constitution of the Australian Commonwealth* (Sydney, 1901), pp. 807-810.

39. *Official Records of the Debates of the Australasian Federal Convention*, Third Session, Melbourne, 1898, 352.

agreed with Barton's interpretation, but Barton's amendment passed and eventually became s. 80 of the Constitution.[40]

Recalling, no doubt, the opinions that had prevailed at the constitutional conventions, Higgins, by then a justice of the High Court, described the effect of s. 80 as being simply that "if there be an indictment, there must be a jury; but there is nothing to compel procedure by indictment."[41] Some years later this interpretation was questioned by Mr. Justices Dixon and Evatt. "It is a queer intention," they said of Higgins' dictum,

to ascribe to a constitution; for it supposes that the concern of the framers of the provision was not to ensure that no-one should be held guilty of a serious offence against the laws of the Commonwealth except by the verdict of a jury, but to prevent a solecism, namely, the use of an indictment in cases where the legislature might think fit to authorize the court itself to pass upon the guilt or innocence of the prisoner.[42]

On their interpretation of s. 80, the federal Parliament would not have it within its power to exclude jury trial unless the punishment and mode of prosecution it prescribed were not the kind of punishment or method of prosecution that went with indictments. There were, they said, two basic ingredients in the indictment procedure: "that some authority constituted under the law to represent the public interest for the purpose took the responsibility for the step which put the accused on his trial" and "the liability of the offender to a term of imprisonment or to some graver form of punishment."[43] So if Parliament prescribed imprisonment as the penalty and then authorized the attorney-general or some other public officer to prosecute, it could not then provide that the offense was triable summarily. The Dixon and Evatt view of s. 80 was not necessary for decision of the case before them, and though it has not been directly refuted, most other judges of the High Court appear to have been better satisfied with the Higgins interpretation.[44] So the guarantee of jury trial is indeed illusory.

40. *Ibid.*, 1894-1895.
41. *R.* v. *Archdall*, 41 C.L.R. 128, 139, 140 (1928).
42. *The King* v. *Federal Court of Bankruptcy; ex p. Lowenstein*, 59 C.L.R. 556, 581-582 (1938).
43. *Ibid.*, 586.
44. *Ibid.*, 571 per Latham C.J. See also *Sachter* v. *Attorney-General for the Commonwealth*, 94 C.L.R. 86 (1954); *The Queen* v. *Kirby; ex p. Boilermakers' Society of Australia*, 94 C.L.R. 254, 294, 313-314.

V

Since its inception the Australian federal Constitution has undergone very little change. The Constitution may be amended by federal legislation which has been approved by a majority of all electors and also by a majority of electors voting in a majority of states,[45] but only a few amendment proposals have been approved by the requisite majorities. None of these amendments has been directly concerned with fundamental human rights. In 1944 a Labour government brought in a bill to extend federal legislative powers for a five-year period; subsequently civil rights clauses were added to allay fears that the proposed increases in federal power would enable the Commonwealth to create a socialist state. One of these clauses provided that "neither the Commonwealth nor a State may make any law abridging the freedom of speech, or of the Press." The other purported to extend the freedom of religion guarantee in s. 116 to bind the states. Neither became law. As on previous occasions, the electors showed themselves suspicious of moves to enlarge Commonwealth power. Given a choice between accepting the proposed amendments *in toto* and rejecting them, they cast a negative vote. Majorities were obtained in two states only: South Australia and Western Australia.[46]

Two years later the Labour government sought and obtained approval for a more limited amendment; this time one enabling the Commonwealth to dispense a wider range of welfare benefits and services. But in the case of dental and medical services there was a qualification. Commonwealth laws making provision for such services were not "to authorize any form of civil conscription."[47] The provision was added on the suggestion of R. G. Menzies, then leader of the Opposition, to meet the criticism that Commonwealth power to provide dental and medical services might result in a system of socialized medicine, something which the medical profession would have resisted at all costs.[48]

---

45. Constitution, s. 128.
46. On the Constitution Alteration (Post-War Reconstruction) Bill of 1944, see Convention of Representatives of the Commonwealth and State Parliaments, *Record of Proceedings* (1942), 11-12, and H. V. Evatt, *Post-War Reconstruction: A Case for Greater Commonwealth Powers* (Canberra, 1942), pp. 41, 45, 83, 84, 105-107, 111, 163. See also Geoffrey Sawer, *Australian Federal Law and Politics, 1929-1949* (Melbourne, 1963), pp. 171-173.
47. Constitution, s. 51 (xxiiiA).   48. Sawer, pp. 173-174.

Twice the federal Constitution has been the subject of general review. On both occasions constitutional changes were recommended but never put to the vote. The first general inquiry was entrusted to a Royal Commission which sat between 1927 and 1929; the second to a joint committee of the Senate and House of Representatives, appointed in 1958. Neither body was prepared to recommend adoption of a comprehensive bill of rights. The Royal Commission contented itself with a bare statement outlining the differences between the Australian Constitution and United States Constitution and cataloguing the several provisions in the former which had a rights-entrenching effect.[49] The Joint Committee on Constitutional Review took a more positive approach. It had heard representations from a number of parties urging the virtues of bills of rights and, having heard them, felt constrained to explain why it thought such provisions were unnecessary. "The absence of constitutional guarantees in the Commonwealth Constitution," it explained, "had not prevented the rule of law from characterizing the Australian way of life."[50] Its view was "that as long as governments are democratically elected and there is full parliamentary responsibility to all electors, the protection of personal rights will, in practice be secure in Australia."[51] But it was not satisfied that the Constitution adequately secured these things and accordingly recommended "a constitutional amendment to protect the position of the elector and the democratic processes essential to the proper functioning of the Federal Parliament."[52]

What the committee wanted was constitutional provision to ensure that the value accorded to votes of electors in each of the states, and each electoral division should, as near as possible, be uniform. As it stands, the Constitution does insist on a degree of equality in voting power, for s. 24 declares that the number of members of the House of Representatives in the states should be proportioned to state populations. But the determination of electoral districts (divisions) and the number of members to be chosen for each district is wholly within Parliament's discretion. The Commonwealth Electoral Act provides for single member constituencies, and for the erection of electoral

49. Commonwealth of Australia, *Report of the Royal Commission on the Constitution* (Canberra, 1929), p. 18.
50. Commonwealth of Australia, Parliament, *Report from the Joint Committee on Constitutional Review* (1959), para. 328.
51. *Ibid.*   52. *Ibid.*

divisions by distribution commissioners. The number of electors in each division is supposed to be roughly the same; it must never exceed or fall short of a quota, arrived at by dividing the total number of electors for the state by the number of members to be chosen for the state, by more than one-fifth of that quota. The act further requires redistribution if this permissible margin is exceeded or if there is an increase of members for the state. Even having regard to the peculiarities of population distribution in Australia, the committee felt that the permissible margin of difference was too great. What it recommended was amendment of the Constitution to entrench the principle of single member electorates and to require that the number of electors in each division of a state should not rise or fall below the quota by more than one-tenth. It further proposed mandatory review of electoral divisions at least once every ten years. The actual erection of divisions should remain Parliament's responsibility, but parliamentary action would be controlled by the minimum requirement provisions and by the further requirement that no division be authorized until the receipt of the report from the relevant electoral commission.[53]

The assumptions underlying the committee's recommendations on apportionment are perhaps more significant than the recommendations themselves. The desirability of constitutional safeguards was considered concurrently with the question of a bill of rights. The committee's reasoning was simply this: that given constitutional "provisions ensuring the regular review of the electoral divisions" and ensuring that the value accorded to the votes of electors are nearly uniform, democratic processes are protected, and inasmuch as they are protected, individual liberties are not likely to be impaired. "In making possible minority governments," the committee concluded, "the majority can be deprived of the government of its choice and the way is open for arbitrary action impairing the freedom of the individual even though the action stands condemned by the majority of people who comprise the electors of the Commonwealth."[54] This line of argument comes dangerously close to saying that there can be no such thing as an unjust majority and that freedom of the individual is what the majority would have it mean and no more.

53. *Ibid.*, Ch. 8.   54. *Ibid.*, para. 330.

VI

On reading the Australian federal Constitution as it was originally framed, one might easily gain the impression that Australians were racial supremacists. Sec. 51 (xxvi) enabled the federal Parliament to make laws with respect to "the people of any race, *other than the aboriginal race in any State,* for whom it is deemed necessary to make special laws."[55] Sec. 127 provided that: "In reckoning the numbers of the people of the Commonwealth, or of a State or other part of the Commonwealth, aboriginal natives shall not be counted."[56] As a result of a constitutional amendment in 1967, the italicized words in s. 51 (xxvi) and the whole of s. 127 were deleted.[57]

The avowed purpose of the draftsmen of s. 51 (xxvi) was to give the Commonwealth power to make discriminatory laws, laws of a kind which before federation had been passed to deal with "the Indian, Afghan and Syrian hawkers; the Chinese miners, laundrymen, market-gardeners, and furniture manufacturers; the Japanese settlers and Kanaka plantation labourers of Queensland, and the various coloured races employed in the pearl fisheries of Queensland and Western Australia."[58] The colonial laws had diverse aims: to restrict immigration, to promote repatriation, to confine the "alien" races to certain areas, to limit their choice of occupation, and, in some cases, to give them special protection. Sir Samuel Griffith, who first suggested the clause, emphasized the importance of immigration control,[59] though if this was his only concern, the requisite federal control was to be had by exercise of the immigration and external affairs powers.

Why was the Commonwealth expressly excluded from making legislation respecting the aboriginal race? The matter was not even debated, but the assumption was that since aboriginal affairs were already the subject of special regulation in the states, federal policy and action was not necessary. Besides, few of the powers that were to be reposed in the Commonwealth seemed to have any direct bearing on

55. Emphasis supplied.
56. On the history of this section, see Geoffrey Sawer, "The Australian Constitution and the Australian Aborigine," *Federal Law Review*, II (1966), 16, 25-30.
57. Constitution Alteration (Aborigines) Act 1967.
58. W. Harrison Moore, *The Constitution of the Commonwealth of Australia* (2nd ed.; London, 1910), p. 462.
59. National Australasian Convention Debates, Sydney, 1891, 703; *Official Records of the Debates of the Australasian National Convention*, Third Session, Melbourne, 1898, 240.

the sorts of questions on which special legislation for aborigines was required. The national government, unlike the national government in the United States, had no jurisdiction over public lands and its powers concerning welfare benefits originally extended only to invalid and old age pensions.

Once it might have seemed that the aborigines were destined to become a forgotten people. But circumstances have conspired to resurrect them from obscurity and to accord them new importance in both state and national policy. Australian governments have begun to recognize that the policies they have pursued in the past, not only in relation to the aborigines, but in relation to immigration, have given the country something of a bad name. They know too that criticisms and pressures from outside cannot be countered simply by saying that race relations are a purely domestic concern. There have been pressures from inside as well, though not so much from established political parties as from individuals and small groups. Protest on behalf of the aborigines is a relatively new phenomenon and both in its objectives and strategies owes a good deal to the example of the civil rights movement in the United States.

Inevitably, the awakening of a public conscience about the condition of the Australian aborigine has led to demands for national policy and action on aboriginal affairs—inevitable, because nowadays any new program which concerns the country at large and which requires substantial expenditure of public money is apt to be regarded as a federal responsibility. Federal initiative in aboriginal affairs has been wanting. Before the amendment of s. 51 (xxxvi) in 1967 the federal government certainly had no power to legislate generally with respect to aborigines, but it did make particular and special provision for them in relation to the franchise and probably could have done likewise in relation to welfare benefits. The move to amend the Constitution to enable the federal government to legislate for aborigines without restriction initially came not from the government but from a Liberal backbencher, W. C. Wentworth, M.H.R. Wentworth's proposal went considerably further than the constitutional amendment eventually proposed by the government and entailed constitutional prohibitions against discrimination. In a sense, Wentworth forced the government's hand, for although his bill was not one the government was prepared to adopt as its own, it could not appear to be opposing the purposes behind it. Whether the passage of the amendment marks the beginning of a new deal for the aborigines remains to be seen. The Commonwealth's intentions at this moment are not clear, but there has been no suggestion that it will exercise its power to the full and thereby oust state jurisdiction. Meanwhile, the states have begun to review their policies and administrations, some more searchingly than others. To date, only one, South Australia, has specifically legislated against discrimination on grounds of race or color. The act in question, the Prohibition of Discrimination Act, 1966, relates to discrimination in admission to shops, hotels, bars, and public places, in the supply of services, letting of accommodation, employment, and restrictive clauses in agreements for sale of land.

VII

The Australian state constitutions have never at any time included bills of rights. The Tasmanian Constitution Act, 1934, contains a section dealing with religious freedom,[61] but like most provisions in state constitutions, it does not have the force of fundamental law and may be repealed or amended like any other statutory provision, even by implication.[62] There is no doubt that the state parliaments could, if they wished, entrench civil rights by passing legislation declaring those rights and then providing that laws repealing or amending the declaration of rights should not be effective unless passed according to some special legislative procedure. A state parliament could, for example, provide that no bill altering or abridging the statutory guarantees

60. The Commonwealth always has made special provisions for aborigines in the federal electoral laws. Under the Commonwealth Franchise Act of 1902 they were denied the right to vote unless already entitled to vote in elections for a state lower House. Aborigines who were or had been members of the defense forces were enfranchised in 1949 (Commonwealth Electoral Act 1949, s. 3); in 1962 the franchise was extended to all adult aborigines (Commonwealth Electoral Act 1962, ss. 2 and 3).

61. Sec. 46 provides:
  (1) Freedom of conscience and the free profession and practice of religion are subject to public order and morality, guaranteed to every citizen.
  (2) No person shall be subject to any disability or be required to take an oath on account of his religion or religious beliefs and no religious test shall be imposed in respect of the appointment to or holding of any public office.
Judging by the marginal note, the section was intended to restate the British Roman Catholic Relief Act (1829) which had been extended to the colony by the Imperial Act, 10 Geo. IV, c. 5 (1830). The inclusion of the provision in the Constitution Act was not debated but was brought about by a general consolidation of Tasmanian legislation in 1934.

62. See *McCawley* v. *The King*, [1920] A.C. 691.

should be presented to the governor for the royal assent unless it had been passed by both houses and approved by a majority of electors voting at a referendum.[63]

A civil rights bill incorporating entrenching clauses of this kind was actually brought down in the Queensland Parliament in 1959 following the premier's pre-election promise to introduce legislation giving effect to the principles of the United Nations Universal Declaration of Human Rights.[64] The bill—the Queensland Constitution (Declaration of Rights) Bill—was far from comprehensive and included a number of clauses the only effect of which would have been to preserve the political status quo. The individual rights guaranteed were few. The right to vote at parliamentary elections was guaranteed to all persons qualified to vote under existing law. A person arrested or detained was to have the right to be informed promptly of the reason, to engage a lawyer without delay, and if his detention was unlawful, the right to obtain release by habeas corpus. When a person's property was compulsorily acquired by a public authority, he was to be entitled to just terms of compensation. Oddly enough, this guarantee was expressed not to apply to acquisition of primary products, the reason for this being that a constitutional requirement that just terms of compensation should be provided in this kind of case might upset schemes for organized marketing.

The bill never became law; indeed, it was never even voted upon. No sooner had it been introduced than it was withdrawn by the government for further consideration. Having been withdrawn, it was shelved indefinitely.

VIII

The High Court's approach to constitutional adjudication has been very much that of a common law court. This is hardly surprising when one considers that most of its business is common law work. Unlike the United States Supreme Court, it sits as a general court of appeal from state supreme courts[65] and its appeal jurisdiction is not limited to cases presenting a federal aspect. The Court recognizes that

63. See *Clayton* v. *Heffron*, 105 C.L.R. 214 (1960).
64. See Ross Anderson, "The Queensland Bill of Rights," *Australian Political Science Association News* (1960), No. 2, 1.
65. Constitution, s. 73.

constitutional interpretation ought to be approached rather differently from the interpretation of ordinary statutes. On the other hand, it has repeatedly stressed that the Constitution took effect within a common law system and should be read accordingly.[66] What this means in practice is that where the language of the Constitution is general and open-textured, the Court will attribute to it a meaning conformable to common law principle and in particular will construe grants of legislative power consistently with common law values. It is as if the common law—or that part of it delimiting public authority and defining fundamental human rights—has a moral superiority which entitles it to be used as a standard both in determining what powers the Constitution was intended to confer and in determining the limits of power supplied by ordinary statute.

The extent to which the High Court is prepared to write common law standards into the Constitution is particularly well-illustrated by its interpretation of Commonwealth executive power. The Constitution merely vests the power in the Crown, makes it exercisable by the governor-general, and declares that it shall extend to the maintenance and execution of the Constitution and Commonwealth laws. The Court has held that, apart from the powers specifically mentioned, e.g., the power to summon, prorogue, and dissolve Parliament, the Constitution does not give the executive branch wider authority than the Crown would be entitled to exercise under the common law.[67] It cannot therefore, by virtue of the Constitution, empower royal commissioners to compel the attendance of witnesses, the giving of testimony, or the production of documents. Such powers may be supplied but only by parliamentary enactment.[68]

Consider also the High Court's interpretation of the Commonwealth defense power. The words of the Constitution are general, but they have been held not to authorize federal legislation interfering unduly with individuals' liberty of association. A federal regulation made in wartime to empower the government to confiscate premises of

66. *Amalgamated Society of Engineers* v. *Adelaide Steamship Co. Ltd.*, 28 C.L.R. 129, 152 (1920); *Federal Commissioner of Taxation* v. *Official Liquidator of E. O. Farley Ltd. (In Liquidation)* 63 C.L.R. 278, 304 (1940).

67. *The Commonwealth* v. *Colonial Combing, Spinning and Weaving Co. Ltd.*, 31 C.L.R. 421 (1922).

68. *Attorney-General for the Commonwealth* v. *Colonial Sugar Refinery Co. Ltd.* [1914] A.C. 237. Likewise the Commonwealth executive cannot tax without parliamentary authorization: *The Commonwealth* v. *Colonial Combing, Spinning and Weaving Co. Ltd.*, 31 C.L.R. 421 (1922).

subversive associations was held unconstitutional, and associated regulations empowering the governor-general to decide which associations were to be illegal and defining the legal consequences flowing from such declaration were held *ultra vires the* enabling act.[69] The lawmaking power given by the enabling act was expressed in such vague terms that it is almost certain that had the regulations in question been included in a statute, they would have been held unconstitutional.

This conclusion is reinforced by the High Court's decision in the *Communist Party Case*.[70] In 1950, the federal Parliament passed an act banning and dissolving the Australian Communist party and any other Communist association which the executive chose to bring within the act. All of such bodies were liable to be deprived of their property; taking part in their activities was made a criminal offense, and "declared" Communists were disabled from holding certain offices. The chief consideration which moved the High Court to hold the act invalid was that the statutory provisions were not of a kind which would permit the Court to decide whether the act could be subsumed under defense or any other head of federal power. The facts upon which the existence of the power to legislate depended—the threat of Communism to national security—had been determined by Parliament or were left to be determined by the executive. On that basis of assumed fact, Parliament had proceeded to impose sanctions on Communists and Communist organizations, not in respect of particular acts committed, but in respect of their mere existence. In ascertaining the constitutionality of the legislation, the Court began, as always, by considering the act's purported effect on antecedent rights. The rights here in question were "the right of association, the common property and the civil rights of the members."[71] The assumption was that they were rights entitled to legal recognition and not lightly to be overridden by legislation. "The Constitution," Justice Dixon observed, "is an instrument framed in accordance with many traditional conceptions, to some of which it gives effect, as, for example, in separating the judicial power from other functions of government, others of which are simply assumed. Among these I think it may fairly be said that the rule of law forms an assumption."[72]

69. *Adelaide Company of Jehovah's Witnesses Inc.* v. *The Commonwealth*, 67 C.L.R. 116 (1943).
70. *Australian Communist Party* v. *The Commonwealth*, 83 C.L.R. 1 (1951).
72. *Ibid.*, 193.   71. *Ibid.*, 200.

In its capacity as the supreme court of common law, the High Court exercises a creative function which in some respects parallels that of the United States Supreme Court in the application of the Bill of Rights. So far as individual liberties derive legal support from decisional rules, the High Court's judgments are just as instrumental in forming and maintaining standards as judgments of the American court. The High Court's decisional rules may of course be negated by statute, but governments are not likely to embark on a course of legislative action if the result would be to overturn principles which the High Court has commended on grounds going to the moral foundations of a democratic society. The role of the High Court is therefore partly educative and partly regulatory.

The kinds of criticisms that have been levelled against judicial enforcement of fundamental law guarantees in some respects apply with equal force to legal systems such as Australia's, in which the legal definition and vindication of individual liberties is left largely to common law processes. And this is a point which the critics of judicial review often ignore. In the United States, Bill of Rights issues come before the Supreme Court as disputes *inter partes*. At this point, a decision has to be made which will affect interests other than those immediately represented before the Court. The Court, after all, is deciding principally with reference to the concrete case in hand. But inasmuch as the Court is making law for the whole, it must consider interests other than those represented and endeavor to arrive at a decision which will conciliate the competing claims and still maximize liberty. "This kind of calculus," Paul Freund comments, "which is a commonplace of the legislative process, raises philosophical and practical problems of the first importance. The question for us is whether the calculus is an appropriate one for the jurisdiction of judges in applying the guaranties of the Constitution."[73] But is it appropriate even for the jurisdiction of judges who make law about liberty without the guidance of constitutional guarantees?

A further criticism sometimes made of the system whereby the Supreme Court pronounces on the application of the Bill of Rights is that the kind of decision involved in such cases is political rather than legal and that policy-making in this area, because of its con-

73. "The Supreme Court and Fundamental Freedoms," in Leonard W. Levy, ed., *Judicial Review and the Supreme Court: Selected Essays* (New York, 1967), p. 133.

troversial nature, is more properly left to legislators. No realist today would deny that in applying the Bill of Rights, the Supreme Court is performing the part of a policy-maker or that the words of the Constitution preclude discretion or choice. The real problem to my mind is how the discretion is to be guided: whether, for example, the Court should presume in favor of legislative judgment and evaluation. In many ways, the problems confronting a court deciding civil liberties questions without a bill of rights or statutory definitions of rights is more acute. There is no legislative judgment to which it can defer. It is obliged to make value judgments and establish law guided only by judicial precedent. The one difference is that its resolution of the issues is not final. Its policies are liable to legislative review and alteration. This very want of finality reduces the pressure upon the judiciary to come up with final answers and discourages attempts to lay down broad principles going beyond the immediate requirements of the case. Courts in this situation are relieved of the necessity of having to lay down guidelines which can be acted upon by the legislature in the future, and though they may think it desirable to give direction about the standards to which officials ought to conform—e.g., standards that ought to be observed by police in interrogation of suspects—any standards they do lay down or suggest are in a sense tentative and provisional: they are subject to legislative revision.

W. D. K. *Kernaghan* / Civil Liberties in the Canadian Community

I. Civil Liberties and the Constitution

The single most noteworthy achievement in the sphere of civil liberties in Canada during the one hundred years since Confederation was the enactment in 1960 of the Canadian Bill of Rights.[1] This statute of the federal Parliament marked the culmination of four decades of continuing efforts to secure improved legal guarantees to Canadian rights and freedoms. It also heralded the beginning of a campaign for the constitutional entrenchment of a bill of rights embracing a wide range of civil liberties and extending its application to the provincial level of government. The focus of this essay will be the factors leading to the achievement of the existing Bill of Rights and the need in Canada today for further legislative and constitutional safeguards to civil liberties.

Central to this examination is an understanding of the meaning of "civil liberties" in the Canadian context. Professor (now Mr. Justice) Laskin has classified Canadian civil liberties into (1) the traditional political liberties—the freedoms of speech, press, religion, assembly, and association; (2) legal liberties—the freedoms "from arbitrary arrest, or arbitrary search and seizure; protection of fair and impartial adjudication"; (3) egalitarian civil liberties—positive governmental action to ensure "equality of employment opportunity or of access to service or amenities without discrimination on account of religion or colour or origin"; and (4) economic civil liberties—"a transfer to the economic sphere of the notion of individual rights developed in the political sphere."[2] Professor F. R. Scott has set forward a similar classification but has added the category of minority or group rights, which in his estimation "rank ahead of nearly all other rights in the minds of most people in Quebec."[3] Mark MacGuigan has argued

1. *An Act for the Recognition and Protection of Human Rights and Fundamental Freedoms.* Canada, *Statutes*, c. 44 (1960).
2. *Canadian Constitutional Law* (3rd ed.; Toronto, 1966), p. 974.
3. *Civil Liberties and Canadian Federalism* (Toronto, 1959), p. 29.

persuasively that the term "civil liberties" should be restricted to the political, legal, and egalitarian liberties which "1) are wholly negative in their scope and 2) relate directly to the human person."[4] Nevertheless, a broad classification encompassing the fourfold Laskin division supplemented by the class of minority rights is the most practicable demarcation of the field since it closely approximates the classification adopted by the federal government in its civil liberties dialogue with the provinces and the United Nations.

In the United States the terms "civil liberties" and "civil rights" are often used interchangeably by both scholars and the general public. In Canada, however, the use of the term "civil rights" to refer to human rights and fundamental freedoms has given rise to much popular confusion and legal controversy since the British North America Act grants to the provinces authority over "Property and Civil Rights in the Province."[5] Both the justices of the Supreme Court and legal scholars are divided among themselves as to the extent to which this provision bestows jurisdiction in the civil liberties field upon the provinces. There appears, however, to be a growing consensus among leading constitutional experts in Canada that the term "civil rights" refers

only to private law rights between individuals, and not to those public rights, such as freedom of religion, of speech, of the press, of association and of the person, which are really only attributes of citizenship and the limits of which are set in the criminal law.[6]

The failure of Canada's Founding Fathers to make extensive provision in the British North America Act for the protection of civil liberties was not motivated by a considered decision to reject a bill of rights modeled on that of the United States. Rather, the occasional, almost incidental, allusions to civil liberties during the Confederation Debates[7] demonstrate that the Fathers of Confederation believed that

4. "Civil Liberties in the Canadian Federation," *University of New Brunswick Law Journal*, XVI (May, 1966), 4.

5. Section 92(13).

6. Scott, p. 24. See also Bora Laskin, "An Inquiry into Mr. Diefenbaker's Bill of Rights," *Canadian Bar Review*, XXXVII (March, 1959), 116, and MacGuigan, p. 12. Note the more detailed discussion of this question in D. A. Schmeiser, *Civil Liberties in Canada* (London, 1964), pp. 74-78, and in W. S. Tarnopolsky, *The Canadian Bill of Rights* (Toronto, 1966), pp. 9-12.

7. See *Parliamentary Debates on the Confederation of the British North America Provinces* (Quebec, 1865), pp. 1, 29, 31, 44, 833, and 1027.

"a Constitution similar in Principle to that of the United Kingdom"[8] would furnish adequate safeguards to individual liberties. It is incorrect to assume, however, the complete absence of constitutional protection of civil liberties in Canada. Those sections of the British North America Act which may be viewed as touching upon aspects of civil liberties are those providing for an annual session of Parliament (s. 20); for representation by population (ss. 51, 51A, and 52); for the limitation of unqualified provincial authority over education through guarantees to separate schools (s. 93); for the independence of justices of the Superior Courts in the provinces through the assurance of tenure during good behavior (s. 99); and for the use of the two languages, English and French, in the federal and Quebec legislatures, in the courts of Quebec, and in those courts created by the federal government (s. 133).

It is remarkable that almost a century after Confederation a number of opponents to the enactment of a Canadian bill of rights based their arguments on Canada's close historical and constitutional links with Great Britain. Such legal watersheds in British history as the Magna Carta of 1215, the Petition of Rights of 1628, the Habeas Corpus Act of 1674, and the Bill of Rights of 1689 were offered as pillars of defense for Canadan civil liberties. These declarations of rights and freedoms marked progress in the struggle of Parliament and the citizen against the arbitrary exercise of royal authority and have been a source of inspiration to civil libertarians in Britain, Canada, and elsewhere. Such charters of liberties do not, however, provide Canadian courts with the legal powers needed to deter and punish periodic transgressions of civil liberties today.

Moreover, it is not realistic to suggest that a transnational implantation of such a culture-bound characteristic as exceptional regard for the preservation of individual and collective liberties could take place between Great Britain and Canada. The less enviable record of the Canadian community in the realm of civil liberties has been conditioned by Canada's distinctive social and political characteristics. Since persons of ethnic origins other than Anglo-Saxon predominate among the Canadian population, a much smaller proportion of Canadian than British citizens possess the Anglo-Saxon heritage of respect for civil liberties. It is significant also that many infringements of Canadian freedoms have occurred in sections of Canada inhabited

8. Preamble to the British North America Act.

largely by persons of British ancestry. Furthermore, in contrast to
Great Britain where Parliament is supreme over the whole field of
civil liberties, freedom-conscious citizens in Canada must oversee the
legislative activities of the federal government and ten provincial governments.

II. Civil Liberties Disputes Preceding the Bill of Rights

The Canadian Bill of Rights did not issue from a single civil
liberties transgression of an exceptional nature. Indeed, the decade
before the enactment of the bill in 1960 was a period of relative qui-
escence in the area of Canadian civil liberties. The Bill of Rights was
the outcome of a number of encroachments on Canadian freedoms
extending over the span of years from World War I to the early fifties.
Although specific proposals for a Canadian bill of rights date only
from 1945,[9] civil liberties problems have plagued the Canadian federation from its very beginning. Before 1914, however, aside from occasional civil liberties controversies of a political and legal nature, the
matter of greatest concern was minority rights, with particular reference to the constitutional, linguistic, and cultural rights of French-
speaking Canadians. During World War I, the budding consciousness
among Canadians of the need for more vigorous defense of personal
freedoms was manifested in opposition to the violations of civil liberties
committed by the Conservative government under the War Measures
Act[10] and allegedly justified by the emergency conditions. Strong exception was also taken to laws enacted as an aftereffect of the Winni-
peg General Strike in 1919. An addition to section 98 of the Criminal
Code[11] provided that any organization which attempted to effect "governmental, industrial or economic change" by forceful means was an
illegal association and that membership in or public support of such
a group was an offense. Under this law, the Ontario Court of Appeal
in 1931 declared the Communist party of Canada an unlawful association.[12] Widespread disapproval in Canada of the sweeping restrictions imposed upon traditional political liberties by section 98 led to

9. The first formal motion requesting a bill of rights was introduced in the House
of Commons on October 10, 1945, by Alistair Stewart of the Co-operative Commonwealth
Federation (now the New Democratic Party).

10. Canada, *Revised Statutes*, c. 288 (1952).

11. Canada, *Statutes*, c. 46, s. 1 (1919).   12. *Rex* v. *Buck*, 3 D.L.R. 97 (1932).

its repeal in 1936.[13] Significantly, the content of section 98 resembled that of the 1940 Alien Registration Act (Smith Act)[14] in the United States aimed originally against pro-Nazi and pro-fascist elements but since employed, together with subsequent statutes, to restrict the activities of Communists.

The Liberal party came to power in Canada in 1926 and except for the years 1930 to 1935 held office until its defeat by the Progressive Conservative party in 1957. The performance of the Liberal government during this period in the defense of human rights and fundamental freedoms was far from praiseworthy. The burden of keeping Parliament and the public informed of important civil liberties issues fell to the members of the federal opposition parties, and notably to the members of the Co-operative Commonwealth Federation. Among the members of the Progressive Conservative party, only John George Diefenbaker, both before and after his elevation to the office of Prime Minister in 1957, merits acclaim for his accomplishments in the preservation of individual liberties. Indeed, he is primarily responsible for the achievement of the existing Bill of Rights.

It is common in Canada to hear the assertion that in the sphere of civil liberties the record of certain provincial governments is even less commendable than that of the federal government. The large number of civil liberties controversies which have occurred and the difficulty of obtaining a precise measurement of the implications and reverberations of even a single dispute preclude the successful testing of such an hypothesis. Nevertheless, an account of selected civil liberties issues at both levels of government does suggest that, unlike provincial infringements of civil liberties, federal wrongs tend to occur primarily in times of national emergency.

At the provincial level, the civil liberties debate best known outside Canada's borders centered on the enactment in 1937 of Quebec's Act Respecting Communistic Propaganda,[15] popularly known as the Padlock Act. This act provided for the closing or "padlocking" for one year of any house suspected of being used "to propagate communism or bolshevism" and for the seizure and destruction of written materials espousing these views. The threat to individual liberties lay in the failure of the act to define "communism" or "bolshevism" and

13. Canada, *Statutes*, c. 29, s. 1 (1936).   14. United States, *Statutes*, c. 439 (1940).
15. Quebec, *Revised Statutes*, c. 52 (1941).

in the government's authority to padlock houses and confiscate literature without granting the accused a trial in the courts.

Also in 1937 the Social Credit government of Alberta passed a
bill entitled An Act to Ensure the Publication of Accurate News and
Information. This act purported to restrict and control criticism of
governmental policies by requiring newspapers to print government-
written corrections to news stories and to disclose the sources of these
stories. Violations of the act were punishable by the suspension of the
newspaper's publication or the prohibition of further articles emanating from "any person or source" of a previous offensive article. Alberta's lieutenant-governor exercised his constitutional authority to
reserve such questionable provincial legislation for consideration by
the governor-in-council (i.e., the Canadian Cabinet). The bill was
then referred to the Supreme Court which declared it *ultra vires* the
Alberta government because of its dependence upon the Social Credit
Act[16] which invaded federal constitutional jurisdiction.[17] Three of the
six judges argued in addition that the act encroached upon federal
powers in its interference with freedom of the press. In the form of
obiter dicta, Chief Justice Duff anticipated some of the famous civil
liberties decisions of the fifties with his statement that the provinces
may exercise wide legislative authority over newspapers but that

the limit, in our opinion, is reached when the legislation effects such a
curtailment of the exercise of the right of public discussion as substantially
to interfere with the working of the parliamentary institutions of Canada
as contemplated by the provisions of the British North America Act and
the statutes of the Dominion of Canada.[18]

A final example of provincial incursion on civil liberties involved
the reaction of Quebec's Roman Catholic population to the inflamma-
tory denunciations of the Church by the Witnesses of Jehovah. As a
consequence of attempts to gain converts through public meetings,
door-to-door visits, and the dissemination of written materials, the
Witnesses were subjected to mob assaults and peremptory arrests. The
determined efforts of the Quebec government in the immediate post-
war period to rid the province of the Witnesses were later declared
extralegal, or *ultra vires*, by the Supreme Court.

16. Alberta, *Statutes*, c. 10 (1937).
17. *Reference Re Alberta Statutes*, S.C.R. 100 (1938).
18. *Ibid.*, p. 134.

The Quebec government was not alone in its maltreatment of the Jehovah's Witnesses. The federal government had declared the Witnesses an illegal organization for three years during World War II. The Prime Minister's justification was that

the literature of Jehovah's Witnesses discloses, in effect, that man-made authority or law should not be recognized if it conflicts with the Jehovah's Witnesses interpretation of the Bible; that they refuse to salute the flag of any nation or to hail any man; and, that they oppose war.

The general effect of this literature is, among other things, to undermine the ordinary responsibilities of citizens, particularly in time of war.[19]

The banning of the Witnesses was merely a minor illustration of the conduct of the Liberal government in its execution of the Defence of Canada Regulations passed under the authority of the War Measures Act. In addition to the prohibition of other associations and societies, including the Communist party, the government demonstrated less restraint than either Great Britain or the United States in such areas as the censorship of newspapers and periodicals; the prosecution and imprisonment of persons for alleged subversive statements; the number of internments; the holding of trials in secret; and the suspension of habeas corpus. On the basis of a careful study of these wartime regulations, Professor Lester H. Phillips concluded that

there exists the possibility that an incalculable amount of harm has been done to numerous minority groups, whose confidence in Canadian democracy it may take years to restore. In short, one may raise some doubt as to whether the Liberal war-time government has lived up to a democratic standard of keeping war-time restrictions to a minimum consonant with military necessity and proportionate to the existing danger to the nation.[20]

Both Canada and the United States issued orders during World War II which evacuated all persons of Japanese descent from their homes on the West Coast and relocated them in the central and eastern sections of the two countries. The stress of the economic and social hardships imposed by such measures led almost half of the more than 20,000 Japanese affected by the Canadian relocation to apply for repatriation to Japan. Then, under emergency powers extended into

19. *Debates* (Commons), 1st Sess. 19th Parl. (1940), 1645-1646.
20. "Canada's Internal Security," *Canadian Journal of Economics and Political Science,* XII (Feb., 1946), 29. See also E. W. Murphy, Jr., "The War Power of the Dominion," *Canadian Bar Review,* XXX (Oct., 1952), 791-806, and H. McD. Clokie, "Emergency Powers and Civil Liberties," *Canadian Journal of Economics and Political Science,* XIII (Aug., 1947), 384-394.

the postwar period by the National Emergency Transitional Powers Act,[21] the Liberal government presented to the House of Commons three orders-in-council relating to the Japanese. Although many of those Japanese persons who had requested repatriation wished to remain in Canada, one of these orders[22] stipulated that more than 10,000 Japanese were to be deported. A majority of those Japanese involved were either born or naturalized in Canada. Both the Supreme Court of Canada and the Judicial Committee of the Privy Council in Great Britain upheld the authority of the federal government to take such deportation proceedings under the War Measures Act.[23] Intense pressure exerted by civil liberties associations and the opposition parties in Parliament persuaded the government to reverse its policy, however, and only 3,964 Japanese actually returned to Japan.[24]

The disposition of the Liberal government to abridge traditional liberties in the interest of the security of the state was again revealed in an incident which had critical international repercussions. In early September, 1945, while the Allied powers were preparing for peace talks, Igor Gouzenko, a cipher clerk in the Soviet Embassy in Ottawa, furnished the Canadian government with documents which exposed the presence of a vast espionage network in Canada. This event also had important implications for Canadian civil liberties. Ten days after the appointment of a Royal Commission to investigate and report upon the state of Soviet espionage in Canada, the public was informed of the existence of the commission. Then, after twenty-six persons identified by the Embassy documents were arrested, they were interrogated by the commission, held incommunicado, and denied access to both families and legal assistance. Only thirteen of those arrested were actually charged with any offense. Moreover, in *Rex* v. *Mazerall*,[25] a case arising out of the espionage proceedings, the Supreme Court held that the accused was presumed to know the law and was, therefore, not entitled to a warning against self-incrimination in testifying before the Royal Commission. As a final affront to the normal judicial process, documentation concerning those persons the commission be-

---

21. Canada, *Statutes*, c. 25 (1945).   22. P.C. 7355.
23. *In the Matter of a Reference as to the Validity of Orders in Council . . . in Relation to Persons of the Japanese Race*, S.C.R. 248 (1946), and *Co-operative Committee on Japanese-Canadians* v. *Attorney-General for Canada*, A.C. 87 (1947).
24. F. E. LaViolette, *The Canadian Japanese and World War II* (Toronto, 1948), p. 273.
25. 4 D.L.R. 791 (1946).

lieved to be guilty of espionage was published before the accused ever received a trial in a court of law.[26]

The cumulative effect of these violations of Canadian freedoms was the awakening of many Canadians to the necessity for improved legal safeguards to civil liberties. Other powerful forces leading to the eventual passage of the Bill of Rights were the United Nations' adoption on December 10, 1948, of the Universal Declaration of Human Rights and the creation of special legislative committees of the Canadian Parliament to inquire into the state of human rights and fundamental freedoms in Canada.

In addition to the statements in the Preamble and Article 3 of the United Nations Charter expressing the determination of member states to co-operate in the promotion of civil liberties, one of the purposes of the organization set forth in Articles 55 and 56 is "to take joint and separate action in co-operation with the Organization for the achievement" of such purposes as "universal respect for, and observance of, human rights and fundamental freedoms for all without distinction as to race, sex, language or religion." To meet these obligations, Canada, as a signator to the Charter, established two legislative committees[27] to examine the extent to which the status of civil liberties in Canada measured up to the preliminary and final drafts of the international declaration. The numerous submissions to these committees by associations and individuals pleading for the enactment of a bill of rights received nationwide publicity. The committees' reports were in sympathy with these appeals but pointed to the formidable obstacles created by the imprecise division of constitutional competence in the field.

During the fifties, the Liberal government opposed the enactment of a bill of rights on the grounds that Canadian liberties were effectively secured by existing laws and that the Supreme Court could serve as the guarantor of Canadian civil liberties. Then, in 1957, John George Diefenbaker, leader of the Progressive Conservative party

26. See *Report of the Royal Commission to Investigate . . . the Communication, by Public Officials and Other Persons in Positions of Trust of Secret and Confidential Information to Agents of a Foreign Power*, Ottawa, June 27, 1946. See also W. Eggleston, "The Report of the Royal Commission on Espionage," *Queen's Quarterly*, LIII (1946), 369-378.

27. Canada, *Special Joint Committee of the Senate and the House of Commons on Human Rights and Fundamental Freedoms, Minutes and Proceedings* (1947) and (1948), and *Special Committee of the Senate on Human Rights and Fundamental Freedoms, Minutes and Proceedings* (1950).

and long the parliamentary champion of civil liberties, became **Prime** **Minister**. Following extensive debate, both in committee[28] and in Parliament, on Diefenbaker's draft bill of rights, the Canadian Bill of Rights became law on August 10, 1960, under the formal title of **An Act for the Recognition and Protection of Human Rights and Fundamental Freedoms**.

III. The Canadian Bill of Rights

Sections 1 to 4 of the act are contained in Part I, and Section 5 and 6 in Part II. Section 1 recognizes and declares that certain rights and freedoms, most of which fall within the classification of political and egalitarian liberties, "have existed and shall continue to exist without discrimination by reason of race, national origin, colour, religion or sex." Section 2 instructs the judiciary that unless specific legislative exception is made, Canadian laws must be interpreted and applied so that these liberties, together with a list of legal liberties enumerated in Section 2, shall be preserved. Section 3 does not go far toward implementation of the recommendation of certain legal experts and special interest groups that Canada establish a civil liberties section in the Department of Justice equivalent to the civil rights division in the United States Department of Justice. Provision is made, however, for the minister of justice to direct the examination of every proposed statute and regulation to ensure its consistency with the terms of the Bill of Rights. Any inconsistencies are to be reported to the House of Commons, but since all government legislation is drafted in the Department of Justice, it is highly unlikely that any government bills which are obviously incompatible with the bill will be introduced in the House. Section 4 states that Part I of the act is to officially constitute the Canadian Bill of Rights.

The principal clauses of Section 5 stipulate that nothing in the first part of the act "shall be construed to abrogate or abridge any human rights or fundamental freedom not enumerated therein that may have existed in Canada at the commencement of this Act" and that "the provisions of Part I shall be construed as extending only to matters coming within the legislative authority of the Parliament of

28. See Canada, *Special Joint Committee of the Senate and the House of Commons on Human Rights and Fundamental Freedoms, Minutes and Proceedings* (1960).

Canada." Finally, Section 6 alters certain clauses of the War Measures Act to allow Parliament to debate and possibly to effect the revocation of the Cabinet's declaration that "war, invasion or insurrection, real or apprehended, exists." Then, in the face of stiff resistance from the opposition parties in Parliament and from many of those Canadians who made submissions on the draft bill, the government added the concluding statement to Section 6 that

any Act or thing done or authorized or any order or regulation made under the authority of this Act, shall be deemed not to be an abrogation, abridgement or infringement of any right or freedom recognized by the *Canadian Bill of Rights.*

Therefore, the Bill of Rights can be rendered impotent when the War Measures Act is in force.

By the adoption of the bill in the form of an ordinary statute of Parliament, the Conservative government rejected several other alternatives. The political realities of Canada's federal system prohibited the enactment of a federal statute which would simply override any provincial legislation in conflict with its provisions. Furthermore, the absence of federal-provincial agreement on a domestic procedure for constitutional amendment would have complicated any attempt to imbed a federal bill of rights in the British North America Act. Legal scholars in particular were bitterly disappointed that no sustained effort was made to achieve the consent of the provinces to a constitutional amendment limiting the powers of both levels of government or to complementary federal and provincial legislation embracing the total field of civil liberties. Thus, the Bill of Rights is operative on the federal level alone and imposes no direct limitations on the legislative powers of the provincial governments.

IV. Civil Liberties and the Supreme Court

One of the most weighty arguments presented against the enactment of a bill of rights was the outstanding performance of the Supreme Court in the defense of civil liberties. On the basis of the Court's decisions between 1950 and 1959 it is understandable that many Canadians should regard the enactment of a bill of rights as superfluous. The Judicial Committee of the Privy Council, which was the final court of appeal in Canadian cases until 1949, had no opportunity to pronounce upon the allocation of legislative powers over civil liberties. Immediately after the abolition of these appeals, however, the Canadian Supreme Court heard several cases involving the delimitation of the boundaries of federal and provincial authority over Canadian rights and freedoms.

As in the United States, so in Canada, several momentous civil liberties cases have arisen from the activities of the religious sect, the Witnesses of Jehovah. The Canadian Supreme Court upheld the right of the Witnesses to distribute literature containing impassioned and provocative criticism of Quebec's religious and governmental authorities.[29] Damages were awarded to Witnesses against police officers who disrupted a religious meeting in a private home[30] and against other police officers who held a lady Witness for two days without laying a formal charge or permitting her legal counsel.[31] Moreover, the Premier of Quebec was personally required to pay damages for ordering the cancellation of the liquor licence held by a Witness who owned a Montreal restaurant and who had been providing bail for the Witnesses on a mass basis.[32] In a series of cases since 1938, the Witnesses in the United States have helped to strengthen constitutional guarantees to the traditional political liberties and particularly to freedom of religion. Similarly, the Witnesses in Canada have obliged the Supreme Court to enunciate the law on questions of religious liberty never before examined by that Court. In this way, the Jehovah's Witnesses have contributed to the enrichment of Canadian constitutional law. Other important decisions of the Court included the rulings that Quebec's infamous Padlock Law[33] and another Quebec law which authorized municipalities to force storeowners to close their establishments on days coinciding with Roman Catholic holy days[34] were beyond provincial jurisdiction.

A notable aspect of these celebrated cases involves the distribution of constitutional competence over civil liberties between the federal government and the Province of Quebec. The judges of Quebec courts and the representatives on the Supreme Court from Quebec are normally French-speaking Roman Catholics trained in the civil law. Members of the Supreme Court from other Canadian provinces are

29. *Boucher* v. *The King*, S.C.R. 255 (1951), and *Saumur* v. *City of Quebec*, 2 S.C.R. 299 (1953).
30. *Chaput* v. *Romain*, S.C.R. 834 (1955).   31. *Lamb* v. *Benoit*, S.C.R. 321 (1959).
32. *Roncarelli* v. *Duplessis*, S.C.R. 121 (1959).
33. *Switzman* v. *Elbling*, S.C.R. 285 (1957).
34. *Birks* v. *City of Montreal*, S.C.R. 799 (1955).

English-speaking judges of varying religious affiliations educated in the common law. Most of the cases, however, have involved issues of criminal law or constitutional law, both of which are applicable to all provinces, including Quebec. Consequently, the several occasions on which the Supreme Court has overruled decisions of Quebec courts on civil liberties questions and has divided along French-English lines in its own decisions are not easily explicable on any other grounds than that of the racial and religious background of the individual judges. Indeed, these decisions appear to reflect as much a conflict of culture as a conflict of law.[35] Since the majority of the justices of the Supreme Court are appointed from provinces other than Quebec, the "English-Canadian" view of political and legal liberties has consistently triumphed over the dissenting opinions of the "French-Canadian" members. Those Canadians who see this judicial clash as a threat to minority cultural rights within the Canadian federation have recommended the establishment of a special judicial tribunal to hear cases involving constitutional disputes between Quebec and the federal government.

The civil liberties judgments of the fifties manifest the force and the eloquence of Justice Ivan C. Rand as the leading advocate of a Canadian civil liberties jurisprudence. Justice Rand, who has been described as the "greatest expositor of a democratic public law which Canada has known,"[36] attempted to bring into judicial being the concept of " 'inherent rights of the Canadian citizen' which will be immune from abridgment by the provinces of Canada, and which will include 'freedom of speech, religion and the inviolability of the person.' "[37] The most explicit statement of this concept came in Justice Rand's contention that

a Province cannot, by depriving a Canadian of the means of working, force him to leave it; it cannot divest him of his right or capacity to remain and to engage in work there: that capacity inhering as a constituent element of his citizenship status is beyond nullification by provincial action. . . . He may, of course, disable himself from exercising his capacity

35. For an elaboration of this hypothesis, see W. D. K. Kernaghan, "Freedom of Religion in the Province of Quebec with Particular Reference to the Jews, Jehovah's Witnesses and Church-State Relations, 1930-1960," unpublished Ph.D. thesis, Duke University, 1966, pp. 201-208.

36. Laskin, "An Inquiry," p. 124.

37. Edward McWhinney, *Judicial Review in the English-Speaking World* (3rd ed.; Toronto, 1965), p. 21.

or he may be regulated in it by valid provincial laws in other respects. But that attribute of citizenship lies outside of those civil rights committed to the Province, and is analogous to the capacity of a Dominion corporation which a Province cannot sterilize.[38]

Through the succession of civil liberties decisions, the Supreme Court moved purposefully toward the creation of a judicial bill of rights for Canada. Following Justice Rand's retirement from the Court in 1959 and the passage of the Bill of Rights in 1960, however, the libertarian trend of judicial decision-making so characteristic of the fifties has not been sustained.[39] Moreover, defense counsel in Canada's courts have been repeatedly frustrated by the refusal of judges to apply the Bill of Rights so as to declare ineffective any prior legislation incompatible with the bill.[40] The assessment by legal experts of the judicial merit of the bill may be succinctly summarized in the words of Canada's Minister of Justice who wrote in a government white paper that the bill

has in practice had a limited application because the Courts have held that it does not expressly over-ride any provisions inconsistent with it which may be contained in earlier federal statutes. While conceivably the 1960 Bill could have been interpreted so as to alter previously enacted statutes, the courts have not done this. There have been some conflicting opinions in various lower courts, but there has on the whole been a strong judicial tendency to assume that Parliament did not intend by the Bill of Rights to alter specific, pre-existing, inconsistent statutory provisions. The Courts have said instead that Parliament would have made an express amendment had it intended to alter its own previously enacted laws.[41]

On the basis of the Supreme Court's decisions and the writings of Canadian law professors,[42] a provisional determination as to the general distribution of powers over civil liberties may be made. The federal Parliament has primary legislative authority over political and legal liberties through its power over criminal law. To enable the

---

38. *Winner* v. *S.M.T. (Eastern) Ltd.*, S.C.R. 887 (1951) at pp. 919-920.
39. See, for example, *Oil, Chemical and Atomic Worker's International Union* v. *Imperial Oil Ltd.*, S.C.R. 584 (1963); *Robertson and Rosetanni* v. *The Queen*, S.C.R. 651 (1963); and *Saumur* v. *A.-G. of Quebec*, S.C.R. 252 (1964). Two other cases which could be viewed as libertarian were decided by a five to four majority of the Court. See *Brodie* v. *The Queen*, S.C.R. 681 (1962), and *McKay* v. *The Queen*, S.C.R. 798 (1965).
40. For a summary of the cases involving judicial interpretation of the Bill of Rights, see Schmeiser, pp. 36-53, and Tarnopolsky, pp. 89-111.
41. Pierre Elliott Trudeau, *A Canadian Charter of Human Rights* (Ottawa, 1968), pp. 13-14.
42. See Laskin, *Canadian Constitutional Law*, pp. 974-975; MacGuigan, pp. 12-14; and Tarnopolsky, pp. 26-59.

enforcement of provincial laws, however, the provinces exercise substantial powers in the area of legal liberties. The provinces also possess dominant, but not exclusive, authority over the categories of egalitarian and economic liberties. The class of minority or group rights touches so many areas of federal and provincial law that no specific conclusions as to the division of legislative authority can be drawn. On many occasions, and particularly in the case of the rights of French-speaking Canadians, complementary federal-provincial legislation is essential to the satisfaction of minority needs.

V. Existing Civil Liberties Issues

This overview of the past and current status of civil liberties in Canada does not allow for detailed examination of the numerous problems which now challenge the capacity of the population for tolerance and accommodation. Prevailing difficulties include control of the propagation of hate literature; the censorship of films by provincial officials; the discretionary, secret, and final decisions of certain administrative boards at both levels of government; the demands of Mennonite and Doukhobor subgroups for religious liberties; allegations of police brutality; and the treatment of such minority groups as the Indians, the Eskimos, the Hutterian brethren, and the Negroes. By way of illustration of the variety and complexity of these civil liberties disputes in Canada, three instances of special interest to American scholars have been selected for brief discussion.

In early 1963 hate propaganda began to be distributed in various sections of the country. This propaganda was disseminated in written form by mail and personal handouts and in oral form through public assemblies of extremist groups, "open-line" radio programs, and interviews on radio and television. This hate campaign has been concentrated primarily in the Province of Ontario but has extended to seven other provinces. The *Report of the Special Committee on Hate Propaganda in Canada* noted that the written materials originated largely in the United States and that among the several ideas that pervaded this literature were the statements that

"Communism is Jewish"; that Hitler was right in his policy of racial extermination; that a Jewish conspiracy exists to get control of the Canadian as well as of the world economy; that the Negro race is an inferior one which can weaken our society; that there is a deliberate campaign to mongrelize the races; and that Negroes should be returned to Africa.[43]

At the same time as this hate propaganda was being spread throughout Canada, the activities of a small number of neo-Nazis in the early sixties led to the formation of the Canadian Nazi party (now the Canadian National Socialist party) in April, 1965. This group received nationwide publicity from its attempts to use the public parks in the city of Toronto to speak against the Jews and the Negroes, from the assaults made upon members of the group by sections of the Jewish population, and from court action taken against its members under restrictive legislation passed by the Toronto municipal council.[44]

The Special Committee on Hate Propaganda reported that "the amount of hate propaganda presently being disseminated and its measurable effects probably are not sufficient to justify a description of the problem as one of crisis or near crisis proportions. Nevertheless the problem is a serious one."[45] On the basis of this conclusion, the committee proposed a number of additions to the Criminal Code to restrict the actions of purveyors of hate propaganda. These recommendations have been incorporated in Bill S-5 which has been introduced into the Canadian Senate. The draft bill provides that anyone who advocates or promotes genocide is liable to imprisonment for five years. Furthermore, anyone who publicly or wilfully promotes hatred or contempt against any identifiable group on the basis of race, color, or ethnic origin may be imprisoned for up to two years. The bill also authorizes the seizure of hate literature. To meet the strenuous objections of those Canadians who fear that legislation against group defamation might be employed to restrict the freedom of legitimate expression, the bill provides that no person can be convicted of wilfully promoting hatred if his statements are true or if they are relevant to a subject of public interest and on reasonable grounds he believes them to be true. Still, debate as to the possible abuse of such legislation continues in the press, scholarly journals, and in a Senate committee established to examine the implications of the draft bill.

Both American and Canadian citizens are aware of the recent conflicts that have arisen in North America over the relationships of cer-

43. Ottawa, 1966, p. 11.
44. See Mark MacGuigan, "Hate Control and Freedom of Assembly," *Saskatchewan Bar Review*, XXXI (Dec., 1966), 232-250.
45. *Report of the Special Committee on Hate Propaganda in Canada*, p. 59.

tain Mennonite groups with all levels of government in the spheres of education and participation in systems of social insurance. In Canada, despite the opposition of the Mennonites to military service during wartime on the grounds of religious belief, their interactions with Canadian governments have until the sixties been generally amicable. In the Province of Ontario the conservative element among the many branches making up the Mennonite religious and cultural family is represented by the Old Order Mennonite and Amish groups. To this date, the Ontario government has permitted these groups to operate their own schools despite evidence that the quality of education achieved there is inferior to that of the public schools.

These Ontario Mennonite groups are in open conflict with the federal government, however, over compulsory participation in the Canada Pension Plan.[46] In a submission to the federal government in late 1967 the Old Order and Amish bishops argued that

it is not only the Canada Pension Plan but the whole series of recent compulsory governmental programs of elementary centralized education, hospitalization, and workmen's compensation as well as the pension plan that by gradual stages is attempting to force our people to conform to what we consider a threat to our understanding of the Christian way of life. . . . We . . . have appreciated Canada's good government and we would not leave this country lightly. We confess, however, we have entertained that possibility if the only alternative to remaining here is to be forced by gradual steps to conform to an ever increasing number of worldly patterns of behaviour.[47]

Under the Social Security Amendments of 1965 Act, the United States government has permitted exemption from participation in compulsory government-sponsored welfare programs to any person who

is a member of a recognized religious sect or division thereof and is an adherent of established tenets or teachings of such sect or division by reason of which he is conscientiously opposed to acceptance of the benefits of any private or public insurance which makes payments in the event of death, disability, old-age, or retirement or makes payments toward the cost of, or provides services for, medical care (including the benefits of any insurance system established by the Social Security Act).[48]

46. Canada, *Statutes*, c. 51 (1964-1965).
47. Submission to the Government of Canada entitled *Re: The Old Order Mennonite and Amish Basis of Objection to Government Sponsored Social Security Programs*, dated at Kitchener, Ontario, Oct. 16, 1967, p. 2.
48. United States, *Statutes at Large*, c. 79, s. 319 (1965).

In Canada, both the Prime Minister[49] and the Minister of National Revenue[50] stated publicly that no exemptions from the Canada Pension Plan would be allowed. Indeed, the Department of National Revenue has seized milk checks belonging to approximately two hundred Old Order and Amish farmers in one area of the Province of Ontario to pay for the obligatory contributions to the plan. The federal government explained that exemptions from the plan must be authorized by the agreement of two-thirds of the provinces containing two-thirds of Canada's population and that such arrangements must be made at a federal-provincial conference on the plan. Since the government is now studying the American scheme for exemptions of religious groups from social security programs, the requests of the Ontario Mennonites may soon be satisfied. The Canada Pension Plan is, however, only one element of the successive welfare programs being established by the federal and provincial governments in Canada. There is little doubt, therefore, that similar controversies will continue to arise unless Canadian governments recognize the incompatibility of universally applied welfare schemes with the religious convictions of certain minority groups.

The insignificance of civil liberties questions involving Negroes in Canada as compared with the United States is reflected in the paucity of literature on the problems and characteristics of Canadian Negroes. Unquestionably, the difference in the extent of the problem of racial discrimination in the two countries is explainable primarily in terms of the size of the Negro population. In 1960 a total of 18,871,831 Negroes in the United States accounted for 10.5 per cent of the population, and the percentage by states ranged from below 1 per cent in such states as Maine, New Hampshire, and Vermont to 42 per cent in Mississippi and 53.9 per cent in the District of Columbia.[51] By way of contrast, in 1961, a total of 32,127 Negroes made up only .18 per cent of the Canadian population. Moreover, 11,900 of these Negroes, or more than 37 per cent of the total, were concentrated in the Province of Nova Scotia. Even in this province Negroes amounted to only 1.6 per cent of the population, and the highest proportion of Negroes

49. Kitchener-Waterloo *Record* (Aug. 14, 1967).
50. *Ibid.* (Aug. 17, 1967).
51. United States, Bureau of the Census, *1960 Census of the Population,* vol. PC(1)-1B.

found in any of the Canadian municipalities was only 4 per cent in the Nova Scotia municipalities of Halifax County and Truro.[52]

Dean W. A. MacKay has asserted that the continued existence in Nova Scotia of a small number of segregated schools for Negroes is a result of unique circumstances in particular areas and not of discrimination or provincial laws.[53] On the basis of a comparative study of Negro communities in Nova Scotia, Pennsylvania, and Virginia in 1964, however, the conclusion was reached that in Nova Scotia

despite the absence of any segregation laws, *de facto* segregation (or isolation) has been known extensively not only in education, but in employment, housing, and human relations as well. Therefore, rural Nova Scotia of the 1950's was not different in socio-economic development, at least apparently, from King and Queen County of Virginia of the 1930's.[54]

A study of the province's capital city of Halifax in 1962 revealed also that "the negroes of Halifax City are under-employed, under-educated, and ill-housed; that their employment and housing opportunities are restricted and that they have been living under a form of segregation."[55]

Progressive measures recently adopted by the government of Nova Scotia manifest an understanding that remedies to the problems of racial discrimination cannot be divorced from those of socioeconomic development. The Inter-Departmental Committee on Human Rights, established in 1962 to recommend improvements in minority rights, urged the consolidation of the province's anti-discrimination laws into the Nova Scotia Human Relations Act.[56] Violations of the act are punishable by fines of $100 for an individual and $500 for a corporation or trade union. The act has been subjected to frequent criticism on the grounds that it is not strictly enforced and that few prosecutions have taken place under its provisions. Dean MacKay has argued that such critical commentary is unjustified because the Department of Labour which administers the act has investigated many complaints

52. Canada, Dominion Bureau of Statistics, *1961 Census of the Population*, vol. 1, part 2.
53. "Equality of Opportunity: Recent Developments in the Field of Human Rights in Nova Scotia," *University of Toronto Law Journal*, XVII (1967), 186.
54. F. W. Jones, "The Interrelation of Socio-Economic Status and Academic Achievement in Nova Scotia, Pennsylvania, and Virginia," unpublished Ed.D. thesis, Pennsylvania State University, 1964, p. 4.
55. Institute of Public Affairs, Dalhousie University, *The Condition of the Negroes of Halifax City* [Nova Scotia]. Bulletin no. 27 (Halifax, 1962).
56. Nova Scotia, *Statutes*, c. 5 (1963). See also MacKay, pp. 180-182.

and has often brought about solutions to alleged instances of discrimination through a conciliation procedure.[57] The government has combined this anti-discrimination legislation with both governmental and private initiatives to promote equality of opportunity in the areas of education, employment, housing, and general community welfare.

The Negro population in Nova Scotia is represented primarily by the Nova Scotia Association for the Advancement of Coloured Peoples (NSAACP), which has no affiliation with the NAACP in the United States. The Nova Scotia organization works closely with the government in the implementation of diverse assistance programs. There is also a so-called "black power" movement in the province with a negligible membership and little influence. Both groups have warned of the possibility of race riots if the socioeconomic position of Negroes does not improve. It appears, however, that the provincial government is taking the positive steps necessary to avert such drastic action by the province's Negroes. The very small Negro population in other Canadian provinces accounts for the comparative lack of tension arising from discrimination against Negroes elsewhere in Canada.

Judicial decisions related to discriminatory practices against Negroes in Canada are rare in comparison to the large body of law which has developed on this subject in the United States. The few sporadic cases involving discrimination against Canadian Negroes in restaurants, taverns, and theaters[58] furnished no redress to the Negroes and demonstrated that little protection exists in the common law in Canada against discrimination in public places. The federal Parliament and most of the provincial legislatures have since filled this gap with the enactment of anti-discrimination legislation.

VI. Constitutional Entrenchment and a Charter of Human Rights

Many sections of the Canadian community argue that the numerous civil liberties disputes, either past or extant, combined with judicial refusal to utilize effectively the Bill of Rights in its present form, demonstrate the need for more far-reaching protection of civil liberties. It is evident that the achievement of comprehensive protection of

---

57. MacKay, pp. 182-183.
58. *Loew's Montreal Theatres Ltd.* v. *Reynolds,* 30 Que. K.B. 459 (1919); *Franklin* v. *Evans,* 55 O.L.R. 349 (1924); *Christie* v. *York Corp.,* S.C.R. 139 (1940); *Rogers* v. *Clarence Hotel Co. Ltd.,* 2 W.W.R. 545 (1940); and *Rex* v. *Desmond,* D.L.R. 81 (1947).

Canadian freedoms depends largely on federal-provincial co-operation and enthusiasm for a constitutionally enshrined bill of rights. To the American reader, the tendency of Canadian scholars and judges to look upon the Canadian Bill of Rights as an ineffective instrument of protection to civil liberties after only eight years of testing doubtless seems premature. Professor Tarnopolsky has pointed out that "it was not until after the Civil War . . . and some would say not until after World War II, that the American Supreme Court began to protect civil liberties through the medium of the *Bill of Rights* and the Fourteenth Amendment."[59] Nevertheless, even since World War II, the Supreme Court of the United States has judged a large number and variety of civil liberties cases, and, unlike Canada, has had recourse to a constitutionally entrenched Bill of Rights.

There is strong governmental and popular support in Canada today for amendment to the Canadian Constitution which will restrict the powers of both levels of government to encroach on civil liberties and which will extend protection to those liberties not embraced by the existing bill. The worth of the bill as a declaratory statement of desirable goals has been demonstrated by the greatly increased concern of provincial governments since 1960 for statutory guarantees of individual liberties. The majority of the provinces now have anti-discrimination legislation in the form of fair employment and fair accommodation practices acts. The Province of Saskatchewan has had a bill of rights since 1947, and the provinces of Alberta, Nova Scotia, and Ontario have recently consolidated their anti-discrimination statutes into human rights acts.

In early February, 1968, the Liberal government issued a white paper on human rights as a basis for discussion at a federal-provincial conference on the Constitution.[60] In its proposal for the entrenchment of a constitutional charter of rights, the government adopted a classification of civil liberties into political, legal, egalitarian, economic, and linguistic rights. Then, the government suggested a division of human rights into two broad categories:

(I)   rights which are expressed in terms of restrictions on the power of Parliament and the legislatures, and which require no enabling or

59. *The Canadian Bill of Rights*, p. 95.
60. *A Canadian Charter of Human Rights* (Ottawa, 1968).

implementing legislation in order to become effective (the rights described as "political" and "legal" fit into this category), and

(II) rights which in order to be fully effective must rely on the support of enabling or implementing legislation because they either anticicipate sanctions for their enforcement or require positive governmental assistance, (the rights described as "egalitarian" and "linguistic" fit into this category).[61]

The government's recommendation that discussion of economic rights be postponed was motivated by a consciousness of the obstacles to reaching agreement on the inclusion and subsequent implementation of such rights. Similarly, the 1960 Bill of Rights, unlike the United Nations Declaration of Human Rights, did not recognize such economic and social rights as those to social security, to work, to an adequate standard of living, to education, and to participation in the cultural life of the community. The single reference to economic rights in the bill declares "the rights of the individual to life, liberty, security of the person and enjoyment of property."[62]

The proposal for the incorporation of "linguistic" rights followed the recommendations of the first volume of the *Report of the Royal Commission on Bilingualism and Biculturalism* that the special needs of the French-speaking population in Canada be given constitutional recognition.[63] According to the government white paper, linguistic rights embrace

(a) *Communication with governmental institutions*—guaranteeing the right of the individual to deal with agencies of government in either official language. It would be necessary to decide whether this should apply to all agencies—legislative, executive, and judicial—and to all governments—federal, provincial and municipal.

(b) *Education*—guaranteeing the right of the individual to education in institutions using as a medium of instruction the official language of his choice.[64]

The federal government's awareness of the impediments to provincial endorsement of a constitutionally entrenched charter of human rights was reflected in the flexible approach set out in the white paper. Only very general suggestions concerning the form of the charter were made and no specific terms of a draft charter were outlined. More-

61. *Ibid.*, p. 29.   62. Section 1(a).
63. Book I, *The Official Languages* (Ottawa, 1967).
64. *A Canadian Charter of Human Rights*, p. 27.

over, at the federal-provincial conference, the Minister of Justice indicated the government's willingness to draft a charter of rights applicable to the federal government and to those provinces wishing to be bound by its provisions. Five of Canada's provincial premiers expressed support for the embodiment of human rights in the Constitution. The other five premiers did not reject the proposal altogether but voiced strong reservations founded in large part on the implied move from the doctrine of parliamentary supremacy to that of judicial supremacy characteristic of the United States. Canadians are certainly mindful of the recurrent criticism of the United States Supreme Court arising from its review of legislation affecting individual liberties.

The meeting of the federal and provincial governments at which the charter of human rights was proposed marked the beginning of continuing discussions on the desirability of amending or rewriting the Canadian Constitution so as to resolve fundamental issues threatening the survival of the federation. Among these critical problems are the extension of language and educational rights of French-speaking Canadians outside Quebec; the demands of Quebec, among other provinces, for an unprecedented transfer of powers to its legislative jurisdiction; and the regional economic disparities in the country. In comparison with the magnitude of these questions, the constitutional entrenchment of human rights may appear to many Canadians to be of less immediate importance. Yet further deliberations on the feasibility of such a charter have been referred to one of the several committees established by the conference to examine in detail the implications and content of possible amendments to the British North America Act. Furthermore, the apparent enthusiasm of the Canadian community for constitutional protection of civil liberties is unsurpassed in Canadian history. This fact augurs well for the incorporation of a charter of human rights in the Constitution during the early years of Canada's second century.

Publications of Robert Stanley Rankin

"The Constitutional Basis of Martial Law." *Constitutional Review*, XIII (April, 1929), 75-84.

"The Future of the Democratic Party." *South Atlantic Quarterly*, XXVIII (July, 1929), 225-235.

"Impeachments and Politics." *South Atlantic Quarterly*, XXIX (October, 1930), 374-393.

"President Hoover and the Supreme Court," *South Atlantic Quarterly*, XXX (October, 1931), 427-438.

"Recent Federal Legislation and Its Effect Upon Building and Loan Associations." *Annual Report of the North Carolina Building and Loan Association*, 1933.

"The Presidency Under the New Deal." *South Atlantic Quarterly*, XXXIII (April, 1934), 152-164.

"Is There a Time Limit for Impeachment?" *American Political Science Review*, XXVIII (October, 1934), 866-872.

"The County Manager Plan Proves Itself." *National Municipal Review*, XXIII (October, 1934), 511-513.

"The Ladder of the Law." *Popular Government*, II (1935), 12-13.

Editor, *When Civil Law Fails.* (Durham, N. C., 1939.)

Readings in American Government. (New York, 1939.)

Editor, *A Century of Social Thought.* (Durham, N. C., 1939.)

"The Importance of Good Government." *The Tarheel Banker*, XVIII (February, 1940), 30-34.

"Roots of the Tree of Liberty." *South Atlantic Quarterly*, XXXIX (July, 1940), 275-280.

"The Graduate Student: Teacher of Technician?" *Proceedings, Schoolmen's Week, University of Pennsylvania*, 1941.

"Hawaii Under Martial Law." *Journal of Politics*, V (August, 1943), 270-291.

"Trials and the Tax Payer." *We the People*, I (September, 1943), 21, 29-30.

"Martial Law and the Writ of Habeas Corpus in Hawaii." *Journal of Politics*, VI (May, 1944), 213-229.

"Presidential Succession in the United States." *Journal of Politics*, VIII (February, 1946), 44-56.

"Robert L. Doughton: Hard Work With No Vacations." In John T. Salter, ed., *Public Men In and Out of Office*. (Chapel Hill, 1946), pp. 167-180.

Political Science in the South. (Tuscaloosa: Bureau of Public Administration, University of Alabama, 1946.)

Editor, *The Presidency in Transition*. (Gainesville, Fla., 1949.)

The Government and Administration of North Carolina. (New York, 1955.)

With C. B. Gosnell and L. W. Lancaster, *Fundamentals of American National Government*. (New York, 1955.)

"An Agenda for the State of North Carolina." *Tarheel Social Studies Bulletin* (Winter, 1955), 11, 3-5, 17.

With C. B. Gosnell and L. W. Lancaster, *Fundamentals of American Government: National, State, Local*. (New York, 1957.)

"The Bill of Rights." In W. B. Graves, ed., *State Constitutional Revision*. (Chicago, 1960), pp. 159-175.

State Constitutions: The Bill of Rights. (New York: National Municipal League, 1960 [State Constitutional Studies Project #5].)

With Winfried R. Dallmayr, "Rights of Patients in Mental Hospitals." In *Constitutional Rights of the Mentally Ill*. Hearings before the Subcommittee on Constitutional Rights of the Committee on the Judiciary, United States Senate, 87th Congress, first session (Washington: Government Printing Office, 1961), Pt. I, pp. 329-370.

"The Impact of Civil Rights Upon Twentieth-Century Federalism." *University of Illinois Bulletin*, LX (May, 1963), 3-23. Edmund J. James lecture on government, 1963 (Urbana: Department of Political Science, University of Illinois).

With Winfried R. Dallmayr, *Freedom and Emergency Powers in the Cold War*. (New York, 1964.)

Index

Abel v. *United States*, 38n
Abram, Morris B., 147
academic freedom, 207-225
Adagogo, Emanuel, 278n
Adamson v. *California*, 148n
Adelaide Company of Jehovah's Witnesses Inc. v. *The Commonwealth*, 320n
Ademola, Sir Adetokunbo, 289n
Adorno, Theodore W., 202n
advertising and public policy, 250-251
African Commonwealth: communications in, 276; communications, table, 277; development problems of, 269-272; environment of, 272-279; executive powers in, 283-292; fundamental rights in, 269-294; fundamental rights or socioeconomic stability, 280-283; government structures of, 283-292; legal systems of, 288-292; legislatures of, 284-287; population figures, tables, 275
Aguilar v. *Texas*, 31n, 150n, 157
Alabama Supreme Court, position on juvenile offenders, 122-124
Alaska, bill of rights, 169, 177
Albert ex rel. Rocin v. *Gougen*, 52n
Almond, Gabriel, and James Coleman, 283n
Amachree, G. K. J., 281n, 282n
Amalgamated Society of Engineers v. *Adelaide Steamship Co. Ltd.*, 319
American Legion, support for Speaker Ban Law, 214
American Voter, The, quotation from, regarding experience, 134
Anderson, Mrs. William, 87
Anderson, Ross, 3, 318n
Andrain, Charles F., 107n
Angelo v. *The People of the State of Illinois*, 123n
Annett v. *United States*, 60n
appellate review, provision for juvenile courts, 130
Aptheker, Herbert, 220n, 220-221
Articles of War, 16
Arver v. *United States*, 55n
Ashanti, 279
Ashauer v. *United States*, 59n
Asians in Africa, 274-275
Attorney-General for the Commonwealth v. *Colonial Sugar Refinery Co. Ltd.*, 319n
Austin v. *Tennessee*, 250n
Australia: constitutional model adopted, 302-304; legal controls through imperial administration, 298-290; legal tradition of, 297-322

Australian Communist Party v. *The Commonwealth*, 320n
Australian constitution, draft of, 305; federal convention, 305-311
Awa, Eme O., 291n

Badger v. *United States*, 68n
Baggett v. *Bullit*, 223n
Baker, R. W., 306n
Baker v. *Carr*, 136n, 137
Baldwin, R. W., 190n
Banks, A. S., 283n
Baptists, 64, 66
Barenblatt v. *United States*, 153n
Barnes, H. E., 193n
Barnes, Judge, 59, 61
Barrett, W., and H. D. Aiken, 193n
Barron v. *Baltimore*, 163n
Barton, Edmund, 310
Basutoland, 281
Baxley v. *United States*, 50n
Bell, Daniel, 104n
Bell, Derrick A., 57, 58n
Bell, Judge Spencer, 61
Berger v. *New York*, 30n
Berlin, Isaiah, 191n, 201n
Bernd, Joseph L., 139n
Berns, Walter F., 85
bill of rights: analysis of state, 165-178; and the Canadian Supreme Court, 333-337; Australian criticism of American, 303-305; Australian state constitutions, 317-318; common provisions of, table, 166-167; contents of, 164-178; dispute over in Canada, 326-332; enactment of Canadian, 323-324; existing issues in Canada, 337-342; functions of, 162; impact on Australian constitution, 303-304; issues in, 178-180; lack of in Australia, 295; legal status of Canadian, 336-337; omissions in, 178-180; opposition to including in constitutions, 164; pressures to make applicable to the provinces of Canada, 343-344; provisions of Canadian, 332-333; relationship of state to federal, 163-164; relationship to the provinces in Canada, 333; trends in, 178-180
Birks v. *City of Montreal*, 334n
Biron et al. v. *Collins*, 52n
Black, Justice, 29, 51, 136, 149n, 157
Black v. *United States*, 52n
Blalock v. *United States*, 59n
Blankard v. *Galdy*, 298n